THE MUSIC PRACTITIONER

The Music Practitioner

Research for the Music Performer, Teacher and Listener

Edited by
JANE W. DAVIDSON

ASHGATE

Published by
Ashgate Publishing Limited
Wey Court East
Union Street
Farnham
Surrey GU9 7PT
England

Ashgate Publishing Company
Suite 420
101 Cherry Street
Burlington, VT 05401-4405
USA

Ashgate website: http://www.ashgate.com

British Library Cataloguing in Publication Data
The music practitioner : research for the music performer,
   teacher and listener
   1.Musicology 2.Music – Performance 3.Music appreciation
   4.Musicology – Methodology
   I.Davidson, Jane W.
   780.7'2

5910092447

Library of Congress Cataloging-in-Publication Data
The music practitioner : research for the music performer, teacher and listener / edited by
   Jane W. Davidson.
        p. cm.
   Includes bibliographical references and index.
   Contents: The practitioner and research – Theory and experimentation :
understanding pitches, tuning and rhythms – Practitioners investigating their daily
work – Researching musician identity and perception – Adopting innovative
research approaches – A final note.
   ISBN 0-7546-0465-9 (alk. paper)
   1. Music–Psychological aspects. I. Davidson, Jane W.

ML3830.M9815 2003
781'.11–dc21

2003052349

ISBN 978-0-7546-0465-5

Reprinted 2009

Typeset by Manton Typesetters, Louth, Lincolnshire, UK.
Printed and bound in Great Britain by TJI Digital, Padstow.

Contents

List of Figures

List of Tables

List of Music Examples

Notes on Contributors

Editor

Jane W. Davidson is a Reader in the Department of Music at the University of Sheffield. Jane currently teaches undergraduate courses on the development of musical ability; psychological approaches to performance; gender issues in western art music; the relationship between music, dance and drama; and music therapy. She also teaches components of the MA in Psychology of Music course offered at Sheffield and runs the MA in Music Theatre Studies. She has published work on musical expression, gesture, music practice, and the determinants of musical excellence. From 1997 to 2001, Jane was editor of the international music journal *Psychology of Music* and is associated with a number of other academic publications, sitting on editorial boards. Besides her teaching and research work, Jane performs as a vocal soloist and music theatre director and has appeared at the Queen Elizabeth Hall, St Paul's Cathedral, and the London International Opera Festival.

Authors

Nicholas Bannan is Director of the Music Teaching in Private Practice Initiative, a distance-learning Diploma and Masters programme at the University of Reading. A graduate of Cambridge University, he taught in several schools, including Eton College. He continued to develop his work as a composer, winning the Fribourg Prize for Sacred Music in 1986. He has carried out research into the use of electronic resources in vocal education and the means by which vocal potential can be released in singers of all ages and abilities. He is investigating the role of singing in human development from an evolutionary perspective.

Bernhard Billeter, pianist and organist, graduated in Musicology from the University of Zurich. He leads an organ class at the Hochschule für Musik und Theater Zurich and is Lecturer at the University of Zurich. His publications include books on contemporary Swiss composers (Frank Martin, Adolf Brunner, Willy Burkhard), volumes of complete editions (Hindemith, Schoeck) and studies on music theory, the interpretation of early music, musical ornamentation, historical tuning, and so on.

Sture Brändström took his piano pedagogic certificate and soloist diploma at the School of Music in Gothenburg. For more than 20 years he has combined piano teaching with public appearances as a pianist. During the 1980s Sture was engaged in research. In 1995 he defended his doctoral thesis in pedagogy at the

University of Umeå. He is currently Research Professor in Music Education at Luleå University of Technology, Sweden. His areas of specialization include instrumental training, action research and education sociology. Sture has published in journals such as the *Bulletin for the Council for Research in Music Education*, the *Canadian Music Educator, Research Studies in Music Education*. His recent presentations include International Society for Music Education (ISME) Research Commission 1994, 1998; ISME conferences 1996, 1998, and Australian Society for Music Education (ASME) 1997.

Karen Burland studied Music and Music Psychology at BMus and MA level at Sheffield University. She is currently finishing her PhD there under the supervision of Jane Davidson. As a performer, Karen is a frequent solo clarinettist in classical and jazz ensembles. She also plays saxophone and performs backing vocals in a rock band.

Daniela Coimbra graduated in Music Education from the Polytechnic Institute of Porto, Portugal. After some experience as a classroom teacher, she went on to study for a Masters degree in Psychology of Music at the University of Sheffield, where she studied for her PhD looking at performance evaluation. She is involved in societies such as the Society for Research in Psychology of Music and Music Education, and European Society for the Cognitive Sciences of Music. She has written a number of journal articles and conference presentations on her PhD topic. Currently she is lecturing in Music Psychology in Portugal.

Franz-Josef Elmer is Privatdozent in Theoretical Physics at the University of Basel, Switzerland. His subject areas include nonlinear dynamics and friction. He is also working as a software engineer in the IT industry.

Heiner Gembris studied Music and Music Education at the Music Academy of Detmold (Germany), Musicology at the Technische Universität, Berlin and at the Freie Universität, Berlin. In 1985 he was awarded a doctorate from Hamburg (thesis title: 'Musikhören und Entspannung' ['Music Listening and Relaxation']). From 1985 to 1990, he worked in the Music Department at the University of Augsburg. From 1991 to 1997, Heiner was Professor of Musicology at the University of Münster and from 1997 to 2001, Professor at the Martin-Luther-Universität, Halle-Wittenberg. He is currently Professor at the University of Paderborn. Heiner's main research interests are music perception and effects of music listening, and development of musical abilities. In 1998 he published *Grundlagen musikalischer Begabung und Entwicklung [Foundations of Musical Ability and Development]* (Augsburg; 2nd edn., 2002).

Jane Ginsborg studied music at York University and trained as a singer at the Guildhall School of Music and Drama, London. She was a professional singer and teacher of singing for a decade before studying Psychology with the Open University. She then undertook a PhD in Music Psychology, under the supervision of John Sloboda, at Keele University. She is currently a Lecturer in Psychology at Leeds Metropolitan University. She has reported her research findings at the British Psychological Society (BPS), Society for Research in Psychology of Music and Music Education (SRPMME) and European Society for the Cognitive Sciences of Music (ESCOM) conferences.

Anna-Karin Gullberg graduated in Psychology, Music Psychology and History of Science and Ideas in 1993. Between 1993 and 1997 she taught Psychology and undertook PhD research in Engineering Psychology at Luleå University of Technology in the field of human–computer interaction. Her graduate studies were in Dance (classic, contemporary) and Music (piano, singing) and her postgraduate studies were in Neurology and Music Pedagogy. Since 1995, Anna-Karin has been engaged in doctoral studies at Piteå School of Music. In 1999, she was awarded a Fil. Lic. in the research area of Formal and Non-formal Music Education. She presented a paper about Rock as a Research Field at NorFA, Copenhagen in 1997: 'Rock music making within and outside the School of Music' (published in 1999 as 'Playing by the rules: A study of music-making within and outside the School of Music', Luleå University of Technology, Sweden). In 1996, her paper 'Performance anxiety and coping strategies for musicians' was published in the *Proceedings of the First International Conference on Engineering Psychology and Cognitive Ergonomics*, Stratford-upon-Avon.

Ingrid Maria Hanken graduated in Pedagogy from the University of Oslo. Since 1976 she has been Associate Professor of Music Education at the Norwegian State Academy of Music. Her publications include the textbook *Musikkundervisningens didaktikk* [*The Theory of Music Education*], which she co-authored with Geir Johansen (Cappelen Akademisk Forlag, 1998), *Research in and for Higher Music Education. Festschrift for Harald Jørgensen*, co-authored with Siw Graabræk Nielsen and Monika Nerland (Norwegian Academy of Music, 2002), which includes the chapter, 'Academies of Music as Arenas for Education: Some Reflections on the Institutional Construction of Teacher-Student Relationships', co-authored with Monika Nerland. Ingrid has served on several national committees concerned with music education and teacher training. She was a commission member/chair of the ISME Commission on Community Music Activity 1984 to 1994, a member of the Board of the Nordic Association for Music Education 1986 to 1993, and Chair of the Norwegian Affiliation of ISME 1986 to 1993.

Peter Johnson is Head of Research at Birmingham Conservatoire, UK, and has been responsible for establishing one of the first practice-based research degree programmes in the UK. He is an experienced conductor and keyboard player and has published on Webern and Performance Studies, including chapters in *Theory* *into Practice* (Leuven University Press, 1999), and *Music Performance: A Guide to Understanding* (Cambridge University Press, 2002).

Kari Kurkela achieved a Piano Diploma from the Sibelius Academy in 1978 and a PhD from Helsinki University in 1986. He has held the post of Piano Teacher in several music schools in Finland. From 1984 to 1989, he held the posts of Junior and Senior Researcher at the Academy of Finland, and in 1987, was Acting Professor of Musicology at Helsinki University. From 1988 to 1989, Kari was Acting Professor of Music Theory at the Sibelius Academy, where he subsequently held the following posts: Professor, Musical Performance Research (1989), Head of the Research Unit (1988–94), Head of the Unit for Doctoral Studies, Solo Department (1994–98), Head of DocMus, Department of Doctoral Studies in Musical Performance and Research (1999–2001), Head of the Graduate School for Performing Arts, Theatre Academy, Helsinki University (1995–2001). Kari has given piano recitals in Finland, Sweden, Germany and France and made recordings for the Finnish Broadcasting Company and television. His main publications are: 'Note and Tone. A Semantic Analysis of the Conventional Notation' (doctoral dissertation), *Ajan herkkä kosketus* [*The Sensitive Touch of Time. A Study of Micro-timing in Piano Performances*], *Mielen maisemat ja musiikki* [*Scenes of Mind and Music. Psychodynamics of Performing Music and Creative Attitude*]. He has also written numerous articles on performing music, music philosophy and music education in different countries.

Daina Langner graduated in Professional Performance from the Rostock Music Academy and began her career as a violinist in the Berlin Symphony Orchestra in 1993. She combined orchestral playing with Psychology studies at Humboldt University. In the summer of 1999 she worked as an assistant during masterclass and performance training for advanced college and conservatory students in Morris, New York. At present she is a post-doctoral research fellow at the University of Paderborn.

Matthew M. Lavy, MA PhD ARCM LTCL, studied Music at Cambridge University, where he stayed on to write a doctoral thesis under the supervision of Dr Ian Cross. His primary research interest is emotional response to music; his PhD models ways in which listening to music can be an emotionally evocative experience. He also has a keen interest in research methodology, particularly that concerning the impact of computer technology on empirical research methods in music psychology.

Jerrold Levinson is Professor of Philosophy at the University of Maryland, College Park. His interests in aesthetics include aesthetics of music and film, ontology and definition of art, emotion in art, interpretation in art, the nature of humour, the nature of aesthetic properties, and relations between aesthetics and ethics. He is the author of *Music, Art, and Metaphysics* (Cornell University Press, 1990), *The Pleasures of Aesthetics* (Cornell University Press, 1996), and *Music in the Moment* (Cornell University Press, 1998), as well as editor of *Aesthetics and Ethics* (Cambridge University Press, 1998), co-editor of *The End of Art and Beyond* (Humanities Press International, 1997), co-editor of *Aesthetics Concepts* (Clarendon Press, 2001) and editor of the *Oxford Handbook of Aesthetics* (Oxford University Press, 2003). A volume of Jerrold's essays has appeared in French translation (*L'art, la musique, et l'histoire*, 1998), and he has contributed articles to *The Dictionary of Art, The Blackwell Companion to Aesthetics, The Handbook of Metaphysics and Ontology, The Encyclopedia of Aesthetics* and *The Routledge Encyclopedia of Philosophy*. Jerrold is on the Editorial Board of the *Journal of Aesthetics and Art Criticism*, and was President of the American Society for Aesthetics from 2001 to 2003.

Kacper Miklaszewski was awarded an MA in Piano at the Rimski-Korsakov Conservatory in St Petersburg after which he took graduate studies in Music Education at the Music School, University of Illinois at Urbana-Champaign. He also has a PhD in Theory of Music from the Chopin Academy of Music, Warsaw. From 1974 to 1992, he undertook research work in the Psychology of Music Department, including projects on tests and measurements of musical achievement and the process of learning in music, at the Institute for Research in Music Education, Chopin Academy of Music, Warsaw. From 1974 to 1980, he held the post of Piano Teacher at the Jozef Elsner Music School in Warsaw, and from 1980 to 1981 he held an Assistantship at the Council for Research in Music Education, School of Music, University of Illinois at Urbana-Champaign. From 1992 to 2003, he taught music at the Nonpublic Elementary School no. 34 in Warsaw. From 1993 to 1999 he was editor (evaluation of audio equipment) of *Studio*, a recording and radio magazine in Warsaw. Now he is an editor at *Ruch Muzyczny*, a music journal in the same city. His permanent collaboration with the Chopin Academy of Music in Warsaw includes working with the Department of Musical Acoustics (training listeners-evaluators) and Department of Psychology of Music (musical tests, learning music). Kacper is currently a member of the Editorial Board of Psychology of Music as well as a founding member of the European Society for the Cognitive Sciences of Music (ESCOM).

George Papadelis graduated in Musicology from the School of Musical Studies (Aristotle University of Thessaloniki). He has also studied Electrical Engineering at the Polytechnic School of Thessaloniki. During the last five years he has been working on rhythm perception as a PhD candidate at the School of Musical Studies. Since 1988 he has also been a research assistant at the Laboratory of Electroacoustics, Music Technology and Television Systems (University of Thessaloniki) and he participated in many research projects. He is a member of the European Society for the Cognitive Sciences of Music (ESCOM) and the Acoustical Society of America.

George Papanikolaou is Associate Professor (PhD in Electronic Engineering) at the Department of Electrical and Computer Engineering (Polytechnic School – Aristotle University of Thessaloniki). His teaching duties include courses on Musical Acoustics and Music Technology at the School of Musical Studies, as well as courses on Electroacoustics and Television Systems at the Department of Electrical and Computer Engineering. He is the Director of the Laboratory of Electroacoustics, Music Technology and Television Systems (established in 1976), which is supported by both the above departments. He is a member of the Acoustical Society of America, the Audio Engineering Society, the Polish Acoustical Society, the Greek Acoustical Society and the American Association for the Advancement of Science.

Richard Parncutt graduated in Music (piano performance) and Science (physics) from the University of Melbourne. His doctoral research at the University of New England, Australia addressed the perception of harmony. He is currently Professor in the Department of Musicology at the University of Graz in Austria. His publications include *Harmony: A Psychoacoustical Approach* (Springer-Verlag, 1989), *Science and Psychology of Music Performance* (Oxford University Press, 2002) and research articles on perception of tonality and rhythm, psychoacoustic/cognitive theories and models, and music performance. He is a member of the editorial advisory boards of *Musicae Scientiae, Psychology of Music, Journal of New Music Research, Music Perception, Jahrbüch Musikpsychologie,* and *Research Studies in Music Education.*

Stephanie E. Pitts is a lecturer at Sheffield, where she directs the MA in Psychology for Musicians and teaches on a range of musicological subjects including Mozart's Operas. She is author of *A Century of Change in Music Education* (Ashgate, 2000), and is currently writing a book about amateur participation in musical groups. In addition she is co-editor of *British Journal of Music Education.* Stephanie is a pianist who has worked in the past as a repetiteur for amateur opera companies, and is now involved in church music and performs regularly as an accompanist.

Andrzej Rakowski is one of Poland's distinguished researchers in the fields of music psychology, musical acoustics and performance. He currently works at the Chopin Academy in Warsaw where he was president from 1981 to 1987. With many internationally cited publications to his name, Andrzej has been a key innovator in the development of the interface between research and practice. He has stood on many prestigious committees and was President of the European Society for the Cognitive Sciences of Music (ESCOM) from 2000 to 2003.

John Rink is Professor of Music and Head of Department at Royal Holloway, University of London. He works in the fields of performance studies, theory and analysis, and nineteenth-century studies. He has produced three edited books for Cambridge University Press, *Chopin Studies 2* (1994; with Jim Samson), *The Practice of Performance: Studies in Musical Interpretation* (1995), and *Musical Performance: A Guide to Understanding* (2002), and has published a Cambridge Music Handbook entitled *Chopin: The Piano Concertos* (1997), which draws upon his experience in performing these works. He is currently preparing another book for Cambridge University Press and is one of three Series Editors of *The Complete Chopin – A New Critical Edition* as well as director of two major online Chopin editions.

Jaan Ross graduated in music theory from the Tallinn State Conservatoire in 1980, and undertook PhD research at the Moscow State Conservatoire. He earned his first PhD in Music Theory in 1988 and second PhD in Psychology in 1992 from the Abo Akademi, Finland. His publications include a number of papers on psychoacoustics, music acoustics, and psychology of music, in the *Journal of the Acoustical Society of America*, *Perception and Psychophysics*, *Music Perception*, *Language and Speech*, *NeuroReport*, and elsewhere. He now combines teaching and research at the University of Tartu and at the Estonian Academy of Music, Tallinn, with administrative work as the Dean of the School of Humanities at Tartu. He is a member of the European Society for the Cognitive Sciences of Music (ESCOM).

António G. Salgado graduated in Philosophy from the University of Oporto and at the same time completed the Superior Diploma in Singing at the National Conservatory of Lisbon, Portugal. In 1989, he completed his Master's degree in 'Lied und Oratorium' at the Hochschule für Musik und Darstellende Kunst, Salzburg, with a thesis entitled 'Aus der Mythologie', an essay on the meaning of mythology in Franz Schubert's Lied works. Since 1993, António has been Vocal Teacher in the Music Department, University of Aveiro, Portugal, and in 2003 completed a PhD in Performance Practice at the University of Sheffield. His published works include 'A Formação do Cantor Profissional' ['Rethinking the "Teacher–Student" Interactive Relationship in the Singing Learning Process'], paper presented during the 'First Latino–Americano Meeting of Musical Education', Salvador, Bahia, Brazil, and published by *ABEM* magazine, October 1998; 'Prolegómenos a uma Teoria do Gesto Vocal' ['Introduction to a Theory of the Vocal Gesture'], paper presented during the 'Second Conferencia Iberoamericano de Investigación Musical', Lanús, Buenos Aires, Argentina and published by the University of Lanús (Universidad Nacional de Lanús), in June 1998.

Stefanie Stadler Elmer is Lecturer of Psychology at the University of Zurich and of Education at Lucerne, Switzerland. Currently, she teaches music and language development, and research methods. Since the early 1980s she has been doing research in Developmental and Music Psychology (Switzerland, Germany, USA), which has been supported by several grants and fellowships. She has published two books (in German), *Play and Imitation – Development of Musical Activities* (2000), and *Children Sing Songs – Cultivating One's Vocal Expression* (2002) and many articles and chapters in German and English. Her main interests concern the development of consciousness and identity, the symbols used to express these by vocal means (speaking, singing), and cultural diversity. Since her childhood, she has played the piano and sung in choirs.

Sam Thompson is a graduate of the University of Cambridge and holds an MA in Psychology for Music from the University of Sheffield. He is currently studying for a PhD at the University of London while working as a researcher investigating music and performance at the Royal College of Music, London. He is an active clarinettist and composer, having had many of his arrangements of the major opera repertoire performed by the English Touring Opera Company.

Allan Vurma graduated in Opera and Recital Singing and Voice Pedagogy from the Estonian Academy of Music in 1990 and in Radio Engineering from Tallinn Polytechnic Institute in 1978. He is working as a soloist in the professional Estonian Philharmonic Chamber Choir and is teaching Voice Methodology in the Estonian Academy of Music. During the last few years he has researched singing voice acoustics with the support of the Estonian Science Foundation.

Aaron Williamon initially studied in the USA, but moved to England for PhD work at the University of London. He currently works in the Centre for the Study of Music Performance (CSMP), Royal College of Music. He has published widely, and is currently editing a book for Oxford University Press entitled: *Enhancing Musical Performance*. Besides his academic career, Aaron is a keen jazz trumpeter.

Foreword

John Sloboda

Contemporary western music psychology can trace its roots to the 1960s and the rise of cognitive psychology as a dominant paradigm for exploring and understanding the human mind. These roots gave the discipline some very important positive attributes: scientific rigour, well-established methodologies, and theoretical incisiveness. Experimental psychologists, working in the main in traditional psychology departments, spearheaded the development of new scholarly bodies, new specialist journals, and the acceptance of high academic standards through such mechanisms as anonymous peer review.

These same roots, however, gave rise to some limitations which the field has needed to address. The first of these was a focus on the listener rather than the practitioner. The second was a concentration on processes that span a few seconds, rather than those spanning minutes, hours, or years. The third was a priority for fundamental and basic research over applied research. It has been heartening to see researchers taking productive steps to overcome all these limitations in recent years. First, the study of music performance is now a rich and diverse research sub-discipline that is undoubtedly one of the major success stories of the last 15 or so years. Second, researchers have developed ever more ingenious ways of tapping processes that take place over long time spans, both within an extended musical work, but also over significant time periods within the life-span of an individual. Third, researchers have begun to take seriously the needs and priorities of practitioners (the people who produce, perform, and support musical outputs of all kinds). These three developments are linked. It is hard to undertake research of real relevance for practitioners unless it addresses music performance, and unless it has something to say about the long-term factors that influence the acquisition and growth of music performance skills.

This book represents an important new step on the road to a truly applicable music psychology. Its primary focus is on the development of the professional performing adult musician, and throughout its pages are unique glimpses into the world of young adult performers, often reflecting incisively on aspects of their own experience and training. These insights are not, in the main, provided by researchers 'parachuting in' from the detached heights of a nearby psychology department. The majority of contributors in this book are 'at the coal face', delivering music training and education in the context of music colleges, conservatoires and university music departments. The issues they address are often exactly the ones that they need solutions for in their everyday work of shaping tomorrow's professional musicians. The result is doubly authentic – representing the concerns of both the teacher and also those being taught.

This book is, in fact, the outcome of initiatives which go wider than the authors of the 25 chapters. Many of these authors were participants at an international conference on 'Research Relevant to Music Conservatoires and High Schools' held at the Lucerne Conservatoire in Switzerland, under the auspices of the Swiss Science Ministry and the European Society for the Cognitive Sciences of Music (ESCOM). This conference, jointly chaired by Thüring Bräm, Jane Davidson, Hubert Eiholzer, and myself, came about in response to a growing international realization that those involved in the training of professional musicians needed to define and grasp research opportunities which reflected their own needs and priorities, rather than attempting pale imitations of what was going on in nearby university psychology or musicology departments. This conference was supported by the European Association of Conservatoires (AEC), and it is heartening to see the increasing number of conservatoires around the world that now consider music psychology to be an integral part of their work, and take it for granted that psychologists should be included among their staff.

What we seem to be seeing is an increasing acceptance within the music profession that the training and support of professional musicians is a multidisciplinary endeavour, requiring, alongside the central inputs of experienced music practitioners, the contributions of a range of other disciplinary specialists, including health professionals, psychologists, exercise specialists, and those with expertise in business, management, and public relations. Such expertise has long been available within the training and support systems in sport and athletics. Performing musicians, who are athletes of the hand and voice, deserve the support of the full range of disciplines that can help them achieve and maintain the high standards which are integral to their success. This book is a small, but significant, sign of a new determination on the part of both practitioners and researchers to make their relationship really work to the direct benefit of performing musicians and, indirectly, therefore, to all those who are affected and inspired by their performances.

Acknowledgements

Several people deserve special mention for the assistance they have contributed to the preparation of this book. Thüring Bräm, the Director of the Luzern Konservatorium, for hosting the meeting out of which this project grew; the Scientific Committee of the European Society for the Cognitive Sciences of Music (ESCOM) for helping to select the authors for this project; Rosie Burt and Martin Haywood in Sheffield and Amy Eiholzer-Silver in Lugano for their assistance with the layout and content of the chapters; and Rachel Lynch and Kristen Thorner from Ashgate and the copy-editor Sarah Price, who supported the book's production. Without the skill, organization, endeavour and patience of Hubert Eiholzer – especially in the early stages of the project – *The Music Practitioner* would not exist, so my deepest thanks go to him.

Chapter 1

Introduction

Jane W. Davidson

In recent decades there has been an increasing interest in the psychology of music, music education, musicology and music philosophy, with publications of books such as *The Musical Mind* (Sloboda, 1985); *Sound and Structure* (Paynter, 1992); *Music Education: Trends and Issues* (Plummeridge (ed.), 1996); *The Practice of Performance: Studies in Musical Interpretation* (Rink (ed.), 1995); *The Social Psychology of Music* (Hargreaves and North (eds), 1997); *Music in the Moment* (Levinson, 1997); *Music and the Emotions* (Juslin and Sloboda (eds), 2002) and *Musical Identities* (Macdonald et al (eds), 2002); *Musical Performance: A Guide to Understanding* (Rink (ed.), 2002); *The Science and Psychology of Music Performance* (Parncutt and McPherson (eds), 2002). For the most part, these books have been heavily discipline-based. The psychology books, in particular, have largely ignored what practical benefits research can bring to the practical musician. Practical musicians of all descriptions are serious about their profession and are constantly looking for ways and means of assessing their own practices, thus the time seemed ripe for an academic book which is of direct relevance to the music practitioner. The explicit aim of this book is to engage music practitioners and demonstrate the many potential links between research and practice.

The book comprises 25 chapters in which research largely from the academic area of music psychology brings a range of practical questions into focus. In the context of this book, research might be regarded as critical, systematic enquiry into topics of specific interest. The spectrum of topics covered is deliberately broad, with issues ranging from historical performance practice to career choice amongst music graduates. A central concern in this brief introduction is to suggest ways in which the reader may dip in and out of the book. It is suggested that three different aspects become the central focus.

The first aspect to consider is that research questions themselves are of interest, and the findings of each chapter provide a useful source of information. For instance, Anna-Karin Gullberg and Sture Brändström (Part 3, Chapter 13) demonstrate that rock musicians trained in music college compose works that are very different in style and form from those rock musicians who learn in informal contexts, and that listeners with different degrees of formal music education appreciate these different styles of composition in different manners.

The second aspect to contemplate is that research findings can have direct educational or general implications which in all cases the authors in this book highlight. In the rock musician chapter, for instance, critical questions for educators include: what happens to a musical genre like rock music when it is taught at a formal learning institution? What are the specific factors that are influential in the individual development of the musician?

The third relevant aspect to be considered is that the research methodologies applied to specific questions in each chapter may have broader applications which may be of interest to a reader wanting to undertake research him- or herself. For instance, Daniela Coimbra and Jane Davidson (Part 4, Chapter 16) describe a large-scale study in which they designed questionnaires requiring quantitative and qualitative analysis. In the former case, this involved them in asking participants specific questions, usually requiring forced-choice answers. From these questions it was possible for them to calculate statistical interpretations of the responses, such as how many of the participants had a particular behaviour, or which of the participants was rated as being better than the others. Thus, the frequency and/or the likelihood of a behaviour being the product of change or some critical variable could be assessed. Qualitative responses can also be quantified and statistical information extrapolated, but the principal advantage of qualitative data is that participants can be asked open-ended conversational-style questions so that they can determine the interview content themselves, with themes of relevance to them being pursued. The qualitative data generated by Daniela and Jane were richly informative, allowing insights into individual behaviour. Thus, the methodologies are juxtaposed yet seen as complementary. In principle, the difference in the two approaches is that the quantitative data provide information that is generalizable to the group of participants studied, whereas qualitative data provide data about an individual. In summary, the current volume is not focused on explaining the methodological principles of research techniques, but the chapters included in the book contain many different styles of research, and thus show the reader the broad range of approaches that can be adopted.

The book is divided into five main parts. In Part 1, different ways in which practitioners can use research is explored by authors who are all both performing musicians and researchers. Aaron Williamon and Sam Thompson are both researchers at the Centre for the Study of Music Performance at the Royal College of Music, London, where they specialize in teaching and researching performance from a psychological perspective. Their chapter defines the ways in which psychological techniques and findings can be applied to the practitioner's work. Kacper Miklaszewski from the recording company DUX in Warsaw is also a music psychologist, and is particularly focused on suggesting ways in which instrumental teachers might benefit from this kind of research knowledge.

John Rink is a pianist and Professor of Musicology at Royal Holloway, University of London, and contributes Chapter 4 of the book. His research over the years has provided critical insights into matters of interpretation, focusing principally on the piano repertoire of Chopin. A central concern for him at the moment is that it may be possible to identify a specific research domain that concerns itself centrally with 'performance studies' and he draws the reader's attention to the elements that such a domain might include. The thrust of the chapter is to suggest that rather than being a specialist single domain, 'performance studies' should integrate historical, theoretical and psychological work in order to provide the performer with a many-toned palette on which to construct his/her own interpretation of a work. Rink gives an exciting exposé of his ideas in the presentation of a case study of Chopin's E minor Prelude Op. 28 No. 4.

Kari Kurkela, Director of Research at the Sibelius Academy in Helsinki, makes a case study of the courses on offer at his institution as an example of how practitioners can be trained to undertake relevant and focused research. Initially, he points out that music colleges and conservatoires are ideal locations to investigate practical music. A key feature of this chapter is that he discusses research data that rely on the opinions of the students. In other words, the students provide data about the strengths and weaknesses of their learning environment. Thus, a feature of the chapter concerns what elements of the musician's education in this institution can be improved upon to advance them as player-researchers. In summary, this first part of the book looks at ways in which practitioners might draw on research to assist their practice, and it also considers ways in which practitioners might train to become systematic researchers.

In Part 2, research approaches that are largely focused around perception and cognition are explored from very different perspectives. Andrzej Rakowski of the Chopin Academy in Warsaw opens the section (Chapter 6) examining how the performer and listener can help the psycho-acoustician to understand how mental operations in perceiving musical pitches might occur. In the following chapter, Peter Johnson from Birmingham Conservatoire presents a highly focused research question about expressive intonation in string quartet playing: What does 'good intonation' in this context imply? This is both an important practical and theoretical issue. He discusses an investigation which analyses professional recordings of Beethoven's String Quartet Op. 135 using the technique of Fourier analysis adopted from physics. In Chapter 8, Bernhard Billeter also enquires into tuning, but from a historical perspective by looking at compositions from the fifteenth to eighteenth centuries. Billeter, from the University of Zurich, notes that there were many difficulties facing musicians at that time and that issues of tuning may well have had an impact on compositional approaches. So, again, his research has significant implications for performers concerned with tuning authenticity. He poses specific questions about tuning related to Bach's use of 'well-tempered' keyboards.

Richard Parncutt of the University of Graz in Austria offers another perspective on musical understanding in Chapter 9, proposing how computer-based teaching might enrich music theory learning. Although speaking about a hypothetical curriculum, Parncutt discusses which elements of music theory can be best explored via these means. Part 2 closes with George Papadelis and George Papanikolaou of the Aristotle University of Thessaloniki investigating how the rhythm categories of a piece of music are perceived. They report a detailed study in which participants were taken through a series of rhythm identification and discrimination tasks in order to explore what mental operations were occurring for perception of the rhythmical categories to occur.

Part 3 of the book demonstrates how practitioners have explored their everyday work. Jane Davidson of the University of Sheffield, for instance, is an active opera director and she uses her work – a production of Purcell's *Dido and Aeneas* – as an opportunity to assess how the creative process operates. Thus, she turns her regular working practice into a research exercise. Jane Ginsborg from Leeds Metropolitan University is a singer, and as such was intrigued to explore how singers approached the memorization of words and music in a song. Adopting a highly systematic approach she is able to investigate not only what strategies people adopt, but which ones seem more useful. The implications of such a research approach for teaching are obvious. As discussed in the opening of this Introduction, Anna-Karin Gullberg and Sture Brändström from Luleå University in Sweden look at how rock musicians learn, with the implications of the research being highly significant: innovation largely happens in non-formal learning contexts, whereas those rock musicians who are formally taught in music college produce less creative works. Again working in a music college, Allan Vurma and Jaan Ross from Estonia (Chapter 14) use objective spectographic analyses of singer's tones to investigate what a vocal training actually does for a voice over the course of a vocal training ranging from one to ten years. The major implications of this systematic enquiry are obvious, for it is demonstrated that the singer's formant (the voice's spectrum) increases with training, but that timbral qualities of the voices are not altered by training. These results present a conundrum for teachers when singers are often evaluated in terms of their vocal timbres.

Part 4 of the book presents research which has focused on how being a musician impacts on an individual's sense of self and how others perceive them. In Chapter 15, António Salgado from the Universidade of Aveiro in Portugal considers the issue of self-identity for opera singers. The research question is of critical importance because of the strong personal identification between musical instrument (the singer's own voice) and their sense of self (who they are as a performer). The research technique adopted is in-depth qualitative interviewing which shows how rich such data can be. Daniela Coimbra and Jane Davidson of the University of Sheffield present the findings of a large-scale investigation of how young opera singers are evaluated in a music college setting in Chapter 16. Their largely exploratory approach reveals intriguing results: singers are principally evaluated in terms of attractiveness and presentation of 'a performing personality', rather than in terms of their vocal characteristics. Evident contrasts and parallels can be drawn between the findings of Chapters 14, 15 and 16 and should stimulate personal reflection for the reader in the contradictory and unexpected findings these systematic enquiries produce.

In Chapter 17, Stephanie Pitts of the University of Sheffield investigates the life transition of music students from school to university. Not only does her study demonstrate how to undertake detailed qualitative enquiry, this kind of research also shows that a gulf exists between what school and universities know and understand of their students Working in the same university as Stephanie Pitts, Karen Burland and Jane Davidson consider a larger time-scale life transition, that from school to professional musician life. In an eight-year longitudinal study they demonstrate that key environmental factors seem to discriminate out those students who will go on to a professional performing career as opposed to those who will either give up music altogether or keep it as an amateur interest. Although their study is exploratory, requiring further data to validate their findings, it does demonstrate the power of research in pinpointing factors that may contribute towards a particular outcome. Part 4 of the book closes with Daina Langner of the University of Paderborn exploring what personality characteristics are displayed by musicians, and in particular what differences exist between a soloist and a group player. She makes some intriguing points concerning training and the selection procedures for various roles within the current music profession.

In Part 5, innovative research methodologies are used to illustrate that creative researchers can find ways of enquiry which provide new types of data for analysis and interpretation. In Chapter 20, computer-based research is discussed as a means of reducing the researcher's cultural biases in the assessment of phenomena in the experimental context. The topic is children's singing and the research is undertaken by Stefanie Stadler Elmer and Franz-Josef Elmer from Switzerland. Ingrid Maria Hanken of the Norwegian State Academy of Music raises important issues in Chapter 21 about how to undertake research that is both useful and 'acceptable'. Working in collaboration with her students, she looks at how student evaluation can be developed as a means of improving the quality of instrumental teaching. Similarly working alongside individuals, Nicholas Bannen from the University of Reading examines a method for teaching general musicianship. The particular emphasis of the chapter is on the action research method used. In this technique, a spiral of cycles of planning, acting, observing and reflecting are put into operation. This means that the devising of a general musicianship syllabus becomes an act of research, and so again the appropriateness of the methodological approach for the teacher/practitioner is to be emphasized. In Chapter 23, Heiner Gembris of the University of Paderborn in Germany discusses how a longitudinal study was devised and analysed, and, most importantly, discusses the findings which examine what music graduates go on to do in their future lives. The section closes with a provocative chapter by Matthew Lavy of the University of Cambridge in which he notes that existing studies can only take us only so far in our explanations of phenomena. He considers how music elicits emotional responses in us and suggests the extent to which we can explain this through empirical enquiry.

We close the book with a final note from Jerrold Levinson of the University of Maryland. This chapter is juxtaposed next to Matthew Lavy's work as it also looks at emotional response, but we use it to conclude the book, for it tackles the most over-arching question of all: What makes music affect us as it does? The writing allows the reader to reflect on empirical work and philosophical induction and what each approach can offer. More specifically, it engages us in the debate of how something experienced as essentially physiological (tingles down the spine, for instance) can have an aesthetic value which may be regarded as a refined and culturally determined cognitive act. So, in the end we are reminded of the objective and subjective elements which need to be considered in order for critical insight to be gained.

Looking over the broad range of work contained in these 25 chapters, we know that this book will provide the reader with an engaging and important exploration of music research relevant to the music practitioner and demonstrate several different empirical approaches to collecting and analysing data. Readers are encouraged to take from it as much as possible and apply its theories and methods and results to their own everyday musical concerns. We hope the reading and reflecting is enjoyed by all!

References

Hargreaves, D.J. and North, A.C. (eds) (1997) *The Social Psychology of Music*, Oxford: Oxford University Press.

Juslin, P. and Sloboda, J.A. (2002) *Music and the Emotions*, Oxford: Oxford University Press.

Levinson, J. (1997) *Music in the Moment*, Cornell: Cornell University Press.

Macdonald, R., Miell, D. and Hargreaves, D.J. (eds) (2002) *Musical Identities*, Oxford: Oxford University Press.

Parncutt, R. and McPherson, G.E. (eds) (2002) *The Science and Psychology of Music Performance*, Oxford: Oxford University Press.

Paynter, J. (1992) *Sound and Structure*, Cambridge: Cambridge University Press.

Plummeridge, C. (ed.) (1996) *Music Education: Trends and Issues*, London: Institute of Education Press.

Rink, J. (ed.) (1995) *The Practice of Performance: Studies in Musical Interpretation*, Cambridge: Cambridge University Press.

Rink, J. (ed.) (2002) *Musical Performance: A Guide to Understanding*, Cambridge: Cambridge University Press.

Sloboda, J.A. (1985) *The Musical Mind*, Oxford: Clarendon Press.

PART 1

The Practitioner and Research

Chapter 2

Psychology
and the Music Practitioner

Aaron Williamon and Sam Thompson

As a seemingly universal human behaviour, the practice of making and listening to music has long been the subject of psychological enquiry (see, for example, Seashore, 1910, 1912, 1919; Bartholomew, 1934). The accomplished music practitioner displays a wide range of 'psychological' skills that are of interest to psychologists working within a number of different subdisciplines. Perhaps as a result of music's multifaceted nature, however, it is only over the last 30 years or so that psychology of music has emerged as a unified field of study, with the appearance of four discipline-specific journals (*Psychology of Music* in 1973, *Psychomusicology* in 1982, *Music Perception* in 1983 and *Musicæ Scientiæ* in 1997) and a host of international societies spanning several continents.

In this chapter we aim to highlight reasons for, and benefits of, this emergent unification and to demonstrate how practitioners can potentially use the methods of modern psychology to further their understanding of the mental and physical demands of music practice and performance. We do so, first, by placing music psychology in context, providing a general overview of psychology and some of its methodological limitations. Second, we explore why psychologists are interested in music and why music practitioners might be interested in psychology. Finally, we detail two ways in which psychologists have investigated music practice and performance – namely, by systematically *observing* musicians as they practise and perform and by *asking* them about their experiences. By doing so we hope to encourage music practitioners to explore the possibilities of employing these methods for themselves.

Psychology: An Overview

Psychology, broadly defined, is the study of the mind and behaviour of humans and other animals (Valentine, 1992). From such a broad definition, one can easily conjure an assorted list of issues that qualify as the subject of psychological research. Indeed, psychologists themselves have carved the domain into a number of diverse subdisciplines, ranging from the study of long-term memory to the treatment of disordered behaviour to the analysis of attitudes and interpersonal relations (see texts by Seamon and Kenrick, 1992 and Butler and McManus, 1995, for introductory reviews).

Aside from the common goal of understanding the mind and behaviour, these seemingly disparate subdisciplines of modern psychology are bound together – to varying degrees – by science. Strictly, science means 'knowledge', but it has come to mean (at least in the modern western world) knowledge acquired as a result of employing empirical methods. Empiricism requires that information be verifiable through experience, as opposed to being generated merely through a priori reasoning. That is, 'it must be possible for different individuals in different places at different times using a similar method to produce the same results' (Ray, 1993, p. 9).

Empiricism typically involves observation, measurement and experimentation. The possibility of applying these procedures to psychological subject matter has been questioned by many (for example, Kant, 1974[1781]; Wundt, 1862). *Observation*, for instance, has been deemed problematic for psychology because much of what is of interest (thoughts and feelings) is not open to direct observation. Hence, almost all psychological statements must be inferred. Inference is, in fact, required of all sciences, but the gap between data and theory is arguably greater in psychology than in many others (Valentine, 1992). Also, it is now clear from years of research across scientific disciplines that neither the observer nor the observed are passive, non-interactive entities in the experimental situation. This is of particular relevance in psychology, where the experiment itself is a social situation.

Measurement also presents difficulties for psychological research. The late nineteenth century witnessed an increase in attempts to measure such factors as intellectual ability. In some cases, this was carried out by assigning individuals scores on constructed scales, such as that for IQ (Intelligence Quotient; see Binet and Simon, 1905; Terman and Merrill, 1972). Researchers in this area have been able to achieve standardization (by delivering tests under uniform conditions to comparable groups of people), reliability (by establishing consistency of results from the same test) and concurrent and predictive validity (that is, agreement between different types of tests given at the same time, and between test scores and other measures of academic success or capability). However, even after a century of progressive research in this area, a large degree of uncertainty still remains as to what the precise values on such scales actually mean, since not all test-makers agree on a single theory or definition of intelligence (Cronbach, 1984).

Finally, *experimentation* harbours some challenges for psychological research. Although empirical investigations of social phenomena and situations are possible, difficulties inevitably emerge in proving that one specific aspect of a situation caused another. Isolating or achieving sufficient control over such aspects can be impossible for a variety of reasons, including the number of factors affecting the situation, how those factors interact and the history of the variables involved.

Moreover, practical and ethical considerations limit the extent to which control can be achieved. Researchers cannot create deprived environments or brain damage in order to study certain behaviours or cognitive processes (Valentine, 1992).

The difficulties with observation, measurement and experimentation are virtually inevitable in psychology. As Valentine (1992) concludes, however, 'psychology does have particular problems but generally these represent differences in degree rather than kind from those of other sciences. Most are capable of resolution to a greater or lesser extent' (p. 7).

Psychology and Music

Like language, some recognizable form of music has been observed in all known human societies (Blacking, 1995). Moreover, it has often served a functional status within society (particularly in less developed cultures) as, for example, an adjunct to religious ceremony, a part of celebration or a preparation for battle.

In the modern western world, a day without music is virtually unknown. When people are asked to list their hobbies and interests, some sort of musical enthusiasm is usually acknowledged, making it the most popular of all avocations (Coslin, 1980; Roe, 1985). One study of university students reported that 28 per cent listened to music for over five hours per day (Toohey, 1982). Music even features as prominently as family and sex amongst individuals' primary values, and it usually rates higher than religion, sport and travel (Cameron and Fleming, 1975). 'Passive' music consumption, such as exposure to music while shopping, is another (some would say regrettable) feature of modern life. Although one may only just be aware of the presence of such music, its effects can be powerful. Recent studies have demonstrated that different genres of so-called 'muzak' can play a significant role in consumer behaviour, even to the extent of influencing purchase intentions (North and Hargreaves, 1998; North et al., 1999).

Given the extraordinary hold music appears to have over us, both consciously and subliminally, it is no surprise that psychologists have devoted considerable time to investigating the relationship between music and the mind. Moreover, the knowledge gained through studying exceptional musical performances can serve to redefine the upper limits of human achievement and provide advice to novices on how to acquire specialized skills (Staszewski, 1988).

Likewise, modern psychology has much to offer musicians. According to Wilson (1994), it can:

1. help explain the instinctual origins of the impulse to make music;
2. examine the relationship between a performer and his/her audience, including social processes such as identification, charisma, idolization and group facilitation;

3. describe the ways in which ideas and emotions are transmitted to an audience by non-verbal processes such as posture and facial expression;
4. test theories about the power of music to influence our ideas and emotions;
5. tell us what kind of people are attracted to performing and why, and the particular stresses they are subject to when doing so; and
6. suggest how optimum performance can be achieved and how such conditions as stage fright and memory lapses can be managed.

To what extent has psychology, to date, provided information on these processes? In *The Musical Mind* (1985), Sloboda suggested that research in music psychology offers considerable knowledge in some of these areas but admitted that there were a number of issues of great importance to musicians that had been left relatively unexplored. He proposed several reasons for this. First, some psychologists studying music have not received extended musical training and so have a limited range of musical insights and intuition to guide their work. Second, theoretical developments in psychology of music have been slow, with researchers tending to construct micro-theories to account for their own results and failing to synthesize research findings from different sources. Third, psychological research is 'dominated by the view that one must understand the most peripheral and simple aspects of intellectual functioning as a prelude to the study of more central and complex aspects'; therefore, the study of topics that are of the most direct relevance to musicians – such as 'large-scale musical structure, performance, and composition' – has been limited (p. v). Fourth, writers in music psychology have tended to address themselves exclusively either to professional psychologists or to music educators and educational researchers.

Sloboda, however, writes optimistically about the emerging state of affairs in psychology of music, noting that researchers well grounded in both psychology and music have 'begun to construct psychologically interesting theories of musical functioning which might be capable of unifying and giving direction to a wide range of research endeavours' (p. v). We would argue that, since the publication of *The Musical Mind* in 1985, research in music psychology has indeed provided better theoretical and pedagogical understanding of many issues within music and that the potential for further growth is perhaps now greater than ever (see Williamon, 2004, for examples and further discussion).

One reason for this is the increasing interest in performance-related research, which has brought with it an influx of researchers with first-hand, practical experience of music-making. We see this experience as an essential element in establishing beneficial collaborative ventures between various types of psychologists and musicians and a rich source for practical, hypothesis-driven research initiatives. A second reason is that the mutual suspicion between the musicological and psychological communities, as discussed by Cook (1994), has largely dissipated as both camps have come to better understand and respect each other's positions. Finally, increased interest in, and awareness of, research in music psychology has enabled a wider dissemination of findings through academic and popular forums, including the media of newspaper, radio and television (for example, 'A musical performance that is all in the mind', *The Times*, 7 Sept 2000; 'Players can calm nerves with a little exercise', *The Daily Telegraph*, 7 Sept 2000; 'Relax, then do it', *New Scientist*, 16 Sept 2000).

It is beyond the scope of this chapter to provide an exhaustive review of recent psychologically interesting theories of musical functioning (for reviews, see other chapters of this volume; Wilson, 1994; Hargreaves and North, 1997; Deutsch, 1999; Parncutt and McPherson, 2002). Rather, in the section to follow, we aim to explore two general approaches that have been used to make both theoretical and practical headway into understanding music performance. More importantly, we hope to demonstrate how music practitioners can use these methods with scientific rigour to gain insight into areas of immediate interest to them.

The Music Practitioner and Performance-related Research

Making music is a psychologically complex behaviour that draws on numerous (nominally independent) skills and processes. For the psychologist interested in studying human intellectual and motor achievement, the domain of music performance can be a particularly rich source of information. Much of the music we listen to – at least in terms of the western art music tradition – is performed by musicians deemed to be in some way 'expert' or 'talented'. These performers must often demonstrate the simultaneous, fluent execution of a variety of cognitive, perceptual, motor and social skills. Such skills may include, but are certainly not limited to, acute motor control (that is, fine motor skills that enable a command of the instrument; see Shaffer, 1980, 1981), flexible control of attention (that is, the ability to control and switch between musical parameters simultaneously; see Allport, Antonis and Reynolds, 1972; Keller, 2001), and specialized memory skills (for example, the retrieval and execution during performance of entire musical works, often containing thousands of notes and complex musical structures; see Chaffin and Imreh, 1997, 2001; Williamon, 2002; Williamon and Valentine, 2002).

It follows, then, that the more detailed knowledge we possess concerning the nature of these skills, the better we will be able to understand the intricacies of expert musical performance. This has clear benefits for music pedagogy. By empirically identifying and delineating the key components of successful performance, it should be possible to develop training programmes that emphasize particular skills (see Williamon, 2004). Research into memorization, for example, has provided evidence that expert performers, as opposed to lesser skilled musicians, use musical structure more frequently to organize their practice sessions in order to aid the learning of music 'by heart' (Williamon and Valentine, 2002).

Rich as this area of research may be, however, it is not without its methodological problems. The principal difficulty rests in maintaining *ecological validity*. Laboratory examinations of how, for instance, chess experts decide upon the 'best next move' or recall the exact positions of presented chess pieces offer relatively suitable measures of chess performance. Consequently, direct evidence can be obtained – from measures such as reaction times and error rates – to reveal specific characteristics of performance (see Chase and Ericsson, 1981, 1982). However, a musician's completion of equivalent tasks in the laboratory would hardly qualify as a 'musical' performance. Musicians may be able to respond to such tasks as a result of their training, but empirical investigations of musical ability should examine the primary skills that are a direct result of that training (that is, the actual practice and performance of music). Although valuable insight has been, and will continue to be, gained from laboratory-based examinations of various musical skills (for example, Halpern and Bower, 1982), researchers, on the whole, have been forced to use less direct methods to obtain information about the mechanisms governing practice and performance.

A second difficulty becomes apparent when trying to reveal characteristics of human functioning that will generalize across all musicians. The vast differences in musicians' training, experience, learning styles and instrumental techniques appear, at first glance, to present an insurmountable number of permutations and variations in skill between performers. This, in turn, makes expert–expert and expert–novice comparisons potentially problematic. In fact, struggling to evade this problem is often what leads to experimental studies lacking ecological validity. In attempting to reduce the complex behaviour of musical performance to a number of shared components, researchers are frequently forced to remove from their experiments just those aspects of performance that seem to make it interesting and worth studying in the first instance. But individual differences between performers clearly are important. Were this not the case, the classical music recording industry could have no reason to produce, say, 20 or more recordings of the Beethoven Piano Sonatas. If there were no discernible differences between the performances, who would buy them? However, individual differences between performers need not be viewed as a hindrance to psychological research; they can tell us much about the processes underlying successful performance (Ericsson and Kintsch, 1995). For example, two expert pianists playing the same musical work may vary constantly in terms of tempo, such that the performances will be of different lengths and sound totally different (think, perhaps, of Glenn Gould and Alfred Brendel playing the same Bach fugue). Moreover, it is unlikely that the same performer will ever play the same work twice in precisely the same way (again, think of Gould's various recordings of Bach's *Goldberg Variations*). However, it has been shown that for most expert performers these tempo fluctuations (commonly referred to as expressive timing deviations) occur predictably within a broad framework determined by the temporal structure of the work in question, from the level of the individual phrase right up to the level of form (Clarke, 1988). The fact that myriad individual differences can exist within this framework seems to suggest something about the way in which a piece of music is represented in the mind of the performer.

These are only two of the methodological obstacles that pervade the study of music performance. How, then, might researchers proceed to examine exceptional musical skill? This has been done effectively by (1) systematically observing musicians as they practise and perform and (2) asking them about their experiences.

Systematically Observing Practice and Performance

The systematic study of behaviours and actions has long served as a principal mode of data collection within psychology. The methods by which music researchers have done this have changed progressively over the last century. In early studies of musicians' practice, for example, researchers were often physically present in the practice room, hurriedly collecting data (making notes and counting errors) as musicians learned short, prescribed pieces (see Rubin-Rabson, 1937, 1939, 1940a, 1940b, 1941a, 1941b). More recently, researchers have had the luxury of portable audio and video recording equipment and, thus, have had enormous advantages over their predecessors, gaining the flexibility to study practice of standard repertoire works when and as often as they like, and giving their participants the freedom to decide for themselves where and when to practise.

A notable example of such work is that of Gruson (1988). She studied the practice strategies of 40 piano students and three concert pianists to determine how those strategies changed with increasing skill. She audio-taped all of the pianists' practice on three musical selections during a single practice session. She then asked a subset of the original 43 players to continue practising the three pieces for nine additional practice sessions. The participants' practice was assessed according to the 'Observational Scale for Piano Practising' (OSPP); a sample of the names and definitions of terms used in the OSPP is listed in Table 2.1. Gruson counted the frequency with which the designated behaviours occurred in practice, finding a number of differences in the practice of pianists at various levels of skill (for example, errors, repeated notes and pauses decreased with competence; self-guided speech, total verbalizations, playing hands separately, time spent practising on each piece and repeating sections increased). She concluded that 'it appears to be many hours of practising a wide variety of music pieces that influences practising behaviours' rather than specific pieces themselves (p. 104).

With this approach to studying behaviour, several logistical challenges must be taken into account. First, the act of recording practice, be it by audio or video,

Table 2.1   A sample of the terms from the Observational Scale for Piano Practising

Term	Definition
Playing without interruption	S plays the piece for 5s interval during which no other behavioural categories occur
Error	S plays incorrect note
Repeat note	S repeats a note on which an error may or may not have occurred with or without correction
Repeat measure	S repeats a measure, or part of a measure, in which an error may or may not have occurred with or without correction
Repeat section	S repeats a section of the piece longer than a measure in which an error may or may not have occurred with or without correction
Repeat piece	S repeats whole piece from beginning after completing previous practice of entire piece
Slow down	S slows the musical tempo beyond the range permitted by the music
Pause	S stops playing for at least 2s in a 5s interval
Speed up	S increases the musical tempo from the normal tempo for a part of the piece
Frustration	S verbalizes or emits signs of frustration
Hands separately	S plays a piece or section of a piece with one hand only
Total time	The duration of time spent in practising
Mean time/piece	(Total time)/(no. of pieces practised)
Tempo	No. of note/s of first practice in each session, averaged over pieces

Source: Gruson, 1988

can be intrusive and unwelcome for some musicians, causing increased levels of general anxiety and unnaturally sharpened self-awareness. Nevertheless, this approach is arguably still less intrusive than having a researcher stand close by, hastily jotting down notes and marking errors. Moreover, with prolonged usage, the impact of the recording device on levels of anxiety and self-awareness should diminish (although never disappearing for some), providing researchers with a near-realistic, and so ecologically valid, practice situation. At any rate, many performers already actively record their practice as a learning tool. Second, deciding how to *transcribe* the recorded practice (that is, turn it into usable information) and extract the desired details from the transcription can often require creative thinking. Gruson (1988) categorized and counted the frequency of behaviours according to the OSPP (below, in 'An Integrated Approach', we review another method of transcription). Regardless of the precise technique, transcriptions should be carefully planned according to pre-determined research objectives and hypotheses, so that adequate answers to research questions can be obtained. Third, listening to and transcribing data will almost inevitably be a labour-intensive endeavour. Depending on the type of transcription being carried out, one may spend many times the amount of actual practice time transcribing the recordings, starting and stopping audio or video tapes repeatedly to ensure that each detail has been documented accurately. To lessen the burden placed on a single researcher, several transcribers are sometimes recruited in order to distribute the workload. In doing this, reliability between researchers must be maintained and demonstrated using established statistical procedures (for example, Cohen's kappa; see Tabachnick and Fidell, 1996). Despite these challenges, systematic studies of practising behaviours in general have proven to be fruitful, providing first-hand, objective data in realistic practice settings (see also Miklaszewski, 1989, 1995; Williamon and Valentine, 2002).

While studies of practice routine and interviews with musicians can be enlightening, it is also important to understand, in as much detail as possible, precisely what musicians do during a performance. This poses something of a problem for the researcher. Perhaps the main difficulty with performance research lies in the method of observation. Particularly, ways must be devised in which realistic performances can be observed without the process of data collection actually interfering with the playing. In other words, how can the performance situation be made ecologically valid? One approach is to video live performances for subsequent analysis. Davidson (1995), for instance, used video recordings in studying the body movements of musicians during performance.

Suppose, however, a researcher wishes to investigate factors such as rhythm and timing during performance. A video recording may not yield sufficiently detailed information for such an analysis. The process of transcription itself would be hugely time-consuming, and in any case, the precision of such a transcription would be limited by a number of factors, not least of which being the relatively slow frame rate of the recording (around 24 frames per second).

It seems that some more direct intervention is necessary if data with the required level of detail is to be collected. The obvious solution is to have performers play on instruments capable of recording the necessary information, and it is probably for this reason that the great majority of detailed performance studies have concentrated on piano playing. It is not that pianists display any particularly interesting musical behaviour per se – simply that the best digital pianos are actually real pianos with various electronic sensors and machinery discreetly added. The realism of the instrument thus ceases to be a factor in experimental design, and the process of recording the data does not necessitate any physical intervention in the performance (other than having the pianist play the right piano). The performer can – in principle – be completely unaware of the data collection taking place. The same cannot be said, however, for even the most advanced electronic wind or string instruments, although this will surely change as the technology improves.

The data collected on digital pianos contains a wealth of information concerning the timing, dynamics and articulation of a given performance. The time interval between, for example, consecutive notes in a melodic line can be easily extracted and used to provide insight into the degree of rubato, the length of phrases and so on. Additionally, the dynamic level of each key-press is recorded and can be subject to similar analyses. Using data such as these, a substantial body of work has built up aiming to discover some of the factors involved in musical expression (see Clarke, 1999, for a review).

Questionnaires and Interviews

The methods outlined above have proven indispensable as tools for discovering 'what goes on' during music practice and performance. However, from the psychological perspective this is only part of the story. It seems important for the music psychologist to understand not only what musicians *do*, but what they *think* they do – in other words, to understand the feelings, attitudes and thought processes that musicians associate with practising and performing music.

Questionnaires are frequently employed in all kinds of psychological research, especially as a preliminary to some more complex experimental procedure. Most consist of a list of questions with either 'yes/no' responses or a range of possible answers over a fixed scale (say one to seven, or 'poor' to 'excellent'). Over the years, a variety of 'standard' questionnaires have been developed to measure factors such as state and trait anxiety (Spielberger et al., 1983), and these have sometimes been adapted specifically to music (for example, 'The Musical Performance Anxiety Self-statement Scale'; Craske, Craig and Kendrick, 1988). Of course, it is possible to create novel questionnaires. Sloboda (1991) developed a detailed questionnaire in which participants were asked to rate how often they experienced various physiological responses (for example, shivers and tears) while listening to music.

Questionnaires have the advantage of being relatively quick and easy to administer. Furthermore, since the questions are often answered by indicating the appropriate category from a fixed list, the data yielded are highly suited to statistical analysis. Some research has suggested that answers given to questionnaires may not be stable over time (Kendall et al., 1987); however, questionnaires can be useful for gathering demographic information about a group of people and assessing (to a limited degree) their attitudes toward certain issues.

Still, the information gleaned from questionnaires is often not sufficiently detailed to allow adequate insight into subjective experience. For this, we require a *qualitative* approach. Qualitative research is that which attempts 'to understand and represent the experiences and actions of people as they encounter, engage, and live through situations' (Elliott et al., 1999, p. 216). Qualitative techniques are explicitly concerned with people's subjective experience of the world, and how this experience affects their behaviour. Until relatively recently, qualitative research was rather out of favour. The rapid developments in 'computational' psychology during the 1960s encouraged a tendency towards methodological elitism, with the unfortunate consequence that directly *asking* people about their experiences was seen as unscientific. As phenomenological accounts of behaviour became unpopular, so too did methods that attempted to investigate the subjective experience of the participant. Fortunately, it is now generally accepted that qualitative measures can provide data that are rigorous and convincing, and as has been observed, 'the past 5 years have seen a dramatic increase in the use of qualitative research methods' (Elliott et al., 1999, p. 215). This is just as well for the music psychologist, as the nature of music performance and listening is such that it is often informative to ask people, more or less directly, about their own thoughts and feelings. While the number of qualitative techniques available to the researcher is too great to review fully here, the following discussion will consider one that is commonly used within music research: the interview.

Broadly speaking, interviews in psychology can take one of three forms: *structured, open-ended* or *semi-structured* (see Ray, 1993, for a review). *Structured* interviews follow a strict format, with little or no deviation from a pre-determined list of specific questions. These questions are usually simple and straightforward, leaving minimal scope for elaboration by the participant. Structured interviews have the advantage that the data are relatively unambiguous and so relatively unsusceptible to subjective interpretation. However, they are limited in their range of application. For example, a structured interview might be useful for finding basic information on practice habits – such as frequency and duration of practice sessions – but less suitable for, say, assessing the strategies employed by a musician to combat anxiety during solo performance.

Open-ended interviews, by contrast, have no set questions. Rather, the interviewer has a general list of themes that they wish to discuss during the interview. This approach to interviewing gives the participant complete freedom of response and places considerable pressure on the interviewer, who must be skilled in guiding the conversation as necessary. Open-ended interviews are notoriously difficult to conduct in such a way as to yield the most useful data and are not usually attempted except by the most experienced of interviewers. Even then, they are generally avoided except in cases where there is a clear need for such an approach (for example, when dealing with particularly sensitive issues).

Arguably the most frequently used type of qualitative technique is the *semi-structured* interview. Like structured interviews, semi-structured interviews are based around a particular list of questions. However, these questions will be phrased so as to allow scope for longer, more personalized answers than in a structured interview. Each question will usually be followed by a number of subsidiary 'probe' questions, either pre-determined or arising directly from the answer given to the initial question. These probe questions are used at the interviewer's discretion to clarify the participant's answer, to gain more information if they are not forthcoming, or to keep them on track if their answer moves too far away from the original question.

Semi-structured interviews have been used extensively in music research. Susan Hallam, for example, has employed the technique in her work on the performance attitudes of expert and novice musicians. In one study (Hallam 1994), she used semi-structured interviewing to 'enable an in-depth analysis of the practising modes' of 22 professional musicians (p. 5). The following is a list of the fixed questions posed by Hallam (often known as the interview script or schedule):

- Is your practice regular?
- Do you practise every day?
- Do you enjoy practising?
- Does your practice follow a regular routine?
- Do you have a warm-up procedure?
- Do you practise studies, scales or exercises?
- How do you practise to overcome difficulty?

Note that while the questions may be answered quite specifically, they are phrased so as to invite further comment. 'Do you enjoy practising?' could be answered simply as 'yes' or 'no', but seems more likely to provoke a response which discusses, for example, different types of practice or good and bad practice sessions. In this study, Hallam did not use pre-determined probe questions, preferring to 'explore … issues arising from the responses by generating further questions' (p. 5).

There are various methods of 'scoring' the data from semi-structured interviews, which enable the use of statistical techniques. Commonly, this kind of analysis will involve looking for particular trends in the participant's responses, counting their frequency and then using a statistical procedure, such as the Chi-square test, to draw inferences from the data. Since the process of interpreting and analysing conversation is itself unavoidably subjective, it is important that the transcription and its interpretation be checked for inter-rater reliability, usually by having a number of people perform the analysis independently.

Qualitative techniques can be invaluable in finding out about aspects of music performance not open to external observation. Despite the recent resurgence of interest in qualitative research, however, it is not without its problems. Chief amongst these is that the interviewer must be able to verify whether the participants are telling the truth – people are often loath to give answers that they feel may give a poor impression of themselves, and so can be tempted to 'say the right thing' rather than respond honestly. Nevertheless, this can be done with careful question-setting designed to minimize the temptation for participants to give misleading information. Related to this is the possibility that participants have never thought about the issue in question, have no real opinion about it or, on a more basic level, simply do not know the answer to a question but do not wish to appear ignorant.

An Integrated Approach

The above discussion has considered the study of music practice and performance from two apparently distinct perspectives. However, one might easily argue that this dichotomy is false, at least in the sense that music practitioners do not usually recognize such a distinction. The question seems to be, then, to what extent can the two modes of enquiry sketched above inform and complement each other to produce a rounded view of the psychology of music-making? Some recent work suggests that a more integrated approach to the subject matter may indeed provide insights that are not only interesting to the psychologist, but useful to the music practitioner.

Chaffin and Imreh (1997, 2001; see also Chaffin et al., 2002) systematically observed the practice of a concert pianist as she memorized and performed the Presto movement of Bach's *Italian Concerto* and Debussy's *Claire de Lune*. The majority of their analyses focused on the more complex of the two pieces, the Presto. Practice for this piece was divided into 57 sessions, aggregated into three learning periods and spread over ten months. Sessions were video-taped, and cumulative records were created showing the pianist's starting and stopping points in the music. Figure 2.1 displays one of Chaffin and Imreh's cumulative records from practice on section C of the Presto from Bach's *Italian Concerto*. The x-axis represents bars of the music, and the y-axis depicts the cumulative number of practice segments. The beginning of each horizontal line indicates the point in the music at which the pianist started playing the piece. The end of each line denotes the point in the music at which the pianist stopped playing. Each new line, reading from bottom to top, indicates that the pianist stopped and restarted.

Using the cumulative records, Chaffin and Imreh compared the number of times that the pianist started and stopped at boundaries in the formal structure (both sections and subsections) with the number of times that she started and stopped at other locations. They found that starts and stops occurred more frequently at structural boundaries than in the middle of sections. From this, they suggested that she organized her practice and subsequent retrieval of the Presto according to its formal structure.

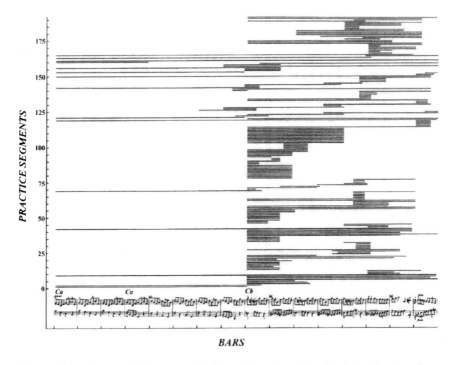

Figure 2.1   A cumulative record of practice of section C of the Presto of Bach's *Italian Concerto*

Source: Chaffin and Imreh, 1997, p. 329

Chaffin and Imreh used comments made by the pianist during and after each practice session and in interviews to confirm their interpretation of the data. In her commentary in session 17, for instance, she focused on sections of the formal structure in which the same theme was repeated. Specifically, she spent a considerable amount of time in comparing differences between the various repetitions of the A and B themes. She then put the two themes together, remarking: 'I think I am going to work on these larger sections. There are definitely a lot of conflicts going on between the first two pages and then the last page and a half ...' (p. 324). Chaffin and Imreh concluded that 'in order to monitor transitions between sections consciously, [she] needed to retrieve a conceptual representation of the next section from memory as she played' (p. 325).

By using qualitative methods in tandem with systematic observations, these authors were able to interpret their data according to existing theories of expert memory and situate their findings within a meaningful musical context. We believe that an integrated approach such as this offers a clear path for future investigation, be it by psychologists or music practitioners. However, researchers must be aware of the methodological problems that accompany the study of music practice and performance, and should be cautious in making specific assertions or predictions based on their data.

References

Allport, D.A., Antonis, B. and Reynolds, P. (1972) 'On the division of attention: A disproof of the single channel hypothesis', *Quarterly Journal of Experimental Psychology*, 24: 225–35.

Bartholomew, W.T. (1934) 'A physical definition of "good voice-quality" in the male voice', *Journal of the Acoustical Society of America*, 6: 25–33.

Binet, A. and Simon, T. (1905) 'New methods for the diagnosis of the intellectual level of subnormals', *Annals of Psychology*, 11: 191–244.

Blacking, J. (1995) *Music, Culture, and Experience*, Chicago: University of Chicago Press.

Butler, G. and McManus, F. (1995) *Psychology: A Very Short Introduction*, Oxford: Oxford University Press.

Cameron, P. and Fleming, P. (1975) 'Self-reported degree of pleasure associated with sexual activity across the adult life-span', mimeographed report: Division of Human Development, St. Mary's College of Maryland, MD.

Chaffin, R. and Imreh, G. (1997) '"Pulling teeth and torture": Musical Memory and Problem Solving', *Thinking and Reasoning*, 3: 315–36.

Chaffin, R. and Imreh, G. (2001) 'A comparison of practice and self-report as sources of information about the goals of expert practice', *Psychology of Music*, 29: 39–69.

Chaffin, R., Imreh, G. and Crawford, M. (2002) *Practicing Perfection: Memory and Piano Performance*, Mahwah, NJ: Lawrence Erlbaum Associates.

Chase, W.G. and Ericsson, K.A. (1981) 'Skilled memory', in J.R. Anderson (ed.), *Cognitive Skills and Their Acquisition*, pp. 141–89, Hillsdale, NJ: Lawrence Erlbaum Associates.

Chase, W.G. and Ericsson, K.A. (1982) 'Skill and working memory', in G.H. Bower (ed.), *The Psychology of Learning and Motivation* (Vol. 16), New York: Academic Press.

Clarke, E.F. (1988) 'Generative principles in music performance', in J.A. Sloboda (ed.), *Generative Processes in Music: The Psychology of Performance, Improvisation, and Composition*, pp. 1–26, Oxford: Clarendon Press.

Clarke, E.F. (1999) 'Rhythm and timing in music', in D. Deutsch (ed.), *The Psychology of Music*, pp. 473–500, San Diego: Academic Press.

Cook, Nicholas (1994) 'Perception: A perspective from music theory', in R. Aiello (ed.), *Musical Perceptions*, pp. 64–95, Oxford: Oxford University Press.

Coslin, P.G. (1980) 'The adolescent through the works of the Research Group on Juvenile Adjustment on the University of Montreal', *Bulletin de Psychologie*, 33: 627–9.

Craske, M.G., Craig, K.D. and Kendrick, M.J. (1988) 'The musical performance anxiety self-statement scale', in M. Hersen and A.S. Bellack (eds), *Dictionary of Behavioral Assessment Techniques*, Oxford: Pergamon.

Cronbach, L.J. (1984) *Essentials of Psychological Testing* (4th edn.), New York: Harper and Row.

Davidson, J.W. (1995) 'What does the visual information contained in music performances offer the observer? Some preliminary thoughts', in R. Steinberg (ed.), *Music and the Mind Machine: The Psychophysiology and Psychopathology of the Sense of Music*, pp. 105–13, Berlin: Springer-Verlag.

Deutsch, D. (1999) *The Psychology of Music* (2nd edn.), San Diego: Academic Press.

Elliott, R., Fischer, C.T. and Rennie, D.L. (1999) 'Evolving guidelines for publication of qualitative research studies in psychology and related fields', *British Journal of Clinical Psychology*, 38: 215–29.

Ericsson, K.A. and Kintsch, W. (1995) 'Long-term working memory', *Psychological Review*, 102: 211–45.

Gabrielsson, A. (1999) 'The performance of music', in D. Deutsch (ed.), *The Psychology of Music*, pp. 501–602, San Diego: Academic Press.

Gruson, L.M. (1988) 'Rehearsal skill and musical competence: Does practice make perfect?', in J.A. Sloboda (ed.), *Generative Processes in Music: The Psychology of Performance, Improvisation, and Composition*, pp. 91–112, Oxford: Clarendon Press.

Hallam, S. (1994) 'Novice musicians' approaches to practice and performance: Learning new music', *Newsletter of the European Society for the Cognitive Sciences of Music*, 6: 2–10.

Halpern, A.R. and Bower, G.H. (1982) 'Musical expertise and melodic structure in memory for musical notation', *American Journal of Psychology*, 95: 31–50.

Hargreaves, D.J. and North, A.C. (1997) *The Social Psychology of Music*, Oxford: Oxford University Press.

Kant, I. (1974[1781]) *Kritik der reinen Vernunft*, trans. J.M.D. Meikeljohn, London: J. M. Dent & Sons.

Keller, P.E. (2001) 'Attentional resource allocation in musical ensemble performance', *Psychology of Music*, 29: 20–38.

Kendall, P.C., Hollon, S.D., Beck, A.T. et al. (1987) 'Issues and recommendations regarding use of the Beck Depression Inventory', *Cognitive Therapy and Research*, 11: 289–99.

Miklaszewski, K. (1989) 'A case study of a pianist preparing a musical performance', *Psychology of Music*, 17: 95–109.

Miklaszewski, K. (1995) 'Individual differences in preparing a musical composition for public performance', in M. Manturzewska, K. Miklaszewski and A. Bialkowski (eds), *Psychology of Music Today: Proceedings of the International Seminar of Researchers and Lecturers in the Psychology of Music*, pp. 138–47, Warsaw: Fryderyk Chopin Academy of Music.

North, A.C. and Hargreaves, D.J. (1998) 'The effect of music on atmosphere and purchase intentions in a cafeteria', *Journal of Applied Social Psychology*, 28: 2254–73.

North, A.C., Hargreaves, D.J. and McKendrick, J. (1999) 'The influence of in-store music on wine selections', *Journal of Applied Psychology*, 84: 271–76.

Parncutt, R. and McPherson, G. (2002) *Science and Psychology of Music Performance: Creative Strategies for Teaching and Learning*, Oxford: Oxford University Press.

Ray, W.J. (1993), *Methods: Toward a Science of Behaviour and Experience* (4th edn.), Pacific Grove, CA: Brooks/Cole.

Roe, K. (1985) 'Swedish youth and music: Listening patterns and motivations', *Communication Research*, 12: 353–62.

Rubin-Rabson, G. (1937) *The Influence of Analytical Pre-study in Memorizing Piano Music*, New York: Archives of Psychology.

Rubin-Rabson, G. (1939) 'Studies in the psychology of memorizing piano music: I. A comparison of the unilateral and the coordinated approaches', *The Journal of Educational Psychology*, 30: 321–45.

Rubin-Rabson, G. (1940a) 'Studies in the psychology of memorizing piano music: II. A comparison of massed and distributed practice', *The Journal of Educational Psychology*, 31: 270–84.

Rubin-Rabson, G. (1940b) 'Studies in the psychology of memorizing piano music: III. A comparison of the whole and part approach', *The Journal of Educational Psychology*, 31: 460–76.

Rubin-Rabson, G. (1941a) 'Studies in the psychology of memorizing piano music: V. A comparison of pre-study periods of varied length', *The Journal of Educational Psychology*, 32: 101–12.

Rubin-Rabson, G. (1941b) 'Studies in the psychology of memorizing piano music: VI. A comparison of two forms of mental rehearsal and keyboard overlearning', *Journal of Educational Psychology*, 32: 593–602.

Seamon, J.G. and Kenrick, D.T. (1992) *Psychology*, Englewood Cliffs, NJ: Prentice Hall.

Seashore, C.E. (1910) 'The measurement of pitch discrimination', *Psychological Monographs*, 13: 21–63.

Seashore, C.E. (1912) 'The measure of a singer', *Science*, 35: 201–12.

Seashore, C.E. (1919) *Manual of Instructions and Interpretations of Measures of Musical Talent*, Chicago: C.H. Stoelting.

Shaffer, L.H. (1980) 'Analysing piano performance', in G.E. Stelmach and J. Requin (eds), *Tutorials in Motor Behaviour*, Amsterdam: North-Holland.

Shaffer, L.H. (1981) 'Performances of Chopin, Bach, and Bartok: Studies in motor programming', *Cognitive Psychology*, 13: 326–76.

Sloboda, J.A. (1985) *The Musical Mind: The Cognitive Psychology of Music*, Oxford: Oxford University Press.

Sloboda, J.A. (1991) 'Music structure and emotional response: Some empirical findings', *Psychology of Music*, 19: 110–20.

Spielberger, C.D., Gorsuch, R.L., Lushene, R., Vagg, P.R. and Jacobs, G.A. (1983) *Manual for the State-trait Anxiety Inventory (Form Y1)*. Palo Alto, CA: Consulting Psychologists Press.

Staszewski, J.J. (1988) 'Skilled memory and expert mental calculation', in M.T.H. Chi, R. Glaser and M.J. Farr (eds), *The Nature of Expertise*, Hillsdale, NJ: Lawrence Erlbaum Associates.

Tabachnick, B.G. and Fidell, L.S. (1996) *Using Multivariate Statistics* (3rd edn.), New York: Harper Collins.

Terman, L.M. and Merrill, M.A. (1972) *Stanford-Binet Intelligence Scale – Manual for the Third Revision, Form L-M*, Boston: Houghton-Mifflin.

Toohey, J.V. (1982) 'Popular music and social values', *Journal of School Health*, 52: 582–85.

Valentine, E.R. (1992) *Conceptual Issues in Psychology* (2nd edn.), London: Routledge.

Williamon, A. (2002) 'Memorising music', in J. Rink (ed.), *Musical Performance: A Guide to Study and Practice*, pp. 113–28, Cambridge: Cambridge University Press.

Williamon, A. (ed.) (2004) *Musical Excellence: Strategies and Techniques to Enhance Performance*, Oxford: Oxford University Press.

Williamon, A. and Valentine, E. (2002) 'The role of retrieval structures in memorizing music', *Cognitive Psychology*, 44: 1–32.

Wilson, G.D. (1994) *Psychology for Performing Artists: Butterflies and Bouquets*, London: Jessica Kingsley Publishers.

Wundt, W. (1862) *Beiträge zur Theorie der Sinneswahrnemung* [*Contributions to the Theory of Sensory Perception*], Leipzig: Winter.

Chapter 3

What and Why Do We Need to Know about Music Psychology Research to Improve Music Instrument Teaching?[1]

Kacper Miklaszewski

I would account for my career in 99 percent to my work, and only in one percent to my talent – Ignacy Jan Paderewski (cited in Lawton, 1939)

Playing a musical instrument is a complex skill. Musicians know this because they remember how just much practice they needed to invest in order to achieve proficiency. Psychologists attempt to understand musical skills, but realize that the complex interaction of many factors make it a difficult phenomenon to explain. For example, when Sloboda applied the terms of Production System Theory (which is based on the fundamental concept that in order to learn and develop a skill, habits need to be formed, and the habits need to become automatic, using little conscious effort – see Anderson, 1981, for more details), he found that performance demands many habits, skills and forms of knowledge. To attempt to show how a learner acquires procedural knowledge (know-how) in playing a musical instrument, Sloboda (1985) concluded that:[1]

> to get to middle C from any other note would require about 30 [...] rules. To get from any note to any other note would require about 900. (Sloboda 1985, p. 228)

So, any attempt to describe musical activity precisely will need to face the problem of the overwhelming complexity of the task itself. Thus it is not surprising that musicians differ very much in their opinions on how they play, and therefore that psychologists have tackled questions about music learning and performance with varying degrees of success to date.

Here are some of the contradictory opinions of musicians and psychologists:

> When I learn a composition, which I have listened to many times before, I never start to play it at the piano ... (Jakov Zak, cited in Vicinski, 1950, p. 182)

> Maria Grinberg (ibid., p. 179) 'simply start(s) to play'.

Psychologist Gordon (2000) says that the worst thing we can do when teaching good performance of rhythmic structures is to ask students to count aloud, while Newman (1974) strongly advises all pianists to count 'with the metronome at a slow tempo' (p. 166). Similar diversity of opinions can be found both in old and more recent sources (see for example Brower 1915, 1917; Marcus, 1979; Miklaszewski, 1983).

In light of all the above, it is no wonder that the role of music instrumental teacher is perceived to be quite demanding (Hallam, 1995). Performance proficiency consists of many skills developed in the aural/oral, aesthetic, expressive and motor domains which all converge in the act of performance. The teacher's objective is, however, not to equip the learner with separate skills, but with a composite: the unique ability to perform music fluently, with technical accuracy, creativity and personal expression. To attain this goal he/she has to provide a student with a richly varied and stimulating experience in order to develop his/her desire to learn, and thus encourage him/her to practise. It seems from the research literature and everyday experience (Hallam, 1995) that teachers usually ask their learners to prepare a task and to evaluate it.

Developing motor skills and skills of critical reflection seems to be the best approach. In trying to explain to a student what he/she should feel (in aural, aesthetic, expressive or motor domains), teachers primarily refer to their own experience, having no access to the experience of their learners. Serious problems appear if verbal advice, imagery and metaphor – the tools typically used to stimulate the creative imagination (see Correia, 1999) – do not work for a particular student.

The aim of this chapter is to point out some of the findings discussed in research on musical behaviour as well as psychology, with the belief that, having them in mind, music teachers may be helped to broaden their repertoire of teaching tools about technical and expressive matters, and in doing so it is hoped that the teacher's work may become more effective.

What Researchers Think They Know about Music Practice

Memorization and Practising

The question of how musicians learn to play their instruments has interested scholars for a century. Kovacs (1916) and Rubin-Rabson (1937, 1945) pioneered the study conditions for effective memorization. They stressed the importance of auditory memory and mental rehearsal during practising, as opposed to purely mechanical memorization. A large range of studies on practising has been recently summarized by Hallam (1997b). She has related the existing findings to a model of practising, derived from Biggs and Moore's (1993) model of general learning. In the model, three groups of factors have been outlined, and labelled *presage*, *process* and *product*.

Hallam shows that many of the relations included in the model have been supported in the research literature; however, some aspects still remain under-researched. Among the latter there are the topics of the individual differences between learners; the effects of the nature of the task to be learned and the relationship between practice and the qualitative aspects of performance; the effects of curriculum and performance requirements on practice and motivation; and the processes involved in developing aural representation of music and how these are used to monitor performance (Hallam, 1997b, p. 217).

People achieving mastery in music performance clearly practise a lot, reaching thousands of hours accumulated during ten or more years of training (Sloboda et al., 1996; Ericsson, 1997). During that time music students not only learn how to play but also how to learn, memorize and so master new repertoire and how to improve their technical proficiency. Hallam (1994, 1997a) found big differences between practice strategies applied by experienced musicians and novices. Professionals, despite individual differences, 'appeared to draw on a musical knowledge base which enabled them to assess the task, identify task difficulties, recognise errors, monitor progress, and take appropriate action to overcome problems' (Hallam, 1997a, p. 103). They think primarily of music (precise sequences of sound events) even though they do it unconsciously, having technical goals in mind (Chaffin, 2000).

Nielsen (1999) points out that specific strategies are used to select relevant information to master the task, to organize the selected information and to integrate it with existing knowledge. He suggests that music teachers should instruct their students to develop their strategic competence accordingly.

From this research literature it seems that an immediate implication for the teacher is to understand that large numbers of hours of practice are required, but this process can be facilitated by the introduction of a range of practice skills (rehearsing small sections, practising individual elements, and so on) which – given that different individuals prefer to work in different ways – will hopefully suit some or all of the individuals' needs. In order to memorize music, the student needs to be taught how to 'hear' the music in their mind and to develop their memory whilst practising.

Internal Representation (a Mental Plan or Template) of Music

Ericsson (1997, p. 40) points out the need for an 'internal representation to mediate expert music performance and its continued improvement during practice'. A good example of this is Lehmann's (1997) discovery that approaching a task will depend on former training and experience. In a memorization experiment, Lehmann discovered that transposition was the most difficult task for all participants, and a correlation between speed of memorization and transposition performance was found. That is, those who could memorize new material quicker were better at performing the transposition task. The author concluded that this finding showed the critical need to possess the ability to represent music mentally: 'Certainly, memorisation manifests itself when the music is memorised, for it is apparent in efficient memorisation as well as in the successful manipulation of the memorised material' (cf. Lehmann, 1997, p. 152).

Mental representation of music has been attracting the attention of researchers and music philosophers for many years. Meyer (1956) and Lerdahl and Jackendoff (1983) related mental representation of music to the structure of music. Theoretically, the essence of musical knowledge for them was the fulfilling or violating of listeners' expectations concerning the development of the musical structure in time. Jones (1990) proposed a theoretical approach in which 'attentional biases and experience with a culture's music shape a listener's responses to some music events'. Using the neuronal network paradigm, Bharucha (1992) successfully modelled the acquisition of tonal structures with the hierarchy of tonic, dominant, subdominant, mediant, submediant and leading note, as a function of the repetitive presentation of stimuli.

In performance studies mental representation of music has been discussed as a performance plan (or intention) which is realized on an instrument through the execution of carefully matched motor programs (Shaffer, 1981; Sloboda, 1982, 1985). It seems that a plan can be either stable – when we perform a well-rehearsed piece of music – or flexible, as in performance at sight. However, effective motor procedures must be easily accessible and predictable.

The role of an internal representation of music interested Miklaszewski (1983), who analysed published interviews with professional performers. Among nine players who explicitly spoke about the development of internal representation of a rehearsed piece of music, seven reported evolutionary changes of the 'ideal form' of music during the practice period, while two claimed knowing all the details of how music should sound just at the beginning of their work. Later on, Miklaszewski and Sawicki (1992) correlated hierarchically weighted measures of the compositions (tonal, rhythmic, melodic 'strength') with the numbers of times that these measures were selected as start and end points of sections practised separately by musicians. A moderate positive relationship between segmentation of music and its form was found. Closer analysis of the criteria used for the segmentation and selection of very short sections indicated that musicians 'think' in terms of formal units of the composition, and departed from this rule only to overcome technical and fingering difficulties rather than to clarify how music should sound.

Thus, this section has indicated that audiences and performers appear to have a mental representation of musical structure which shapes their listening, performing and rehearsing behaviours. It is evident that the music teacher can use this knowledge to assist in structuring tasks for students, both to strengthen their existing representations and to develop new knowledge and skill. Working with western tonal music in its structural units will clearly facilitate the memorization process.

Audiation

Audiation is a term developed by Gordon:

> Audiation takes place when one hears and comprehends music silently, that is when the sound of the music is not physically present. [...] It may seem contradictory that one may listen to (hear) music and at the same time audiate that music. The fact is that as one listens to music, he is aurally perceiving sound the moment that it is heard. It is not until a moment or so after the sound is heard that he audiates and gives meaning to that sound as he is aurally perceiving additional sounds that follow in the music. As one audiates, he may also be recalling (anticipating) the music. ... Although musicians are capable of hearing all of the music that they audiate, it cannot be assumed, unfortunately, that they are capable of audiating all of the music that they hear. (Gordon, 1989, pp. 7–8)

Audiation is then the foundation for learning musical terminology and the symbolic representation of musical events (musical notation). Audiation is also fundamental to playing an instrument. The essence of instrumental proficiency is to transfer musical ideas into acoustical events in order to guarantee reception of these ideas by listeners. Competent performance is impossible without having audiational experience of music prior to its execution on the instrument. In this case audiation is a term analogous to a performance plan.

Many empirical investigations have shown that those who do not 'audiate' with fluency are slower at learning and are weaker at pitch skills such as tuning and other forms of pitch-matching (see McPherson, 1996). Thus, developing training programmes in which students are encouraged to 'think in sound' will evidently have benefits in the learning and understanding of music.

Assigning Meaning to Music

The meaning of music has been discussed by many musicians. Controversially, Clynes (1977) postulated the existence of biologically programmed spatio-temporal patterns for the non-verbal communication of specific emotional characters in music. According to this theory, emotion and its expression form a single existential entity – a vital part of music. Sloboda (1998), however, argues that the dynamics of experience – sensations of tensions and resolutions – are vital in bringing musical meaning. He points out that emotions and moods are usually either positively or negatively valued, 'but the dynamic feelings or sensations of tension are essentially unvalenced' (p. 25), and so could be meanings brought by music. Both Lavy and Levinson (in this volume) provide more possible explanations. However, the one focused upon here is that proposed by Watt and Ash (1998), who supposed that when:

> we experience the sound of music ... we are consciously aware of the acoustic structure of the sound (at least when we attend to it). However, when we listen to

music we are aware of more than just this. We are aware of a significance to the pattern of sound. (p. 34)

Their experiment with 180 musically naïve subjects suggested that listeners tend to attribute so-called 'disclosure' meaning to music, rather than meaning associated with taste or features of physical objects. Disclosure meaning covers cues which tell us about the personality of a person delivering an utterance. Watt and Ash conclude that music is probably perceived as if it were a person making disclosure. Moreover, individual compositions have their own unique patterns and structures. Therefore, the music itself is possibly analogous to a specific personality with highly individualized traits and characteristics.

When we listen to different performances of the same composition (for example, Prelude Six from *The Second Book of Preludes* ('Général Lavine' – excentrique) by Debussy, as performed by Krystian Zimerman (CD reference: DG 435 773-2) and Francine Kay (CD reference: Audio Ideas AI-CD-005)) we experience two different 'disclosure' meanings of the same music. In the different performances, rhythmic and timbral patterns are executed in a significantly different manner, but the execution is coherent throughout each performance. This indicates that each performer assigned an interpretation to the music's patterns and structures in a highly coherent way. Thus, tonal and rhythmic patterns, and even separate sounds, are given an 'identity' by the performer. This identity secures recognition of the performer's interpretation. Thus, the performer's interpretation may be regarded as an expression or manifestation of their personality.

The approach to meaning given here is only one of many explored; however, it implies that teachers can help students to understand both compositional and interpretational style in an immediate and personalized manner.

Meaning of Music and the Self-controlling Brain

The pianist Vladimir Ashkenazy told the reporter of *Clavier* that for him learning is:

> An emotional process … Emotional is to put the significance of the piece into the complex of your personality, so to speak it's done, then you don't have to memorise as such because then the piece memorises by itself, by the significance of its content. (Stone and Parsons, 1976, p. 12)

When discussing the meaning of music, it is possible to think about the meaning assigned to acoustical structures by a person. Perhaps it is only in this moment that these acoustical structures become music. When listening to music performed by a musician who willingly assigns some meaning to it, the listener's expertise is used to detect this meaning from the performance. The precise knowledge the listener has of the performer's meaning is an attractive research problem and one which has been pursued by some researchers (for example, Sloboda, 1985;

Gabrielsson et al., 1983); but in this context, the meaning of music appears to be a result of attentive listening as well as intentional shaping of acoustical structures during performance.

The brain scientist Sir John Eccles has been interested in voluntary attention for a long time. He stresses that 'perception is dependent on a *directed attention'* (1994, p. 108) and voluntary movements are dependent on our conscious will to act. Thus '... there is no need to consider all of ... activity as being *primarily* induced by the task ...' (p. 164). Attention can enhance and embellish perceptions:

> This can be appreciated when we listen attentively to music or examine a beautiful picture or enjoy some beauty in nature. Attention is specially related to the appreciation of beauty ... *consciousness is experienced in the brain where you evoke it by your attention*, which plays on selected areas of the cerebral cortex to give excitation. (p. 176)

Following this hypothesis, it would be possible to think that musicality and interests may govern the perception of music and modulate processes involved in learning music. Musicians would probably agree that focusing attention on music – perceived as well as performed – and a will to act musically are very important in the development and acquisition of musical skills. Here is yet another possible implication for the teacher: to train the student's attention to unfold the many possible levels of interpretation, structure, form and thus emotion and expression in the piece, and in themselves.

Playing Musical Instruments and the Will to Act

Whatever we know about the anatomy of hands and fingers, lips and lungs, we are still unable to describe precisely what we do when playing a musical instrument. Having a model by Shaffer (1981) in mind, we could suppose that the more precise the plan we possess, the easier it is to execute a performance. For Shaffer, a key task of the performer is to shape the timing and loudness of the musical sounds, patterns and phrases in a manner that remains in agreement with the musical form (Shaffer, 1984, 1987, 1993). Unfortunately, brain research still gives us no direct knowledge of how the mental representation of the music to be performed is transferred into precise sequences of neuronal signals and sent to our hands and fingers; how, in fact, our will to act becomes an action.

We know, however, that there are different motor areas in a human brain cortex. Besides the primary motor cortex, in which the chain of motor impulses leading to muscles starts, there exist a supplementary motor area and a pre-motor area. The supplementary motor area is thought to participate in planning highly complex coordinated sequences of movements, and the cells of the pre-motor area activate much earlier than the cells in the primary motor area. This anticipation increases with the growing complexity of motor response and its intended precision. Another part of our brain – the cerebellum – is assumed to be responsible for the comparison of what was to be attained by the movement with what has been actually attained. Thus it plays a significant role in movement control (Górska and Majczyński, 1997). However, much of the processing of coordinated movements is placed in parts of the brain that are not accessible by human conscious control. It means that our minds can execute movements only by setting the goals for them and controlling how the goals are attained. The consequence of this is that a lot of practice is needed in order to learn to perform highly coordinated motor sequences, such as those involved in playing a musical instrument. It is not possible to master piano playing only by thinking about finger movements. Happily, we are able to plan the results of an intended action and then evaluate them, audiate, and express emotions stemming from the performance. Undoubtedly, the more that we use the 'self' to control our brain, the more effectively we learn.

The hint here for the teacher is obvious: what we are lacking in one domain, we can make up for in another. Therefore, the teacher needs to encourage the student to develop as many conscious and reflective strategies for learning, listening and performing as possible.

Conclusion

In a chapter as brief as this, it is not possible to cover a large number of points for discussion. However, by focusing on what is known about some elements of performance, it seems that the music practitioner, and most specifically the teacher, can learn how to refine their own approaches to learning music.

Note

1. The author would like to thank Jane Davidson and the Ashgate editorial staff for their creative help and assistance in the preparation of the final version of this chapter.

References

Anderson, J.R (1981) *Cognitive Skills and their Acquisition*, Erlbaum: Lawrence Erlbaum Associates.

Bharucha, J.J. (1992) 'Tonality and learnability', in M.R. Jones and S. Hallam (eds), *Cognitive Bases of Music Communication*, pp. 213–14, Washington, DC: APA.

Biggs, J. and Moore, P.J. (1993) *The Process of Learning*, New York: Prentice Hall.

Brower, H. (1915) *Piano Mastery: Talks with Master Pianists and Teachers*, New York: Stokes.

Brower, H. (1917) *Piano Mastery: Talks with Master Pianists and Teachers – Second Series*, New York: Stokes.

Chaffin, R. (2000) 'Characteristics of expert performance: A case study', paper presented in the symposium *Does Practice Make Perfect?* S. Hallam (Chair), at the *5th International Conference on Music Perception and Cognition*, 7 August 2000, University of Keele, UK.

Clynes, M. (1977) *Sentics: The Touch of Emotions*, New York: Anchor Press/Doubleday.

Correia, J.S. (1999) 'Embodied meaning: All languages are ethnic ...' *Psychology of Music*, 27: 96–101.

Eccles, J.C. (1994) *How the SELF Controls its BRAIN*, Berlin: Springer.

Ericsson, K.A. (1997) 'Deliberate practice and the acquisition of expert performance: An overview', in H. Jørgensen and A.C. Lehmann (eds), *Does Practice Make Perfect? Current Theory and Research on Instrumental Music Practice*, pp. 9–51, Oslo: Norges musikhogskole.

Gabrielsson, A., Bengtsson, I. and Gabrielsson, B. (1983) 'Performance of musical rhythm in 3/4 and 6/8 meter', *Scandinavian Journal of Psychology*, 24: 193–213.

Gordon, E.E. (1989) *Learning Sequences in Music,* Chicago: GIA.

Gordon, E.E. (2000) 'Teoria uczenia się muzyki' ['Music learning theory'], in E. Zwolińska (ed.), *Podstawy teorii uczenia się muzyki według Edwina E. Gordona [Fundamentals of Music Learning Theory according to Edwin E. Gordon]*, Bydgoszcz: WSP.

Górska, T. and Majczyński, H. (1997) 'Mechanizmy sterowania ruchami dowolnymi' ['Mechanisms of voluntary movements'], in T. Górska, A. Grabowska and J. Zagrodzka (eds), *Mózg a zachowanie [Brain and the Behaviour]*, pp. 214–32, Warsaw: PWN.

Hallam, S. (1994) 'Novice musicians' approaches to practice and performance: Learning new music', *Newsletter of the European Society for the Cognitive Sciences of Music*, 6: 2–9.

Hallam, S. (1995) 'Professional musicians' orientations to practice: Implications for teaching', *British Journal of Educational Psychology*, 12: 3–19.

Hallam, S. (1997a) 'Approaches to instrumental music practice of experts and novices: Implications for education', in H. Jørgensen and A.C. Lehmann (eds), *Does Practice Make Perfect? Current Theory and Research on Instrumental Music Practice*, pp. 89–107, Oslo: Norges musikhogskole.

Hallam, S. (1997b) 'What do we know about practising? Toward a model synthesising the research literature', in H. Jørgensen and A.C. Lehmann (eds), *Does Practice Make Perfect? Current Theory and Research on Instrumental Music Practice*, pp. 179–231, Oslo: Norges musikhogskole.

Jones, M.R. (1990) 'Learning and the development of expectancies: An interactionist approach', *Psychomusicology*, 9(2): 193–228.

Kovacs, (1916) 'Untersuchungen über das musikalische Gedachtnis' ['Research into Musical Memory'] *Zeitschrift für Angewandte Psychologie*, 11: 113–35.

Lawton, M. (1939) *The Paderewski Memoirs* (Polish edition 1984), Kraków: PWM.

Lehmann, A.C. (1997) 'Acquired mental representation in music performance: Anecdotal and preliminary empirical evidence', in H. Jørgensen and A.C. Lehmann (eds), *Does Practice Make Perfect? Current Theory and Research on Instrumental Music Practice*, Oslo: Norges musikhogskole.

Lerdahl, F. and Jackendoff, R. (1983) *A Generative Theory of Tonal Music*, Cambridge, MA: MIT Press.

Marcus, A. (1979) *Great Pianists Speak with Adele Marcus*, Neptune, NJ: Paganiniana.

McPherson, G.E. (1996) 'Five aspects of musical performance and their correlates', *Council for Research in Music Education*, 127: 115–21.

Meyer, L.B. (1956) *Emotion and Meaning in Music*, Chicago: University of Chicago Press.

Miklaszewski, K. (1983) 'Praca muzyka instrumentalisty nad utworem przygotowywanym do publicznej prezentacji – próba analizy' ['Musician instrumentalist's work on musical composition prepared for public performance – an attempt at analysis'], unpublished doctoral dissertation, Warsaw: Chopin Academy.

Miklaszewski, K. and Sawicki, L. (1992) 'Kryteria segmentacji materiału muzycznego dokonywanej przez pianistów w utworze przygotowywanym do publicznej prezentacji' ['Criteria of segmentation introduced by pianists into a composition prepared for public performance'], in J. Krassowski (ed.), *Muzyka fortepianowa IX* [*Piano Music vol. IX*], pp. 181–95, Gdańsk: Moniuszko Academy of Music.

Newman, W.S. (1974) *The Pianist's Problems: A Modern Approach to Efficient Practice and Musicianly Performance*, New York: Harper and Row.

Nielssen, S.G. (1999) 'Learning strategies in instrumental music practice', *British Journal of Music Education*, 16(3): 275–91.

Rubin-Rabson, G. (1937) 'The influence of analytical prestudy in memorizing piano music', *Archives of Psychology*, 220 (monograph): New York.

Rubin-Rabson, G. (1945) 'Mental and keyboard overlearning in memorizing piano music', *The Journal of Musicology*, III(1).

Shaffer, L.H. (1981) 'Performances of Chopin, Bach, and Bartok. Studies in motor programming', *Cognitive Psychology*, 13: 326–76.

Shaffer, L.H. (1984) 'Timing in solo and duet piano performances', *The Quarterly Journal of Experimental Psychology*, 36A: 577–95.

Shaffer, L.H. (1987) 'The interpretive component in musical performance', in A. Gabrielsson (ed.), *Action and Perception in Rhythm and Music*, Stockholm: Royal Swedish Academy of Music.

Shaffer, L.H. (1993), 'Performing the F# minor Prelude Op. 28 No. 8 by Chopin', unpublished manuscript.

Sloboda, J.A. (1982), 'Music performance', in D. Deutsch (ed.), *The Psychology of Music*, New York: Academic Press.

Sloboda, J.A. (1985), *Musical Mind. The Cognitive Psychology of Music*, Oxford: Clarendon Press.

Sloboda, J.A. (1998) 'Does music mean anything?', *Musicae Scientiae*, II(1): 21–32.

Sloboda, J.A., Davidson, J.W., Howe, M.J.A. and Moore, D.G. (1996) 'The role of practice in the development of performing musicians', *British Journal of Psychology*, 87: 287–309.

Stone, G. and Parsons, A. (1976) 'Vladimir Ashkenazy talks', *Clavier*, 15(1): 10–13.

Vicinski, A.V. (1950) 'Psichologičeskii analiz processa raboty pianista-ispolnitielia nad muzkalnym proizviedieniiem' ['Psychological analysis of a piano performer's work on music composition'], *Izviestiia Akademii Pedagogičeskich Nauk RSFSR Vyp.* 25: 171–215.

Watt, R.J. and Ash, R.L. (1998) 'Psychological investigation of meaning in music', *Musicae Scientiae*, II(1): 33–53.

Chapter 4

The State of Play in Performance Studies

John Rink

Scholarly research on musical performance has been gaining in momentum to the point that 'performance studies' might now be regarded as a musicological discipline in its own right. Evidence for this exists in the burgeoning books and articles on performance from recent years, and in the remarkable number of conferences devoted at least in part to performance issues. More and more universities and conservatoires offer courses encouraging the interaction of theory and practice, rather than their traditional separation, while professional performers increasingly present themselves as both 'doers' and 'talkers' (Kerman, 1985, p. 196).

This healthy state of affairs partly reflects changes within musicology at large – among others, challenges to the 'work concept' and the presumed identity between score and music; thus, there is a renewed emphasis on music as sound and event, an ontological status lost in the mid-nineteenth century, when music's notation gained the upper hand. Of course, the study of musical performance has a long tradition within musicology, mostly in the fields of 'historical performance practice' and the psychology of performance. The chief differences today are a broader remit and a simultaneous dismantling of boundaries between performance-related research domains. In José Bowen's words (1999, p. 445), 'the study of music in performance offers a common ground, where "new" and "traditional" musicology can meet'.

But can we legitimately speak of a discipline – or even a subdiscipline – of performance studies? In the strict sense, perhaps not, or not yet – if a 'discipline' requires a community of scholars, institutions to support their work, a body of research and established modes of dissemination, shared beliefs and values, a common discourse, and a perceived identity.[1] Performance studies scores higher on some of these counts than others, although the past decade's achievements have at least put this field of enquiry firmly on the musicological map.

Bowen similarly professes faith in 'a new, unexplored subdiscipline, the study of music *as* and *in* performance'. He argues 'not that musicology should abandon ... its current methodology or goals', but that it should strive for 'an understanding that music is heard, analysed, and even conceived in terms of individual, period, and geographic performance styles, ... work-specific traditions, and individually innovative performances'. For Bowen, to study the performance tradition of a musical work is to study the musical work itself (1999, pp. 424, 430 and 451). Jonathan Dunsby, on the other hand, is more circumspect – or so he was in *Performing Music: Shared Concerns* from 1995. Claiming that 'little sense has emerged of a discipline', he describes performance studies as 'fragmentary' and marked by a 'relatively random scattering' of contributions, many of which fail to engage with 'real, pragmatic issue[s]' or to address 'even preliminary matters ... usefully' (1995, pp. 23, 25 and 27).

Although greater consolidation has been achieved since 1995, certain problems plague performance studies as currently practised (which might explain Nicholas Cook's reference (2001, p. 40) to a 'faltering advance towards a performance studies paradigm' within musicology). These include a lack of common understanding as to what properly belongs within that umbrella term (a simple comparison of the many degree programmes in 'performance studies' reveals great disparity as to content and curriculum); an almost exclusive bias towards western art music; a secondary bias towards solo piano repertoire, particularly in two of the three principal domains within performance studies; and a further bias towards the study of tempo and dynamics, mainly because these lend themselves to more rigorous modelling than intractable parameters like colour and bodily gesture.[2] How these problems will be overcome remains to be seen; much depends on their clear recognition by practitioners of this putative discipline. With that in mind I shall conduct a survey of its constituent parts, briefly summarizing the main aims of three overlapping domains: historical performance practice, the psychology of performance, and analysis and performance. Within each, I shall identify both fundamental dichotomies and constraints imposed on the performer. A case study of Chopin's E minor Prelude Op. 28 No. 4 will follow.

The first dichotomy – in the field of historical performance practice – exists between 'pure' research and its hands-on application. In Joseph Kerman's view, historical performance practice research reconstructs features 'that conventional musical notation leaves out' – including absolute pitch level, tuning, tempo, rhythmic nuance, embellishment, timbre, articulation, playing techniques and even type of instrument. Little wonder that 'so much more seems to be written about musical performance from a historical standpoint than from any other' (Kerman, 1985: 187–8). Although such scholarship tries 'to determine "What was done", not "What *is* to be done", let alone "*How* to do it"' (Taruskin, 1988, p. 201), direct application to actual performance has of course often been attempted – at times with musically catastrophic results, in a quest for an historical 'authenticity' both chimerical and inimical to individual interpretative freedoms. I wrote some years ago that the urtext playing style advocated by some has 'threaten[ed] the pursuit of individual artistic convictions to an unprecedented extent' (Rink, 1994, p. 214), turning the performer into little more than a museum curator whose main task is to dust the exhibits left by the great composers without really touching, let alone altering, them. More recent

developments in historical performance research include the study of recordings
– whether 'positivistically' in the form of discographic spadework, or 'critically'
in, say, the investigation of how tempo has changed within the performance
traditions of individual pieces. For instance, so-called 'tempo maps' provide
synchronic snapshots of given recordings which, when juxtaposed with one
another, show how 'average' tempo has evolved over the years (whatever 'average'
might mean).[3] The value of this research to performers is less than clear, although
Bowen for one believes it could enhance their realization that performing styles
are 'neither natural nor absolute' but merely conventional, while introducing
them to new interpretative parameters (1999, p. 438). At least the accent is on
individual interpretation, as opposed to the normative thrust of a strain of
historical research denying performers their voice.

This latter dichotomy – between the normative and the interpretative – also
characterizes some work on the psychology of performance, which, in Eric
Clarke's judgement (1995, p. 52), typically focuses on 'general mechanisms'
rather than 'individual manifestations'. Such mechanisms include 'the formation
of conceptual interpretations, retrieval from memory of musical structures, …
transformation into appropriate motor actions[,] … internal timing mechanisms
… [and] perceptual consequences', as Caroline Palmer has shown in a magisterial
survey of empirical research in music performance (1997, p. 115). This research
is fascinating and instructive, but it can seem all too remote from the reality of
performance and the perceptions of the performer, who is often treated more as
a laboratory rat than a sentient being. This is partly for reasons identified by
Clarke, that cognitive studies of performance reveal 'little or nothing about the
specificities of interesting and exceptional performance', instead proposing
'extremely blunt' models which are based on 'a vast range of adequate or
competent performances' and may be significant 'for those studying general
cognitive processes, but … [are] less interesting to musicians' (1995, p. 52).
Even psychologists have yet to gauge the musical import of their data – in
particular, about how music is heard and felt. For instance, like the 'tempo maps'
referred to above, graphs of tempo and dynamic fluctuation empirically derived
from MIDI data produced on a Yamaha Disklavier[4] or on the basis of other data
beg the question of whether such fluctuations are literally perceived by either
performers or listeners. Performed music is, of course, rarely metronomic, but
musically trained listeners – and performers – tend to sense a fictitiously constant
tempo even during the obligatory ritardando at cadence points (a slowing which
was discerned as such only by untrained listeners in experiments conducted by
Bruno Repp (1992)). The incontrovertible 'facts' of the performance as expressed
by the data thus reveal only a partial and perhaps misleading truth – which is a
salutary lesson both for psychologists and for those studying recordings.

Unlike the psychology of performance, the field of analysis and performance
deals mostly with specificities, not generalities – or so it did when Kerman
lamented the lack of a 'coherent theory in this area', its 'whole thrust' being (in

his opinion) 'to focus the attention of its practitioners on the single score that happens to be in front of them' (1985, p. 197). Much has changed since then, but only after a few wilderness years marked by problematic interventions like those of Eugene Narmour, who wrote that 'performers, as co-creators, ... must acquire theoretical and analytical competence ... [P]erformers can never plumb the aesthetic depth of a great work without an intense scrutiny of its parametric elements' (1988, p. 340). Even Edward Cone – whose *Musical Form and Musical Performance* (1968) repays many rereadings – once proposed that 'an analysis is a direction for performance' (1960, p. 174), a comment suggesting to Kerman anyway that 'the principal function of performance is to articulate relationships ... brought out by analysis' (1985, p. 98). Wallace Berry (1989, p. 44) likewise maintained that 'every analytical finding has an implication for performance' – a contentious statement I later qualified on his behalf to 'every analytical finding *of musical significance* ...' (Rink 1990, pp. 334–5).

Indeed, my 1990 review of Berry's *Musical Structure and Performance*, like Jonathan Dunsby's editorial in *Music Analysis* the previous year, challenged prevailing views about the relation between analysis and performance in what amounted to a personal manifesto and an agenda for further research. A decade later, I see the emergence of yet another dichotomy within this domain: between analysis of individual performances (an analytical mode essentially descriptive in nature), and analysis prior to, and serving as the basis of, a given performance (an analytical mode essentially prescriptive in nature). The former category – analysis *of* performance – might take the form of tempo and dynamic maps of recorded or live performances, like the ones discussed above, whereas my own work has quite differently depicted the 'contents' of performance by employing the diagrammatic tools of 'rigorous' analysis.[5]

As for the second, prescriptive mode of analysis – analysis for the sake of performance – I have written the following:

> That one can execute a 'serious analysis' of a piece and then extract all the interpretive implications latent therein to formulate a meaningful basis for the work's performance is a widespread assumption in the literature ... which I find less than convincing. Attempting to recast the findings of analysis into a performance mould is ... not unlike translating a book into another language word-for-word, without regard to ... idioms, inflections, grammar and syntax... [G]enerally the result would be stilted, contrived, and possibly nonsensical. (1990, p. 320)

I remain dubious about the musical viability of 'one-to-one mappings' between rigorous analytical methodologies and performance, though I do believe that performers continually engage in a kind of analysis as an integral part of building an interpretation. In other words, all performance requires analytical decision of some sort. My most recent work has investigated the nature and methodological assumptions of such a 'performer's analysis' – an analytical mode which allows performers to be performers rather than mere agents of the theorist (see Rink, 2002).

If I had one criticism to make of performance studies to date, therefore, it would be that certain authors have all but robbed performers of their musical personae and artistic prerogatives, transforming them into museum curators, laboratory subjects, theorists and analysts, at the expense of their identities as musicians. What conviction can performers hope to have when thus constrained? And if such constraint is the end result, can we claim that performance studies has much to do with actual performance? If this would-be discipline is to exist in more than the 'fragmentary' state alleged by Dunsby, its practitioners must somehow attend to the performer's concerns, to 'real, pragmatic issue[s]', to 'preliminary matters'. That does not at all mean forsaking the research pursuits of the last decades, but it may require a re-evaluation of motive, a refocusing of activity and an abandonment of any claim that we have touched upon the reality of performance unless or until we have done so. It may also necessitate a wider scholarly awareness of the spectrum of performance-related research being conducted – not least because performance is itself highly variegated and resistant to explication in one and only one vein. We can be sanguine about the future of performance studies perhaps only to the extent that performers themselves come to assume greater priority within the discipline.[6]

Case Study: Chopin, E Minor Prelude

The following case study of Chopin's E minor Prelude will suggest how the research strands I have identified can be interwoven in building an interpretation. It derives from my previous work on nineteenth-century piano music, while reflecting an increased attention in general to performance-practice issues post-1800.

Chopin published his Twenty-Four Preludes Op. 28 in 1839, having completed the set on Majorca by late January that year, when he sent the autograph manuscript to Julian Fontana in Paris for eventual use as a *Stichvorlage* for the French first edition.[7] This manuscript survives, likewise a sketch from late 1838 or early 1839. Adolphe Catelin published the French first edition (see Example 4.1), a second, revised impression of which followed almost immediately.[8]

Issues germane to performing the E minor Prelude arise from these sources, and I shall identify them in defining a performance conception which, while 'historically informed', recognizes the breadth of the performer's musical awareness. One such issue concerns a recurrent notational idiosyncrasy of Chopin's: the downward stem directions used throughout the sketch and autograph of this Prelude (except for the anacrusis in the autograph, its counterpart in bar 12, and from bar 20 to the end). This might have no musical import, but Carl Schachter for one believes that 'Chopin's calligraphy conveys the continuity of

Ex. 4.1 Chopin, E minor Prelude Op. 28 No. 4

the long melodic line far better than any of the printed editions with their alternating up and down stems'. He notes: 'pianists would do well to project that visual continuity in a long, legato, *espressivo* line' (1994, p. 180) – a line enhanced by the broad slurs. All of this suggests that a composer's notation can have expressive, or semiotic, significance to the performer, as we shall see again later.

Other relevant notational features include the long appoggiaturas in bars 11 and 19, and the 'long accents' in bar 8 and (possibly) bars 12 and 16. The intended realization of the appoggiaturas may be implied by paired quavers in the sketch – that is, played in eighteenth-century style, in line with Chopin's *bel canto*-inspired performance approach in general. As for his long accents, the ones here fulfil a variety of functions,[9] among others to prolong a stress over tied notes (bar 8); to convey a sense of 'leaning', that is, directional impulse to an appoggiatura (bar 12); and to emphasize an expressively important dissonance just before the climax (bar 16).

Although Chopin provided no metronome marking, his 'Largo' operates within a 2/2 time signature – which, astonishingly, some editions change to 4/4. Many pianists take far too slow a tempo, luxuriating in the rich harmonic palette of the modern piano, whereas the Pleyel favoured by Chopin allows a steady stream of colour within the left-hand counterpoint when a proper *alla breve* prevails. And Chopin's distinctive rubato comes into its own within a fluid tempo, the right hand as it were being freed from the pulsing left-hand quavers.

Chopin's intentions with regard to pedalling are elusive. My own approach reflects the capabilities of period pianos: namely, to use pedal throughout while striving for the lighter left-hand attacks and seamless colour I have referred to. Tempo, articulation and pedalling thus work symbiotically – as do factors like dynamics and *Affekt*. Both the key of E minor and the slow, chromatically descending bass convey a lamentational quality derived from baroque archetypes (see Eigeldinger, 1994, p. 176), inviting an understanding of the piece as elegy or lament, not merely as prelude. Such an awareness of genre should perhaps serve as a starting point in building an interpretation – along with the other factors I have identified.

My historical approach thus far has been traditional, focusing on sources, notational problems, the composer's own performing style, period instruments and genre. One could conduct a quite different investigation of 'historical performance practice' by studying the successive recordings of this work in the manner of Bowen and others. I shall not do so here,[10] but I will refer to three performances that illuminate the issues just raised. The first two are Alfred Cortot's from 1926 and 1942, the third Raoul Koczalski's from *c*. 1938. Cortot's earlier rendition is quite slow and, by modern standards, indulgent, with rolled left-hand chords, wilfully out-of-sync parts, textual alterations and secco harmonies at the end. His second reading retains these features buts coheres better, thanks to a fluency of pace and a less mannered articulation which serve rather than thwart the performance conception. It is possible that Cortot's 1942 interpretation was influenced by Koczalski's, itself no doubt indebted to his teacher Carl Mikuli, who studied with Chopin. Koczalski maintains a true 2/2, keeping the pace through bar 17's climax while shading the melody with dynamic swells and a pedal intriguingly reserved for points of melodic activity – sometimes prolonging dissonances to intensify expression (as in the reprise). The grace notes might be unstylistically short, but Koczalski's conception is cogent and coherent.

Some 90 years ago, Koczalski published short biographical and critical essays on the composer as well as analytical vignettes on the pieces he performed in four recitals. His comments on the E minor Prelude[11] remind us that design in performance – and musical form in general – should be conceived as a process, not as static architecture. It seems appropriate to turn now to larger issues of form, having felt our way into the piece as performers themselves do, scanning the score for points of interest which may or may not be explained on the basis of an existing knowledge of the genre, contemporary notational conventions, the composer's style and so on. The 'sight-reading' we have carried out leaves us ready to contemplate the whole – as understood by performers. Dunsby comments that 'performers know about "form" in the sense that they know it helps to be aware where they are in a piece when playing it' (1995, p. 24). But there is more to it than that. Performers 'feel' form not necessarily in terms of the structures demonstrated by analysts, but in the sense of musical 'shape' – an elusive but vital concept.[12] Indeed, David Epstein (1995, p. 130) asserts that 'shaping, as every musician knows, is the essence of interpretative performance'. Although in my view analogous to structure, shape is 'more dynamic' in conception: defined in terms of 'momentum, climax, … ebb and flow' and so on, it comprises 'an outline …, a set of gestures unfolding in time. Attaining a coherent, intelligible "shape" in performing a work is one of the principal goals of practice' (Rink, 1990, pp. 323–4), as also implied by both Erwin Stein (for whom 'the act of artistic creation consists in the shaping of the material' (1962, p. 17)) and Edward Cone (who wrote, 'the performer must … carefully consider the rhythmic shape of the composition, and of its parts' (1968, p. 49)). Cone similarly claims that 'valid and effective performance' can be achieved 'by discovering and making clear the rhythmic life of a composition' (1968, p. 31) – 'rhythmic life' amounting to 'shape' as I have defined it.

The 'shape' of the E minor Prelude has various manifestations at different levels, ranging from the 'end-accented', 'iambic' melodic motive announced at the start to the distinctively handled ending 24 bars later, after the virtually constant quaver motion ceases in bar 23 in 'a palpable sign that announces closure', followed by 'a stock cadential figure' (Agawu, 1987, p. 14). Jim Samson sees the path between these points as a 'continuous form' 'expressed through a simple bipartite design, a statement with conflated response', whose subtlety resides 'in Chopin's control of the "intensity curve"' (1996, p. 183). The high-point along that path is the emphatic bar 17, which reaches dynamic, registral and textural peaks over a dominant pedal. Although climactic, this bar should not be allowed – in Schachter's opinion – to disrupt the flow, as it is transient within a prolonged subdominant harmony, the true 'structural dominant' being reached only in bar 19 (Schachter, 1994, p. 178).

Whether or not one accepts that rationale, it makes sense to carry the momentum beyond bar 17's downbeat towards bar 19, where the 'futile', resigned melody returns. More problematic, perhaps, is the treatment of the reprise at bar 13. Eric Clarke and Jane Davidson (1998, p. 80) identify two conflicting views of the Prelude – either as 'a binary A A' structure' (bars 1–12 and 13–25) or as 'a more singular and unified' entity. From their different interpretations arise three 'critical structural issues for a performer': first, the amount of emphasis to give the melodic return and potential 're-start' at bar 13; second, 'the extent to which the first twelve bars are treated as a relatively closed, self-contained unit'; and third, the handling of the final cadence, whether as an overall goal or an 'almost parenthetical, though conventionally necessary, framing device'.

These issues invite disparate performance strategies, and Clarke and Davidson analyse two accordingly distinct renditions of the Prelude.[13] In particular, they examine how the pianist uses his body as an agent of expression in each 'take', presenting 'tracking data' for his head position throughout the two performances, as well as evidence of other 'expressive gestures'. Noting a 'high correlation between … head and hand gestures', they propose neither 'that body movement determines the interpretation of structure, nor that a performer's conception of musical structure determines body movement', but simply that 'gesture and physicality play a much more integral role than has hitherto been recognized in specifying the character of a performance' (1998, pp. 82, 88 and 89). This may seem obvious, but it is worth remembering that much of the psychological and analytical literature on performance presupposes a physical 'neutrality': the music and its 'structure' (however conceived) are somehow disembodied and thus dehumanized. Furthermore, the prevailing view is that musical expression itself comprises (in Clarke's words (1995, p. 22)) 'systematic patterns of deviation from the "neutral" information given in a score' – in other words, that 'expression is a departure from some norm'.[14]

How then might performers build from their first impressions of the music a sense of its shape and expressive content? How do they even conceive the latter – in the terms used by Samson, Schachter, Agawu, Clarke and Davidson? And how can 'valid and effective performance' of this Prelude be achieved? It is my belief that from the performer's perspective, 'the music' is paradoxically more simple and more complex than the previous citations imply. 'The music' as played results from a synthesis developed through extensive contact with a piece, in rehearsal and in actual performance – a synthesis of many of the features identified thus far, and others yet to be discussed.

William Rothstein (1995, p. 237) asserts that 'The performer's aim … [is] to discover, or create, a musical narrative' based on 'all he or she knows and feels about the work'. I too regard performances in terms of 'musical narratives', which to my mind involve:

> the creation of a unifying thread, a *grande ligne* linking the constituent parts of a performance into a rhythmically activated synthesis. Vital for intelligible, effective performance, it means giving the music a sense of shape in time by devising a hierarchy of temporally defined musical gestures from the small to the large scale. While playing, the performer engages in a continual dialogue between the comprehensive architecture and the 'here-and-now', between some sort of goal-directed impulse at the uppermost hierarchical level (the piece 'in a nutshell' [see Stein, 1962, p. 71]) and subsidiary motions extending down to the beat or sub-beat level, with different parts of the hierarchy activated at different points within the performance. (Rink, 1999, p. 218)

In the E minor Prelude, one aspect of Chopin's score suggests, or even specifies, the music's 'shape in time' and a strategy for realizing it: in my view, the notation's semiotic signification extends not only to the stem directions within Chopin's autograph (as mentioned before) but, more importantly, to the very contours etched by both melody and bass as registral levels rise and fall, wax and wane. A *grande ligne* can be drawn for this Prelude simply by connecting all the right-hand pitches in a single line; likewise the principal bass notes, which fall into two broad sweeps. Figure 4.1 presents an image of the registral flux implicit within the score but brought to the fore by removing staves, noteheads and so on.

This image captures the music as 'sung' by the pianist: that is, not as discrete attacks or fixed points more or less joined despite the physical gaps between them (as in the score), but as a continuous sonority, as line, as gesture. This is not to say that a pianist literally has such an image in mind when playing

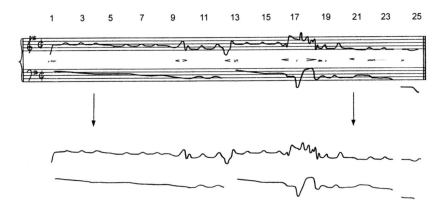

Figure 4.1   Chopin, E minor Prelude Op. 28 No. 4: registral contour in profile

through the music; but my simple diagram of registral activity, when experienced diachronically, approximates the moment-by-moment narrative of the performance while also synchronically illustrating its profile and topography, in what amounts (for this piece) to a sort of 'intensity curve'. In a sense, it both prescribes and describes, inspires and captures musical process in a work where registral trajectory is of paramount significance.

Here we see what the performer allows us to hear: an inexorable left-hand descent, followed by gentle inflections; another attempt to descend which is interrupted, giving way to violent swings before gradually regaining the lowest tessitura as the music ends, after a momentary but telling hiatus. The right hand's course is one of alternation between small-scale inflection and jagged fluctuation: the drawing of breath at the opening occurs again in the middle, although more markedly; similarly, wider oscillations follow the initially gentle undulations, becoming urgent and destabilizing when they re-enter, sooner than before, at the point of climax. In the diagram, the return of the steady inflections at the end suggests containment as clearly as the performance itself does.

I do not wish to claim that my simple diagram stands for a performance or represents it in its full complexity. On the contrary: it is little more than a 'skeleton' derived (ironically) from the neutral score – a 'skeleton' which will, of course, experience considerable manipulation in the hands of every pianist, with a unique result each time. But despite these shortcomings, the diagram helps us imagine a fundamental aspect of performance: that is, the discovery of an inner thread within the music – a *grande ligne* based, in this instance, on registral activity above all else – which in turn shapes and is shaped by a host of factors weighed up while assimilating a work.

As we have observed, the factors impinging on one's ultimate interpretation are diverse – among others:

- the Prelude's generic character as elegy or lament;
- its performing history (perhaps including the recordings I have referred to);
- Chopin's notational idiosyncrasies (including long accents, long appoggiaturas and stem directions);
- other features of his style (such as 'breathing' from the wrist; long, 'sung' phrases; independent right and left hands joined in a unique rubato);
- structure as 'shape' (whether 'continuous form', the play of register, or the course of other parameters);
- the physical dimension (keeping the left hand light, in a seamless flow of colour; expressive use of the body, and so on).

These factors – and no doubt many more – feed into an interpretation when filtered through a kind of 'prism' defined by the performer's artistic prerogatives.

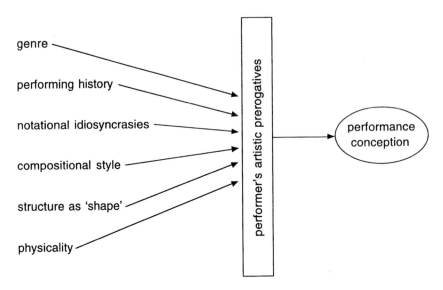

**Figure 4.2   Chopin, E minor Prelude Op. 28 No. 4: 'refraction' in
                interpretation**

The process of refraction implied by Figure 4.2 leads to a performance in which
the performer can at last believe: one reflecting personal conviction and individual
choice, at the same time demonstrating historical and analytical awareness and a
given 'programming' (both physical and psychological). This process of refraction
is to me the essence of interpretation, the reality of performance (at least, piano
performance). It is 'shaping' writ large.[15]

The synthesis I have sketched here could possibly serve as a model-in-microcosm
for the budding discipline of performance studies. Those of us working in the
field must of course continue the historical, analytical and psychological research
on performance that has occupied us during the past few decades. But we would
do well to heed Dunsby's advice that performance studies should engage with
'real, pragmatic issue[s]' and 'preliminary matters' – and the most important of
these is surely the decision-making process implicit in the interpretative act. The
re-evaluation of motive and refocusing of activity that I have already encouraged,
in conjunction with an increased knowledge of the range of performance research
being produced, will combat 'fragmentation' within the discipline and help to
give the actuality of performance due consideration. Thus, like the performer,
will we succeed in weighing up the manifold factors implied by a score, ultimately
giving them musical shape in striving for valid and effective interpretations of
our own.

Notes

A version of this chapter appears as 'Chopin and performance studies' in Irena Poniatowksa (ed.) (2003), *Chopin and his Work in the Context of Culture*, 2 vols (Cracow: Musica Iagellonica).

1. See Nettl (1999).
2. This obsession with tempo and dynamics is a latter-day counterpart to the obsession with pitch relations in traditional analysis.
3. See Bowen (1999), pp. 435, 440 and 449.
4. See Clarke (1995), pp. 32–3, 35 and 40–41.
5. See Rink (1994), pp. 232 and 239; see also Rink (1999), pp. 231–2 and (especially) 236, where an 'intensity curve' traces the topography of a particular performance.
6. Cf. the somewhat different prognosis for performance studies in Cook (2001) (which perhaps underemphasizes the role of performers themselves).
7. The paragraphs that follow derive from Rink (2001).
8. Breitkopf & Härtel issued the German first edition, based on a copy by Fontana; and Wessel brought out the English first edition, prepared from Catelin's revised impression.
9. See John Rink, 'Les concertos de Chopin: notation et exécution' (in press).
10. Rink (2001) surveys 14 recordings of this Prelude.
11. Koczalski (1909), p. 167; see the translation in Rink (2001), p. 444.
12. For discussion see Rink (2002).
13. See Clarke (1995), pp. 32–3 and 35.
14. Performers – and their teachers – can also fall prey to such a view. Roy Howat for one (1995, p. 3) laments 'the results of regarding music as the symbols on the page, which one must then "make interesting". "Put some expression into it!" is still a ubiquitous cry even at conservatories, notwithstanding the contradiction in terms.'
15. Figure 4.2 is not a comprehensive model of performance conception but a visual reminder that many elements influence an interpretation and that the performer (not the scholar) must be the final arbiter as to their respective roles therein.

References

Agawu, V. Kofi (1987) 'Concepts of closure and Chopin's Opus 28', *Music Theory Spectrum*, 9: 1–17.

Berry, Wallace (1989) *Musical Structure and Performance,* New Haven, CT: Yale University Press.

Bowen, José (1999) 'Finding the music in musicology: Performance history and musical works', in N. Cook and M. Everist (eds), *Rethinking Music*, pp. 424–51, Oxford: Oxford University Press.

Clarke, Eric (1995) 'Expression in performance: Generativity, perception and semiosis', in J. Rink (ed.), *The Practice of Performance: Studies in Musical Interpretation*, pp. 21–54, Cambridge: Cambridge University Press.

Clarke, Eric and Jane Davidson (1998), 'The body in performance', in W. Thomas (ed.),

Composition, Performance, Reception: Studies in the Creative Process of Music, pp. 74–92, Aldershot: Ashgate.

Cone, Edward T. (1960) 'Analysis today', *Musical Quarterly*, 46: 172–88.

Cone, Edward T. (1968) *Musical Form and Musical Performance*, New York: Norton.

Cook, Nicholas (2001) 'Between process and product: Music and/as performance', *Music Theory Online* 7(2), available at: <http://societymusictheory.org/mto/issues/mto.01.7.2/toc.7.2.html>.

Cortot, Alfred (1926) Recording of Chopin, Prelude in E minor Op. 28 No. 4 (EMI CZS 767359 2).

Cortot, Alfred (1942) Recording of Chopin, Prelude in E minor Op. 28 No. 4 (EMI CZS 767359 2).

Dunsby, Jonathan (1989) 'Guest editorial: Performance and analysis of music', *Music Analysis*, 8: 5–20.

Dunsby, Jonathan (1995) *Performing Music: Shared Concerns*, Oxford: Clarendon.

Eigeldinger, Jean-Jacques (1986) *Chopin: Pianist and Teacher as Seen by His Pupils*, trans. Naomi Shohet with Krysia Osostowicz and Roy Howat, ed. Roy Howat, Cambridge: Cambridge University Press.

Eigeldinger, Jean-Jacques (1994) 'Placing Chopin: Reflections on a compositional aesthetic', in J. Rink and J. Samson (eds), *Chopin Studies 2*, pp. 102–39, Cambridge: Cambridge University Press.

Epstein, David (1995) 'A curious moment in Schumann's Fourth Symphony: Structure as the fusion of affect and intuition', in J. Rink (ed.), *The Practice of Performance: Studies in Musical Interpretation*, pp. 126–49, Cambridge: Cambridge University Press.

Howat, Roy (1995) 'What do we perform?', in J. Rink (ed.), *The Practice of Performance: Studies in Musical Interpretation*, pp. 3–20, Cambridge: Cambridge University Press.

Kerman, Joseph (1985) *Musicology*, London: Fontana.

Koczalski, Raoul (1909) *Chopin-Zyklus: Zum hundertsten Geburtstag Frédéric Chopins*, Leipzig: Pabst.

Koczalski, Raoul (*c.* 1938) Recording of Chopin, Prelude in E minor Op. 28 No. 4 (Archiphon ARC-119/20).

Narmour, Eugene (1988) 'On the relationship of analytical theory to performance and interpretation', in E. Narmour and R.A. Solie (eds), *Explorations in Music, the Arts, and Ideas*, pp. 317–40, Stuyvesant, Pendragon.

Nettl, Bruno (1999) 'The institutionalization of musicology' in N. Cook and M. Everist (eds), *Rethinking Music*, pp. 287–310, Oxford: Oxford University Press.

Palmer, Caroline (1997) 'Music performance', *Annual Review of Psychology*, 48: 115–38.

Repp, Bruno H. (1992) 'Probing the cognitive representation of musical time: Structural constraints on the perception of timing perturbations', *Cognition*, 44: 241–81.

Rink, John (1990) Review of Berry 1989, *Music Analysis*, 9: 319–39.

Rink, John (1994) 'Authentic Chopin: History, analysis and intuition in performance', in J. Rink and J. Samson (eds), *Chopin Studies 2*, pp. 214–44, Cambridge: Cambridge University Press.

Rink, John (1999) 'Translating musical meaning: the nineteenth-century performer as narrator', in N. Cook and M. Everist (eds), *Rethinking Music*, pp. 217–38, Oxford: Oxford University Press.

Rink, John (2001) 'The line of argument in Chopin's E minor Prelude', *Early Music*, 29: 434–44.

Rink, John (2002) 'Analysis and (or?) performance', in J. Rink (ed.), *Musical Performance: A Guide to Understanding*, pp. 35–58, Cambridge: Cambridge University Press.

Rink, John (in press) 'Les concertos de Chopin: notation et exécution', in Jean-Jacques Eigeldinger (ed.), *Frédéric Chopin: texte, interprétation, récéption*, Geneva: Droz.

Rothstein, William (1995) 'Analysis and the act of performance', in J. Rink (ed.), *The Practice of Performance: Studies in Musical Interpretation*, pp. 217–40, Cambridge: Cambridge University Press.

Samson, Jim (1996) *Chopin*, Oxford: Oxford University Press.

Schachter, Carl (1994) 'The Prelude in E minor Op. 28 No. 4: Autograph sources and interpretation', in J. Rink and J. Samson (eds), *Chopin Studies 2*, pp. 161–82, Cambridge: Cambridge University Press.

Stein, Erwin (1962) *Form and Performance*, London: Faber.

Taruskin, Richard (1988) 'The pastness of the present and the presence of the past', in Nicholas Kenyon (ed.), *Authenticity and Early Music*, pp. 137–207, Oxford: Oxford University Press.

Chapter 5

A Case Study of a Practical Research Environment: Sibelius Academy, Helsinki

Kari Kurkela

This chapter is a case study of how a higher education institution which specializes in the training of musicians to a professional standard has developed opportunities for practical musicians to engage in research. The case study is highly relevant to this book for not only does it give details of how research can be undertaken by practising musicians, it also shows that the practical musician is a potential candidate to become a researcher. Indeed, implicit in the text is the belief that musicians should make a reflexive turn and investigate their own practices in order to develop their skills and find out more about their domain. The case study focuses on the Sibelius Academy in Helsinki, Finland, and especially on the DocMus – a doctoral degree offered to musicians wishing to research an aspect of practical music-making.

Background

Three doctoral programmes were started at the Sibelius Academy in 1982. However, it was not until the beginning of the 1990s that activities really got under way. For clarity, the programmes that currently exist are shown Table 5.1. They were developed to make a national and international contribution to:

1.   a high standard of musical *performances*;
2.   the growth of *knowledge* about different phenomena in music; and
3.   high-quality music *pedagogy*.

The institutional intention is that art, pedagogy and research and development work can challenge and stimulate each other. It should be stated from the outset that, although this chapter considers the approach to research at the Sibelius Academy, much of what is discussed can be applied to the teaching, learning, performing and creating interests of professionals. Consider, for example, the lower part of Table 5.1 where a justification is made for the role, degree and purpose of research for the musician.

Table 5.1 Doctoral programmes at the Sibelius Academy (Doctor of Music)

	Studies in General		
	A. Art Study Programme	**B. Research Study Programme**	**C. Development Study Programme**
1. The principal aim of the studies	High artistic proficiency	High scholarly proficiency	Expert level in some practical (professional) field of music
2. The criteria for evaluation	Capacity for independent, high-level artistic activity; soloist capability; artistic profile and creativity	Capacity for independent research work; knowledge of the subject matter; integrity and depth in the treatment; originality of results	Capability to offer expert services (skills, methods and knowledge) in a specified area; original approach in treatment; unity of theory and practice
3. Main relevance of the studies for the society	Artistic products (development of humanitarianism, quality of life …)	Scholarly tested knowledge (explanation, control, critique, transformation, emancipation, understanding …)	New methods, means and practices; expert level services
4. Work for degree qualification	Five recitals or corresponding artistic productions plus a short thesis	A dissertation	A portfolio of relevant products, such as recordings, compositions, pedagogical material, a manual for professional use, software and/or a new device plus an obligatory research report on the object of development

The Role of Research

	A. Art Study Programme	B. Research Study Programme	C. Development Study Programme
4. Extent of research-oriented studies (regulatory time span of full-time studies)	Thesis: 4 months; ancillary subjects (artistic and academic) 8.5 months; usually much more time is needed	4–5 years; usually much more time is needed	4–5 years; usually much more time is needed
5. Student's special contribution to research	Practical experience in the subject matter, capability for artistically relevant questioning and treatment; see also A7	Main concern focused on research (acquisition and possession of methods, traditions, literature, etc.)	Inclination to apply existing research findings, development of applied research, practical relevance of findings
6. The role of research for the student	Supports the optimal artistic development (see A7 and B3)	Is the main interest of the student	Supports the acquisition of skills and knowledge; a means for developing and testing methods, practices, etc.
7. The relevance of research for society	Provides documents on artistic functioning (practices and principles); support in producing and receiving art; see also A3	See B3	See C3

In the research study programme, however, the research activities are filtered through the presentation of a thesis, with the scholarly criteria for this procedure being the same as in a traditional research-oriented university: work that makes a unique contribution to the field and that reveals independent research and high-level (publishable in peer-review journals) critical insight. These criteria also fit with Davidson and Smith's (1997) belief that a reflexive turn can be made so that musical practices can become regarded as research activity. In order for this to happen in a manner which also allows for verification, typically through replication, a formalized written presentation of findings is necessary.

In the art study programme, the principal aim of studies is to promote the student's artistic capabilities. It has its own aim and content and, therefore, it differs markedly from the research study programme. It is important to understand that this study programme has not been designed to transform artists into researchers. However, a certain amount of academic study and a thesis of limited scope are also required in this programme. I will discuss the rationale behind these requirements later in this chapter.

In the development study programme, theoretical and practical studies lead to a readiness to develop new practices, methods and other innovations for different fields of music. Of equal importance is the student's own professional specialization in a selected area. An intimate connection between practice and theory is central. For example, some of our students – when they have acquired the relevant skills and knowledge – develop new pedagogical methods that are tested and modified in action research projects. Another example is the student who studies the performance conventions of a certain early music style in connection with his or her own artistic training in the same subject; the result is a manual and a recital – born together and sustained by each other.

Strengths and Challenges of Research at a Music Academy

There has been a clear gap in Europe between conservatories, arts or vocationally-oriented universities where the emphasis has been on practice, and the traditional book-based research universities. Even if a certain division of main interests and duties does continue in the future, the roles of these institutions seem to be changing, with the partially artificial separation of practical and academic approaches diminishing.

Certain possibilities and limitations direct research education and research activity whatever the context, but the following facts, for instance, must be constantly taken into account when planning the research education in the DocMus at the Sibelius Academy:

1.   The master's degree of our students is usually based on artistic and so very practical requirements.

2. Therefore, many of our students – even those applying for the research study programme at doctoral level – have little prior formal training in research work.
3. Not surprisingly, more than half of our doctoral applicants opt for the art study programme.
4. When beginning the doctoral programme, many of the students have significant artistic and pedagogical experience of, and practical knowledge about, the research subjects.
5. The students also have high motivation to undertake high-quality work and the potentiality to learn.
6. In addition to the Sibelius Academy's own resources, the activities of the other art- and research-oriented universities in Helsinki partly intersect and complement our activities. They represent expertise in other performing arts (such as theatre and dance) as well as traditional academic competence in philosophy, aesthetics, psychology, education, musicology, technology, and so on.

It is easy to see that among the most important questions in developing the research work in the Sibelius Academy unit are the following:

1. How can students' exceptional artistic and pedagogical experience and enthusiasm be nurtured in the best possible way?
2. How can the educational resources available be used to the best possible advantage in order to provide the students with sufficient readiness for research work? That is, the research education is based on the conviction that the students with extraordinary musical experience and a well-focused research training can achieve valuable results.

In summary, to support the research activity of the students on the DocMus, we have to:

- Be aware of the students' personal research interests as well as their exceptional artistic and pedagogical experience; this will manifest itself in individual study plans.
- Create a supportive environment that gives space for creative potential which sometimes means taking conscious risks to develop projects outside of the usual research traditions, for example, when posing questions and trying to find methods of inquiry.
- Organize sufficient individual tutoring and courses which provide support in philosophy, methodology and other areas that are indispensable for research work. For instance, students are encouraged to join thematic research groups which offer conceptual and theoretical background as well as opportunities for critical discourse (at the moment, four thematic

groups exist: performance practices of early music, other historical approaches to the performance of music, systematic studies in the performance of music and instrumental pedagogy).

- Create sufficient interplay between art, research and development to encourage the students to develop projects – for instance, in seminars and cross-disciplinary and cross-artistic meetings.
- Take artistic expertise into account when planning and evaluating the research activities.

At the Sibelius Academy, we believe that what this art school lacks in its basic preparedness for research work is at least to some extent compensated for by partly non-conceptualized and extensive practical experience and knowledge. The main challenge is to find a way to transform this intuitive knowledge into academically appropriate questions and results. Two important factors guide research work: the intimate nature of reality (whatever it is) and research traditions. Tradition can be a force, but it can also be a limiting factor by assimilating reality into existing approaches, questions, methods and concepts. The lack of a strong research tradition can be a weakness, but it can also help research to accommodate itself to reality in innovative ways.

Can an Artist Attain a Doctorate?

In many European countries there is ongoing discussion about the relationship between artistic education and the doctoral degree. This discussion has also taken place at the Sibelius Academy. The majority of our art students take Bachelor of Music and Master of Music degrees. These degrees are formal goals of the systematic artistic education which mark the students' personal growth. It is not difficult to understand that this kind of progressive artistic training can go on even beyond the master's degree. It is true that some talented artists feel they do not need doctoral education – or even undergraduate schooling. However, there are more very talented artists interested in our programme than the number we can accept because of our limited resources.

It is naturally very beneficial for different universities and corresponding schools to consider carefully what the most natural and supporting educational choices are for attaining good results in their field. Therefore, it is essential that the staff responsible for planning education analyse very carefully, and with as little prejudice as possible, the characteristic features of their field, and that the curricula be designed accordingly.

This being the case, as we develop the curriculum for our *art* study programme at the Sibelius Academy, we constantly keep in mind the fact that it needs to support the student's *artistic* development in an optimal way. The major question is how the education should be designed in the artist's study programme in order to provide maximum opportunity for artistic development. And correspondingly, what kind of academic readiness should be expected from artists as Doctors of Music? It would be damaging to get stuck in the traditional view that *only* a researcher can hold a doctorate; this would be too limited a conception of the qualification as a university degree. At least as damaging might be a belief that if an artist has a doctorate, that he or she should look or sound like an academic scholar. At the Sibelius Academy, we think that if an *artist* is given a doctoral degree, he or she must primarily be an excellent artist. Therefore, the emphasis in education is on independent artistic work leading to five demanding recitals or other results comparable to that. Practical expertise is typically achieved by practising, usually in cooperation with an instrumental teacher, and gaining other skills and insights through master classes, other tuition and practical courses connected with the very act of performing. But for the doctoral student, even more is required.

The Role of Research in the Doctoral Art Study Programme

As already mentioned, the principal aim of the art study in the Sibelius Academy's doctoral programme is to promote the student's artistic capability and not to transform an artist into a researcher. Why, then, are academic studies and a thesis included in this study programme at all? We believe it is beneficial for an artist to strengthen his or her relationship with reality by articulating thoughts and ideas through a thesis. Put in a slightly different way: it is of great advantage to an artist if he or she can develop a conscious, critical and creative relationship with the principles that determine his or her conception of the unknown that we call reality. It is the reflexive turn of Davidson and Smith (see 'Background' earlier in this chapter), with the thesis being a formalized medium through which the practical insights are articulated and documented. This is why our students in the art study programme are encouraged to work conceptually and analyse critically as well as adopt, modify and even create new principles that are associated with their work and interests. In this way, we hope that our students will also be well equipped for further personal development as well as flexible and innovative activity in their professional fields.

Formally, we expect that in addition to their artistic capabilities, all the graduates from the art study programme:

- are able to seek knowledge that concerns their work as an artist (skills in the acquisition of existing knowledge);
- relate constructively (that is, in a systematic, critical and empathic way) to different artistic and scholarly ideas that might be relevant to their activity as artists (skills in analysing knowledge, flexibility in understanding);

- are ready to seek, conceptualize and test new ideas related to their artistic activity (creativity);
- can express themselves linguistically in an articulate way (skills in verbal expression).

How can the students in the art study programme obtain sufficient training for managing the scholarly goals discussed above? The students are recommended to attend a variety of seminars and courses as a part of their studies. Even if art students are not expected to attain the research results equal to the demands of the research-oriented students, both groups need clarification of, and support in, the same topics. Naturally, the work with a thesis (corresponding to 16 weeks of full-time work) also supports the aforementioned development. Our experience shows that studies of this kind effectively strengthen students' critical and innovative attitude and, consequently, support their development as artists and as pedagogues.

The formal requirements do not imply that the thesis of an art student has to be an innovative product from the point of view of research. However, critical and systematic procedures are required due to educational aims. And when an activity, which tests principles that determine a student's conceptions of the unknown, is carried out in a sufficiently critical, systematic and creative way, it is research. Therefore, the scholarly work that our art students do in order to become better artists has sometimes produced results that can be regarded as innovative and valuable from the point of view of professional research. Of course, not all theses represent such a high standard of research – which is not the point, since (allow me to repeat myself) the primary purpose of the thesis in the art study programme is to support the optimal growth of the student as an artist. However, as persons having long and irreplaceable practical experience in the field of music, many artists are able to pose valid questions and approach them freshly – and also communicate about the results with other music professionals.

In this connection, I would like to deal briefly with a question formulated as follows: 'Under what conditions – if any – can a performance be considered a result of research work?' My opinion is that, in many cases, a performance can be seen as being partly influenced by the findings of research activity. However, we have to keep 'result' and 'application' as concepts separate from each other. A practical application of research findings may not be enough as a result of research work itself. However, we are approaching the field of development work, where the emphasis between research and art – or result and application of research work – can vary considerably.

But if this were the whole story, it would be too simple. It might be important to note that artistic activity can be, should be and actually is being used as a *method of research*. In the DocMus we are very interested in developing methods of this type. Thus, practising a Nocturne by Chopin can have a double function:

it can be a method for attaining artistic aims, but the act of playing can also function as a research method in different ways. Correspondingly, the result of the activity can be art or research or both. If the result is art, then the performance has to speak for itself: it gives the audience experiences that may function as the main argument for its existence. But if playing is used as a method of research, then the result is usually transmitted by linguistic means (perhaps supported by musical examples) and follows the argumentation required in the research work. For instance, if performing has been used as a method for attaining research results, this method should be explained and critically evaluated in a research report, similarly to any other method (see Figure 5.1).

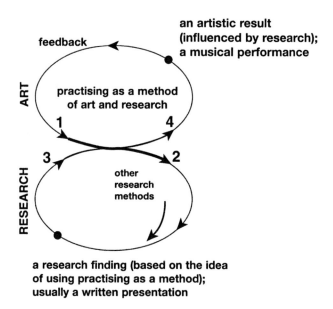

Figure 5.1   Interaction between artistic and research activities

Difficulties in the Past and Challenges for the Future

It is not difficult to imagine what kind of ideological difficulties the adoption of research by an art school can call forth. 'Music does not need words'; 'Knowledge can damage artistic intuition'; 'How could an artist ever say anything scientifically reasonable about reality?'; and so on. Additionally, the idea of an artist as a doctor has been challenging for some people. It is often easier to keep one's own prejudices than to find out how things really are (even for the press). But this is normal with new phenomena. And, of course, many people have understood the potential value of this activity. A good strategy is to be patient and to try to do everything as well as possible.

Today, there is a rather nice division of labour among the different university departments of musicology and the Sibelius Academy, each of them concentrating on some areas that are not so well represented elsewhere.

One difficulty, to which I have already referred, is the educational background of our research-oriented students. It is not unusual that we have to operate simultaneously on the basic level of research education and on the postgraduate level of results. This demands much of our students. And it demands much of teaching and supervision as well. As far as the interaction between art and research students is concerned, I have recently noticed that the depth of treatment of certain issues puzzling our research-oriented students may put disadvantageous demands on some artistically-oriented students attending the same seminars. This may lead to some minor rearrangements in the future. However, my trust in our interactive environment has remained firm.

Every year we have many more applicants than we can accept into our unit. We have been compelled to create a rather selective audition and entrance examination procedure to restrict the numbers and maintain the high level of our students. In spite of all this, the department has grown rapidly. A critical point has been reached. On the other hand, it is very difficult to reject highly talented candidates. In addition, the precondition for an internal research community and group teaching is that there are enough active students interested in the same field of research.

From a personal point of view, developing our activities has been a challenging project. Supervising art and research students is rewarding in many ways and keeps me in touch with art and research. At the moment, however, I would like to find more time for my personal projects. It is very important that in a music academy, research and other creative activity are not limited to doctoral students. We should have enough resources for postdoctoral research, and our staff must have enough time for their own creative work – be it art, research or something else that differs from everyday teaching and management and supports the diversity of the department in a sensible way. We must find a reasonable balance between short-term efforts that provide concrete results on a yearly basis and long-term development of our interactive community. This is not possible without time and space devoted to creative uncertainty, experiments, trials and mistakes, which may finally lead to the maturation of new ideas and practices.

Some Ideas for the Future

I conclude with some ideas which I have at the moment about doctoral education, and research especially, in a music academy. In particular:

- The roles of art, pedagogy and research have to be clearly differentiated (that is, not confused with each other) and then integrated in a beneficial and reasonable way. The best place for a reasonable integration is in the mind of the student.
- Art students can do research. They are interested in the same studies as research students and vice versa. Scholars and artists can learn from each other in seminars and elsewhere.
- A lot of tutoring and courses are needed. Even if the standards for the theses of the art students are much lower than for the dissertations of the research-oriented students, the former may need as much or even more instruction than the latter.
- It is important to be open to new approaches that the students may have and to try to adjust them to conform to the demands of a realistic research project and the student's research potentiality.
- It is important to find research questions that satisfy the needs of a community and may not have been dealt with elsewhere.
- The effect of the critical mass should be remembered.
- The quality and quantity of professional teachers and other staff must be adequate. It is beneficial if, in addition to their own scholarly competence, academically-oriented teachers have personal experience of or otherwise understand artistic work. The teachers should have time for their own creative work.
- The general public is not always very quick to understand new ideas. Dissemination of information about the doctoral programmes and their different aims is needed.
- It is important to be patient and realistic. It takes considerable time to create a new culture.

Note

1. For more about the different study programmes, see <http://www.siba.fi/>

Reference

Davidson, J.W. and Smith, J.A. (1997) 'A case study of newer practices in music education at conservatoire level', *British Journal of Music Education*, 14(3): 251–69.

PART 2

Theory and Experimentation: Understanding Pitches, Tuning and Rhythms

Chapter 6

From Acoustics to Psychology: Pitch Strength of Sounds

Andrzej Rakowski

Introduction

Music is the art of creating constructions of sound sequences. Patterns of these constructions depend strongly on the one hand on physical patterns of sound produced by nature, and on the other on the psychophysiology of human perception. *Acoustics* is a science that deals with sound and its applications. *Acoustics of music* deals not only with sound, but also with the way it is produced, organized and perceived in music (and also, to some degree, with the way it travels from the source to the listener). The production of sound, as it reaches the listener's ears, incorporates the action of musical instruments, and also, to a significant degree, the modification of sound waves through their multiple reflections from the walls, ceiling and floor of a concert hall or practice room. In contemporary life, the vast majority of music reaches the listener through loudspeakers or headphones, and these electronic sound transmissions and spatial projection of sound stand as a prolongation of original room acoustics. Indeed, in many cases, electronic devices replace traditional musical instruments.

Most of the material compiled in this book presents research that might have been or actually has been undertaken in the environment of music schools at university level, working with live musicians, and addresses either performance or perception of live performance issues. In the three chapters that follow the present chapter, the authors concentrate on three various stages of the musical message: cognitive (categorical perception of time in music), acoustic (with sound reflections in a traditional concert hall), and electroacoustic (with electronic sound transmission). In this chapter, I illustrate briefly the results of some investigations that were conducted in a music-acoustics laboratory situated within an academy of music. The research concerned the perception of pitch, and may be classified as *psychoacoustics of music*. I am deeply convinced that, though similar laboratory work could have been conducted in any psychological or acoustical research institution, the most convenient and most effective aspect of the current project was that it took place in a music school, and that it was with the constant cooperation of musicians in their own environment that the current results were obtained. Thus, I emphasize that settings where feedback from expert practitioners is possible do help to develop relevant and real-life context results. Bearing this in mind, I outline the research question and background literature below to situate the research project.

The Concept of Pitch Strength and Pitch Level

Percussive musical instruments are usually classified in two groups: those of 'definite' and those of 'indefinite' pitch. Intuitively, such a dichotomic division may seem strange to anyone familiar with the rather continuous distribution of value in most perceptual phenomena. So in the 1970s first concepts were formulated which recognized pitch strength as an independent factor of sensation (Wightman, 1973; Rakowski, 1977; Fastl and Stoll, 1979). Pitch strength may appear to have a very large value (as in a pure tone or the tone of the oboe) or a very small value (such as in short clicks or in uniform, 'white' noise). It is assumed that the value of pitch strength (or pitch salience) is distributed continuously in various acoustic signals and the term 'indefinite pitch', for example, as a feature of the sound of a bass drum, means only that the accuracy of defining its pitch by ear is not sufficient to locate that sound precisely within a western-music chromatic pitch scale. It does not mean that the sound of the bass drum is deprived of any pitch at all. In order to check this concept, it would be enough to compare the sound of the bass drum with that of another 'indefinite-pitch' instrument, say the orchestral triangle, and ask whether they differ in pitch. They certainly do, and surely it would be impossible to differ in something that does not exist or is totally indefinite.

In existing research approaches, two methods of measuring pitch strength have been proposed. Firstly, the 'indirect' method (Rakowski, 1977; Rakowski et al., 1996; Kiuiła et al., 1998) is based on adjusting the frequency of a comparison pure tone to the investigated sound at an equal pitch. The procedure is based on the following assumption: the more salient the pitch of the investigated sound, the easier it is to compare its pitch with that of a comparison pure tone. The comparison is performed by adjusting the frequency of a pure tone to a pitch equal to that of the investigated sound. The compared sounds are presented one after another. After a number of such matchings are performed, the frequencies of the 'equal-pitch tones' are more closely distributed when the pure tones are matched to a sound with a strong pitch than when they are matched to a sound with a weak, less definite pitch.

Pitch strength is operationally defined as a reciprocal (inversion) of a measure of dispersion of 'equal pitch' frequencies of the comparison pure tones. The so-called interquartile range, or IQR, has been taken as a measure of dispersion. In the present experiment IQR means the distance (interval) between two frequencies computed in cents (1/100th parts of a semitone). Those two frequencies are selected in the following way: the higher one is the frequency over which exactly 25 per cent of the total number of matchings took place, and the lower one is the one under which exactly another 25 per cent of matchings occurred.

The second method for measuring pitch strength, a 'direct' one, employs direct numerical assessments of pitch strength by a group of listeners. In the best known variant of this method, the assessments are made in relation to a number arbitrarily attached to a comparison sound (an 'anchor') presented before each measured sound (Fastl and Stoll, 1979; Fastl, 1988).

The present research was performed with the indirect method of measuring pitch strength. Its advantage over the direct method is that it enables one not only to estimate the value of the pitch strength of the sound (PS), but also to assess the pitch level (PL), that is, the real value of the pitch itself. In this experiment pitch level is defined as a median of the frequency distribution of pitch matchings. The median value of a distribution of pitch-matching tone frequencies is the value representing a mid-point between two groups of frequencies, one above the mid-point and one below it.

The Pitch-matching Procedure and Presenting the Results in a Visual Form

Fifteen sounds composed a group of stimuli for the experiment. There were three violin tones played with various kinds of vibrato or without vibrato, a violin tap tone, the sounds of marimba, xylophone, kettledrum, bass drum, snare drum, orchestral triangle and a 1000-Hz pure tone. All sounds were stored in the computer and reproduced monaurally through high-quality headphones (Koss HV-PRO) with the loudness level of 60–65 phons. Nine music students with normal hearing took part in the experiment as listeners. None of them possessed absolute pitch. Experimental sessions were conducted individually with each listener in turn seated in an acoustically treated, sound-insulated booth.

The listening task was to compare the pitch of an experimental sound with that of a pure comparison tone and to regulate the frequency of the comparison tone to make the pitch of both sounds equal. The initial frequency of the comparison tone before the adjustments started was chosen at random. The participant could listen at will to the experimental and/or comparison stimuli before and after any frequency correction. The listener's final decision was recorded as a result.

The series of 15 experimental sounds was presented to each participant ten times in a random order of stimuli to prevent any effects of constant mutual influence among stimuli. Each listener was allowed to perform matchings of no more than two series daily, with at least one hour of intermission to avoid exhaustion. Results of the first two series of matchings were excluded from further processing to compensate for the effect of learning, so the pitch of every experimental sound was estimated on the basis of 72 results of pitch matching (nine subjects, eight replications). Such a number of pitch-matching frequencies was considered sufficient to draw fairly robust conclusions about the investigated parameters of pitch. The results were pooled together and used for calculations.

To visualize the results of matchings, the 72 'equal pitch' tone frequencies obtained for each experimental sound were shown in histograms along a frequency scale of equal octaves. The histograms were organized by grouping the individual results (individual pitch-matching frequencies) in 20-cent (one-fifth of a semitone) sections. The number of results gathered in a single section was represented by the height of a corresponding column of a histogram. Pitch-matching histograms obtained in this way for all instrumental sounds investigated are shown in Fig. 6.1.

As can be seen in Fig. 6.1, for most instruments except the bass drum (14) and, to some extent, the orchestral triangle (11), frequencies of pure tones tuned to 'equal pitch' with a given instrumental sound were concentrated near to some specific frequency (the 'main frequency'). In most cases, such as in the sound of the violin played with a bow (1, 2 and 3), of marimba (5), xylophone (6), vibraphone (8, 9 and 10), cymbals (12) and snare drum (13), whose physical spectra are composed of a number of distinct pure tones, the main frequency corresponds to the frequency of the strongest or most important tone of that sound's spectrum (for example, 'first harmonic', the 'fundamental tone' in a violin's sound). In the violin 'Tap tone' (4), produced by knocking an instrument's belly, or in the kettledrum sound (7), the 'main frequency' corresponds to that of the air resonance inside the instrument. The sound of a triangle is composed of a chaotic mixture of a very great number of component tones, and choosing the one which is most representative for pitch may be a difficult matter. Still more difficult for the listeners appeared to be choosing a pure-tone frequency to match the pitch of the bass-drum sound (14). A number of chaotically distributed pure tones in the physical spectrum of this instrument are accompanied by very strong, reverberating low-pitch noise, whose pitch may be only approximately estimated by matching to it a pure tone.

In the case of the instrumental sounds investigated in the present research, the main frequency attracting most of the equal-pitch matchings was always connected with a real, physical component contained in the sound's spectrum. In some other cases, the main concentration of pitch-matching frequencies may occur even without the presence of a corresponding physical component in the spectrum, due to a particular psychoacoustic effect known as a 'virtual pitch phenomenon' (Terhardt, 1979).

The accuracy of tuning (opposite to the width of dispersion of pitch-matching frequencies, as mentioned earlier) is an important 'indirect' measure of the pitch strength. Whenever the main frequency can be selected from the pitch-matching histogram, the pitch strength may be computed as an inverse value of the measure of dispersion of those frequencies that form a 'zone of concentration' around it. The maximum width of such a zone of concentration, which contains a set of data for computing both pitch strength and pitch level of a given sound, has been arbitrarily established as 300 cents, or three equally tempered semitones.

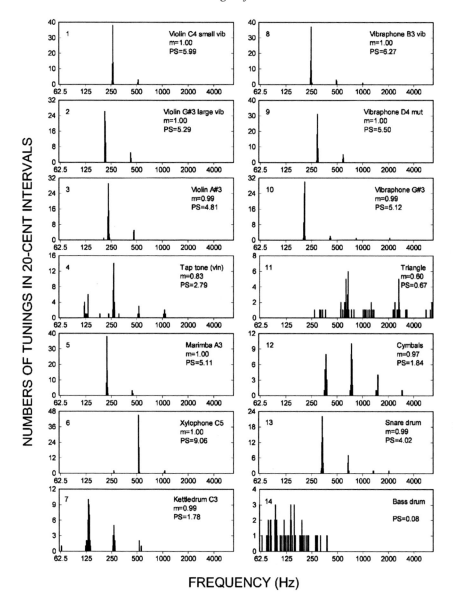

FREQUENCY (Hz)

Individual pitch-matching frequencies were connected in groups within one-fifth of a semitone sections. The number of pitch matchings within each section is represented by the height of a corresponding vertical bar. Frequency values ... 250 ... 500 ... correspond roughly to ... C4 ... C5 ... etc.

m = factor of monochromaticity

PS = pitch strength

Figure 6.1 **Results of tuning a pure tone in equal pitch to the investigated instrumental sound**

The remaining, very important problem concerns the pitch matchings that fell outside the concentration region of the main frequency. For most sounds investigated within the present research, a typical distribution of those pitch matchings is such that they form regions of concentration at a distance of one or more octaves from the main frequency. The usual approach to this phenomenon is to treat such decisions in estimating pitch by the listeners as 'octave errors'. For reasons which will be discussed in the final section of this chapter, pitch matchings that fall in such distributed regions of concentration will not be treated as errors, but as data confirming the existence of a dominating musical pitch class (pitch chroma) in the investigated sound sensation. Consequently, all octave-related zones of pitch-matching concentration (including the main-frequency zone) are called 'monochromatic zones', and the 'factor of monochromaticity' (m) is introduced as a relation of the number of pitch matchings contained in all monochromatic zones to the total number of pitch matchings. The factor of monochromaticity is a quantitative measure which may be used in first estimations as to whether a given sound may be treated as one of 'definite pitch' or of 'indefinite pitch', and later in more exact computations of the pitch strength.

For most of the sounds investigated within the present research the factor of monochromaticity (m) was 1.00 or 0.99; for the remaining sounds, factor m had the following values: 0.97 (cymbals, 12), 0.83 (tap tone, 4), and 0.60 (triangle, 11). It was arbitrarily and provisionally decided that sounds with a factor of monochromaticity (m) lower than 0.50, or those where that factor is impossible to assign, would be treated as sounds of indefinite pitch. Pitch strength and pitch level of these sounds were computed from the whole distribution of pitch matching frequencies in the full frequency range.

Presenting the Results in Numbers

As has been mentioned earlier, the factor of monochromaticity may be used to estimate whether the investigated sound should be treated as that of *definite* or of *indefinite* pitch. In the present research only the sound of the bass drum turned out to belong to the latter category, as in its pitch-matching distribution no trace of an octave-related structure could be found. The pitch strength of this sound was calculated as an inversion of the measure of dispersion (IQR) of the pitch-matching distribution in the whole frequency range. In all other sounds the factor of monochromaticity could be established with a value higher than 0.50; this could lead to the conclusion that from the perceptual point of view they were all sounds of definite pitch. It should be noted that some of those instruments (triangle, cymbals and snare drum) are classified by traditional musicology as instruments of indefinite pitch.

To establish the numerical value of *pitch strength* in sounds of experimentally found definite pitch, both the width of pitch-matching distribution within the

Table 6.1   Pitch level (PL) and pitch strength (PS) of sounds determined in the experimental series of pitch matchings

	Sound Parameters				Experimental Results		
No.	Sound	f_1 (Hz)	m	n_1	PL (Hz)	PL/f_1 (cents)	PS
1	Violin C4 small vib	263.9	1.00	68	261.9	−13.2	5.99
2	Violin G#3 large vib	214.4	1.00	65	211.3	−25.3	5.29
3	Violin A#3	233.6	0.99	62	230.9	−20.3	4.81
4	Violin tap-tone	271.2	0.83	40	266.6	−29.4	2.79
5	Marimba A3	222.4	1.00	68	220.7	−13.3	5.11
6	Xylophone C5	529.2	1.00	66	525.6	−11.9	9.06
7	Kettledrum C3	134.2	0.99	50	133.7	−7.1	1.78
8	Vibraphone B3 vib	247.8	1.00	66	247.0	−6.0	6.27
9	Vibraphone D4 mut	296.4	1.00	62	293.3	−18.6	5.50
10	Vibraphone G#3	208.4	0.99	66	206.6	−15.3	5.12
11	Triangle	668.8	0.60	22	656.4	−32.3	0.67
12	Cymbals	371.8	0.97	30	368.6	−14.8	1.84
13	Snare drum	339.1	0.99	57	334.9	−22.0	4.02
14	Bass drum	–	–	–	134.6	–	0.08
15	Pure tone	500.0	1.00	72	500.1	0.3	27.95

vib = vibrato
mut = muted
f_1 = main frequency, frequency of a physical component in the spectrum of sound around which the main concentration of pitch matchings occurred – centre of the main zone
n_1 = the number of matchings contained in the main zone
m = factor of monochromaticity, a ratio of the number of pitch matchings contained in the main zone (n_1) to the total number of matchings (72)
PL/f_1 = microinterval between the pitch level and main frequency of a given sound

main zone and the value of the factor of monochromaticity must be taken into account. So it was decided that the pitch strength of these sounds would be computed as the inversion of a measure of dispersion (IQR) of pitch matchings within the main zone, multiplied by the factor m. Pitch-matching frequencies concentrated in all monochromatic zones outside the main zone confirm a musically meaningful selection of a given pitch class (pitch chroma) represented by the distribution of pitch matching frequencies within the main zone.

Important additional information that may be acquired by the use of the indirect method of measuring pitch strength (we may call it simply a method of pitch matching) is the information about the psychologically relevant value of pitch itself, the *pitch level* of a given sound. Pitch level of sound (PL), a physical representative of the value of psychological pitch magnitude, is the median value of the distribution of frequencies of comparison tones tuned to equal pitch with the sound. As has already been described, the median value of a distribution is a central value situated exactly in the middle of a given set of data. For indefinite pitch sounds (for example, with factor of monochromaticity below 0.50), the set of data is composed of all the pitch-matching frequencies obtained

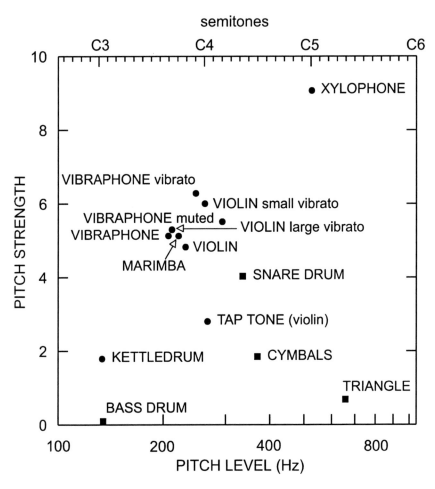

Circles = instruments of 'definite pitch'
Squares = instruments of 'indefinite pitch', according to the existing theoretical classification

Figure 6.2   Pitch level and pitch strength in sounds of musical instruments

in the course of a pitch-matching experiment. For sounds of definite pitch, a set of data means only those pitch matching frequencies that are contained in the main zone of concentration.

The parameters used in calculating pitch strength and pitch level of investigated sounds, together with the results of calculations, are shown in Table 6.1. The two-dimensional display of pitch strength and pitch level of instrumental sounds is shown in Fig. 6.2.

Discussion and Conclusions

The most important outcome of the research performed is the conclusion that in trying to match the pitch of a pure tone to that of an instrumental sound, musicians subconsciously perform operations on two independent components of musical pitch value: pitch class and pitch height (Rakowski 1996, 1999). The expression 'musical pitch class' in the tonal system of western music means a pitch unit used for musical tonal constructions; in other words, it means a pitch category of about one semitone width (sometimes a little wider, when tuning accuracy is not perfect). Due to the properties of our musical memory and musical imagination, pitch classes are easily connected in melodic sequences and enter into hierarchical tonal relations. An extremely important feature of a pitch class is its octave circularity. It means that octave replications of a given pitch class preserve a certain kind of identity and, to a large degree, have the same meaning in tonal constructions.

There is a small but interesting difference between the notions of musical pitch class and musical chroma. The difference consists in the kind of auditory memory engaged in the functioning of these two phenomena. The concept of pitch chroma was put forward by Révész (1913), who formulated the two-element theory of musical pitch. One element, the tone height, is the continuously rising, unstructured sensation of pitch (we prefer now to call it 'pitch height', or simply 'natural pitch'). The other element is a sequence, repeating with octave circularity, of distinct musical chromas; C, C#, D, D#, E ... and so on. The problem is that if we give such names to musical chromas, we also assume that they will have constant, absolute values of pitch, represented by definite constant frequencies. However, such constant values of pitch may only be stored in the long-term memories of those people who have so-called 'absolute pitch'. The overwhelming majority of other listeners and musicians, who do not have absolute pitch and presently do not use any instrument with a fixed tuning, perform the operations of structuring musical pitch without referring to any fixed-pitch tonal system. They may adopt any incidental pitch as a point of reference and develop in their short-term memory a system of pitch classes that may not be 'in tune' with the fixed chromas, but that play exactly the same part in the creation and perception of musical structures. The notion of a pitch class seems to be more general than that of a chroma, and the meaning of them is slightly different; however, it seems that on many occasions the two terms may be used interchangeably, or a combination of both can be applied.

The sequence of operations performed by the listener during the pitch-matching experiment seems to be as follows. Having listened to the investigated sound, the listener chooses a point along the natural pitch scale to make a decision concerning the pitch value. This chosen natural pitch value is located in the short-term memory and immediately transformed into a musical-pitch category (a chromatic pitch class). The next stage of the operation consists of trying to find the best match between the pitch class remaining in the memory and the pure comparison tone. Here, however, several solutions may be accepted with varying probability. Due to the nature of the chromatic pitch dimension, a given pitch class may appear in any of several octaves along the scale of natural pitch. The matching not only requires the equalization of pitch, but also possibly finding a good match for the timbres of the two sounds compared. Such a matching is not always easy, and quite often results in the 'octave errors' between the main frequency of the investigated sound and that of the matched pure tone. The above reasoning leads, however, to the conclusion that the 'octave errors' should not be treated as 'errors' as far as the dimension of pitch chroma, the most important dimension of pitch in music, is concerned. Consequently, all concentrations of pitch-matching frequencies appearing in one or more octave relations with the main frequency add to the strength of the sensation of pitch.

The method of measuring pitch strength and pitch level of sound used and described in the present investigation differs in many aspects from most of the methods proposed thus far which have the same goal (for example, Terhardt et al., 1982). Its point of departure was not in theoretical assumptions and calculations based on measurement of the physical spectrum, but in asking musicians what they really hear as pitch in a given auditory stimulus. Ultimately, a theory of multidimensional structure of musical pitch was selected on the basis of psychological facts – monochromatic distribution of pitch-matching frequencies.

As seen in Table 6.1, the highest value of pitch strength was obtained for a pure tone at 500Hz. Such a result was expected, as in this particular case both stimuli compared had the same timbre. Some experiments should be performed in future using a more 'musical' sound, that is, a harmonic complex tone as a comparison stimulus: it must be remembered that when tuning orchestral instruments, musicians choose this kind of sound (the sound of an oboe) rather than a pure tone. Nevertheless, pure tones seem to be the most universal stimulus for pitch comparisons with various kinds of sound.

It has been suggested in theoretical considerations and shown in experiments (Wightman, 1973; Rakowski, 1977; Fastl, 1998) that the larger the pitch strength of a given sound, the more precise the perceptions of differences of its frequency (in other words, the smaller the frequency differential threshold of that sound). Following the above reasoning, the results of the present experiment give information about the precision of differentiating the pitch of sound in various musical instruments. Furthermore, they bring a first suggestion (now confirmed in recently performed experiments) of the increase of pitch strength and frequency selectivity with rising frequency of sound up to some optimum value. (See high value of the pitch strength in the sound of a xylophone, played about an octave higher than other instruments' sounds, Figure 6.2.)

The method proposed here will be improved and verified in further experiments by comparing its results with those obtained by means of other methods. Observation of the results obtained so far (with a limited number of sounds) leads to the conclusion that psychologically justified division of sounds into 'definite-pitch' and 'indefinite-pitch' classifications, if at all necessary, might be grounded on the existence or non-existence of a monochromatic structure of their pitch-matching histograms.

Acknowledgement

The work was supported by the State Committee for Scientific Research, Grant No 1 H01F 045 18. The author wishes to thank Ilia Kiuila and Piotr Rogowski for help in taking measurements and for performing calculations.

References

Fastl, H. (1988) 'Pitch and pitch strength of peaked ripple noise', in H. Duifhuis, H.W. Hoot and H.P. Wit (eds), *Basic Issues in Hearing*, pp. 370–79, London: Academic Press.

Fastl, H. (1998) 'Pitch strength and frequency discrimination for noise bands or complex tones', in A.R. Palmer, A. Rees, Quentin M.R.C. Summerfield and R. Meddis (eds), *Psychophysical and Physiological Advances in Hearing*, London: Whurr Publishers.

Fastl, H. and Stoll, G. (1979) 'Scaling of pitch strength', *Hearing Research*, 1: 293–301.

Kiuiła, I., Rakowski, A. and Rogowski, P. (1998) 'Pitch and pitch strength of cello vibrato tones', *Proceedings of the International Symposium on Musical Acoustics ISMA'98*, Leavenworth: 321–5.

Rakowski, A. (1977) 'Measurements of pitch', *Catgut Acoustical Society Newsletter*, 27: 9–11.

Rakowski, A. (1996) 'Pitch strength, pitch value and pitch distance', *Acustica*, 82: S80.

Rakowski, A. (1999) 'Perceptual dimensions of pitch and their appearance in the phonological system of music', *Musicae Scientiae*, 3: 23–39.

Rakowski, A., Kiuiła, I. and Rogowski, P. (1996) 'Pitch and pitch strength of violin vibrato tones', *Proceedings of the 4th International Conference on Music Perception and Cognition*, Montreal: 507–12.

Révész, G. (1913) *Zur Grundlagen der Tonpsychologie*, Leipzig: Veit.

Terhardt, E. (1979) Calculating virtual pitch, *Hearing Research*, 1: 155–82.

Terhardt, E., Stoll G. and Seewann M. (1982) 'Algorithm for extraction of pitch and pitch salience from complex tonal signals', *Journal of the Acoustical Society of America*, 71: 679–88.

Wightman, F.L. (1973) 'The pattern-transformation model of pitch', *Journal of the Acoustical Society of America*, 54: 407–16.

Chapter 7

'Expressive Intonation' in String Performance: Problems of Analysis and Interpretation

Peter Johnson

Introduction: 'Expressive Intonation'

For the singer, string- and wind-player, good intonation is not a matter of conforming to some mathematically determined temperament but is 'a dynamic process, expressing the organic relationship between notes in a musical context' (Blum, 1977, p. 103). So writes David Blum in his account of Casals' approaches to performance and interpretation. He proceeds to describe 'expressive intonation' (EI) in some detail: any passing or auxiliary tone can be altered in the direction of the next tone, so that, in the most familiar instance, leading-notes are sharpened to 'express' their progression to the tonic.[1] I propose to examine this practice in the context, first, of a Casals recording, and subsequently in recordings of the slow movement of Beethoven's last string quartet.

If the sharpening or flattening of a tone can be expressive in Blum's sense, the listener must be aware of some normative intonation, either previously defined in the performance or known a priori. Blum is curiously silent about what this could be, but by examining Casals' recordings, we can deduce a probable standard. We shall find that this relates interestingly to Seashore's well-known study of intonation among pre-war violinists. A related question raised by EI concerns ensemble performance. If tones such as the leading-note are routinely sharpened, how does this affect their harmonic relationship with other tones? Is the function of the leading-note as third of the dominant sacrificed in the interest of melodic syntax, and if so, how does this affect the expressive qualities of the performance? And are there circumstances in which performers would tend to favour pure intonation over EI by emphasizing its consonance over its syntactical function? Beethoven's Lento assai proves to be one such case, although individual recordings display strikingly different solutions to this problem.

First, however, we shall look at the relatively straightforward example of Casals' own unaccompanied playing of the Sarabande from Bach's C minor Suite, an example Blum chose to illustrate EI (Blum, 1977, p. 108). As well as clarifying Blum's methods, an analysis of Casals' recording provides a suitable context for a critical review of our methods of intonation analysis.

Ex. 7.1   Casals: Bach, Cello Suite V (BWV 1011) Sarabande, bars 1–8

According to Blum, the recurring minor seconds in this movement invite EI (Example 7.1). Actual intonations can be determined by spectrum analysis,[2] and Figure 7.1 shows the spectra of the third and fourth notes of bar 1, the B2 and C3 respectively, in Casals' recording.[3] The y-axis shows relative decibel levels for each peak frequency, the strongest signal taken as 0 dB. In these spectra, no readable harmonics appear above 1200 Hz, although the upper frequency-limit of electric shellac recordings of the pre-war era was about 5 kHz; the frequency-range of our analyses is up to 11 kHz.

In Figure 7.1, each fundamental shows a clearly defined principal frequency: 125.0 Hz for B2 and 131.2 Hz for C3. The accuracy of these readings is < 0.17 Hz, which is < 2 cents at this register (Johnson, 1999a). Such spectra can furnish

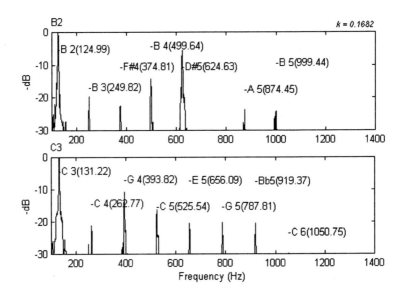

Figure 7.1   Spectrum analysis of Bach's C minor Sarabande at bar 1: B2, C3

a good deal of data about what is happening within any sounding event, but cannot represent the tone itself. One immediate problem is that the harmonics of a tone are rarely exact integer multiples of the fundamental, and psychoacoustic tests have long demonstrated the importance of the lower-order harmonics in the perception of frequency (see Butler, 1992, for a useful general discussion and recorded test samples). However, we shall see that the fundamentals provide a useful working approximation of perceived frequency, a conclusion also reached by Hagerman and Sundberg in their study of Barbershop singing (Hagerman and Sundberg, 1980, p. 198).

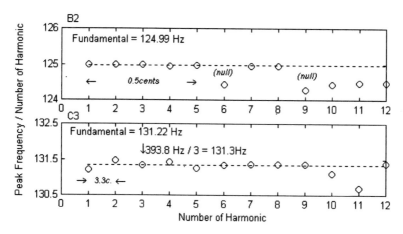

Figure 7.2   Bach's C minor Sarabande at bar 1: Harmonics of B2 and C3

Figure 7.2 presents sets of harmonics for B2 and C3, as revealed in the spectra of these tones. Here, the set of theoretical harmonics was first derived as integer multiples of the shown fundamental, and the spectrum searched for the peak frequencies nearest to each harmonic. To allow easy comparison between the fundamental and peak frequencies, the latter are divided by their respective harmonic number, so that, were each peak to correspond exactly to the theoretical harmonic, the data would form a straight line. In the plot for C3, for example, the peak p at 393.8 Hz represents the third harmonic, and this is accordingly plotted at $p/3$ = 131.3 Hz. This is about one cent sharper than the actual fundamental, well within our margin of error (< two cents). Figure 7.1 shows that this is a strong harmonic and may be the focal point for the ear's reading of frequency for this tone. The fundamental is lower by about three cents, where the precision of our data is in the order of < two cents. In the upper plot, however, all the data closely correspond to the harmonics of the fundamental except for obvious anomalies: in the region of the sixth harmonic and from the ninth upwards, there are no discernible peak signals. In both these examples, therefore, we may assume that the fundamental adequately represents perceived frequency within suitable working limits. This proves generally to be the case.

The next stage is to read the intervals between tones. From Figure 7.1, we can calculate the interval between the fundamentals of B2 and C3 as 84 cents.[4] This is 16 cents narrower than Equal Temperament (ET) and a massive 28 cents narrower than the just minor second at 112 cents. For comparative purposes, it is useful to plot each tone of a recording in terms of its deviation from Just Intonation (JI). To do this, we must first construct a just scale of frequencies in which the perfect fifths are formed of the ratio 3:2, the major thirds as 5:4, and so on. Chromatic tones such as *f#* are calculated as pure major thirds from an appropriate pitch of the diatonic scale. The leading-note/tonic minor second is 16:15 if tuned as a just major third from the dominant. Once this scale is set from an appropriate frequency as tonic, the frequency of each successive fundamental in the sample can be plotted in terms of its deviation from it. Any sample tuned exactly to JI will show zero deviation, resulting in a single horizontal line.

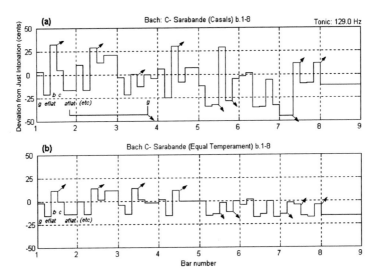

Figure 7.3   Tunings compared with Just Intonation

Figure 7.3(a) shows how Casals' tuning in the first eight bars compares with the theoretical tuning of Just Intonation. Each step represents a single tone, as indicated by the pitch-class names shown in bar 1, and the vertical lines connecting each step indicate the size of deviation of each interval from JI. The rising semitone B2–C3, 28 cents narrower than JI, is represented as the gap between the third and fourth steps, and is measurable by the length and direction of the connecting vertical line. All the conjunct rising minor seconds are indicated by the upward-pointing arrows, and it can be seen that, in each case, the first of the pair of tones is tuned significantly sharper than the second, relative to JI, by margins in excess of ten cents. Falling semitones, marked by the down-arrows, are similarly 'expressed' by narrow semitones. Longer-term voice-leadings are also indicated, as, for example, the A-flat2 in bar 1, which is relatively flat compared to the G2 at the fifth quaver of bar 3, and this conforms exactly to the Casals/Blum performance recommendations for this movement.

Figure 7.3(b) shows how the same passage would appear if performed exactly in ET. The minor seconds of ET appear to fulfil admirably the function of 'EI', suggesting that ET may not be entirely unmusical. Nevertheless, each of Casals' semitones is significantly narrower than ET, and tends more closely to resemble those of Pythagorean tuning (22 cents narrower than JI). This recalls Seashore's contention that violinists of the pre-war era tended to use Pythagorean tuning (Seashore, 1967 [1938]). I have noted elsewhere that the wide variations of intonation shown by Seashore's data suggest, on the contrary, that no single temperament was used by his violinists, and this is also suggested by the above results from Casals (Johnson, 2000). On the other hand, they do show a consistent application of EI. Figure 7.3 further indicates that Casals' 'non-expressive intonation' could well have been ET, since his semitone steps are always narrower, though not always excessively narrower, than the 100 cents of ET. Plots of the repeat of bars 1 to 8, and of the two playings of the second section of the Sarabande, confirm these conclusions.

In unaccompanied or monophonic performance, of course, there is no strong reason to conform to the natural intonation of JI. In ensemble performance, on the other hand, the application of EI would appear to be problematic in so far as it creates harmonic dissonance with other tones. How do string players in ensemble handle the potential conflicts between vertical consonance and EI? My next example will also bring the question of normative practices and the differences between the extremes of Just and Pythagorean tunings sharply into focus.

The theme of the slow movement of Beethoven's last quartet begins in bar 3 with stepwise quavers falling from tonic to dominant and rising back to the tonic. Whereas the first leading-note is dissonant, the second forms the major third of the sustained dominant chord (Example 7.2). Bar 5 is an exact repeat of bar 3. This is music that has often been described as 'sublime' (Kerman, 1967), a description perhaps not unconnected with the consistency with which quartets have adopted very slow tempos over the last 70 years. The average is well below 60 quaver beats per minute, so that the duration of each beat is significantly more than 1 second. The listener is thus afforded plenty of time to savour the colouring and intonational inflection of each sonorous event. How, then, have violinists managed the tuning of the falling and rising leading-notes in these bars?

Ex. 7.2 Beethoven's Lento assai (Op. 135iii), bars 1–6

Figure 7.4 indicates the relative tuning of rising and falling leading-notes in bar 3, taken from 25 recordings. The data are plotted chronologically, from the Flonzaley Quartet's 1927 recording to the Leipziger Quartet's of 1998. The relative tuning of the falling leading-note is shown by the down-arrow (∇) and of the rising tone by the up-arrow (Δ). The upper plot shows the relative tuning of each leading-note expressed as a major third from the second violin's dominant, reading fundamentals derived by spectrum analysis. The interval is shown in terms of its deviation from the just major third, so that an entry on the zero line indicates a just major third between the A-flat3 and C4 fundamentals. For the lower plot, the interval measured is the semitone between leading-note and the adjacent tonic in the first violin; in this case, it is the deviation of this interval from the just minor second that is plotted. Assuming that the tonics and dominants are more or less constant in pitch, the two plots should appear to be inverted, since, if the leading-note is tuned sharp, it will create a correspondingly narrow semitone against the tonic.

The upper plot in Figure 7.4 shows that the majority of quartets tune their leading-notes as significantly sharp major thirds from the dominant, sometimes exceeding the 22 cents of Pythagorean tuning. However, the falling leading-notes are on average tuned higher than the rising leading-notes by a factor of about four cents. The rule of EI is thus tending to be reversed in performances of this extract (numbers in parentheses are the equivalent readings for bar 5):

Falling leading-note sharper than rising leading-note:	64% (52%)
Rising leading-note sharper than falling:	16% (32%)
Same tuning for both (< 5 cents deviation):	20% (16%)

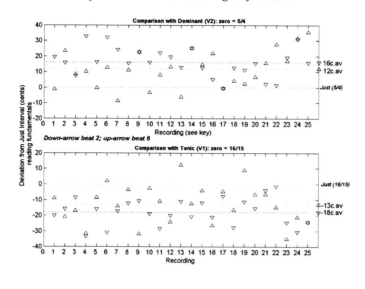

Key:

1	Flonzaley Quartet (1927)	14	Melos Quartet (1984)
2	Busch Quartet (1934)	15	Vermeer Quartet (1985)
3	Budapest Quartet (1941)	16	Guarneri Quartet (1987)
4	Loewenguth Quartet (1947)	17	Lindsay Quartet (1987)
5	Hungarian Quartet (1957)	18	Emerson Quartet (1988)
6	Hollywood Quartet (1957)	19	Alban Berg Quartet (1989)
7	Fine Arts Quartet (c.1960)	20	New Budapest Quartet (1991)
8	Italian Quartet (1968)	21	Medici Quartet (1991)
9	Amadeus Quartet (1969)	22	Arr. Bernstein, VPO strings (1991)
10	Vègh Quartet (1973)	23	Juilliard Quartet (1996)
11	La Salle Quartet (1976)	24	Vanbrugh Quartet (1996)
12	Tallich Quartet (1977)	25	Leipziger Quartet (1998)
13	Amadeus Quartet (1982)		

Figure 7.4   Tuning of falling and rising leading notes: Op. 135iii, bar 3

It is also of interest to note that all the major thirds equal to, or narrower than, JI occur with the rising leading-notes.

Figure 7.4 indicates, however, that in a number of recordings quite exceptional intonational strategies are adopted. Recordings in the 1990s show a somewhat inconsistent tendency to tune the leading-note exceptionally sharp. Two earlier recordings, nos 9 and 14, show identical yet very sharp readings for leading-notes: these are from the Amadeus Quartet's 1969 LP and the Melos Quartet's recording of 1984 respectively. Given the reputation of these quartets, and indeed of their recordings, these results cannot lightly be dismissed as accidental or indicative of error. And in striking contrast to all of these is sample no. 17, from the Lindsay Quartet's recording of 1987: here, each leading-note is shown to form an exact just major third with the dominant, and the semitones with the tonic are only marginally narrower than JI. But can we hear these differences, and if so, how do they affect our understanding of the performance or even the work? I propose to compare the Melos Quartet's recording with the Lindsays', and make some general interpretative suggestions as to how the experienced and receptive listener may respond to these divergent performance strategies.

The Melos Quartet's Recording of the Lento Assai

Figure 7.5 shows three of the harmonic series constituting the tones in the last quaver beat of bar 3, as recorded by the Melos Quartet. It is drawn from the same spectrum as the data for sample no. 14 in Figure 7.4. The three tones are the cello's double-stopped A-flat2, the second violin's A-flat3, and the first violin's rising leading-note, C4. The interval between the fundamentals in the first and second violins, as plotted in Figure 7.5(a), is 418 cents, or 32 cents sharper than JI. As with our analysis of the Casals recording, this plot shows that, although the lower-order harmonics present some complexity, this does not significantly affect the reading of intervals as measured from the fundamental frequencies.

Since the several series relate to one sonorous spectrum, we would expect to find certain peaks doubling as the harmonic of two or more fundamentals. In fact, all the peaks corresponding to the even-numbered harmonics of A-flat2 should appear as the entire series of A-flat3, and this is indeed the case. However, we

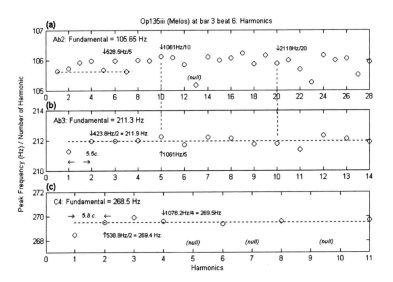

Figure 7.5   Melos Quartet: Harmonics of three tones

might also expect the tenth harmonic of A-flat2 and the fifth harmonic of A-flat3, both at C6, to be represented by the same peak as the fourth harmonic of C4. The latter is shown to be at 1078 Hz, whereas the former are both at 1061 Hz, 29 cents flatter. The two identifiable peaks in the region of C6 are visible in the spectrum, and confirm the exceptionally wide tuning of the A-flat3/C4 interval.

Many of the harmonics shown for A-flat2 (Figure 7.5 plot (a)) are clearly anomalous. We note that E-flat2 and G-flat3 are also sounding in this chord, and the cello's A-flat shows that every harmonic above the seventh is either masked or non-existent. Those of C4 are more consistent, but the fundamental is significantly flatter than the average by some seven cents. From current psychoacoustical theory, we must assume that the true reading of the frequency of this tone is in the order of 270 Hz. However, by the same argument, the second violin's fundamental should also be read as some five cents sharper than its fundamental, leaving the interval between the two, as indicated in Figure 7.4, to be about two cents too low, a negligible error.

What we hear from this performance is a richly intoned melody, projected by the first violin above the accompanying ensemble and marked by a wide and fairly slow vibrato; the tempo is relatively slow. The lack of acoustic consonance, as indicated by the asynchrony of common harmonics such as C6, probably contributes to the sense we have of the soloist singing, as it were, above the ensemble, a detached and independent voice.

The Lindsay Quartet's Recording of the Lento Assai

Figure 7.6 allows direct comparison of the sample from the Melos Quartet's recording with the same extract in the Lindsays' recording.[5] Here, the peak frequency at C6 (1049 Hz) serves as harmonic for A-flat2, A-flat3 and C4. Apart from one null datum at the seventh harmonic, the peaks in plot (c) correspond closely to the integer multiples of the C4 fundamental, with a maximum deviation of a negligible three cents.[6]

An obvious anomaly in Figure 7.6 is the second violin's A-flat3. Measuring fundamentals, this forms an exact just major third with the first violin (386 cents), but the lower-order harmonics indicate a wider tuning by some 11 cents. This suggests that the interval plotted for sample no. 17 in Figure 7.4 is wrong, and that the first and second violins in fact form an equal-tempered major third at this point. This point must be conceded, but it is not the whole story. The second violin's fundamental is an exact second harmonic of the cello's A-flat2, and, with this tone, the C4 does indeed form a just major third, as also indicated by the synchrony of the tenth and fourth harmonics respectively. In fact, the harmonics of the cello's A-flat2 are shown to be more persistent than in the Melos Quartet's sample, confirming the clearly audible presence of this tone in the Lindsays' ensemble.

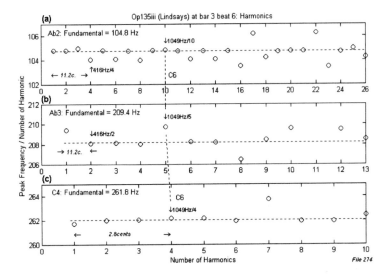

Figure 7.6   Lindsay Quartet: Harmonics

Interpretation

I have elsewhere discussed the Lindsays' recording in some detail, noting the
marked *tenuto* on the rising leading-note which exaggerates the effect of the
wide semitone to the ensuing tonic (Johnson, 2000). I interpret this as effectively
denying the potential of this music to flow freely, to capture the gentle lullaby
movement implied in Beethoven's score. Yet, before we condemn the Lindsays'
interpretation as inauthentic, it is worth noting how Beethoven develops the
movement over the first two variations of this four-variation movement. Already
in the first variation, there are chromatic appoggiaturas which draw us steadily
away from the uncomplicated world of tonic and dominant harmony. But the
second variation, at bar 22, thrusts us without preparation into a dead-slow
funeral march in the tonic minor, marked *Più Lento* and characterized by a
dragging double-dotted rhythm. In many performances this is presented as
unprepared, as indeed it appears to be in the score. But the Lindsays manage the
opening 32 bars in such a way as to make the *Più Lento* seem inevitable, the
focus of the movement. It is specifically in the playing of the opening theme,
with its very slow tempo, marked *rubato*, balance, styles of *vibrato*, and, as
shown here, the unusual intonational strategy, that the expressive coherence
between the theme and the *Più Lento* variation is created.

But why should tunings close to JI contribute to the emotional intensity of this
music? One answer may be that JI, with its inherently natural properties, has
come to signify difference from the normative expressive world of ET and the

wide variations of EI.[7] Perhaps JI imparts an impersonal, non-subjective quality to the expression, particularly where the melodic tones are drawn into an acoustic consonance with the resonant accompaniment (Johnson, 2000). It is as if the Lindsays' leader, Peter Cropper, is expressing the will, the *vouloir,* to deny the natural salience of the uppermost voice (Tarasti, 1994). To this extent, the somewhat desultory vibrato indicates a voice that is singing against its will. There is thus a darkness but also a complexity in this playing, and the music we hear speaks not of lullaby but of introspection, of an awareness of the possibility of the tragic, such as will find full expression in the Lindsays' playing of the *Più Lento* variation.

Conclusion

The study of intonation in ensemble contexts is both possible and profitable. Fundamentals give a working approximation of the perceived tuning of tones, but the harmonic spectra reveal subtle variations which are arguably of interpretative significance. Accomplished performers are able to use intonational strategies to colour their interpretation of the composer's score. Intonation is thus one of the means by which our leading performers can say something new about an established work, and it is surely through such processes that the canon itself survives, not as a museum of musical works, but as living, contemporary music.

Notes

1. The term 'tone' refers here to the sounding event corresponding to a note in the score.
2. I am using purpose-built software within the Matlab environment, utilizing its powerful Signal Processing and graphics functions (Johnson, 1999b). All my samples are recorded at 22.05 kHz. The spectrum analyses use a frame-size of 2^{17} samples, allowing a maximum duration of c.6.5s. Zero padding is used for shorter samples. A Hanning Window is applied.
3. Pitches are named using the American Standard nomenclature, where the cello open C string is C2, middle C is C4 and A440 is A4. Italicized lowercase letters refer to pitch-classes. The readings at the peaks represent the maxima of the internal data, rather than the much less accurate cursor position.
4. An interval in cents, c, is calculated from frequencies $f1$ and $f2$, by the formula

$$c = 1200 \times \log_2(f1/f2).$$

5. See Johnson (2000) for the spectrum from which these data are derived.
6. In Johnson (2000), I state that the cello is flatter than the second violin. This minor inaccuracy illustrates the importance of close examination of complete lower-order

harmonic series. From the listener's perspective, of course, my point stands that the composite tone is complex.

7.   This would only be true for mainstream performance, since just major thirds are nowadays standard in period instrument performance. To this extent, the use of JI as a special effect is style-dependent. See Johnson (2000) for further discussion.

References

Blum, D. (1977) *Casals and the Art of Interpretation*, Berkeley, Los Angeles, London: University of California Press.

Butler, D. (1992) *The Musician's Guide to Perception and Cognition*, New York: Schirmer Books.

Hagerman, B. and Sundberg, J. (1980) 'Fundamental frequency adjustment in barbershop singing', *Journal of Research in Singing*, 4(1): 3–17.

Johnson, P. (1999a) 'Performance and the listening experience', in P. Dejans (ed.), *Theory into Practice: Composition, Performance and the Listening Experience*, pp. 55–101, Leuven: Leuven University Press.

Johnson, P. (1999b) 'SPAN: spectrographic analysis of musical extracts in the Matlab environment', Birmingham Conservatoire.

Johnson, P. (2000) 'Intonation and interpretation in string quartet performance: The case of the flat leading-note', in C. Woods, G.B. Luck, R. Brochard, S.A. O'Neill and J.A. Sloboda (eds), *Proceedings of the Sixth International Conference on Music Perception and Cognition* (CD-ROM), Keele: University of Keele.

Kerman, J. (1967) *The Beethoven Quartets*, London: Oxford University Press.

Makeig, S. (1982) 'Affective versus Analytical Perception of Musical Intervals', in M. Clynes (ed.), *Music, Mind and Brain: The Neuropsychology of Music*, pp. 227–50, New York and London: Plenum Press.

Morrison, S.J. and Fyk, J. (2002) 'Intonation', in R. Parncutt and G.E. McPherson (eds), *The Science and Psychology of Musical Performance*, pp. 183–98, Oxford: Oxford University Press.

Rakowski, A. (1990) 'Intonation variants of musical intervals in isolation and in musical contexts', *Psychology of Music*, 18: 60–72.

Seashore, C. (1967[1938]) *Psychology of Music*, New York: Dover Books (1938 edn.: McGraw Hill).

Tarasti, E. (1994) *A Theory of Musical Semiotics*, Bloomington and Indianapolis: Indiana University Press.

Chapter 8

Do Compositions Reveal Information about Historical Tuning?

Bernhard Billeter

Our knowledge of the tuning of keyboard and fretted instruments in earlier centuries is incomplete. How are we to know which tuning serves for which compositions? This question has important practical consequences for the interpretation of early music. There are three sources of information available to practitioners and scholars to help answer this question: surviving instruments, tuning treatises, and the compositions themselves. In this chapter the first and second sources are briefly treated before taking a more detailed look at several compositions and considering which, if any, indications about historical tunings may be derived from them.

Surviving Instruments

Preserved organs never retain their original tunings. Disused organ pipes are very rare and only in special cases do tracks in the metal or wood of stopped pipes show the original position of the plate. Even these only allow inexact measures of tuning. The same may be said about the tuning measures of the *clavecin brisé* (dismountable harpsichord) of Jean Marius, which is housed today in the Museum of Historical Instruments in Berlin. The measures given by Helmut K.H. Lange and Konstantin Restle are not exactly the same and they each interpret the tuning differently.[1]

Tuning Treatises

Tuning treatises may be divided into practical tuning instructions and theoretical discussions which take place against a mathematical background. Tuning instructions are generally written by organ builders and provide only inexact methods. Theoretical writings do not usually provide a complete account of the tuning of their respective periods either. This is because practising musicians were not interested in exactly pure intervals, such as, for example, pure major thirds: they preferred a system which used only nearly pure intervals. An example of this may be found in Michael Praetorius' 1619 text *Syntagma II*. Discussing meantone temperament, Praetorius wrote: 'The fifths C-sharp – G-sharp and F-sharp – C-sharp should not be so much wrong [that is, a quarter syntonic comma too small] and not pure, but something between.'[2] The reason for this is that the G sharp key should be available in case the minor third of an F minor triad is needed. In the keyboard music of the period of Praetorius, A flats may sometimes be found.

The Compositions Themselves

So far, musicologists have not generally considered the characteristic features of compositions themselves as potentially important sources of information about the historical tuning of particular pieces. This may be due to a general reluctance of researchers to move away from corroborated facts and proofs towards circumstantial evidence and hypotheses. When other methods fail, however, I see nothing objectionable about using a supposition to generate a hypothesis in the critical sense of the word.[3]

In the *Fitzwilliam Virginal Book* there is a piece by John Bull entitled 'Ut, re, mi, fa, sol, la'. It is a fantasy which moves through all 12 major keys. Unlike all other works by John Bull, as well as all other works in the *Fitzwilliam Virginal Book*, it is impossible to play this fantasy in meantone temperament (see Example 8.1).

Ex. 8.1   John Bull, 'Ut, re, mi, fa, sol, la', from the *Fitzwilliam Virginal Book*

It may be that this is an experiment in equal temperament. Many musicians today do not know that fretted instruments had equal temperament, even in the sixteenth to eighteenth centuries, with every fret placed at $\frac{1}{18}$ of the remaining length of the chord. Equal temperament was first described mathematically by Simon Stevin, a Dutch mathematician who developed logarithms (*c.* 1600). We know English viol consorts of the beginning of the seventeenth century played with enharmonic changings, and we know that sometimes a viol consort and an organ played together. This allows the hypothesis that equal organ temperament was used at the English Royal Court in the period before the English Revolution.[4] Afterwards, it seems to have been forgotten for a long time.

During the sixteenth and seventeenth centuries, keyboard music was written in a small number of keys without sharps and flats, or with only few accidentals. Also, the five upper keys of the keyboard were always C sharp, E flat, F sharp, G sharp and B flat. This is because in meantone temperament A flat and D sharp do not exist. But there are exceptions. To understand this it is important to know that it is a historical fact that there was not just one strict meantone temperament – meaning the quarter-syntonic-comma-meantone – but that there were several variations on it. For example, as early as the period in which Arnolt Schlick was composing (late fifteenth to early sixteenth centuries), A flat was sometimes used instead of G sharp. According to Schlick's written tuning instructions, this key is tuned as a fifth below E flat. Unfortunately, the use of A flat cannot be proved by referring to his organ compositions, as they contain neither A flats nor G sharps!

Rare exceptions to meantone tuning, and in particular the use of A flat and D sharp, can be found in some keyboard pieces by Girolamo Frescobaldi as, for example, in his 'Toccata Undecima' (Example 8.2) and his 'Canzona Quinta' (Example 8.3).

In Example 8.3, the 'Canzona Quinta', the A flat is only short and transitional. Similarly, D sharp occurs in two of Frescobaldi's elevation toccatas, but the use is brief and transitional. There was an Italian tradition of writing elevation toccatas in E major. But usually the dominant triad containing D sharp was avoided or used only transitionally, as in Example 8.4.

But in the first example by Frescobaldi, 'Toccata Undecima' (Example 8.2), the A flat is more important, occurring twice as an accented note. For this reason it is assumed by some scholars that Frescobaldi used our modern equal temperament. Patrizio Barbieri recounts the story of a musician, '*un vecchio musicastro*' from southern Italy, who introduced equal temperament to the house of Cardinal Francesco Barberini in Rome in about 1640 and who is claimed to have influenced Frescobaldi.[5] The first part of the story may be true, because equal temperament was also propagated at this time by Joseph Zaragoza, Juan Caramuel Lobkowitz, Juraj Križanić and others. But the claim that this influenced Frescobaldi seems to be wrong, since Frescobaldi uses the notes A flat and D sharp only very rarely. And just as the 'Toccata Undecima' contains many rhythmic experiments, it may very well contain harmonic experiments. This suggestion is supported by the expressive value of the A flat, as well as by the fact that both occurrences are within dissonant chords. Frescobaldi's second book of toccatas seems to have been written more for the organ, and the first book more for the harpsichord – as the title suggests. In the first book there are even occurrences of D flat, as Example 8.5 shows.

Joseph Ratte[6] explains that the seventh E flat – D flat in meantone temperament is a good approximation of the natural seventh with the proportion 4 to 7, but this is irrelevant because this chord, which contains the tritone G – D flat, is

**Ex. 8.2   G. Frescobaldi, 'Toccata Undecima', in *Il secondo libro di toccate*
... (1637)**

**Ex. 8.3   G. Frescobaldi, 'Canzona Quinta', in *Il secondo libro di toccate* ...
(1637)**

Ex. 8.4 G. Frescobaldi, 'Toccata per l'Elevazione', third mass of *Fiori musicali* (1635)

Ex. 8.5 G. Frescobaldi, 'Passacagli from the Balletto Secondo', in *Toccate d'intavolatura di Cimbalo et Organo ...* , *Libro Primo* (1637), bars 4 and 6

regarded by the listener as dissonant. There is a much more crucial part in meantone temperament in the same piece some bars later: here A flat, C and E flat form a triad of A flat major, but the fifth is very bad; so bad that it is called 'the wolf' (see Example 8.6).

A similar effect can be heard in the 'Cento Partite sopra Passacagli', in combination with a D flat which forms a very bad triad of D flat major, with the third D flat – F being much too wide (see Example 8.7).

Also, the end of 'Cento Partite sopra Passacagli' is very experimental in E minor with some dominant chords, but in this example the dissonant D sharp is retarded by the suspended fourth (E). Taking into account the experimental character of these few pieces by Frescobaldi, one can argue that a meantone temperament should be used. I suggest, however, the use of neither a strict

Ex. 8.6   G. Frescobaldi, 'Passacagli from the Balletto Secondo', in
Toccate d'intavolatura di Cimbalo et Organo … , Libro Primo
(1637), bar 13

Ex. 8.7   G. Frescobaldi, 'Cento Partite sopra Passacagli', first *Altro tono*

quarter-comma-meantone nor a regular one-sixth-comma-meantone, but rather
an irregular meantone temperament with a better third C – E than the third E – G
sharp, such as I have described elsewhere.[7]

   As far as I can see, all practical tuning instructions of organ builders suggest
irregular temperaments, even later in the eighteenth century. In my opinion, it is
senseless to give mathematically exact measures in cents for historical tunings,
and even less to give these measures with three decimal figures after the point.
Tuning pure major thirds a little bit too wide, to the point at which the third begins

to beat, permits a less narrow tuning of the fifths than is possible with exactly pure thirds. And tuning the F sharp, C sharp and G sharp just slightly higher and the E flat slightly lower than in a regular one-fifth- or one-sixth-comma-meantone temperament enables the player to give a convincing interpretation of the experimental examples discussed above. An electronic tuning instrument should be used to help tune these irregular measures, and it is a pity that some of these electronic instruments are equipped with the mathematically exact positions of meantone, Werckmeister and other temperaments.

Johann Jakob Froberger continued in the experimental manner of his teacher Frescobaldi. But one should divide his keyboard works into those of Italian and those of French influence. To the former group belong pieces like 'Ricercar', 'Fantasia', 'Capriccio', 'Canzona' and 'Toccata'; to the latter belong the later suites and variations. The Italian-influenced pieces were composed more for the organ and do not use A flat and D sharp more frequently than the works of Frescobaldi. The French-influenced pieces are more individual and personal in style and are best played on the clavichord, which was the instrument Froberger liked best. On this instrument it is possible to slightly raise the pitch of a given note by pressing down more firmly on the key. In this way, an A flat may be helped to sound better when played together with C, F, and even E flat in meantone temperament (see Example 8.8).

Ex. 8.8   J.J. Froberger, Suite XIX, Allemande

With the sharps we do not have this possibility, because we cannot lower the pitch on the clavichord by pressing the keys less firmly. Froberger included many sharps in his French-influenced works, for example D sharp in the Suites in E minor. And these D sharps are part of the dominant triads which end the first part of each movement, where the ear wishes a pure major third (see Example 8.9).

Should we conclude that another tuning was used or intended for these suites? I do not think so. The best solution may be that an instrument with 'broken' upper keys was used. In the sixteenth and seventeenth centuries, many keyboard instruments had both E flat *and* D sharp, G sharp *and* A flat, including some organs. Some harpsichords with broken upper keys survive in museums; for example, there is a spinet and a harpsichord in Leipzig.

Ex. 8.9   J.J. Froberger, Suite VII, Courante

But while this explanation can account for the occurrences of D sharp and G sharp, how are we to interpret the A sharp and even E sharp in the Allemande of the same suite? Broken upper keys were usually in no more than one or two positions per octave, and while there were some harpsichords with 19 or even 31 keys per octave (Zarlino and Vicentino), these were exceptional (see Example 8.10).

Ex. 8.10   J.J. Froberger, Suite VII, Allemande, bars 6 and 7

However, when played using meantone temperament, the result is acceptable to the ear: the two sharps occur in dissonant chords with a tritone, and listeners are much better able to tolerate impure intervals when they occur in dissonant chords.

The same effect was used by Johann Kaspar Kerll, who studied in Rome with Giacomo Carissimi during the same years as Froberger. Kerll's 'Toccata 4', entitled *Toccata cromatica con durezze e ligature*, contains 26 D sharps and 15 A sharps, most of which are very short or occur in dissonant chords with a tritone (see Example 8.11).[8]

Ex. 8.11   J.K. Kerll, Toccata 4

With similar methods, we could now study the *Well-tempered Clavier* by Johann Sebastian Bach. In the first collection of 1722 we would note an important difference between the pieces in C major and C sharp major: in the former the triads are held, in the latter they are not. This suggests that unequal temperament was used. However, in the second collection, written about two decades later, such differences cannot be found. Whether this fact can assist in answering the question, as yet still puzzling scholars, of how Bach tempered his keyboard instruments is a topic worthy of further investigation, although beyond the scope of the present article.

To summarize, adopting a method of research based on looking at the compositions themselves, we have discovered evidence to suggest that the rare occurrences of A flat and D sharp in compositions by Frescobaldi and Froberger do not rule out the use of meantone temperament, but rather emphasize the harmonic tension engendered by the use of these notes, while at the same time suggesting that an irregular alteration of meantone temperament is the correct tuning to use for these works.

Notes

1. Lange (1978) 'Das Clavecin Brisé von Jean Marius in der Berliner Sammlung und die Schlick-Stimmung'; Restle (1997) 'Zur Stimmung des Marius-Cembalos im Berliner Instrumenten-Museum'.
2. Praetorius, Michael (1619), *Syntagma II*, p. 155.
3. After preparing this article I became acquainted with the work of another scholar using this method. See Jira (1997) *Musikalische Temperaturen in der Klaviermusik des 17. und frühen 18. Jahrhunderts.*
4. Otterstedt (1997) 'Vereinbarkeit englischer Gambenconsorts mit Orgelbegleitungen in der ersten Hälfte des 17. Jahrhunderts'.
5. Barbieri (1987) *Acustica, Accordatura e Temperamento nell'Illuminismo Veneto*, p. 295.
6. Ratte (1991) *Die Temperatur der Clavierinstrumente*, p. 342.
7. Billeter, Bernhard (1989) *Anweisung zum Stimmen von Tasteninstrumenten in verschiedenen Temperaturen*, pp. 19–23.

8. The complete keyboard works of Johann Kaspar Kerll, recorded by Bernhard Billeter, Motette CD 12161 and 12171, Düsseldorf, 1997. Played on the main organ of Rheinau, built by Johann Christoph Leu in 1711–15 which, following restoration, is tempered in one-sixth-comma-meantone.

References

Barbieri, Patrizio (1987) *Acustica, Accordatura e Temperamento nell'Illuminismo Veneto* [*Acoustics, Tuning and Temperament in Enlightenment Venice*], Rome: Edizioni Torre d'Orfeo.

Billeter, Bernhard (1989) *Anweisung zum Stimmen von Tasteninstrumenten in verschiedenen Temperaturen* [*Instructions for Tuning Keyboard Instruments in Different Temperaments*], Kassel: Berlin Merseburger Berlin.

Jira, Martin (1997) *Musikalische Temperaturen in der Klaviermusik des 17. und frühen 18. Jahrhunderts* [*Musical Temperaments in the Piano Music of the 17th and early 18th Centuries*], Tutzing: Verlag Hans Schneider.

Lange, Helmut (1978) 'Das Clavecin Brisé von Jean Marius in der Berliner Sammlung und die Schlick-Stimmung' ['The Clavecin Brisé by Jean Marius in the Berlin Collection and Schlick tuning'], *Die Musikforschung*, 31: 57–79.

Otterstedt, Annette (1997) 'Vereinbarkeit englischer Gambenconsorts mit Orgelbegleitungen in der ersten Hälfte des 17. Jahrhunderts' ['The compatibility of English gamba-consorts and organ accompaniments in the first half of the 17th century'], in *Stimmungen im 17. und 18. Jahrhundert: Vielfalt oder Konfusion? 15. Musikinstrumentenbau-Symposium am 11. und 12. November 1994* [*Tunings in the 17th and 18th Centuries: Variety or Confusion? The 15th Symposium on Making Musical Instruments, 11–12 November, 1994*], pp. 80–100, Konferenzenbericht No. 52, Michaelstein: Stiftung Kloster Michaelstein.

Praetorius, Michael (1619) *Syntagma II*, Wolfenbüttel: Bärenreiter Verlag.

Ratte, Joseph (1991), *Die Temperatur der Clavierinstrumente*, Kassel: Bärenreiter Verlag.

Restle, Konstantin (1997) 'Zur Stimmung des Marius-Cembalos im Berliner Instrumenten-Museum' ['The tuning of the Marius harpsichords in the Berlin museum of musical instruments'], in *Stimmungen im 17. und 18. Jahrhundert: Vielfalt oder Konfusion? 15. Musikinstrumentenbau-Symposium am 11. und 12. November 1994*, pp. 28–34, Konferenzenbericht No. 52, Michaelstein: Stiftung Kloster Michaelstein.

Chapter 9

Enrichment of Music Theory Pedagogy by Computer-based Repertoire Analysis and Perceptual-cognitive Theory

Richard Parncutt

Introduction

Theories of harmony and counterpoint vary from the most *deductive* (or reductionist), explaining isolated abstract examples by reference to abstract rule systems and tacitly assuming the existence of a normative style (for example, Fux, 1725; Lovelock, 1956; Krämer, 1991), to the most *inductive* (or historical), based directly on scores from different historical styles and periods (for example, de la Motte, 1988). Both approaches have specific pedagogical advantages: the deductive method allows for the complexity of the tonal system to be broken down into easily learnable steps, while the inductive method refers directly to primary source material, and acknowledges stylistic diversity. Modern harmony texts such as Forte (1974), Aldwell and Schachter (1978), Piston (1978), Pratt (1984) and Levine (1995) are situated at different points between these extremes.

  Both deductive and inductive approaches to music theory may be enriched by the methods, findings and theories of *systematic musicology*: deductive approaches by relevant perceptual theories, and inductive approaches by context-sensitive statistical analyses of notated music. Most music theories refer in some way to both (psycho)acoustics (for example, the harmonic series) and statistical properties of relevant repertoires (for example, any claim that a given procedure is more prevalent than another, in a given style). Several influential music theories have relied heavily on perceptual-cognitive theory (for example, Riemann's 1877 theory of *beziehendes Denken*, or referential thinking; Hindemith's 1942 theory of *combination tones*; Lerdahl and Jackendoff's 1983 theory of *generative grammars*). Statistical analyses of the musical repertoire – or, failing that, subjective considerations of frequency of occurrence, or *prevalence*[1] – are often used as explanatory tools in music theory (Budge, 1943; Jeppesen, 1946; McHose, 1947; de la Motte, 1988; Eberlein, 1994).

  In recent decades, rapid developments in computer technology and psychological research methods have enabled advances in both perceptual theory relevant to music (Terhardt, 1974a, 1976; Parncutt, 1989; Bregman, 1990; Krumhansl, 1990; Tillmann et al., 2000) and the application of statistical procedures to the analysis of musical scores (Huron, 1999). Computers are routinely used to run psychoacoustical experiments (including digital sound synthesis and analysis), to analyse large historical databases of musical scores, and (in both cases) to carry out statistical analyses.

With relatively few exceptions (for example, Lerdahl, 1988; Larson, 1997a), music theorists have been slow to take advantage of these developments – perhaps due to the political landscape of universities, which tends to isolate music theorists from scientific colleagues with similar interests. But given the long music-theoretic tradition of direct or indirect reliance on perceptual theory and statistical analysis, and the evident ability of perceptual-statistical approaches to cast new light on age-old questions of why musical elements function in the way that they do, the gradual incorporation into theory texts and courses of modern improvements in both fields would appear inevitable. Here, I describe specific ways in which this kind of integration may occur.

The materials I will describe lend themselves to either traditional or computer-assisted instruction. A computer-assisted course in harmony and counterpoint might integrate the following four modules:

1. Implementations of relevant perceptual-cognitive models such as roughness and fusion of sonorities, pitch salience, perceived relationships between sonorities, perceptual grouping in the auditory scene, melodic expectancy, tonal stability and tension, key relationships, and so on (details below).
2. Tools for statistical analyses of databases of musical scores (cf. *Humdrum*: Huron, 1999).
3. The theory of *pitch-class sets* (pc-sets; Forte, 1974).[2] Usually applied to atonal music, pc-set theory may also shed light on perceptual and historical aspects of different tonal systems (for example, Parks, 1989). It provides a framework within which all possible pitch patterns in the chromatic scale (chords, functions, harmonic sequences ...) can be systematically investigated with respect to given perceptual parameters and constraints.
4. Sound, so that students can hear the materials they are working with in the above three cases.

Of course, the system would need to be user-friendly and flexible. The various modules would be interconnected in an open design, allowing for unanticipated future extensions. The creation of such a system would be a major, but fruitful, research project.

A course in music theory incorporating perceptual theory and statistical analysis could be designed in various ways and at various levels (high school, conservatory, university undergraduate, graduate). Students might first carry out statistical analyses of scores in a given repertoire (cf. Krumhansl et al., 1999). They would be encouraged to repeatedly refer back to the scores themselves – to study the specific contexts in which musical patterns of interest occur. They would then adjust their analyses to account appropriately for context. Following Meyer (1973), context-dependent analyses of this kind may be regarded as summary representations of the syntax of a given style.

Students might then attempt to simulate their statistical data using perceptual models. The aim would be to test the validity of the models, and to explore the extent to which the perceptual parameters being modelled may have influenced the historical development of tonal syntax.[3] Beginning with the assumption that all possible patterns in the chromatic scale are candidates for musical elements, students might systematically enter selected pc-sets (or T_n-sets: Rahn, 1980)[4] into relevant models. Results would also be compared with the properties and functions of musical elements in conventional harmonic theory, and with students' musical intuitions.

Statistical analyses of musical patterns divide into two broad categories: those that depend on the location of a predetermined tonic (for example, prevalence of scale steps in a major or minor key), and those that do not. Often, a piece of music has no clearly defined tonic, or the exact location of modulations is unclear (Thompson and Cuddy, 1992), making a tonally based analysis problematic. The following presentation of selected teaching materials begins with analyses of music that are not limited by this constraint.

Effects that are Independent of Tonality

The simplest consideration is the *range of absolute pitches* used in music. Most musical pitches are confined to the range of the treble and bass staves.[5] Why? Presumably, because the range of the bass and treble staves corresponds roughly to the range of the human voice (women, men, children). But why is pitch in *instrumental* music mostly confined to the bass and treble staves, even though instruments such as the double bass and piccolo – and, of course, the piano – are not? Perceptual theory provides an answer: the *pitch salience* (clarity, prominence, attention-getting power) of harmonic complex tones is greatest in the range of the treble and bass staves – a consequence of the co-evolution of the ear and the voice (Terhardt et al., 1982; Huron, 2001). If pitch plays an important role in musical structure, as it does in both western and most non-western musics (because of the way the ear is attuned to the non-musical human environment: Parncutt, 1998), musical tones with clearer pitches tend to be favoured over those with less clear pitches.

Next, we may ask whether there are any interesting statistical regularities in *melodic intervals* in music. For example, which are more prevalent in melodies: rising or falling seconds? In advance, one may hypothesize that all intervallic possibilities are regularly tried out by composers. So there should be no big variations in melodic interval prevalence, in a large, representative sample of music. Wrong! Systematic musicological research (for example, Vos and Troost, 1989) has shown that these distributions are far from a flat. First, easily the most prevalent melodic interval in western music is the major second (M2). Minor seconds (m2s) occur about half as often. Beyond the M2, larger intervals are generally less prevalent than smaller (with a couple of obvious exceptions: perfect fifths (P5s) are more prevalent than tritones, and perfect octaves (P8s) than major sevenths (M7s)). Music with many large melodic intervals (for example, Webern) is unusual. Second, smaller intervals (especially seconds) tend to fall more often than rise, and larger intervals (starting with the perfect fourth or P4) more often rise than fall – with the exception of the P5, which (in western music) tends to fall more often than rise. Vos and Troost observed the same two effects in a wide range of non-western melodic styles, suggesting that they are good candidates for musical universals, and motivating us to look for a psychological explanation.

The predominance of M2 intervals in melodies may be explained by Bregman's (1990) theory of stream fusion and segregation (see also Miller and Heise, 1950; Noorden, 1975): in the *auditory scene*, tones that are close to each other in pitch and time (gestalt principle of proximity) are more likely to be grouped perceptually (*melodic fusion*). A musical melody is a good example of such a unit (although melodic coherence also depends on higher-level style-dependent cognitive factors: Deutsch, 1999). The relative rarity of the m2 by comparison to the M2 may be due either to performance limitations (tuning the voice while singing), perceptual limitations (categorical perception of pitch: Burns, 1999), and/or cognitive limitations on memory for scale steps (Rakowski, 1997). The second effect – the asymmetry between rising and falling intervals – is harder to explain. Melodic phrases typically begin low, rise to a peak, and fall again at the end (Huron, 1996), imitating the rising and falling of pitch between breaths in speech. Musically, this pattern could be matched either by a rising leap followed by several falling steps (regarded by Meyer, 1973 and Narmour, 1977 as an implication followed by a realization), or by several rising steps followed by a falling leap. The first of these two patterns better matches speech intonation, in which a fast intake of breath associated with a sudden increase in pitch is followed by a slow exhalation (while speaking) associated with a gradual decrease in pitch known as *pitch declination* (Cohen et al., 1982; Fujisaki, 1983; Ladd, 1984).[6]

Consider now melodic fragments of three tones. Having heard two tones, listeners tend to expect a third tone at certain pitches and not at others. For example, if the first two tones form a rising leap, listeners expect a step in the opposite direction, especially if the second tone is near the top of the tessitura of the instrument or voice (Hippel and Huron, 2000). *Melodic expectancies*, expressed as probabilities of continuation as a function of pitch, can be generated quite accurately by a system of perceptual-cognitive rules (Krumhansl, 1995; Larson, 1997b; Schellenberg, 1997).

Consonance and *dissonance* have been defined in various, sometimes inconsistent, ways, in both music theory (Cazden, 1980; Tenney, 1988) and psychoacoustics (Plomp and Levelt, 1965, give a historical overview). A possible reason is that, like timbre (Grey, 1977), consonance is psychologically multidimensional. One of the most important of these dimensions is the *roughness* that is perceived on the surface of the sound. The roughness of a harmonic interval is associated with beating between almost-coincident partials (pure tone components). The strength of the roughness sensation can depend on the amplitudes and frequencies of all partials in both tones (Plomp and Levelt, 1965; Terhardt, 1974b; Rakowski, 1982). Historically, listeners' tolerance and preference for roughness changed as the syntax of western music developed.

Of the 12 *harmonic intervals* within an octave that can be formed by typical musical tones, the P8 is the least dissonant, followed by the P5. The relative dissonance of the other ten intervals depends on the spectral envelope of the tones, the octave register in which they are presented, the criteria according to which dissonance is judged, and the musical experience of the listeners. According to Malmberg (1918), this order is M6, M3, P4, m6, m3, TT (tritone), m7, M2, M7 and m2.

Consonant harmonic intervals tend generally to occur more often than dissonant ones in tonal music – a fact that can easily be demonstrated using statistical software. Prevalence distributions of harmonic intervals depend further on the number of voices in the texture, and which voices are chosen for the analysis; for example, in mainstream tonal music, the P4 interval occurs more often between upper voices than between an upper voice and the bass (see discussion on chord inversion below).

Harmonic fusion may be defined as the tendency for a harmonic interval or chord to blend perceptually into a single sound (DeWitt and Crowder, 1987). It may be explained in the context of Terhardt's (1974a, 1976) theory of the perception of pitch, consonance and harmony (Parncutt, 1988, 1989, 1993), as follows. A musical sonority (complex tone or chord) generally evokes several different pitches, which may be perceived either simultaneously (*multiplicity*), or separately, at different times and in different contexts (*ambiguity*). If one of these pitches is much more salient than the others, it may be the only pitch to be noticed (consciously perceived), and the sonority will fuse. Terhardt's theory predicts the relative perceptual salience of a sonority's pitches in two stages. First, the salience of each *spectral pitch* (corresponding to an audible partial) is calculated. Second, *virtual pitches* are identified by looking for harmonic patterns among the spectral pitches; their salience is calculated on the basis of the spectral pitch saliences. In this approach, harmonic P8s, P5s and P4s between musical tones fuse better than other intervals because their spectra include a more clearly audible and complete harmonic series, which leads to a more salient main virtual pitch.[7]

Eberlein (1994) counted how often sonorities such as major and minor triads and various kinds of seventh chords occur in tonal music (cf. McHose, 1947). He obtained the following rank order: major triad, minor triad, major-minor (dominant) seventh, diminished seventh, minor added sixth chord (or half-diminished seventh), triad with suspended fourth, minor seventh and diminished triad. Psychologically, these data can be explained if we assume that music-theoretically consonant chords are more prevalent in tonal music, and that harmonic consonance is a combination of smoothness (lack of roughness) and fusion (Terhardt, 1974a, 1976): chords without second intervals (major, minor, diminished triad; diminished seventh) tend to be less rough, and chords with a clear, unambiguous root (major triad, major-minor seventh) fuse more easily (Parncutt, 1988).

In a representative sample of polyphonic keyboard works by J.S. Bach, Huron (1991) found that, while fused harmonic sonorities (the triads and seventh chords just listed) tend generally to be favoured, there is an additional tendency to *avoid* fused harmonic *intervals* (P8, P5, P4) between individual voices within a contrapuntal texture. The reason is presumably that fused intervals threaten the perceptual independence of the voices. The prevalence of thirds and sixths in two-part tonal writing may be accounted for similarly, by combining a general preference for consonant intervals (P8, P4/P5, thirds/sixths) with a tendency to avoid intervals that easily fuse (P8, P5/P4).

The twin ideals of avoiding roughness and promoting fusion can also explain the main *voicing* rules (inversion, doubling, spacing) of conventional harmony theory (Lippius, 1612; Rivera, 1984). Regarding inversion, root positions are generally more prevalent than first inversions, followed by second inversions (Eberlein, 1994). This is presumably because root positions fuse more easily (Parncutt, 1996). According to this argument, second inversions are least prevalent because their root is most ambiguous: it can be either the bass (as in the double suspension from 6-4 to 5-3) or the fourth above the bass (as in a passing 6-4 within a Schenkerian 10-8-6 voice exchange; see Forte and Gilbert, 1982). Regarding doubling, the root of major and minor triads is more often doubled than the other voices; again, this encourages fusion.

Regarding spacing, intervals within the upper three voices of a four-voice texture seldom exceed an octave. But the interval between bass and tenor is limited only by the ranges of those voices; and small intervals between bass and tenor sound muddy (rough) in the lowest register and tend to be avoided. These familiar conventions have physiological origins. Each hair cell on the basilar membrane of the inner ear acts like a filter; it only passes frequencies within an interval proportional to a *critical band*.[8] Critical bandwidth depends on spectral frequency: above about A_4 (a') it lies between two and three semitones, and at lower frequencies it gradually widens (when measured in semitones). Roughness is experienced when two pure tones of about equal amplitude lie within the same critical band (Plomp and Levelt, 1965), such as when thirds are sounded in the bass. On the other hand, the degree of fusion decreases as the number of critical bandwidths between a pair of partials increases.[9] This may be why chord voicings with large intervals between the upper voices tend to be avoided.

Table 9.1   Prevalence of root progressions between root-position triads in eighteenth- and nineteenth-century music

	Rising P4	Falling P4	Rising 3rd[a]	Falling 3rd	Rising M2	Falling M2	Total
Maj-maj	64	19	0	0	6	2	**91**
Maj-min	60	1	2	9	5	0	**77**
Min-maj	5	20	1	15	5	3	**49**
Min-min	21	5	0	0	1	0	**27**
Total	**150**	**45**	**3**	**24**	**17**	**5**	**244**[b]

The numbers in the body of the table are chord counts in Eberlein's (1994, pp. 422–3) sample whose qualities correspond to the left column of the table and whose roots traverse the intervals given in the top row. Notes to the table:

a.   The two chords have one tone in common for P4 progressions, two for third progressions, and none for M2 progressions. For the third progressions, the quality of the interval (M3 or m3) depends on the quality of the triads; e.g., the rising third between major and minor triads is a M3.
b.   The total number of successive pairs of major and minor triads counted by Eberlein in his sample was 251. Omitted from the table are five root progressions of a rising m2 (three from minor to major, two from major to major) and two mode changes on the same root (one major to minor, one minor to major).

The next important statistical property of harmony to consider is the prevalence of specific progressions of two chords. Table 9.1 shows the prevalence of chord progressions between major and minor triads, based on a representative sample of scores composed between 1700 and 1850 by J.S. Bach, Handel, Mozart, Beethoven and Mendelssohn. The first point to notice is that root progressions through a P4 (or P5) are more prevalent than through a third – even though progressions through a third have two tones in common (rather than one). Why? Two contrasting perceptual-cognitive explanations warrant consideration. The first involves the way the brain learns and processes information. In simulations of musical learning with self-organizing neural nets, the cycle of fifths emerges spontaneously among the network units (simulated neurons) corresponding to the 24 major and minor triads or keys (Leman and Carreras, 1997; Tillmann et al., 2000). To achieve this result, it is not necessary to input tonal music to the model; all that is required is the pc-salience profiles or the 24 triads (Parncutt, 1988) or the stability profiles of the 24 keys (Krumhansl and Kessler, 1982, hereafter called the *K-K profiles*). Both are presented in Figure 9.1.[10] An alternative explanation invokes the psychological phenomenon of *categorical perception* (see, for example, Burns, 1999): stimuli that are similar or close in their main perceptual attributes (pitch, loudness, timbre, duration) may be assigned to the

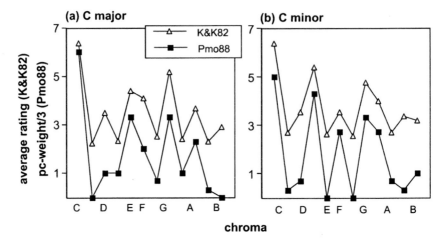

Open triangles: K-K profiles, that is, experimental goodness-of-fit ratings on a seven-point scale, averaged over three cadential progressions (IV-V-I, II-V-I, VI-V-I) and a single tonic triad (I).

Filled squares: *pitch-class weight* according to Parncutt (1988) with root-support weights P1/P8 = 10, P5 = 5, M3 = 3, m7 = 2, M2/M9 = 1, m3 = 0, divided by 3 for ease of comparison.

Figure 9.1   Comparison of major and minor K-K profiles with calculated chroma salience within the corresponding tonic triad

same perceptual category, and hence take on essentially the same meaning. For example, the lexical meaning of the vowel /a/ is independent of the speaker's regional accent or first language. Returning to harmony: triads in third relationships have more tones in common than not, and so may be perceived as a prolongation of the one harmony (a single category), with a melodic change in one voice – consistent with Riemann's concept of *parallel harmony*.[11] But triads in fifth relationships clearly separate into different harmonic categories or functions. And of all possible pairs of harmonically distinct triads, triads in fifth relationships have the strongest harmonic relationship (pitch commonality: Parncutt, 1989).

According to Table 9.1, root progressions of a P4 or M2 between root-position major or minor triads more often rise than fall, but root progressions of a third (M3 or m3, depending on the qualities of the chords) more often fall than rise. This asymmetry may be explained by considering the *subsidiary pitches* of a chord – perceived pitches that are not physically present or notated, but correspond to missing roots of incomplete harmonic series, and are therefore predicted by Terhardt's pitch theory. Figure 9.1 (lower line, filled squares) shows theoretical predictions for the salience of each pc when a major or minor triad is sounded. As a rule, the more salient the pc, the more likely it will function as the root (Parncutt, 1988). The figure shows that both major and minor triads have salient subsidiary pitches at fifth and third intervals *below* the root. As a result, in progressions through a falling fifth, falling third, or rising second, subsidiary pitches in the first chord coincide with actual notes in the second. Extending the theory of Meyer (1973) and Narmour (1977), the subsidiary pitches in the first chord may be regarded as *implications* that are *realized* in the second chord (Parncutt, 1996).

A final aspect of tonal syntax that is largely independent of tonality is *voice leading*. In contrapuntal textures, students learn to avoid leaps between successive tones in upper voices, and to avoid parallel P5s and P8s between any pair of voices (Lippius, 1612; Rivera, 1984). Both these principles may be explained by Bregman's (1990) theory of stream fusion and segregation. The individual parts in a contrapuntal texture will hang together perceptually and be heard as melodies if intervals between successive tones are small (steps), and other familiar melodic procedures are followed (such as following a leap by a step in the opposite direction). Moreover, each melody in the texture will be separately perceptible if intervals between simultaneous tones in different voices are consistently larger than intervals between successive tones in the same voice, and if parallel P5s and P8s are avoided. Parallel motion encourages harmonic fusion (gestalt principle of common fate), which is further enhanced if the intervals concerned are among the lowest in the harmonic series (P8, P5).

Effects that Depend on Tonality

Various authors (Krumhansl, 1990; Järvinen, 1995; Cuddy, 1997; others cited by Krumhansl) have investigated the prevalence of the twelve pcs in major and minor key contexts – how often the tonic tone ($1^\wedge$) is sounded in comparison to the dominant tone ($5^\wedge$), and so on. Prevalence profiles in major and minor keys closely resemble the K-K profiles of those keys. In general, more prevalent tones tend to be perceived as more stable than less prevalent tones, regardless of tonality (church modes, blues scales, North Indian *thats*, and so on: Krumhansl, 1990; Cuddy, 1997; Cooper, 1998).

Prevalence profiles also closely resemble pc-salience profiles of major and minor triads (Figure 9.1). A simple but speculative explanation is that, in major and minor tonalities, it is the final triad – not the final tone – that functions as the tonic (cf. Riemann, 1877; Schenker, 1906); and this triad, in order to achieve closure, needs somehow to *represent* the preceding music, or to *realize the implication* created by the preceding music. Since the tonic triad is the musical element that best follows a musical passage in a major or minor key, Krumhansl's probe tone fits well with a preceding tonal passage if the tone well represents the tonic triad – that is, if it has high salience within that sonority.

The pc-salience profile is historically older, and therefore arguably more fundamental for tonal theory, than the K-K profile. Major and minor triads first became commonplace in the fifteenth century (Old Hall Manuscript, Fauxbourdon, Dufay, Ockeghem), suggesting that their pc-salience profiles were also cognitively internalized at that time; then, as now, pitch salience influenced how well a given tone followed a given chord.[12] But it was not until the early Baroque (seventeenth century, especially Monteverdi) that a range of music-syntactic developments – including changes in the way dissonances were prepared and resolved, a preference for major or minor triads rather than open P5 sonorities at the end of phrases, a stronger feeling of forward progression, the consolidation of the subdominant-dominant-tonic progression, and the clear demarcation of modulations and tonal areas – suggested that major-minor tonality had established itself (Dahlhaus, 1967).

In the previous section, I briefly considered doublings within chord voicings, but without regard to temporal context. In a tonal context, doubling depends on tonal stability as represented by the K-K profile (Huron, 1993): the more stable the tone, the more likely it will appear simultaneously in different octaves. This principle parsimoniously explains why the leading tone ($7^\wedge$) and non-diatonic tones ($\#1^\wedge$, and so on) are seldom doubled – in the K-K profiles, these six chroma are the least stable of the twelve.[13] It also explains why, for example, the best tone to double in the submediant triad (VI) is the third rather than the root, in both major and minor keys: just as doubling the root of a chord clarifies its root and so enhances its consonance, doubling the tonic (or other stable scale degree) clarifies the tonality of a passage.

Voice leading also depends on tonal context: progressions from one scale step to another tend to occur in a particular direction. A familiar example is the progression from leading tone to tonic, which is more prevalent than tonic to leading tone. Generally, a progression from a tonally unstable tone to a tonally stable tone (or from a non-chord tone to a chord tone) is more prevalent than the reverse (Pinkerton, 1956; Youngblood, 1958; both cited in Krumhansl, 1990). Moreover, less stable tones are perceived as more related to more stable tones that follow them, than vice-versa (Krumhansl, 1979, 1990), suggesting that the perception of relatedness (like most other aspects of music perception) is learned from musical experience. The strength of the tendency or expectation to resolve in a particular direction (yearning) depends on the difference in stability and the smallness of the interval between the two tones (Bharucha, 1996). Similarly, chord functions more often progress from unstable to stable than the reverse (McHose, 1947);[14] the same asymmetry is found in perceptual judgements of relatedness (Bharucha and Krumhansl, 1983; Krumhansl, 1990).

A final statistical regularity in this quick overview is the rank order of prevalence of diatonic triads, which according to Budge (1943) is I, V, IV, II, VI, VII and III, in both major and minor keys (Krumhansl, 1990). This pattern cannot be explained by the K-K profiles alone. It is also influenced by the perceptual-cognitive bias toward falling-fifth progressions, and toward progressions from less to more stable chords.

Conclusion

A harmonic theory that takes the chromatic scale as its starting point may be applied to a wider range of styles than more conventional, diatonically-based theories. Lerdahl (1989, pp. 66–7) commented that:

> The conventional wisdom, at least in the United States, holds that Schenkerian theory explains diatonic tonal music and pitch-set theory explains atonal music (chromatic tonal music is a source of discomfort). This scenario is implausible from a psychological standpoint if only because it presupposes two entirely different listening mechanisms. We do not hear *Elektra* and *Erwartung* in completely different ways. There is a good deal of 20th-century music – Bartók or Messiaen, for instance – that moves smoothly between tonality (broadly speaking) and atonality. In short, the historical development from tonality to atonality (and back) is richly continuous. Theories of tonality and atonality should be comparably linked.

A perceptual-statistical approach to harmony based on the chromatic rather than the diatonic scale can help to bridge the gap between music theories based on the major-minor system and music theories associated with other styles: the impressionist tonalities of Debussy and Ravel, serial and non-serial forms of atonality, bebop jazz, and even harmonic and contrapuntal styles from the Middle Ages and Renaissance where clear mappings may be made between diatonic and (hypothetical) chromatic scale steps. Such a pluralistic approach is consistent with trends toward postmodernism and neotonality.

Pluralism also includes tradition. Traditional harmony theory will, of course, never be replaced by the proposed newer methods. But methods such as these could usefully extend, complement, enrich, diversify and revitalize traditional approaches.

Notes

1. In the rest of this chapter, the term *prevalence* means frequency of occurrence; *frequency* is reserved for spectral or fundamental frequency.
2. A pitch class (pc) is a pitch considered without regard to its octave register (for example, all A flats and G sharps belong to the same pc).
3. Recent explorations of the relationship between perceptual theory and music history (Tenney, 1988; Eberlein, 1994) have highlighted social and physical influences on the compositional conventions of different historical periods. These influences limit the extent to which perceptual models can account for musical syntax. Relationships between predictions of perceptual models and statistical properties

of tonal-harmonic syntax are largely *indirect*; directly, our perception of music depends mostly on musical conditioning (Lundin, 1947; Parncutt, 1989).

4. T_n-sets are invariant under transposition but not inversion. For example, major and minor triads belong to the same pc-set, but to different T_n-sets.

5. A good introductory project for students using a statistical analysis program might be to calculate and compare prevalence distributions of musical pitches across different styles and instrumental forces. The shape of the distribution is remarkably constant: an inverted U centred near D4 (d') with most of the area under the curve falling within the treble and bass staves (cf. Huron, 1993b).

6. Of course, the fundamental frequency of a speech utterance rises and falls from word to word. Pitch declination is more precisely defined as a gradual decline in the peaks and valleys of the pitch contour.

7. The music-theoretically familiar explanation that octaves, fifths and fourths are found in the lower reaches of the harmonic series is only *indirectly* correct. The harmonic series cannot meaningfully explain anything about music perception until its own perceptual function is clarified. According to the gestalt principle of closure, the missing elements of a familiar pattern are perceptually filled in. The harmonic series is an example of such a pattern. A perceptual model incorporating this pattern (Terhardt et al., 1982; Parncutt, 1989) can account for the perception of pitch in incomplete harmonic complex tones, such tones with a missing fundamental and tones with only odd harmonics.

8. According to Pickles (1988, p. 264), 'simultaneous masking patterns produce wider resolution bandwidths than do basilar membrane and neural tuning curves'.

9. Fusion has been found to fall as frequency separation increases between both AM pure tones (Bregman et al., 1985) and noise bursts (Turgeon, 2000). An alternative explanation is that the auditory system is familiar with harmonic complex tones, in which intervals between partials are larger in the bass.

10. It is not clear whether this connectionist approach can explain the predominance of fifth progressions in Renaissance and Baroque music, in which not all triads in the chromatic scale are typically available or in use.

11. In a major key, for example, Riemann regarded both IV and II as species of subdominant; see de la Motte (1988).

12. It would be interesting to investigate this claim systematically, for example in the context of the proposed course.

13. The traditional, and equally valid, explanation is that the doubling of leading and chromatic tones normally produces parallel octaves.

14. Typically, a relatively large increase in tension, e.g. I-#IV°, is followed by a series of smaller decreases, for example #IV°-V-I. This is analogous to the previously mentioned asymmetry in melodic interval distributions.

References

Aldwell, E. and Schachter, C. (1978) *Harmony and Voice Leading*, New York: Harcourt Brace Jovanovich.
Bharucha, J.J. (1996) 'Melodic anchoring', *Music Perception*, 13: 383–400.

Bharucha, J.J. and Krumhansl, C.L. (1983) 'The representation of harmonic structure in music: Hierarchies of stability as a function of context', *Cognition*, 13: 63–102.

Bregman, A.S. (1990) *Auditory Scene Analysis*, Cambridge, MA: MIT.

Bregman, A.S., Abramson, J., Doehring, P. and Darwin, C.J. (1985) 'Spectral integration based on common amplitude modulation', *Perception & Psychophysics*, 37: 483–93.

Budge, H. (1943) *A Study of Chord Frequencies*, New York: Teachers College, Columbia University.

Burns, E.M. (1999) 'Intervals, scales and tuning', in D. Deutsch (ed.) *Psychology of Music* (2nd edn.), pp. 215–64, San Diego: Academic Press.

Cazden, N. (1980) 'The definition of consonance and dissonance', *International Review of the Aesthetics and Sociology of Music*, 11: 123–67.

Cohen, A., Collier, R., and Hart, J.'t (1982) 'Declination: Construct or intrinsic feature of speech pitch?' *Phonetica*, 39: 254–73.

Cooper, D. (1998) 'The unfolding of tonality in the music of Béla Bartók', *Music Analysis*, 17: 21–38.

Cuddy, L.L. (1997) 'Tonal relations', in I. Deliège and J.A. Sloboda (eds), *Perception and Cognition of Music*, pp. 329–52. Hove, East Sussex: Psychology Press.

de la Motte, D. (1988) *Harmonielehre*, Kassel: Bärenreiter.

Dahlhaus, Carl. (1967) *Untersuchungen über die Entstehung der harmonischen Tonalität* [*Investigating the Emergence of Harmonic Tonality*], Kassel: Bärenreiter.

Deutsch, D. (1999) 'The processing of pitch combinations', in D. Deutsch (ed.), *Psychology of Music* (2nd edn.), pp. 349–411, San Diego: Academic Press.

DeWitt, L.A. and Crowder, R.G. (1987) 'Tonal fusion of consonant musical intervals: The oomph in Stumpf', *Perception and Psychophysics*, 41: 73–84.

Eberlein, R. (1994) *Die Entstehung der tonalen Klangsyntax*, Frankfurt: Peter Lang.

Forte, A. (1974) *Tonal Harmony in Concept and Practice* (2nd edn.), New York: Holt, Rinehart, and Winston.

Forte, A. and Gilbert, S.E. (1982) *Introduction to Schenkerian Analysis*, New York: Norton.

Fujisaki, H. (1983) 'Dynamic characteristics of voice fundamental frequency in speech and singing', in P.F. MacNeilage (ed.), *The Production of Speech*, pp. 29–55, New York: Springer.

Fux, J.J. (1725) *Gradus ad Parnassum*, trans. A. Mann (1943), New York: Norton.

Grey, J.M. (1977) 'Multidimensional perceptual scaling of musical timbres', *Journal of the Acoustical Society of America*, 61: 1270–77.

Hindemith, P. (1942) *Unterweisung im Tonsatz*, Mainz: Schott.

Hippel, P. von, and Huron, D. (2000) 'Why do skips precede reversals? The effect of tessitura on melodic structure', *Music Perception*, 18: 59–85.

Huron, D. (1991) 'Tonal consonance versus tonal fusion in polyphonic sonorities', *Music Perception*, 9: 135–54.

Huron, D. (1993) 'Chordal-tone doubling and the enhancement of key perception', *Psychomusicology*, 12: 73–83.

Huron, D. (2001) 'Tone and voice: A derivation of the rules of voice-leading from perceptual principles', *Music Perception*, 19: 1–64.

Huron, D. (1996) 'The melodic arch in Western folksongs', *Computing in Musicology*, 10: 3–23.

Huron, D. (1999) *Music Research Using Humdrum: A User's Guide*, Stanford, California:

Center for Computer Assisted Research in the Humanities. Available <http://dactyl.som.ohio-state.edu/Music824/humdrum.index.html>.

Järvinen, T. (1995) 'Tonal hierarchies in jazz improvisation', *Music Perception*, 12: 415–37.

Jeppesen, K. (1946) *The Style of Palestrina and the Dissonance*, New York: Dover.

Krämer, T. (1991) *Harmonielehre im Selbststudium*, Wiesbaden: Breitkopf und Härtel.

Krumhansl, C.L. (1979) 'The psychological representation of pitch in a tonal context', *Cognitive Psychology*, 11: 346–74.

Krumhansl, C.L. (1990) *Cognitive Foundations of Musical Pitch*, Oxford: Oxford University Press.

Krumhansl, C.L. (1995) 'Music psychology and music theory: Problems and prospects', *Music Theory Spectrum*, 17: 53–80.

Krumhansl, C.L. and Kessler, E.J. (1982) 'Tracing the dynamic changes in perceived tonal organization in a spatial representation of musical keys', *Psychological Review*, 89: 334–68.

Krumhansl, C.L., Louhivuori, J., Toiviainen, P., Järvinen, T. and Eerola, T. (1999) 'Melodic expectation in Finnish spiritual folk hymns: Convergence of statistical, behavioral, and computational approaches', *Music Perception*, 17: 151–96.

Ladd, D.R. (1984) 'Declination: A review and some hypotheses', *Phonology Yearbook*, 1: 53–74.

Larson, S. (1997a) 'The problem of prolongation in *tonal* music: Terminology, perception, and expressive meaning', *Journal of Music Theory*, 41: 101–36.

Larson, S. (1997b) 'Continuations as completions: Studying melodic expectation in the creative microdomain *Seek Well*', in M. Leman (ed.), *Music, Gestalt, and Computing: Studies in Cognitive and Systematic Musicology*, pp. 321–34, Berlin: Springer.

Leman, M. and Carreras F. (1997) 'Schema and gestalt: Testing the hypothesis of psychoneural isomorphism by computer simulation', in M. Leman (ed.), *Music and Computing: Studies in Cognitive and Systematic Musicology*, pp. 144–68, Berlin: Springer.

Lerdahl, F. (1988) 'Tonal pitch space', *Music Perception*, 5: 315–50.

Lerdahl, F. (1989) 'Atonal prolongational structure', *Contemporary Music Review*, 4: 65–87.

Lerdahl, F. and Jackendoff. R. (1983) *A Generative Theory of Tonal Music*, Cambridge, MA: MIT.

Levine, M. (1995) *The Jazz Theory Book*, Petakuma, CA: Sher Music.

Lippius, J. (1612) *Synopsis Musicae Novae*, trans. B.V. Rivera (1977), Colorado Springs: Colorado College Music Press.

Lovelock, W. (1956) *Third Year Harmony*, Brundall, Norwich: Elkin.

Lundin, R.W. (1947) 'Towards a cultural theory of consonance', *Journal of Psychology*, 23: 45–9.

Malmberg, C.F. (1918) 'The perception of consonance and dissonance', *Psychological Monographs*, 25: 93–133.

McHose, A.I. (1947) *The Contrapuntal Technique of the 18th Century*, Englewood Cliffs, NJ: Prentice-Hall.

Meyer, L.B. (1973) *Explaining Music: Essays and Explorations*, Berkeley, CA: University of California Press.

Miller, G.A. and Heise, G.A. (1950) 'The trill threshold', *Journal of the Acoustical Society of America*, 22: 637–8.

Narmour, E. (1977) *Beyond Schenkerism*, Chicago: University of Chicago Press.

Noorden, L. van (1975) *Temporal Coherence in the Perception of Tone Sequences* (doctoral dissertation), Eindhoven, NL: Institute for Perception Research.

Parks, R.S. (1989) *The Music of Claude Debussy*, New Haven, CT: Yale University.

Parncutt, R. (1988) 'Revision of Terhardt's psychoacoustical model of the root(s) of a musical chord', *Music Perception*, 6: 65–94.

Parncutt, R. (1989) *Harmony: A Psychoacoustical Approach*, Berlin: Springer.

Parncutt, R. (1993) 'Pitch properties of chords of octave-spaced tones', *Contemporary Music Review*, 9: 35–50.

Parncutt, R. (1996) 'Praxis, Lehre, Wahrnehmung. Kritische Bemerkungen zu Roland Eberlein, *Die Entstehung der tonalen Klangsyntax*', *Musiktheorie*, 11: 67–79.

Parncutt, R. (1998) 'Listening to music in the real world? A critical discussion of Marc Leman's (1995) "Musicology Music and Schema Theory: Cognitive Foundations of Systematic"', *Journal of New Music Research*, 27: 380–408.

Pickles, J.O. (1988) *An Introduction to the Physiology of Hearing* (2nd edn.), London: Academic.

Pinkerton, R.C. (1956) 'Information theory and melody', *Scientific American*, 194: 77–86.

Piston, W. (1978) *Harmony* (4th edn.), New York: Norton.

Plomp, R. and Levelt, W.J.M. (1965) 'Tonal consonance and critical bandwidth', *Journal of the Acoustical Society of America*, 38: 548–60.

Pratt, G. (1984) *The Dynamics of Harmony*, Milton Keynes: Open University.

Rahn, J. (1980) *Basic Atonal Theory*, New York: Schirmer.

Rakowski, A. (1982) 'Psychoacoustic dissonance in pure-tone intervals: Disparities and common findings', in C. Dahlhaus and M. Krause (eds), *Tiefenstruktur der Musik*, pp. 51–67; Berlin: Technische Universität.

Rakowski, A. (1997) 'The phonological system of musical language in the domain of pitch', in J. Steszewski and M. Jablonski (eds), *Interdisciplinary Studies in Musicology*, 3: 211–21, Poznan: Poznan Society for Advancement of Arts and Sciences (PTPN).

Riemann, H. (1877) *Musikalische Syntaxis*, Leipzig: Breitkopf und Härtel.

Rivera, B.V. (1984) 'The seventeenth-century theory of triadic generation and invertibility and its application in contemporaneous rules of composition', *Music Theory Spectrum*, 6: 63–78.

Schellenberg, E.G. (1997) 'Simplifying the implication-realisation model of musical expectancy', *Music Perception*, 14: 295–318.

Schenker, H. (1906) *Harmony*, trans. E.M. Borgese and ed. O. Jones (1954), Cambridge, MA: MIT.

Tenney, J. (1988) '*A history of "Consonance" and "Dissonance"*', New York: Excelsior.

Terhardt, E. (1974a) 'Pitch, consonance, and harmony', *Journal of the Acoustical Society of America*, 55: 1061–9.

Terhardt, E. (1974b) 'On the perception of periodic sound fluctuations (roughness)', *Acustica*, 30: 201–13.

Terhardt, E. (1976) 'Ein psychoakustisch begründetes Konzept der musikalischen Konsonanz', *Acustica*, 36: 121–37.

Terhardt, E., Stoll, G. and Seewann, M. (1982) 'Pitch of complex tonal signals according to virtual pitch theory: Tests, examples and predictions', *Journal of the Acoustical Society of America*, 71: 671–8.

Thompson, W.F. and Cuddy, L.L. (1992) 'Perceived key movement in four-voice harmony and single voices', *Music Perception*, 9: 427–38.

Tillmann, B., Bharucha, J.J. and Bigand, E. (2000) 'Implicit learning of tonality: A self-organizing approach', *Psychological Review*, 107 (4): 885–913.

Turgeon, M. (2000) 'Cross-spectral auditory grouping in the presence of competition among alternative organizations, using the paradigm of rhythmic masking release', PhD Dissertation, McGill University.

Vos, P.G. and Troost, J.M. (1989) 'Ascending and descending melodic intervals: Statistical findings and their perceptual relevance', *Music Perception*, 6: 383–96.

Youngblood, J.E. (1958) 'Style as information', *Journal of Music Theory*, 2: 24–35.

Chapter 10

The Perceptual Space Between and Within Musical Rhythm Categories[1]

George Papadelis and George Papanikolaou

The Problem of Categorization

The concept of 'category' is philosophical in its origin. The term was first introduced by Aristotle in order to define his ten classes of entities: substance, quantity, quality, relation, place, time, posture, state, action and passion (Thomson, 1967, pp. 46–8). The use of the term in contemporary psychology is closely related to its logical–philosophical background, the so-called 'classical view of categories' (Sutcliffe, 1993, pp. 35–6), and it is mainly associated with memory and thought organization (Thomson, 1967, pp. 46–54; Glass and Holyoak, 1986, p. 149; Hampton and Dubois, 1993, pp. 12–13).

Categorization processes play a crucial role in our interaction with the infinitely complex and continuously varying environment, allowing us to organize the continuous flow of incoming information into discrete and manageable units, which are being conceptualized as 'objects'. The term 'object' generally refers to any class of recurring experience, from a concrete entity (for example, a flute or a piano) to an abstract concept (for example, sound brightness or harshness; Harnad, 1987, p. 1). Furthermore, at subsequent levels of cognitive processing, 'objects', on the basis of common properties, or functional similarity, and so on, are treated as members of the same category (Glass and Holyoak, 1986, p. 149). If we consider the previously mentioned examples, it is obvious that a flute or a piano, on the basis of their functional similarity, are both classified in the category of 'musical instruments'. The more abstract notions of 'sound brightness' and 'harshness' are treated as instances of the broader category 'timbral quality'.

Experimental and theoretical work on categorical perception is characterized by a vast diversity of approaches. These form an interdisciplinary research area, which extends from threshold psychophysics to the study of higher-order categories such as object categories, pattern categories and abstract concepts. The basic points of interest that underlie the majority of different perspectives are summarized in the following questions:

- On what basis are stimuli grouped and organized? Or, in other words, how are categories defined?

- How are categories mentally represented? What are the main characteristics of these representations and what processes underlie their formation?
- Is categorical perception a learned or an innate phenomenon, or both? Which categories are innate and which are learned?
- How are categories formed and developed through learning? (Harnad, 1987, p. 2).

Two main category types, *sensory perception* and *generic knowledge categories*, outline two corresponding broad areas of research on category cognition. Although there is not a clear-cut distinction between them, they are generally distinguished according to the abstractness of attributes that define their members (Medin and Barsalou, 1987, p. 456).

Classification with sensory perception categories is directly related to the physical stimulus. Their investigation is focused on the way in which physical energy is transformed and represented in the form of perceptual experience. As an example we can mention the characteristic pluck versus bow distinction between various synthetic music-like sounds, as a result of changes in their attack duration (Cutting et al., 1976).

Generic knowledge or conceptual categories are mainly associated with knowledge representation and processing. The attributes used in classifying an 'object' in a generic knowledge category rather refer to its mental representation than to its actual physical properties. For example, when listeners are asked to classify a certain temporal pattern as rhythmic or arrhythmic, on the one hand, their judgement is unavoidably based on the pattern's physical attributes, but on the other hand, it mainly depends on listeners' conceptualization of rhythmicity.

The Psychophysical Approach to Sensory/Perceptual Categorization

The phenomenon of categorical perception was first observed and investigated with colour perception and the perception of speech sounds, but afterwards research was extended to various sensory modalities, as well as to other species.

According to the classical model of absolute categorical perception, different levels of a physical continuum are initially transduced and transformed in an analogue fashion into corresponding levels of sensory stimulation. That initial transformation of the incoming energy patterns into monotonically related patterns of stimulation is characterized as a pre-categorical stage of information processing. At subsequent stages of processing, sensory information is recoded and organized into discrete categories of perceptual responses (Pastore, 1987, p. 29). Although that model simulates the phenomenon on the basis of variation in a single dimension, it also applies to a multidimensional variation of the physical stimulus. If we approach the phenomenon of categorical perception as a signal-processing task, it can be seen as an analogue to digital transformation, by which certain continuously varying dimensions of the physical stimulus are recoded into sets of discrete perceptual responses (Harnad, 1987, p. 4).

An illustrative example of categorical perception can be drawn from the domain of colour perception. A common fact, that was further supported by the classic colour-scaling experiments, is that the great variability of perceived hues across the visible spectrum, which actually corresponds to a physical continuum of wavelengths, is organized and named on the basis of four basic colour categories (blue, green, yellow and red) or their combinations (Bornstein, 1987, p. 287). This qualitative differential response in the processing of many physical continua was associated with a classic psychophysical problem: 'The relation between an observer's ability to identify stimuli varying along a continuum and his ability to discriminate between pairs of stimuli drawn from that continuum' (Macmillan et al., 1977, p. 452).

The generally accepted experimental approach to demonstrating categorical versus non-categorical (continuous) perception is psychophysical and it is based on identification and discrimination tasks (Liberman et al., 1957; Schouten and van Hessen, 1992). Identification requires subjects to categorize instances along a unidimensional or a multidimensional physical continuum, using labels. Regarding the previously mentioned example of hue categorization, we use the labels 'blue', 'green', 'yellow' and 'red' in order to classify the great variability of perceived hues along the entire colour spectrum. Discrimination is usually performed using pairs of stimuli and a 'same-different' procedure. The criteria for a definition of categorical perception vary among different researchers and various definitions have been expressed in terms of identification performance, discrimination performance or a combination of them (Medin and Barsalou, 1987, p. 458). In general, categorical perception occurs when discrete regions of the physical continuum are assigned different labels. In addition, discrimination acuity is expected to be worse within categories than at boundary regions.

In other words, the perception of discrete categories is assumed to cause a distortion of discriminability along the continuum, which is revealed by a negative correlation between identification and discrimination acuity.

Categorical Perception of Musical Rhythm Patterns

Contemporary theories of musical rhythm have stressed the importance of approaching musical rhythm patterns as multilevel structures, which are actually shaped by the interaction of various durational relationships between their different time levels (Yeston, 1976; Kramer, 1988; Epstein, 1995). Actual durational proportions acquired by the listener constitute one of the major underlying factors in the perception of musical rhythm. From a cognitive point of view, it is important to focus on the strategies used by the human mind for the encoding of the huge number of all possible durational proportions that characterize real musical events, which finally lead to the perception of a limited number of discrete durational and rhythm categories.

When reviewing rhythm perception literature, one notices some early attempts to investigate the categorical perceptual response to various classes of durations and rhythmic structures (see Clarke, 2000 for an overview). This fact is commonly reflected in the western tonal/metric tradition of musical theory and notation, where a limited set of note values is used for representing all possible durations. Similarly, a small number of metres (metre categories) is used to encode the great variability of real rhythmic relations. In opposition to musical notation conventions, temporal analysis of any musical performance reveals that written note values give only an approximate outline of actual durations and consequently a high degree of timing variance is obtained, either as a result of musical expressivity, or due to perceptual and motor limitations (Desain and Honing, 1992, pp. 30–31).

In a paper published in 1987, Eric Clarke formulated a theoretical framework in investigating categorical perception of musical rhythm. This framework was based on the distinction between two qualitatively differing components of information in the perception of musical rhythm: a categorical and a continuous (non-categorical) one. The first component accounts for the encoding of the structural information in terms of a strict metrical framework, and the second one for all continuously varying timing deviations from this 'perfect categorical fit' (Clarke, 1987, p. 30). More precisely, according to Clarke, the process of rhythm categorization is based on a pattern-matching procedure; that is, every acquired temporal pattern is correlated to a 'best-fitting' mental rhythmic schema, whose structure is characterized by small, whole-number durational ratios (for example, 1:2, 1:3, 1:2:3, and so on). Any deviations from that accurate-timing pattern are treated as a kind of non-categorical piece of information, which is considered either as musical expressivity, or just as inaccurate performance of rhythm. In addition to that theoretical formulation, Clarke's study made a major contribution in that he embodied the standard experimental method of correlating identification and discrimination performance for demonstrating categorical perception in the rhythm perception research.

Since the Clarke (1987) paper, there has, in fact, been a limited number of studies to investigate the categorical perception hypothesis as applied to the rhythm perception domain. Moreover, these studies are mainly concentrated on the demonstration of the categorical versus continuous (non-categorical) perception of simple rhythm patterns with respect to certain dimensions of variation of the physical stimulus, which are critical in the sense that they play a significant role in the pattern's classification as a member of a certain rhythm category. Two published works are focused on this specific area: Schulze (1989) and Windsor (1993). Methodologically, they both employ a systematic variation within a certain dimension of the rhythm pattern, and they use the standard experimental trials of identification and discrimination. As evidence for demonstrating categorical perception they adopt the criterion of detecting a peak in discriminative acuity at the category boundaries. The main difference in their approach to rhythm categorization is obtained with respect to the dimension under interest: Schulze (1989) is concentrated on the relative timing domain contrasted to Windsor (1993), which employs a relative dynamic-accent approach.

Structural Aspects for Rhythm Categories: An Experimental Investigation

Earlier investigations on the perceptual categorization of rhythm patterns were mainly concentrated on the question of whether musical rhythm patterns are perceived and internally represented in a categorical fashion, or, in other words, in the form of well-defined rhythm/metre categories. Recent experimental work on various non-musical auditory continua, especially from the domain of phoneme perception, has demonstrated the importance of directing research towards an exploration of the internal category structure, as well as to various related phenomena such as the 'perceptual magnet effect'[2] (Iverson and Kuhl, 1995), typicality effects (Rosch et al., 1976), flexibility of boundaries (Repp and Liberman, 1987), and so on.

In our work (Papadelis, 1999; Papadelis and Papanikolaou, 1999a, 1999b) we stressed the importance of adopting recent experimental methods and findings from the field of the categorical phoneme perception research, into rhythm perception research. Our investigation was directed towards a detailed mapping of the resultant 'rhythm space', which is formed as a consequence of a systematic manipulation of certain stimulus dimensions. Special emphasis was put on the temporal domain, by focusing on timing variations at three different musical tempi (slow, medium and fast). Furthermore, our main concern was also to reveal the role of learning in the acquisition and improvement of rhythm categories, by investigating rhythm categorization behaviour of adult musicians aged between 21 and 30 years.

The basic question addressed by our study was whether a systematic change in durational ratios of a prototypical rhythm pattern that produces a sequence of variations lead to the perception of well-defined rhythm/metre categories along the sequence, as a result of the perception of different metrical interpretations. As a consequence, four specific questions were formulated as follows:

1. What are the basic structural aspects that characterize the mental representation for rhythm categories?
2. What kind of differentiation in their structure is obtained among different musical tempi?
3. How does a pattern's structural complexity affect its categorization?
4. Does a subject's skill in classifying the best exemplars within each category reflect their categorization acuity throughout the category's entire range?

Or, in other words, does that skill reveal the existence of accurate and detailed representations for rhythm categories?

Method

According to the psychophysical experimental methodology for the detection and exploration of categorical perception, a systematic variation of durational relations was introduced to a generative rhythm pattern so as to produce a set of rhythm variations between adjacent rhythm categories.

The generative rhythm pattern and the resultant set of variations were constructed according to the following conditions:

1. Every period of the generative pattern consists of a sequence of five short percussive sounds, which function as time markers and define five corresponding inter-onset time intervals.
2. The durational pattern within each period is shaped through the use of two different values of durations, *a* and *b*; more specifically, each period of the pattern consists of two successive intervals of duration *a*, followed by three of duration *b*. That introduction of two different classes of durations defines two corresponding periodicities or rhythmic levels or rhythmic strata (according to Maury Yeston). At this point it is worth noting Yeston's statement that '... a meter arises from the interaction of two rhythmic strata ...' (Yeston, 1976, p. 67).
3. The entire set of rhythm variations was produced through a systematic perturbation of duration *b* by equal steps at the level of just noticeable difference in duration. Duration *a* was varied accordingly, so as the total period duration throughout the whole set of variations remained constant.

Given that the number of individual sounds per period, as well as period duration, are held constant throughout the whole set of variations, the only factor that varies is *b/a* ratio. Thus, the systematic manipulation of durations *a* and *b* defines a reference grid along the physical continuum of durational ratios *b/a*, which forms a basis for the graphical representation of the resultant 'perceptual rhythm space'. Note also that *b/a* ratio is a numerical expression of the interaction between the two rhythmic strata defined by durations *a* and *b*, and serves as a critical variable that determines pattern's rhythmic interpretation.

In Figure 10.1, a graphical representation of the entire set of rhythm variations at medium tempo is shown in combination with their corresponding durational ratios at the rightmost column. The **x** markers mark attack points of individual sounds within each pattern. Patterns that are characterized by exact whole-number durational ratios are illustrated in musical notation. Similar sets of rhythm variations were also constructed at fast and slow tempo.

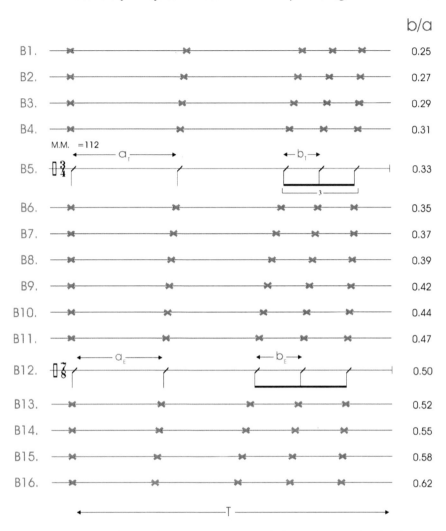

Rhythm patterns, which are characterized by exact whole-number durational ratios, are presented in musical notation. Markers in each rhythm pattern represent attack points of short percussive sounds.

Figure 10.1   Sequence of rhythm variations at medium tempo (B1–B16) and their equivalent durational ratios (*b/a*)

Twenty-one students at a University Music Department – between 21 and 30 years old – participated in the experimental procedure. All of them had considerable performance experience in at least one musical instrument and all reported having no known hearing disabilities. Before they entered the main experimental procedure, they passed through an introductory training session. During their training, participants were also subjected to an evaluation process by which their skill on rhythm detection was determined in terms of their acuity to identify the rhythm of these patterns within each category, whose temporal structure was characterized by exact whole-number durational proportions.

The main experimental procedure was based on a within-subjects design with repeated measures and consisted of the two following tasks:

1. Identification and goodness-rating task: Identification required subjects to detect the rhythm for the total of experimental conditions presented in a random order. Ambiguity in rhythm detection was also reported. In addition to the classical identification task, a category goodness-rating task was further employed,[3] which required subjects to evaluate each pattern's rhythmic precision on a scale from 1 (bad) to 6 (good). Metronomic timing was adopted as a reference for the maximum rhythmic precision within each rhythm category.
2. Discrimination task: This involved an AB same–different forced–choice procedure. The two rhythmic variations within each pair of stimuli were one step apart in the basic set of experimental conditions.

Results and Discussion

The introductory evaluation process of subjects' skill in identifying the rhythm of the accurate metronomic-timing patterns for each different combination of category and tempo provided a percentage success value for each subject. The case of correct identification after listening to the pattern for the first time was adopted as a reference for the maximum identification performance. A final 'quantification' of a subject's skill in rhythm identification was performed by calculating two characteristic parameters: (a) The mean success value for the total of experimental conditions, which was adopted as an indication of subjects' efficiency on rhythm identification; and (b) the corresponding standard deviation, as a measure of subjects' certainty to perform correct identifications. Application of cluster analysis in respect to the above two parameters resulted in a classification of subjects into two performance groups: a high performance group (group A) and a low performance one (group B).

An initial approach to the characteristic aspects of categorization behaviour among different performance groups was performed through an exploratory analysis of identification and goodness-rating data. Frequencies for category identification scores were calculated for all variations within each sequence. Examination of their distributions revealed a high degree of certainty in category identification for group A members, which was indicated by maximum identification percentages for most variations within each category, as well as by an abrupt differentiation in the shape of the corresponding distributions at boundary regions. In addition, small differences were observed in identification performance among different tempi. In contrast, high uncertainty characterizes category identification by group B members, which becomes even higher at extreme values of tempo. Moreover, these differences in identification performance between the two groups are more noticeable at metrical contexts with a more complex structure (for example, 7-beat rhythms).

A more detailed mapping of the resultant perceptual rhythm-space was performed by the calculation of goodness-rating means and the corresponding standard error for all variations within each category. Goodness-rating means were represented in the form of goodness-rating curves similar to those in Figure 10.2, and for the total of experimental conditions (that is, combinations of rhythm category, tempo and performance group). Analyses of the least significant differences among goodness-rating means revealed an increased sensitivity by group A members in the detection of the best exemplars within each category. Equivalently high was the significance of the differences between goodness-rating means among the majority of variations at boundary regions. In addition, slight differentiation was obtained among different tempi. Goodness-rating performance of group B subjects revealed a great influence of tempo and the pattern's structural complexity on categorization acuity: categories were less clearly defined at extreme values of tempo, as well as under high complexity of stimulus's rhythm structure.

The comparative analysis of identification and discrimination data showed that listeners exhibited reduced sensitivity in detecting small timing differences near the best exemplars of each category and increased sensitivity at boundary regions. These discrimination contrasts, which were typical at all different tempi, provide further support to the categorical hypothesis as well as to the existence of the 'perceptual magnet effect' (Papadelis and Papanikolaou, 1999a, p. 3).

Most important, our exploration and mapping of the perceptual rhythm space between and within categories revealed significant similarities to the organization of phonetic categories. The shape of goodness-rating curves within each category revealed that rhythm categories are characterized by a graded structure. Graded structure means that all members within the same category are not perceived as equivalent, but differ in the degree of typicality: some of them are judged as being more representative or typical of their categories than others (Rosch et al., 1976, p. 491; Medin and Barsalou, 1987, p. 471). Several previous studies on the perception of musical rhythm patters (Essens and Povel, 1985; Clarke, 1987) have produced strong evidence that the degree of typicality is a matter of the pattern's proximity to a small whole-number durational proportion. Our results also show a 'migration' of the best exemplars within each category towards small whole-number durational proportions.

Boundary positions are not fixed, but vary according to various factors (for example, tempo, pattern's structural complexity, and so on). A phenomenon

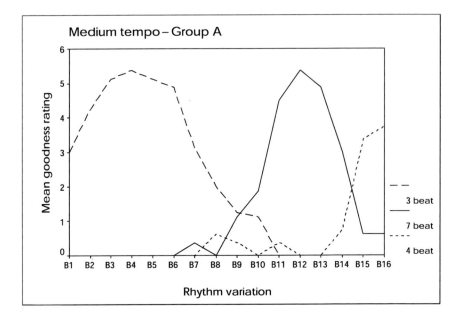

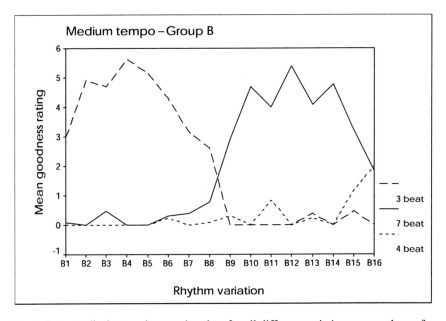

Dashed curves display goodness-rating data for all different variations as members of a 3-beat rhythm category, solid-line curves for their goodness-rating as members of a 7-beat rhythm category and dotted curves for their goodness-rating as members of a 4-beat rhythm category. Separate graphs are plotted for each performance group. Group A corresponds to the high-performance group and Group B to the low-performance group.

Figure 10.2   Goodness-rating means for all metrical interpretations along the sequence of stimuli (B1–B16) at medium tempo

worth noting that affects boundary localization is the competitive action between neighbouring categories. That is, boundary shifts in any rhythm category may occur as a consequence of a diffuse representation of its neighbouring ones (Papadelis, 1999, p. 237). Similar findings are reported in the related research on boundary formation between phonetic categories, where plentiful data have long been collected. These data demonstrated that 'the detection of category boundary is vulnerable to biasing influences of various kinds' (Repp and Liberman, 1987, p. 90).

A high degree of variability in categorization performance was obtained among different musical tempi. Tempo changes result in a considerable structural differentiation within any rhythm category. In particular, tempo changes affect boundary localization, certainty and sharpness of boundary formation and prototype detection, as well as well-formedness of the category's graded structure. Similar effects of speaking rate – the counterpart of musical tempo in the speech production domain – on the perceptual structure of a phonetic category are also reported in the phoneme perception literature (Miller and Volaitis, 1989, p. 511).

Perspectives for Further Research

In this chapter a number of issues relating to rhythm categorization behaviour have been addressed. A major observation of our investigation was that there seem to be significant similarities between phonetic and musical rhythm categories, in respect to certain structural aspects. Obviously, the rich experimental literature on phoneme categorization would serve as a valuable point of reference for the newly established research domain of the musical rhythm categorization.

As a conclusion, we will stress the importance of directing research towards an investigation of the cognitive mechanisms that contribute in the development and refinement of accurate representations for rhythm categories. This developmental approach outlines a promising field of research, which, on the one hand, aims at deepening understanding about the way in which rhythm categories are acquired during childhood and improved through acculturation and musical education, and on the other hand, is expected to provide valuable insights for the improvement of educational methods for the development of rhythmic skills.

Notes

1. Portions of this chapter were presented at the *Joint Meeting 'Berlin 99' (137th regular meeting of the Acoustical Society of America and the 2nd convention of the European Acoustics Association: Forum Acusticum)* Berlin, 1999 and at the *First European Conference on Research Relevant to the Work of Music Academies and Conservatories.*

2. 'Two results are necessary to demonstrate a perceptual magnet effect in speech perception. First, some members of a phonetic category must be judged to be better examples of the category than others. Second, instances that approximate an idealized prototype should be less discriminable than category members that do not closely match the prototype' (Lively and Pisoni, 1997).
3. It was shown from previous psycholinguistic research that goodness-rating metrics give a more detailed outline of the category's structure than frequency curves which are extracted from identification data (Miller and Volaitis, 1989; Hodgson and Miller, 1996).

References

Bornstein, M. (1987) 'Perceptual categories in vision and audition', in S. Harnad (ed.), *Categorical Perception: The Groundwork of Cognition*, pp. 287–300, Cambridge: Cambridge University Press.

Clarke, E. (1987) 'Categorical rhythm perception: An ecological perspective', in A. Gabrielsson (ed.), *Action and Perception in Rhythm and Music*, pp. 19–33, Stockholm: Royal Swedish Academy of Music.

Clarke, E. (2000) 'Categorical rhythm perception and event perception', in *The Proceedings of the 6th International Conference on Music Perception and Cognition*, Keele University.

Cutting, J., Rosner, B. and Foard, C. (1976) 'Perceptual categories of music like sounds: Implications of theories of speech perception', *Quarterly Journal of Experimental Psychology*, 28(3): 361–78.

Desain, P. and Honing, H. (1992) *Music, Mind, Machine: Studies in Computer Music, Music Cognition and Artificial Intelligence*, Amsterdam: Thesis Publishers.

Epstein, D. (1995) *Shaping Time: Music, the Brain, and Performance*, New York: Schirmer Books.

Essens, P. and Povel D.-J. (1985) 'Metrical and non-metrical representations of temporal patterns', *Perception & Psychophysics*, 37(1): 1–7.

Glass, A. and Holyoak, K. (1986). *Cognition*, New York: McGraw-Hill.

Hampton, J. and Dubois, D. (1993) 'Psychological Models of Concepts: Introduction', in I. Van Mechelen, J. Hampton, R.S. Michaelski and P. Thomas (eds), *Categories and Concepts: Theoretical Views and Inductive Data Analysis*, pp. 11–33, London: Academic Press.

Harnad, S. (1987) 'Psychophysical and cognitive aspects of categorical perception: A critical overview', in *Categorical Perception: The Groundwork of Cognition*, pp. 1–25, Cambridge: Cambridge University Press.

Hodgson, P. and Miller, J. (1996) 'Internal structure of phonetic categories: Evidence for within-category trading relations', *Journal of the Acoustical Society of America*, 100: 565–76.

Iverson, P. and Kuhl, P. (1995) 'Mapping the perceptual magnet effect for speech using signal detection theory and multidimensional scaling', *Journal of the Acoustical Society of America*, 97(1): 553–62.

Kramer, J. (1988) *The Time of Music*, New York: Schirmer Books.

Liberman, A., Harris, K., Hoffman, H. and Griffith, B. (1957) 'The discrimination of phoneme sounds within and across phoneme boundaries', *Journal of Experimental Psychology: Human Perception and Performance*, 54: 358–68.

Lively, S. and Pisoni, D. (1997) 'On prototypes and phonetic categories: a critical assessment of the perceptual magnet effect in speech perception', *Journal of Experimental Psychology: Human Perception and Performance*, 23(6): 1665–79.

Macmillan, N., Kaplan, H. and Creelman, D. (1977) 'The psychophysics of categorical perception', *Psychological Review*, 84(5): 452–71.

Medin, D. and Barsalou, L. (1987) 'Categorization processes and categorical perception', in S. Harnad (ed.), *Categorical Perception: The Groundwork of Cognition*, pp. 455–90, Cambridge: Cambridge University Press.

Miller, J. and Volaitis, L. (1989) 'Effect of speaking rate on the perceptual structure of a phonetic category', *Perception & Psychophysics*, 46(6): 504–7.

Papadelis, G. (1999) 'Durational ratios and the categorical perception of musical rhythm patterns', unpublished PhD thesis, University of Thessaloniki, Greece (in Greek).

Papadelis, G. and Papanikolaou, G. (1999a) 'Effect of timing variations on the categorical perception of musical rhythm patterns', in *Collected Papers from the Joint Meeting 'Berlin 99' (137th regular meeting of the Acoustical Society of America and the 2nd convention of the European Acoustics Association: Forum Acusticum)* (available on CD-ROM), Berlin: Deutsche Gesellschaft für Akustik.

Papadelis, G. and Papanikolaou, G. (1999b) 'Mapping the perceptual space between and within musical rhythm categories', unpublished presentation at the First European Conference on Research Relevant to the Work of Music Academies and Conservatories, Lucerne: European Society for the Cognitive Sciences of Music.

Pastore, R. (1987) 'Categorical perception: Some psychophysical models', in S. Harnad (ed.), *Categorical Perception: The Groundwork of Cognition*, pp. 29–52, Cambridge: Cambridge University Press.

Repp, B. and Liberman, A. (1987) 'Phonetic category boundaries are flexible', in S. Harnad (ed.), *Categorical Perception: The Groundwork of Cognition*, pp. 89–112, Cambridge: Cambridge University Press.

Rosch, E., Simson, C. and Miller, S. (1976) 'Structural bases of typicality effects', *Journal of Experimental Psychology: Human Perception and Performance*, 2(4): 491–502.

Schouten, M. and van Hessen, A. (1992) 'Modelling phoneme perception I: Categorical perception', *Journal of the Acoustical Society of America*, 92(4): 1841–55.

Schulze, H.-H. (1989) 'Categorical perception of rhythmic patterns', *Psychological Research*, 51: 10–15.

Sutcliffe, J. (1993) 'Concept, class, and category in the tradition of Aristotle', in I. Van Mechelen et al. (eds), *Categories and Concepts: Theoretical Views and Inductive Data Analysis*, pp. 35–65, London: Academic Press.

Thomson, M. (1967) 'Categories', in P. Edwards (ed.), *The Encyclopaedia of Philosophy*, Vol. II, pp. 46–55, London: Collier-Macmillan.

Windsor, L. (1993) 'Dynamic Accents and the Categorical Perception of Metre', *Psychology of Music*, 21: 127–40.

Yeston, M. (1976) *The Stratification of Musical Rhythm*, New Haven: Yale University Press.

PART 3

Practitioners Investigating their Daily Work

Chapter 11

Making a Reflexive Turn: Practical Music-making Becomes Conventional Research

Jane W. Davidson

Background

Introduction

This brief chapter has been stimulated by the process of editing the current volume and by the many different teaching and research contexts in which I have found myself over the years. Working principally in a university, but also contributing to a course in a music college and both performing and directing in a professional capacity for music theatre, I am acutely aware of the fact that I undertake two very different types of research: that typically disseminated through academic papers where behaviours are observed and quantified so that conclusions can be drawn about how musicians might typically behave in a certain context; and that I engage with when creating a performance. This chapter discusses the latter category as a research area, and describes a study which uses the conventional behavioural research methods I typically draw upon in my academic papers to explore performance preparation as a research topic.

So What is Research?

Any dictionary will define research as involving curiosity, enquiry, experimentation and study. At the moment, historical musicology (I include here issues of performance practice), ethnomusicology, musical acoustics, psychology and sociology, and music analysis are all typically regarded as research domains in music. Indeed, a range of chapters in the current volume draw on methods from these domains to illustrate how research can have important applications for the music practitioner. The current volume tends to focus on systematic study and experimentation, and since much of this type of research comes from the more scientific branch of music studies, the manipulation of variables or detailed observations of behaviour are given as examples of good research. I do not question any of these approaches, or indeed the potential benefits and positive applications for music practitioners. However, I feel that it is important to explore the theoretical potentials in regarding practical musical activities themselves as research. Indeed, if research is to do with experimentation, study, curiosity and enquiry, many practical music-making situations do at some level involve a research process. Here, I focus on *process*. For in the preparation of a piece, many performers investigate what sounds best and why. These performers may engage in some form of musicological research, or use an existing research literature such as the findings presented in the rest of the current volume as a grounding for their own performance. The preparation for performance is often, therefore, a research process: variables being manipulated, as hypotheses are tested.

For me, it is a little more problematic to define performance per se as research. It strikes me that in the western art tradition performance is typically a more presentational than a reflexive activity. I would argue that performance is rather more analogous to the skills and knowledge-base necessary for a written examination. (I am not saying that examinations or performance do not involve moment-by-moment creativity, interpretation and inspiration, but taking an examination or giving a performance are not typically times for totally radical experimentation.) Ideas in free improvisation are typically emergent from previously tried and tested ways of using similar musical materials. What I am suggesting is that the presentational style of an examination or a performance is oppositional to the reflective processes and experimental style involved when a portfolio of critical coursework is created – a more acceptable analogy for the rehearsal process. However, since debate is currently brewing in academic circles about what research status performance might be given, I am not going to attempt to theorize a new definition of practical music as research. All I ask is that practitioners begin to consider their own rehearsal and performance processes and examine why certain elements which contribute towards creating a rehearsal or a performance occur and how they might be different. Additionally, I hope that by engaging in these kinds of processes, practitioners may be inspired by the relevance of the wide and varied research approaches available to extend and develop their own skills and abilities.

Given all of the above, I now turn to a conventional research paradigm to demonstrate how I have used the rehearsal process as a research activity. I do this with the express aim of demonstrating that practitioners can and should participate in research activity themselves, researching topics of direct relevance. Besides providing practitioners with critical insights, as the results of the current study will reveal, undertaking research also provides the practitioner with a means of validating and refining their own practices.

A Traditional Frame of Reference for Research

In 1946, Kurt Lewin coined the term 'Action Research' to describe an approach in which practitioners could make enquiries into their own situations, typically with an 'action for change' outcome. Participants in a particular project became researchers by collecting 'data' (usually thoughts, feelings and other such outcomes about a process) which they analysed to reveal findings which assessed a situation and enabled the implementation of some kind of change as a consequence of their research. A good example of this is when a management committee of a particular social service examines how and why committee decisions are made and how more effective decisions could be made based on an observation of the committee's working practices. An example of action research for developing a tool for music education is found later in this book in Chapter 22 by Bannan. For more details and context for action research, I refer the reader to Robson (1993) for an excellent overview.

From this brief introduction to the principles of Action Research, it is immediately apparent that it has the potential to be adapted to musical rehearsal contexts, especially when large numbers of people are involved, and a democratic way of arriving at a performance outcome is sought. Hence, I adopted Action Research principles to work on a performance project.

The Project

Every year, I work with a group of young singers to devise an opera production. For them, it is often their first experience of such work, but I always get them heavily involved in devising their characters and movements on stage. For me, it is always a fresh process with ideas emerging as I observe interpersonal interactions and work with the individuals moment by moment. It is typically a problem-solving task: how can character x get from A to B? What is motivating him or her and why? The Action Research technique was a simple means by which I could collect data to 'research' the dramatic and musical elements of the opera production being constructed in rehearsal. Thus, the project was a traditional means of collecting data on a form of practice – here, the rehearsal process. It might also be regarded as a piece of research which documents the research process.

Participants

There were 25 participants in all: myself as artistic director, a chorus of 12, 9 soloists and 3 dancers. We all rehearsed at the Guildhall School of Music and Drama for 15 sessions: 12 taking place fortnightly from October to March (each session lasted for 2 hours), and the final 3 rehearsals occurring within the space of 3 days immediately preceding the performance at the end of March. The work being produced was Purcell's opera *Dido and Aeneas*.

Data Collected from the Participants

The following data were collected from the participants:

- Diaries for all rehearsals: a blank page was given with the heading: What did you think about/take away from today's rehearsal?
- Questionnaires about specific aspects of the rehearsals: these were distributed for completion at the end of each rehearsal and included were brief questions which required open rather than closed responses. Examples of the questions included:

  - What was best about the rehearsal today?
  - What was worst about the rehearsal today?
  - If you could change two things about the production process, what would they be?

- Detailed oral reports made during the rehearsals: these were in the form of group discussions at moments of rest during the rehearsal process. Questions similar to those posed in the questionnaires were asked. The group discussion element was pursued in order to explore group versus individual processes and to explore the general group dynamics – who was dominating and why.
- Final feedback on the performance. At the end of the final performance, students were asked to fill in an open-ended feedback form in which they stated what had appealed most/least in the process and why.

Results

In line with Action Research and other qualitative research practices (cf. Robson, 1993), the analysis of all the above described data involved a process by which all data were systematically examined, with emergent like-content being grouped. These groups of data were then arranged according to theme. The themes were then taken back to the participants and their advice was sought about the validity of the categorizations made. This was done by asking them to look the data available, and to explore whether the themes were indeed suitable labels. After this feedback and some further discussion, the following themes were validated.

Atmosphere

Overwhelmingly, the participants in this project referred to the feelings they experienced in the rehearsals, particularly those connected with producing a conducive atmosphere for work. Below are three typical commentaries:

> The rehearsal today was pure enjoyment because I could be me. I felt safe. I was able to explore the character for myself. (Chorus member)

> Here, I've got the courage to offer my ideas. There's a good feeling around. I feel good about the work. I look forward to the rehearsals. (Chorus member)

> Everyone's created an atmosphere. We're all in it together. It's fun! (Soloist)

My own diaries of the sessions show many references to the participants working hard to achieve a constructive atmosphere. Indeed, I began each session with warm-up games to get people moving, interacting, talking and singing together. All the participants undertook these tasks with enthusiasm and energy, so we were all working towards a common goal. These data reveal many obvious examples of group trust and group identity construction. From the data there is evidence of an emergent sense of group as the sessions progress. Here are two brief examples from the same person's diary taken after the first and fifth rehearsals:

> (Week One) I feel good, and it was really different doing so much movement in order to try out how it felt being each character. I don't really know that many people in the class though, so it's a bit weird ... Slightly exposed and alone. (Soloist)

> (Week Five) When we did that witch bit, I could see we were all helping one another. It was good to see it all ticking over. I felt like some sort of witch machine: in there going for it with the others. (Soloist)

In several discussions with the whole group, we reflected on the notion of group growth and many said that they recognized the 'group feeling' as one of the most critical experiences for them as the rehearsals progressed: a sense that they were coming together, getting closer, freer, easier and more able to understand one another.

In order to deepen the concept of *Atmosphere* more, it is useful to contextualize the theme within an existing theoretical context. Foulkes (1973, 1975a) was one of the first psychoanalysts to develop theories about the dynamics of work in groups. The key concepts he explored have clear resonances with the current data. There is the *Group Matrix*: the notion is that people who come together in the context of a group develop a shared psychic life. As relationships become more intimate an ever-deepening dynamic emerges. This is when a *Group*

Association is formed. Here individuals become instinctively able to associate with what another group member has just signalled.

Additionally, there is the *Conductor*; Foulkes used this label for the leader. The *Conductor* does not produce the group's ideas, but does something with them in order to channel information to help produce an integrated whole (Foulkes, 1975b). In retrospect, I can interpret my intentions in the group as being a strong *Conductor*. My method of working attempts to find a means of placing an individual's communication within the whole. Here are some typical examples of my work which can be seen as that of a *Conductor*:

> [Talking about a section of introductory music]
> What's this bit of music about for you?
> In what ways can its meaning be expressed in the action here?
> Well, let's see if we can find a sequence of simple movements which encapsulate your ideas in some way.

Offers were made, these being refined later in the session with me stating:

> Select five movements that you particularly like ...
> Now you've rehearsed them, reject two and preserve the three which show the most contrast.

I was essentially systematizing a way of making decisions that could accommodate individual differences. I was creating the production by generating rules and boundaries within which individual freedom could operate. It was a near-democratic process! I could not allow thoughts and ideas to become too diverse as I needed to keep the concept of a whole in my mind. I was the person with an artistic overview, but I wanted each performer to contribute to the whole.

The attempt to embrace individual needs is reported in much of the psychological research on group function. For example, Douglas (1993) showed that in order for any group to operate successfully, the members need to have a connection between individuals, but one that does not jeopardize sense of self.

Interestingly, there were no interpersonal conflicts within the project. Different people responded to the development of the production in different ways, with some feeling more comfortable than others at particular points in time, but no one ever argued strongly or disputed what emerged. *The Sorceress* preferred to improvise his movements and vocal inflections, whereas *Aeneas* wanted every gesture and inflection monitored, and he rehearsed by checking and double-checking each sequence. It seemed that by developing a group sense – through task-focused work – we all respected the different ways of working each individual preferred, and so the group preserved and supported the individuals within it. There was always a sense of *Association* to the whole.

Of course, it is only in the analysis of these data that I am able to reflect on how these dynamics emerged, but records show that all participants at some level recognized what was going on. Here is a typical example of a summary of a rehearsal given by a chorus member:

> Today's session was about getting the mood right for *Belinda*. We needed to help her, support her if you like, as she sings *Thanks to the lonesome vales*. I think we got hold of our characterization very well. We were lovers, who had made love, but we were not dominating the scene. I'm sure it's *Belinda* who the audience will look at, but we're there just showing people what's happened and what is to come. Actually, I think we're the most important people in this work – holding and supporting the whole thing.

The critical nature of group function certainly strongly interfaces with the next emergent theme, creativity.

Creativity

Beginning the next theme by examining the relevant literature, creativity has been described variously by Gorder (1980), Gordon (1989), Webster (1990) and others as a process which involves a problem-solving approach, or even thinking divergently about an issue in order to come to a conclusion which permits the creation of something new. In this opera group, it was evident that we were finding answers to questions, thinking broadly about issues, then limiting our options in order to come to a conclusion. I surprised myself by my exploratory attitude to work for and within the whole group. The following excerpt of recorded dialogue captures a typical exchange over a major production decision: how to play the characters of the witches.

Me:	How do you view these witches then?
Chorus member 1:	They're more like wild beasts than humans.
Chorus member 2:	I think they're like the living dead or something …
	Isn't that Killer Zombies! [Everyone laughs]
Me:	If that's what they are, how might they sound?
C1 and C2:	[Offer wild cackling and snorting sounds along
	with some spasmodic, shaking movements]
Sorceress:	How am I in here?
Me:	What do you think? Big and bold? Human? Machine? Sexy?
	[Laughter]
Sorceress:	I think I would like to have sex with them ALL!
	[All laugh]
	But maybe I can do it with the words
	– seduce them with my pronunciation …
	The line 'Share in the FAME of a MISCHIEF'.
	[He sings it, slurring and adding a lot of emphasis
	to the words in upper case]
Me:	Well, shall we try it?
	The Sorceress is seducing you with vocal
	inflections and you're all moving around like 'dying'

	mad creatures, responding in a random sort of manner to his presence.
	[They all try the sequence twice]
	So, what's working?
Sorceress:	Do you think this is good?
	[He caresses his own body with his hands as he sings]
C2:	Let's try reflecting that – it looks really wild.
	[All laugh]

So the rehearsal sequence continues. I take the group's ideas, refine them and get them to rehearse the suggestions. It is a dynamic process. It was, certainly, an experimental approach: proposed hypothesis, test, outcome with conclusion. This form of creativity was not only limited to direct forms of social interaction, however. In one scene, I decided to emphasize the allegorical elements of the plot, and whilst the *Second Woman* was singing 'Oft she visits this lone mountain' (a reference to Dido, and additionally an allegorical account of the Greek legend of Acteon's downfall when he is pursued and killed by his own hounds after Diana had transformed him into a stag), I got one of the chorus members (a trained dancer) to dance the part of a dying stag. I deliberately paid homage to Nijinsky at the start of the dance, getting the dancer to hold positions similar to those I had seen of Nijinsky's portrayal of the faun when he first danced the role in Debussy's *Prélude à l'après-midi d'un faun*. I used photographic images as the starting point from which all the other movement ideas emerged. Of course, the extra ideas were developed in collaboration with the dancer. As I saw the dancer make one movement, another possibility to extend the gesture would become apparent, and this would develop into a series of steps. The dancer would add ideas too, often returning to the dance after a week or so having added a few steps himself. Here there was collaboration, but it was less dependent on a group sharing.

Role Flexibility in Rehearsal

As the discussion of the themes listed above reveals, there was much accommodation of musical and social ideas in the rehearsals for this opera. Young and Colman (1979) stress that personal interdependence is critical for a coherent musical whole to be produced, but it seems that such apparent closeness depends on trust and respect of each individual's boundaries. A small number of studies have examined the interactions in large music groups, usually orchestras as social units (cf. Faulkner, 1973; Atik, 1992, 1994, 1995; and Allmendinger et al., 1994), and research findings reveal that:

1. participants must be able to meet the challenges of the tasks (that is, they need to be capable and skilled);

2. individual activity needs to be directed towards achieving group goals;
3. the leader's role must be perceived as being facilitative and democratic.

It is evident that complex and subtle, but above all flexible, interactions are required in order for these three key elements of ensemble functioning to be successfully achieved.

Analysing the data from *Dido and Aeneas*, the single factor which seemed to permit the group dynamics to function was the flexibility between individuals, allowing a constant flux between individual and group needs, especially between me as leader and the others, who often had fantastically spontaneous ideas. Take, for example, the case of a female chorus member who was completely confused about her own abilities to move and sing simultaneously. Her own needs were at the forefront of her mind. In one rehearsal she suddenly looked at me – obviously on the verge of tears – and frustratedly said: 'I just can't do this. I'm no good!' For that instant I could not think of a response, as I was trying to work out a vocal passage with one of the soloists. The dancer who had been in the stag sequence immediately saw my momentary paralysis and voiced an opinion: 'It's great what you're doing, but maybe you could do less moving when you're singing and more when you're not singing?' It was a perfect solution for the woman, and one the dancer felt good about, to have stepped in and taken the initiative to move the individual, and therefore the group, forward (he commented on the event at length in his rehearsal diary).

There was a continual state of flux for me between being in the role of group member and *Conductor*. Indeed, in my diaries, I would report feeling uncomfortable if a session had been 'too dictatorial', that is, if I had given too many 'instructions'. By the time of the final performance, however, I drew a small diagram in my diary to encapsulate how I had felt about my progress within the group over time. This is shown in Figure 11.1. Initially, I saw my role as being apart, but trying to get the individuals to move from their individual positions to more integrated group situations (Figure 11.1(i)). About two-thirds of the way through the rehearsal period (Figure 11.1(ii)), I felt as though I was in a group, but a group which surrounded me, that is one that I was still not completely synthesized into. By the performance, I felt part of a whole (Figure 11.1(iii)).

Several of the other group members came up with similar thoughts and feelings. Belinda also made a figural representation of herself in the project (see Figure 11.2). The similarities are obvious, as is the emphasis on flexibility.

Individual Performer Progress

Here, I focus on a single example, though I could have selected data from any of the participants. The example is of a woman who began very tentatively in the group. This was not through lack of performance experience (she was indeed an

(i) Initially

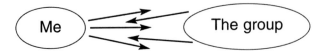

(ii) After two-thirds of the rehearsal time had gone by

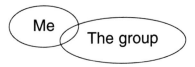

(iii) By the performance date

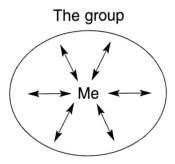

Figure 11.1   Jane in relation to the rest of the group

experienced performer) but, as she explained to me during the first rehearsal, being blind she had never performed with a cast of sighted individuals in a dramatic performance before. When I turned up to the initial rehearsal, I had no previous knowledge that she would be in the group, so took the session as I had planned: movement warm-up, vocal warm-up, brief exploration of all the individual characters in the opera. Immediately I realized that I was going to have to modify things so that this woman could work at a similar pace to everyone else. In the movement session, many of the cues I gave were non-verbal, and when singing, I often depended on my arm gestures to give instructions to change the dynamics and timbre of the vocal sounds. I knew she was having difficulty keeping up, as I occasionally found her in the midst of the others not

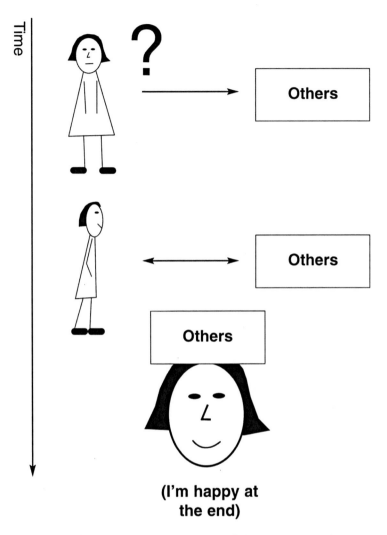

Figure 11.2   Belinda in relation to the rest of the group over time

quite knowing where she was or what she was to do. Initially, she said nothing. After the first session she wrote a very powerful diary, which she quite forcibly handed to me at the beginning of the second session:

> Well, everyone else seemed to enjoy the session. I felt that it was hopeless: How can a blind woman take part in something so oriented around movement with a visual focus? Opera is not for me!

Of course, in the week between sessions one and two, I had thought about how to give information to the group, and was quite determined to facilitate the woman's integration into the action of both the rehearsals and the performance. The second session was slightly better. By session five, things had changed radically; now she was standing in the middle of the floor and quite literally speaking at the top of her voice:

> You guys, just tell me where the hell you're standing! Where are we moving from? Will SOMEBODY show me!

From that point onwards there was no hesitation about where to go or what to do. In retrospect, I see this change as one from the tension of the novelty of the situation, through to this woman deciding that she was part of the ensemble. Indeed, in discussion feelings to this effect became increasingly apparent. She and I decided that it was best to cast her in the role of the *Second Woman*, and then she did not have to do some of the bits she hated: 'that foot tapping stuff' (the Baroque-style dances).

The *Second Woman* became the person to challenge everyone in the group:

> Jane, you've just told me to stand still, so I'm doing that, and now you're telling me that I look stiff and like a statue … Aren't statues still? I'm only doing what I'm being told!

> Why is she grabbing me like that? It feels all wrong being swirled around like that. It MUST look stupid. Gawd, you guys sometimes make me wonder!

My feeling was that this woman challenged everyone, as she was herself facing the most incredible personal challenges. But I was demanding a lot of her. When I decided to include the stag sequence (see the section 'Creativity' above), I thought it would be interesting for the *Second Woman*, as the singer of the aria, to communicate with the other characters as if in a dream-like or visionary state. I decided she would make a sequence of dance-like arm gestures that she and *Dido* could exchange. I was amazed at how difficult the simple but soft, visually aesthetic (to my eye at least) movements were to teach to someone with no visual concepts:

> Does it look nice Jane if I do it like that? I haven't a clue! These movements feel so strange to me.

The *Second Woman*, *Dido* and the dancer worked really hard at perfecting the section. It looked fantastic: the *Second Woman* making tender caresses of her face with her hands, and additional outstretched arm gestures with her and *Dido*'s heads looking skyward were all perfectly coordinated. It was the moment when the *Second Woman* took centre stage. It was a key moment in the performance. For the *Second Woman* it was evident that this scene represented a letting down of barriers and profound personal progress. There was lots of laughing and joy to emerge during those dance sequence rehearsals. In costume, just before the show, the *Second Woman* came to me and said:

> Don't I look gorgeous? What about that make-up (fluttering her long mascara-covered eyelashes)?! By the way Jane, I think the show looks great. I'd say that you're quite a good choreographer, well especially my dancing, it's beautiful!

We both hooted with laughter.

Summarizing Statement about the Emergent Themes of the Project

The more I have examined the data from the opera project and discussed it with the participants, the more I realize how profound and significant the emergent issues were for us all. Many of the processes we went through can be viewed as having powerful psychodynamic elements: personal illumination, self-discovery, accommodation of others' needs, working together as a group. Research has therefore drawn out the role of group process and made all the participants aware of its role. The impact of this information will undoubtedly have consequences for participation in future projects. Indeed, arguably, exploring these issues in real time, because of the Action Research paradigm, made us work more deeply and thoughtfully than we would have otherwise. Feeding back these themes to the participants, it was apparent that all were impressed by the potency of the group work, and also appreciative of the opportunity to reflect upon it.

Clearly, in music-working contexts, psychodynamically informed music therapists work with individual versus group issues in a direct manner on a daily basis; but what is striking in the current project is that we were all chipping away at fundamental issues of communication and presentation throughout the rehearsal process. I am not saying we were engaged in therapy, but rather we embarked on a project with a simple performance goal which then took us on a journey of self-discovery and change. It was certainly a highly valuable experience for me and the others (all of whom have read this chapter, though I have omitted their names here for the sake of confidentiality) to reflect upon the processes that were undertaken, since it led us to a deeper understanding of what was happening to us and why.

In terms of a strict 'Action Research' definition, we were not aiming for change within our current practices, because we were all working together for the first time. However, the rehearsal process shows a clear change over time: the gradual synthesis into and accommodation of individual needs, and a growing understanding of my working practices so that a coherent whole emerges.

Discussing Practice-based Research

Much of what I have written about in the results section of this chapter reflects quite straightforward research practices, with themes emerging in a typical qualitative manner. The written analysis provided an insight into the group and individual processes connected with the project, and I can therefore strongly recommend this kind of research enquiry in practical music-making situations. Indeed, it is perhaps a useful approach for music educators – such as educators working in the music college where I directed *Dido and Aeneas* – to bring this type of research to student and staff practices. Certainly, some sort of critical diary in which working practice, thoughts and feelings and ensemble dynamics could be discussed would be a powerful starting point. For me, the process of documentation and then critical reflection re-enforces the research element of the rehearsal process. It cannot be denied that when we worked on that opera we were researching what the music and movement were for us, moment-by-moment.

References

Allmendinger, J., Hackman, J.R. and Lehman, E.V. (1994) 'Life and work in symphony orchestras: An interim report of research findings', Report No. 7, Cross-National Study of Symphony Orchestras, September 1994: 95–107.

Atik, Y. (1992) 'The conductor and the orchestra: A study in leadership, culture and authority', unpublished Masters Dissertation, University of Manchester Institute of Science and Technology.

Atik, Y. (1994) 'The conductor and the orchestra: "Interactive aspects of the leadership process"', *Leadership and Organization Development Journal*, 13(1): 22–8.

Atik, Y. (1995) 'People factors in the performing arts', *Performing Arts Medicine News*, 3(3): 7–12.

Douglas, T.A. (1993) *Theory of Groupwork Practice*, London: Macmillan.

Faulkner, R.R. (1973) 'Orchestra interaction: Some features of communication and authority in an artistic organization', *The Sociological Quarterly*, 14: 147–57.

Foulkes, S.H. (1973) 'The group as matrix of the individual's mental life', in R.E. Wolberg and E.K. Schwartz (eds), *Group Therapy 1973 – An Overview*, pp. 93–118, New York: Intercontinental Medical Books Corporation.

Foulkes, S.H. (1975a) *Group Analytic Psychotherapy: Method and Principles*, London: Karnac Books.

Foulkes, S.H. (1975b) 'The leader in the group', in Z.A. Liff (ed.), *The Leader in the Group*, New York: Jason Aronson.

Gorder, W.D. (1980) 'Divergent production abilities as constructs of musical creativity', *Journal of Research in Music Education*, 28: 34–42.

Gordon, E.F. (1989) 'Audiation, imitation and notation: Musical thought and thought about music', *Music Teacher*, 59: 15–17.

Robson, C. (1993) *Real World Research*, London: Blackwells.

Young, V.M. and Colman, A.M. (1979) 'Some psychological processes in strong quartets', *Psychology of Music*, 7: 12–16.

Webster, P.R. (1990) 'Creativity as creative thinking', *Music Educators Journal*, 76(9): 22–8.

Chapter 12

Singing by Heart: Memorization Strategies for the Words and Music of Songs

Jane Ginsborg

Introduction

The primary purpose of music academies and conservatoires is to train musicians to perform, compose and teach music. A secondary purpose is emerging, however: to train musicians in skills necessary for performing and preparing to perform. For example, the Alexander Technique and Dalcroze eurhythmics are taught in order to improve posture, the use of the body and rhythmic awareness. Yet practice and learning skills are rarely included in the curriculum. It could be argued that Alexander Technique and Dalcroze eurhythmics are established methods, while little is yet known about effective learning skills for musicians. Nevertheless there is a growing body of psychological research into expert performance, which includes a substantial literature on practice. In the same way that students at school and university can explicitly learn the skills that will help them study, so it should be possible for aspiring musicians to learn the skills that will help them practise most efficiently.

One subset of such skills is memorization. Most solo performers perform from memory on at least some occasions, and singers and pianists are expected to perform from memory on most occasions. Memorization skills are rarely taught formally, for two reasons. First, it is sometimes claimed that memorization ability is somehow mysterious and that it should remain so lest it disappear. However, a more down-to-earth reason for not teaching memorization is that what is known about the theory and practice of effective memorization is not yet available to those who would teach it.

The starting point for the research reported in this chapter was the literature available on the practising, learning and memorization techniques of instrumental musicians. The present research, however, focuses on the memorization strategies of singers. Very little empirical research has been carried out with expert singers, as opposed to expert instrumentalists. Although it might be predicted that singers' memorization strategies would be similar to those of instrumental musicians, the singer's task differs in that he or she must memorize and perform from memory words as well as music. The purpose of the research, then, was to identify effective memorization strategies for singers, with particular attention paid to the memorization of the words as well as the music of songs. The research programme took the form of a pilot interview study and three main studies, one observational and two experimental, which will be outlined in turn.

Interview Study

First, semi-structured pilot interviews were carried out with five professional singers. They reported learning the words and music of songs separately before combining them. Their memorization strategies were primarily for the words rather than the music. These included studying the meaning of the text, translating it into English if necessary, as well as memorizing the words phonetically, by rote. Overall, the singers described a three-stage process:

1. initial study;
2. learning; and
3. deliberate, rather than implicit, memorization.

These findings echo those of an interview study carried out by Wicinski (1950, cited by Miklaszewski, 1989, p. 96) who interviewed ten eminent pianists of the day on the topic of preparing pieces for performance from memory. Seven reported that initial study of the whole piece formed a first stage; this was followed by a second stage in which they worked on technical difficulties, while the third and final stage consisted of rehearsals of the whole piece in order to perfect the final interpretation.

Observational Study

Next, an observational study was carried out whose primary aim was to determine the practising and memorization strategies available to singers, and to compare them with those used by instrumental musicians. A second aim was to compare the strategies used by singers of different levels of expertise, and a third was to try to distinguish more effective from less effective strategies.

How might singers' strategies compare with those of instrumental musicians? According to the literature on pianists of varying levels of expertise practising and learning music, their activities include 'analytic pre-study' and 'mental rehearsal' (Rubin-Rabson, 1937), playing with hands together and separately (Rubin-Rabson, 1937; Gruson, 1988; Miklaszewski, 1989), playing at different speeds (Miklaszewski, 1989) and repeating single notes, bars and sections of music (Gruson, 1988; Miklaszewski, 1989). Singers, too, might well carry out 'analytic pre-study' and 'mental rehearsal'; indeed, some of the activities reported by the interview respondents could be defined as such. Singers, too, might well sing at different speeds and repeat different portions of the music to be learned. However, playing with hands together and separately is clearly not an option for singers. Nevertheless, a comparison might be made, for example, between the pianist learning to play the music for the right hand and the music for the left hand separately, and the singer learning words and music as independent components of a song.

To what extent would the strategies used by singers of different levels of expertise at different times during the learning and memorizing process be different, and to what extent would they be similar? We know that instrumental musicians' practising strategies change with the development of expertise. Would this be the case for singers as well?

For example, in an observational study of expert, intermediate and novice pianists who learned three new pieces over the course of ten practice sessions, Gruson (1988) found that in the first session experts were more likely than the other groups to repeat sections of a piece rather than single notes or bars, to play with left and right hands separately, to spend more time on each piece and to use 'self-guiding' speech. That is, they began by dividing the task into discrete units and working methodically and systematically on them. As the sessions progressed, experts spent more time playing uninterruptedly, repeated fewer notes and slowed down less. While the novice and intermediate pianists increased their speed of playing steadily throughout the sessions, the experts decided on their final tempo at an early stage – which tended to be faster than the tempi used by the other groups – and achieved it by the seventh session. This suggests that they had clearer goals and a better idea of how to meet them than the less expert pianists. In other words, they had better meta-cognitive awareness, which seems to have been confirmed in the course of interviews during which they were able to describe the varied and complex nature of their strategies.

While the focus in Gruson's study was on differences between the strategies of experts and novices for practice and learning, a number of case studies providing more detailed analyses of the practising behaviour and, more specifically, the memorizing behaviour of individual pianists have also been carried out. These include studies by Miklaszewski (1989, 1995), Chaffin and Imreh (1994, 1996a, 1996b, 1997) and Lehmann and Ericsson (1998). Since many instrumental musicians, like singers, perform from memory, they often focus during practice sessions on activities designed to help them memorize, and there is thus a small body of research into effective memorization strategies for pianists and other instrumentalists (Hughes, 1915; Rubin-Rabson, 1937; Ross, 1964; Nuki, 1984; Hallam, 1997).

Hallam's (1997) phenomenographic study of expert and novice instrumental musicians explicitly investigated their memorization strategies. Like the expert pianists in Gruson's study, the expert musicians in Hallam's study showed more meta-cognitive awareness than novice musicians, in so far as the experts were more likely to report using analysis in the course of memorization. This involved, for example, noting features of the material to be remembered, such as key changes, harmonic structure, the length of rests and difficult 'exit points'. However, they sometimes also used the technique of memorization largely without conscious awareness, and then linking short memorized sections together to form longer sections until the whole piece was memorized. Most of the expert musicians reported combining the two approaches as appropriate to the demands of the particular music to be memorized.

To summarize the aims of the present study, then, the first was to find out what activities would be undertaken by singers that might be directly or indirectly comparable to those of instrumentalists which have been identified by Gruson. The second was to compare the activities of singers of different levels of expertise over the course of the learning and memorizing process. For example, would singers of differing levels of expertise work on different lengths of 'practice unit', as Gruson found that pianists did? Third, would expert singers be as aware of their goals for practice and memorization, and how to meet them, as the expert instrumentalists in Gruson's and Hallam's studies were?

Method

Thirteen singers (students, amateurs and a group of experienced professional singers who had not taken part in the pilot interviews) were asked to learn and memorize the same new song over the course of six 15-minute practice sessions, and to provide a concurrent verbal commentary. The practice sessions were recorded on audiotape, and the tapes were transcribed and analysed.

The strategies used by the singers were defined initially as 'modes of attempt'. They included singing the words and music together, either reading from the score or singing from memory; speaking the words without the music; playing or singing the music without the words; playing or vocalizing the melody; playing the accompaniment; counting beats aloud. As suggested earlier, these modes of attempt could not be compared directly with the strategies of instrumental musicians identified in Gruson's and Hallam's studies. However, some similarities were found between the singers in the present study and Gruson's expert pianists, in that the singers – whether experts, amateurs or students – chose to work on practice units that gradually increased in length and corresponded to compositional units such as phrases and verses. The expert singers differed from the other groups in that they used more modes of attempt and were more likely than the other groups to speak the words, count aloud and sing from memory.

The expert singers also appeared to be more goal-oriented, in that, as reported by the interview respondents, they memorized deliberately and from the beginning of the practice sessions. Another strategy that distinguished them from the other groups involved focusing on the words separately from the music. However, although the interview respondents had suggested that this was a strategy to be used in the earliest stages of familiarization with a song, the expert singers in the present study were more likely to study the words and music separately once they had already begun memorizing them together.

The aim of distinguishing more effective from less effective higher-level strategies was met initially by defining the 'best' memorizer and the 'worst' memorizer. The 'best' was the first of the 13 to sing the whole song entirely accurately from memory. The 'worst' was the singer who took longest to memorize and made the most errors when singing from memory. The verbal commentaries provided by these two singers were then analysed along with their practice and error data.

The 'best' memorizer sang the words and music of the song together rather than separately. She started memorization early and tested her memory throughout the practice sessions. She worked on a variety of lengths of practice unit. She made plans and implemented them, monitored and corrected her errors, and explicitly evaluated her practice. Her approach to practising and memorizing thus resembled the approaches of the expert pianists described by Gruson (1988): her strategies were varied and complex; her verbal commentary was detailed and 'self-guiding'. Overall, she appeared to possess a high degree of meta-cognitive awareness. In contrast, the 'worst' memorizer implemented plans, monitored errors and evaluated her practice to a much lesser extent; she preferred to sing the music only, started to memorize comparatively late and consistently repeated the whole song rather than smaller sections.

The hypothesis that the strategies of the 'best' memorizer were indeed more effective than those of the 'worst' memorizer, in that they would consistently produce better performance outcomes, remains to be tested. One way to do this would be to undertake an intervention study in which participants of equivalent levels of expertise would memorize new songs using both types of strategies identified.

Experiment One

The results of the two analyses of data gathered in the observational study included two apparently contradictory findings. The professional singers who took part in the pilot interviews reported learning the words and music of songs separately, and the expert singers in the observational study made more attempts on the words separately from the music than the other groups did. In contrast, the 'best' memorizer in the second analysis preferred to sing the words and music together rather than separately. An experiment was therefore carried out in order to find out whether any advantage, in terms of accuracy and confidence in performance from memory, would be gained by memorizing words and music separately, prior to memorizing them together, or by memorizing them together throughout the whole memorization process.

A new unaccompanied song was constructed and 60 singers were asked to memorize it. The melody was a folk song, 'tweaked' slightly to remove direct repetitions within the melody, and the text was the second verse of an obscure poem. Half the participants were expert and half were novice memorizers of songs. They were randomly divided between three different practice strategies. One group was asked to memorize the words first, then the melody, and then the words and melody together. The second group was asked to memorize first the melody, then the words, and then both. The third group was asked to memorize the words and melody together all the time. At the end of the memorization phase, which lasted 20 minutes, the participants were asked to sing the song from memory. They were then interviewed about their musical experiences and training for 10 minutes. At the end of the interview they were asked to sing the song again. In this second performance, word-only errors (errors in or omissions of the words while recalling the melody accurately), music-only errors (errors or omissions in the melody, while recalling the words accurately), simultaneous word-and-music errors (singing both words and music inaccurately or forgetting both altogether) and hesitations (pauses either because the singer had forgotten what came next, or to correct errors) were scored and analysed.

There proved to be no statistically significant differences between the expert and novice memorizers either in terms of accuracy or confidence. However, participants who had memorized the words and music of the song together throughout the memorization phase made fewer word-only errors than those who had memorized the words and music separately for the bulk of the memorization phase. Thus, if I were asked to offer practical advice to singers on the basis of this finding, I would suggest that, when time is short, singers are better advised to memorize words and music together than to memorize them separately.

Why were there no significant differences between participants with differing experience of memorizing songs? It may be that singers do not become expert memorizers simply by memorizing many songs; expertise is acquired as a result of deliberate practice, and memorization per se is rarely the focus of most singers' practising or memorization activities. On the other hand, many of the participants in this study who were deemed 'novices', on the basis that they were choral singers who rarely memorized vocal music with words, were also instrumental musicians with experience of memorizing music.

In order to test the hypothesis that the ability to memorize songs accurately is related to the ability to learn songs accurately, which in turn is a skill acquired through the development of musical expertise, the participants hitherto deemed expert and novice memorizers were therefore re-grouped on the basis of the extent to which they had undergone musical training. Thirty-five participants had 'high', and 25 participants had 'low' levels of musical expertise.

Although *experience* of memorization had no effect on the ability of singers to memorize a song accurately, musical expertise appeared to have a significant effect. That is, singers with high levels of musical expertise were more accurate in their performances from memory than singers who were less expert musicians: they made significantly fewer music-only errors, and also significantly fewer simultaneous words-and-music errors. Moreover, when participants had memorized the words and music simultaneously they performed most accurately and most confidently from memory: they made significantly fewer word-only errors, fewer simultaneous words-and-music errors, and fewer hesitations. The most accurate and confident performances were given by expert singers who had memorized the words and music of the song together.

The prediction that musically expert singers would demonstrate more accurate and confident recall in performance from memory was upheld. Furthermore, it seems that, for expert musicians at least, memorizing the words and the music of a song together is a more effective strategy, in terms of accuracy and confidence, than memorizing them separately. These findings complement the evidence already presented to suggest that singers who memorize words and music together have better recall for the words when they perform from memory (Rubin, 1977; Hyam and Rubin, 1990).

Experiment Two

The final experiment, undertaken with the help and encouragement of Anders Ericsson and Andreas Lehmann, investigated three questions. First, are the words of songs recalled primarily in terms of their semantic meaning, as suggested by the professional singers who took part in the pilot interviews? Or are they recalled in terms of their 'structural' qualities, emphasized by their setting to music, as suggested by Wallace (1994)? In other words, how important is it to understand the meaning of the words of a song for the purpose of memorizing them? I am not talking about interpretation or performance, for which understanding the meaning of the words of the song is clearly paramount. Rather, the question is whether it is possible to explain the ability of singers to sing from memory, in languages they do not understand or speak, in terms of the relationship of the words to the music to which they are set.

We addressed this question by asking expert singers to memorize songs with semantically meaningful words and non-semantically meaningful words, in this case digit strings, and to perform them from memory within a variety of constraints. If the words of songs are memorized and recalled in terms of their semantic meaning, songs with non-semantically meaningful words should be harder to memorize and recalled much less easily and less accurately than songs with semantically meaningful words.

Second, how separable are the words and music of newly memorized songs when they are recalled? Serafine et al. (1984) played folksongs with inter-changeable words and melodies to non-musically trained listeners and asked them to rate them for familiarity when they were played with different words and melodies. They found what they called an 'integration effect' for the words and music of songs. That is, listeners remembered the songs better when they heard both the words and the music for a second time than when they heard familiar words set to a different melody or a familiar melody with different words. The findings of Experiment One indicated an integration effect, similar to that noted by Serafine et al. for listeners' recognition memory, when singers were asked to recall the words and music of songs, in so far as they were more likely to forget or make errors in the words and music simultaneously than to produce one component accurately and to forget or make a mistake in the other. We aimed to find support for this finding by comparing recall of the texts of the songs with and without melody, and by considering the extent to which text and melody 'triggered' recall for each other.

Third, what is the relationship between speed of acquisition for songs and effective memorization? Lehmann and Ericsson (1995) propose that musicians hold abstract mental representations of the music they perform that underlie both memorization and performance skills. Their finding that pianists who memorize quickly are able to carry out complex tasks from memory, such as transposition, supports this proposal. We used Lehmann and Ericsson's memorization paradigm to explore the relationship between speed of acquisition and the ability to 'manipulate' the texts and melodies of the songs once they had been memorized. This involved showing each participant the musical score of the song to be memorized and simultaneously playing a recording of the melody and accompaniment. The score was then removed and participants were asked to sing as much of the song as they could remember to the recorded accompaniment. These pairs of trials, singing first with the score and then without, were repeated until the participants were able to sing two consecutive accurate performances of the whole song from memory. Speed of acquisition, then, was measured by the number of pairs of trials preceding memorization to the following criterion: the fewer pairs of trials the participant needed, the faster the song was memorized.

Twenty singers with high levels of musical expertise, most of whom had participated in the first experiment, took part in this study. Each carried out two sessions in which they memorized an unfamiliar song, one with a word-text and one with a digit-text, to different but matched melodies. Once each song was memorized to criterion they then performed a series of 15 tasks designed to assess the extent to which they could retrieve the text and melody independently, modify the text and melody, and respond to different types of cues. The experimental sessions were recorded on audiotape and the participants' performance on each task was transcribed and scored. Measures included accuracy, latency and task duration.

The first question was whether the words of newly memorized songs are memorized and recalled primarily in terms of their semantic meaning or as a component of the melody. We predicted that participants would take more time to memorize songs with digits instead of words than songs with semantically meaningful words in English, and that if understanding the meaning of the words of the song was crucial for recall then the songs with word-texts would be recalled more easily and more accurately than the songs with digit-texts. Eight post-memorization tasks measured recall for text.

As predicted, songs with digit-texts took longer to memorize. On the other hand, songs with word-texts were not recalled consistently more accurately or faster than digit-texts. In fact, digit-texts were recalled more accurately than word-texts in one task, and word-texts were not recalled any more accurately than digit-texts in the other tasks. However, recall was slower for digit-texts when participants were asked to recall the text of the whole song at speed both with and without the melody, and in two other tasks. So *understanding* the meaning of the song clearly does play an important part in recall, though perhaps not as much as is sometimes thought.

The second question was how separable the words and music of newly memorized songs are when recalled. Again, the answers were equivocal. We found that participants recalled digit-texts but not word-texts both faster and more accurately with than without the music. The results of the cueing tasks, however, showed that both types of text and melody are more likely to be encoded and retrieved as integrated, rather than independent, components. Although participants were not able to retrieve the appropriate text when cued with a fragment of melody any faster than they were able to retrieve the appropriate melody when cued with a fragment of text, they found it much harder to sing the appropriate melody without also singing the text than they did to speak the words without also singing the melody.

The final question concerned the relationship between speed and effectiveness of memorization. We predicted significant correlation between speed of acquisition and performance such that the faster the participants memorized, the quicker and more accurately they would perform on the 15 tasks devised to show different aspects of memory for the song. We found significant correlation between speed of acquisition and performance on seven tasks, as well as a correlation between memorization ability, as measured in terms of accuracy and confidence in the previous experiment, and performance. Six of these tasks, however, measured speed rather than accuracy of recall: for example, speaking the words of the whole song at speed; retrieving fragments of the text and fragments of the music 'reversed'; responding to cues, both 'forward' and 'reverse'; and singing the phrases of the song in reverse order. The seventh task involved singing the pitches of the melody of the song only, without rhythm, to the regular beat of a metronome.

Lehmann and Ericsson (1995) argue that the ability to form mental representations of a piece of music rapidly, measured as speed of acquisition, underlies the ability to produce performances from memory that are both stable and flexible, as exemplified by their transposition task. It may well be, then, that this same ability to form mental representations rapidly during the process of memorization also underlies the ability to perform from memory at speed and to carry out certain tasks involving 'manipulation' of the memorized song. On the other hand, it may be that performance of the tasks that did not correlate with speed of acquisition, including the accurate performance of the song with accompaniment and at the same tempo as that at which the song was originally memorized (as required in circumstances more usual than that of this study), are better explained in terms of the automatization of performance resulting from the rote memorization of text and melody together.

Conclusion

A comparison of the pilot interview data with the findings of the observational study suggests that, although implicit theories about what constitutes efficient practice and memorization may be held by singers, they either fail to practise according to their theories, or their theories are wrong. This suggests that experienced singers, even those who can also be defined as expert musicians, do not necessarily practise and memorize as efficiently as they might. Given that there is no established theory of memorization for singers based on empirical research, those who devise conservatoire curricula can hardly be blamed for failing to include, and singing teachers can hardly be blamed for failing to teach, efficient memorization skills. However, it is clear that a singer's ability to memorize, which sometimes appears just as mysterious and elusive a process to the memorizer as to his or her audience, is as amenable to deconstruction and demystification as other musical phenomena such as talent, expression and absolute pitch.

As in earlier investigations into the practising and memorization strategies of instrumental musicians, the gathering and comparison of observational data has made it possible to define the main components of practice with a view to memorization, and suggests the strategies that are most likely to prove efficient. The results of the two experiments, meanwhile, show that there is an 'integration effect' for the words and music of songs that holds good for memorization and recall as well as for recognition memory, and that music can enhance recall for the words of songs to the extent that they do not necessarily have to be understood in terms of their semantic meaning. To put the findings of the present programme of research as briefly as possible: the more musical knowledge and expertise singers have, the better they are likely to memorize; the more critically and strategically they think about the way they practise and memorize, identifying and striving to meet interim and ultimate goals, the better they are likely to do; the more accurately and thoroughly they learn the music and use it as a way of structuring their recall for the words, rather than focusing on words and music separately, the better they are likely to memorize. These findings provide the basis for further research to be carried out; meanwhile, it is to be hoped that they will be used also as a basis for encouraging singers, especially those who fear they must be incapable of memorizing, to consider efficient memorization as a skill to be practised and learned, and thus to be mastered.

References

Chaffin, R. and Imreh, G. (1994) 'Memorizing for piano performance: A case study of expert memory', paper presented at 3rd Practical Aspects of Memory Conference at the University of Maryland, Washington, DC, July/August.

Chaffin, R. and Imreh, G. (1996a) 'Effects of difficulty on expert practice: A case study of a concert pianist', paper presented at the 4th International Conference on Music Perception and Cognition, McGill University, Montreal, 11–15 August.

Chaffin, R. and Imreh, G. (1996b) 'Effects of musical complexity on expert practice: A case study of a concert pianist', paper presented at meeting of the Psychonomic Society, Chicago, 3 November.

Chaffin, R. and Imreh, G. (1997) 'Pulling teeth and torture: Musical memory and problem solving', *Thinking and Reasoning*, 3(4): 315–36.

Gruson, L.M. (1988) 'Rehearsal skill and musical competence: Does practice make perfect?', in J.A. Sloboda (ed.), *Generative Processes in Music: The Psychology of Performance, Improvisation and Composition*, pp. 91–112, London: Oxford University Press.

Hallam, S. (1997) 'The development of memorization strategies in musicians; Implications for education', *British Journal of Music Education*, 14: 87–97.

Hughes, E. (1915) 'Musical memory in piano playing and piano study', *The Musical Quarterly*, 1: 592–603.

Hyman, I.E. and Rubin, D.C. (1990) 'Memorabeatlia: A naturalistic study of long-term memory', *Memory and Cognition*, 18(2): 205–14.

Lehmann, A.C. and Ericsson, K.A. (1995) 'Expert pianists' mental representation of memorised music', paper presented at the 36th meeting of the Psychonomic Society, Los Angeles, 10–12 November.

Lehmann, A.C. and Ericsson, K.A. (1998) 'Preparation of a public piano performance: The relation between practice and performance', *Musicae Scientiae*, 2(1): 67–94.

Miklaszewski, K. (1989) 'A case study of a pianist preparing a musical performance', *Psychology of Music*, 17: 95–109.

Miklaszewski, K. (1995) 'Individual differences in preparing a musical composition for public performance', in M. Manturzewska, K. Miklaszewski and A. Bialkowski (eds), *Psychology of Music Today: Proceedings of the International Seminar of Researchers and Lecturers in the Psychology of Music*, pp. 138–47, Warsaw: Fryderyk Chopin Academy of Music.

Nuki, M. (1984) 'Memorization of piano music', *Psychologia*, 27: 157–63.

Ross, E. (1964) 'Improving facility in music memorization', *Journal of Research in Music Education*, 12(4): 269–78.

Rubin, D.C. (1977) 'Very long-term memory for prose and verse', *Journal of Verbal Learning and Verbal Behaviour*, 16: 611–21.

Rubin-Rabson, G. (1937) 'The influence of analytical pre-study in memorizing piano music', *Archives of Psychology*, 31: 220.

Serafine, M.L., Crowder, R.G., and Repp, B.H. (1984) 'Integration of melody and text in memory for songs', *Cognition*, 16: 285–303.

Wallace, W.T. (1994) 'Memory for music: Effect of melody on recall of text', *Journal of Experimental Psychology: Learning, Memory and Cognition*, 20(6): 1471–85.

Chapter 13

Formal and Non-formal Music Learning amongst Rock Musicians

Anna-Karin Gullberg and Sture Brändström

Anyone who has ever attended a rock concert at a college of music knows that you seldom, if ever, witness 'rowdy and chaotic' entertainment. Even though the music college runs courses which cover jazz and rock, offering teaching on both the main instrument and in groups, the odds that the evening will end up with rebellious young people 'stage diving' over the wildly dancing audience are exceedingly small. Phenomena often associated with rock concerts outside of music colleges seldom occur amongst the performing musicians. Neither do the well-behaved, applauding listeners, who are as analytical in their comments about mistakes as about improvements, cultivate such phenomena. Why do these music students in their twenties seem so markedly different from other young people of the same age outside music college? There is much to indicate that students at music college are socialized with a specific set of values which exclusively prevail within colleges of music, and that their time at music college is the final stage in a long process of development.

The overall aim of this chapter is to shed light on the relationship between formal and non-formal learning amongst musicians who play music within the rock and pop genre. The research which is described concerns music students and semi-professional rock musicians who do not primarily make their living from their music. This area of questioning ought to be extremely pertinent for music teachers at different levels, who in their daily work are continually confronted with questions about what attitude they should take in relation to youth music as it emerges outside of educational establishments. The concept of pop or rock music used in this article is a wide and to some extent fluid working definition, which embraces most of the styles of music popular amongst young people, but is usually associated with energetic, rhythmic music and is usually played by ear (Lilliestam, 1995, 1997, 1998).

Formal Learning of Rock Music

The concept of formal learning refers to a form of learning that takes place within the setting of an educational establishment, which is led by a teacher, and where rules and traditions for communicating the teaching are formalized (Säljö,

2000). Students at music colleges in Sweden have been able to choose courses in jazz and rock for a number of years now. This opportunity has not altered to any great extent the type of students applying to undertake courses. The students come from the same type of background and have many common experiences regarding organized and institutionalized activities where formal teaching has been a central feature. An above-average number of the students are members of the Swedish Church or members of a Free-Church organization, and many of them have been active in the Scout movement and in sports clubs whilst growing up. Practically all of the students have had formal pre-training in music, having taken voluntary music classes at municipal music schools and folk high schools (Brändström and Wiklund, 1996; Bouij, 1998; Brändström, 1999a, 1999b).

As well as gaining musical competence, the pupils are educated within a school context with its associated set of values and norms regarding tastes in music, musical form and performance. The pupils who feel at home within the above-mentioned establishments are also those who, having completed their musical education, continue their general educational careers by working as teachers at municipal music schools, on pre-training music courses and at music colleges. This relatively closed system means that a large number of the teaching staff at music colleges in Sweden have travelled along the same route through the system (Brändström and Wiklund, 1996).

A central and perpetually current question for research into music teaching is what happens when a type of music, which by tradition exists outside of and in some cases in opposition to society's institutions, becomes the object of formal teaching.

Non-formal Learning of Rock Music

The learning of rock music usually takes place in a completely different context to formal music teaching. Music in Sweden is, with a certain amount of competition from sport, perhaps the most important leisure activity amongst the children and young people of today. It has been commented on in several different connections by researchers in music psychology (for example, Sloboda, 1985; Hargreaves 1986) as well as by Scandinavian teachers and researchers in youth culture (Lilliestam, 1997; Ruud, 1997; Fornäs et al., 1988) that music plays a very important part in young people's development. The majority of socio-cultural studies that have been undertaken have shown how young people's different social experiences are reproduced in music and in each other's company. Early experiences from the musical climate in their own homes, access to musical instruments in the home and experiences in the company of their friends create a familiarity with different genres and have a long-lasting effect on their tastes in music. The media play a significant role in musical acculturation, and rock and pop music streams out constantly from stereos, television channels and computer games. The widespread use of information technology has also increased access to resounding music as well as to sheet music and song texts.

Rock music is often viewed as a lifestyle (and as an alternative form of learning) which is essentially different from the formal teaching at school. The learning processes of rock can be described as collective, voluntary, spontaneous, informal and open in character. In contrast to this we have school, where the learning processes are depicted as being individual, obligatory, institutionalized, formalized and closed (Fornäs et al., 1988). It has further been demonstrated that rock music as an educational practice is very complex. Besides pure music learning, extensive practical and technical learning also takes place, and, in addition, rich opportunities for social training and other general personal development elements are provided.

The Relationship between Formal and Non-formal Learning

It is, of course, misleading to say that there is a watertight bulkhead between generations or social contexts, and most adults are more affected by youth culture than is usually maintained. Neither is rock music totally isolated from music teaching in Swedish schools. Rock and pop music have lately become a part of music education in Sweden. Municipal music schools have started appointing teachers in this field, and in higher education establishments jazz musicians and, to some extent, rock musicians have been engaged to teach in their respective specialist areas. Although school does not directly breed rock musicians, it does provide plenty of opportunities for musical training (Campbell, 1995). This means that many musicians outside of music establishments have played some musical instrument or have sung in a choir during their time at school. Modern music teaching in compulsory schools is also based more or less on the pupils' own musical experiences.

Despite these integrative tendencies, rock music lives its own life, apparently unaffected by what happens during music lessons at school. Teenagers listen to music more than ever before, and many learn to play an instrument without teachers being involved. In many cases they learn to play their style of music to a very high technical and musical standard. Musicians within the rock and pop genre devote countless hours to practising and rehearsals to an extent fully comparable to the time music students spend on their work.

The increased elements of rock and pop music in music college teaching have not, however, led to any great broadening of the genres, nor has 'tough and hard' rock music gained any pronounced understanding from the music college establishment (Lilliestam, 1995). Even if an open, submissive and non-authoritarian view is taken of how rock music ought to be handled in schools, it becomes obvious how difficult it is to unite rock's 'nature' with the teaching traditions in schools as formalized over time (Ericsson, 1996). As regards the role of musicians, there seems to exist a tension between formally trained jazz and rock musicians, and those who play within these same musical styles but do not possess any formal musical training. Music performed by trained musicians is frequently identified by non-formally trained musicians as being polished and dull, having a blind faith in the quantity of notes played rather than the quality (see, for example, Olsson, 1993, 1997). Teachers and students at music colleges, on the other hand, often display an inadequate understanding and sometimes an open contempt for rock music performed outside the music college establishment. The tension between the institutionalized culture and the milieu that the students will be working in after their training has led to something of an identity crisis for institutional musical education, but can also serve as an incitement to change existing practice within music teaching.

The aim of this study was to investigate *whether* and, if so, *how* jazz and rock students differ from non-formally trained rock musicians in their approach to creating a rock song from a tune and text they have been given. Special attention is directed at possible differences in methods of working and the learning processes.

Method

After much reflection it was decided that two music groups should be approached to create and record a rock song, and the task should be carried out on separate occasions, with observers present throughout. The participants would also be interviewed about their contribution and thought processes before, during and after the recording session. It was further decided that the research should be conducted in a 'real life' situation, and as a relatively neutral backdrop a recording studio was chosen because it was likely that this would be a well-known setting for all those involved. ('Relatively' neutral because the studio was situated at a music school where the music students worked regularly and where the rock group might not feel very much at home. Ideally a studio where none of the groups had played before should have been used, but this would have been very expensive.) Neither of the groups knew that another group was involved. The aim of the research was described by the project leaders as being simply to create a song in any style they liked as long as the result could be called 'rock music'.

The Groups of Participants

The two groups of participants will be referred to as the 'College Group' and the 'Rock Group', but these descriptions must not be taken as having any significance in terms of the relative worth of the two groups. In terms of their socio-cultural background, earlier musical training and musical preferences, the groups can be regarded as being representative of their respective populations, that is to say, 'students of jazz and rock music at colleges of music in Sweden' and 'people who play rock music outside of musical establishments' between the ages of 19 and 24 years.

Process

After talking to teachers and musicians, an approach was made to the vocalists in two groups who were considered able and willing to take part in the research. The task was to arrange and record a finished version of a 'rock song'. The groups had free rein as regards the instrumentation, key, tempo, harmonization, and so on. The only constraint imposed on the groups' interpretation and performance of the song was that the tune given to the groups should be recognizable in the final version of the song. Some time after contact was made with the two groups they came to the recording studio on different occasions and without knowing about each other to record their version. The observers and the sound technician sat almost exclusively in the control room and only entered the studio when the video camera needed adjusting. Both groups were allowed to take part in mixing the recording, so they were able to influence their version until they felt totally satisfied with the result. The interviews were conducted in a separate room immediately after the recording session.

Material

The material consisted of a single pentatonic tune in the key of A minor, composed by K.G. Johansson (doctoral student in music education) for use in this experiment, and the lyrics in English (see Example 13.1). The groups were given the simple tune, programmed with sequencers and recorded on cassette tape in the key of A minor at 120 BPM (beats per minute). Sheet music for the tune, as well as the English text, accompanied the tape. Research data were collected by observing the way the groups worked during the recording and mixing of their respective songs. The whole recording process in the studio was documented on video. The final research data comprised background information from questionnaires, interviews, observations, video films and the completed musical products.

Results

For the purposes of this chapter the results will be presented briefly by describing, group-by-group, the work done before the recording session (information from

Ex. 13.1   K.G. Johansson, *Here I am Again*

the interviews) and the methods of working used during the actual recording sessions (observational notes and interviews). The recordings were compared using the parameters of melody, harmony, rhythm sections and dynamics, based on the material submitted by the participants and on listening to the two versions of the song several times.

The College Group

Work Done prior to the Studio Recording Session

The College Group got together one evening a few weeks before they were due to record the song to discuss the arrangement and a possible style for the song. A few weeks later the group held rehearsals in a practice room after they had listened to the recorded tune. Different variations in the tempo and 'groove' were tried, and the version which everyone in the group felt most comfortable with was a 'soft' and 'cool' version. After a process of trial and error the definitive form was finally found, but a lot of changes were made along the way. During rehearsals the idea arose that the finished song should sound a bit like the Swedish group Bo Kasper's Orchestra, but 'more frothy and more mystical'. The College Group's arrangement comprised vocals, electric bass, electric piano and percussion.

Method of Working during the Recording Session

First thing in the morning they began work by setting up the instruments, microphones, and so on, in the studio. Everyone arrived on time and the day began with general chat. The group decided that they would prefer to try to do everything 'live'. Due to technical reasons, this proved impossible. Instead, it was decided to first lay down the backing tracks and record the vocals later. After playing the song for a while they were ready to do the first recording, which proved to be too 'soft and laid-back'. After recording it four times everyone was happy with the 'sound', which now better reflected the group's intentions. The addition of the vocal tracks soon began and after some discussion amongst those involved it was decided to add harmony parts in both thirds and octaves. The 'sound' of the voice was important for the singer: 'It feels like the tune is quite cool, but quite dirty, and in that case I don't think there should be too many effects or colours.' The percussion was added in the form of maracas, wind chimes, and so on. The percussion was redone when the group became aware of slackness and that certain parts 'were running away', and therefore did not correspond to the 'frothy and insinuating feeling' intended.

After a break for lunch, mixing began, and mainly the vocals were changed. After some turns at mixing and listening to the song, everyone in the group was basically happy with the result. The pianist commented: 'It's turned out something like I imagined it would ... but I think that we all had different ideas and therefore it became a sort of compromise ... but you only notice things like that afterwards.'

The instrumentation, with the percussion instruments which came in and disappeared, vocals which emerged more and more towards the end of the song, and the execution and variations in the rhythm sections implied a 'jazzy' sound and gave rise to a number of dynamic variations. The verses were almost entirely based on an A-minor chord, varied with extensions like Am add9, Am9, Am11, and so on, making the music sound jazz-influenced.

Analysis: The Road to the Finished Result

> Why do you devote yourself to music?
> It's good for the body and soul and it's fun!
> (College group singer)

The whole recording situation for the College Group was permeated with a remarkably good atmosphere, and disputes were conspicuous by their absence. The group's members were relatively far apart in the recording studio and for the most part remained seated during the proceedings. The group worked in a decidedly 'democratic' fashion, showing great respect for their co-musicians' technical skills and musical ability. They each interpreted the basic material and worked out what their contribution was going to be relatively independently of each other. The result was that their individual contributions were largely improvised on location in the studio, and the final arrangement took shape as the group was feeling its way. 'Nothing is written down or definite – there is a lot of improvisation the whole time, and it sounds different each time we play it. There is no arrangement, it's just based on us as musicians, 'cos we know each other', the pianist commented.

Despite there being large amounts of vocals, the singer did not comment on the lyrics during the interview. Her only comments regarding the basic material and her own vocal contribution concerned the musical aspects and never the text she had to sing. This could of course be related to the nature of the task, but also to the fact that it is relatively unusual for music students to compose music and write their own lyrics (cf. Georgii-Hemming, 1999). All the members of the group belong to a culture where the codes are well known, where they are all familiar with the terminology and references used. To record a song in this way is not markedly different from the way they usually work. It did not seem irksome for them to make music using a tune and lyrics they had been given. The group's friendly conversations and relaxed body language reinforced the impression that it did not require any particular exertion or unusually high levels of concentration to carry out the task they had been given.

The Rock Group

Work Done prior to the Studio Recording Session

The Rock Group singer listened to the tune on the cassette tape the night before the day of the recording session and got some ideas regarding chords and the arrangement of the song. These suggestions were presented to the other members of the band during the recording session. The singer further emphasized that as he had not written the song himself, it did not seem as important to work as hard as he otherwise would have done. According to him the arrangement of the song should be identical to the band's other songs, 'a sort of standard approach we always use'. The Rock Group had neither rehearsed nor discussed the arrangement or other details before the recording session. The band consisted of bass, drums and two guitarists, one of whom was also the singer.

Method of Working during the Recording Session

The group assembled in the morning and chatted whilst they completed the questionnaires. One of the guitarists commented, 'Shit, it's the same answers as when you were in seventh grade – it's still punk and being in revolt against society.' The Rock Group wanted to play 'live and have the same "sound" as in the rehearsal room'. The only thing to be added after that was the vocals. 'What record are we using for the guitar sound?' asked the sound technician. They all agreed that it should be 'Chavez, song number two'.

The whole morning was spent trying out various guitar and bass sounds, swapping cables and amplifiers, and getting the microphones in the right places for the drums, which took a long time. Comparisons were made between the guitarists' sounds. They played together in parts of a song and came into the control room to listen. The sound was given the seal of approval and the rehearsing began. The singer showed the others his ideas for the verse and chorus parts, and the group played closely together whilst each band member tried to learn his part. The volume in the studio was very loud. Everyone except the musicians in the band left the studio.

Late in the afternoon they played the song through for the first time to record it, but nobody wanted to keep that version. A proper recording was accomplished and after they had listened to it in the control room everyone seemed quite pleased with it, given the circumstances. 'The tempo is a bit rushed, but we won't do it much better without playing it for a while.' During the evening the production of the song was carried out in the control room. In addition to the singer, the bass-player was present, and he mixed the song. The singer at one point exclaimed, 'It's a long time since I last read music ... is it the right tune?' The bassist suggested 'rock screams' in the chorus and added, 'we had to redo "Waiting in the Rain" because it was off-key'. After that the recording was mixed, but the song could not be considered completely finished. In answer to the question of whether the song turned out the way they had intended, the singer/guitarist answered, 'Yes, sort of ... when you've written a song, you've got everything ready ... I mean how the song should sound, in your head, how it sounds on record ... so it's sort of how I had intended it to be.'

The Rock Group made almost no use of dynamics; instead, the accompaniment was based on a tight structure, a 'wall of sound' which was brought about with the help of a compact eighth-note rhythm from the bass and the guitar. There were also a couple of places with variation in the instrumentation: the first eight bars of the introduction, the first four bars of the bridge and the closing part, the 'outro'.

Analysis: The Road to the Finished Result

> Why do you devote yourself to music?
> To let off steam ...
> > (Rock Group singer)

It is both mentally and physically demanding to be on tour for a long period of time. After having recently come home from a long and exhausting tour of Europe, the members of the band communicated this both verbally and non-verbally. The Rock Group's method of working could best be described as 'playing by ear', with the singer energetically communicating his ideas on chords and arrangement to the other members of the band. As the singer expressed it: 'If I have written a song, then I tell them that it is written in these chords, this is the chorus and these are the verses, etc. I always teach them that it is these chords and these chords. I never sing the tune, but instead show the beat.'

As the material was new, it had to be played a number of times before the bass-player and the guitarist caught on. To record material they had not played before was a strange and evidently irksome situation for them to be in. It was obvious that a lot of concentration was required during the learning process, and a lot more effort than usual was demanded. The singer commented, 'We never write a song and then record it in the studio the day after. We usually check whether it really is a good song.'

Even though the guitarist/singer played the part of leader, the others probably did not see him as an actual teacher. How each of them made their contribution was at the end of the day up to each of them individually, bearing in mind the common codes: 'We are all ... equally idealistic when it comes to sound and such like. We are very thorough about which guitar sound and which drum sound we would like, but it is nevertheless how much energy the songs have which is the most important thing.'

The Rock Group did not seem to improvise at all during the recording session, and this corresponded to their own comments that they never normally improvise or play any solos. Most of the songs are finished off by the singer himself or the bass-player (who in addition to the singer is the one who composes the band's material), including rhythm sections, and that was also the case on this occasion. The members themselves thought that there was more energy in the first few recordings and that additions were unnecessary. 'It's easy to lose the energy', and this also resulted in the song only being recorded a few times, with no additions being made afterwards. The time taken to record was longer in total than for the College Group, and this was probably because it was a more complicated process, with drums and several guitar amplifiers being involved. The singer in the Rock Group returned several times to the character and content of the lyrics which he regarded as being banal and strange for him to sing, when compared to the group's usual repertoire of songs. He did not feel that his own performance had been a great success.

Discussion

This momentary insight into the two groups' methods of working means that subtle aspects regarding their inner communication can only be hinted at. For the students it was no great event to spend a few hours in a studio at the same music college they usually attended. For the Rock Group the element of difference was that the studio was situated at a college, which might possibly have brought in associations which, in their turn, could have influenced the task being undertaken. The factors outside of the music which usually surround the activity of playing music were for obvious reasons not present during the recording session. Both groups saw the tune and lyrics as being neutral and as being something they were able to work with, and the material used can thus be seen as a foundation which worked well in that respect. On the other hand the actual task seemed to some degree alien to the participants, and the singer in the Rock Group also emphasized the difficulty of arranging original material which he had not composed himself. In addition, the task of arranging a song based on a predetermined tune was not the way the Rock Group usually created music, but was a task more familiar to the College Group.

'College Pop' or Rock Music

The College Group made a jazzy pop song with many similarities with what is often called 'typical music college music' or 'college pop' and which is associated with influences from so-called 'slick music'. The notion of 'slick' means well-produced, cleanly arranged, well-played and well-mixed music. Slick music can be associated with the category of 'adult rock' or 'American West Coast music' and inclines in the direction of jazz (Johansson, 1995). The version had obvious similarities with the general trend within the category of Swedish pop music, especially with female vocalists, backed up by professional/studio musicians, who are often connected to music colleges. To go into studio work can be seen as an obvious way of getting into pop after graduating from music college (Steward and Garratt, 1984), and seems perhaps a more obvious choice for an 'afro-oriented' singer than singing rock songs and entering the more alien culture of rock music.

The sound and atmosphere of the Rock Group's version and the lyrics' sentimental elements added to the easily gained impression that the song was from the 1980s. The Rock Group's own definition of the final result was: 'Emocore [emotional hardcore] guitar sound which reminds you of the group Chavez.' The type of modal harmony (so-called Aeolian harmony) in the rock music of the 1980s is an important contributory factor to the 'sound' which characterizes recent rock music (Björnberg, 1984). Recent rock music also applies an often-reversed method of composition, where the background with 'riff', harmonic patterns, drum beat, and so on, is done before the tune is added. That the tune was not seen as being of primary importance for the Rock Group was clearly illustrated by the fact that the other members of the band did not take part in the composition until the recording was finished. As the singer said, 'No, they don't usually know how the tune goes, and often the PA is so bad that they don't know how the tune goes before we've recorded it in the studio. I'm the only one who does.'

The two versions not only sounded completely different, they were also within a musical province which the other group felt strong antipathy for. The College Group did not like the music genre of hard rock, and the Rock Group hated fusion jazz. It is an established fact that many people outside of music establishments do not identify themselves with the musical styles most favoured by music colleges. It is, for example, worth noting that contemporary pop and rock music was not held in particularly high regard amongst members of the College Group. Their musical preferences were easily associated with groups of listeners considerably older than themselves. A survey of university students of the same age as the musicians was conducted, using the song material. The results showed that music school students exclusively preferred the College Group's version, whilst students studying other subjects preferred the Rock Group's version (Gullberg, 1999).

Differences in Learning Environments

As earlier research has stressed (Bouij, 1998; Brändström, 1999a) there are differences between the two groups as regards early musical influences, formal musical training and musical preferences. In the case of the College Group, a socialization process regarding musical preferences has probably taken place over many years, directed at the musical styles which are regarded as valid and which dominate within music establishments. The Rock Group's members stated that during their teenage years it was their friends who had had the most influence on their musical tastes and their own music-making. Of course, the use of the media and the fact that they are involved in a non-institutional musical life at a certain period of time can, to a certain extent, also explain why they play within the genre of music they have chosen. It is possible that differences in temperament and personality can also explain some of the differences, but that discussion is not within the scope of this paper.

One of the biggest differences between rock music outside of and within music institutions is probably that in the school situation one is largely noticed for the mistakes one makes; that one plays a wrong note, holds the instrument incorrectly, intones incorrectly or plays the wrong sort of music. Learning about music outside of music establishments is characterized to a large extent by the participants being involved in creating music. Even though in this case it was the songwriter who showed the others how they should play the song, the whole group had common aims, common motivation and common musical preferences. Creating music thus becomes both an individual and a collective process, and the choice as to whether to take part is voluntary. If the overarching aim of formal teaching overemphasizes the importance of being accomplished and playing 'correctly', this can distance the musicians and teachers from the music listeners who do not view 'playing correctly' as being the primary goal of music-making.

If it is the case that a certain teacher profile and musician profile develops over the years at music colleges, it is important to make people aware of the mechanisms which form the basis for this more or less conscious influence. Teaching methods based on reading music have continued to dominate within most colleges, even within the fields of jazz and rock music. One reason for this could be that students and teachers find it more difficult to express their musical competence in a musical style which perhaps demands more understanding of what is 'written between the lines' than the music styles which emphasize technical ability in a more pronounced way. This fact could be one of many reasons why the general favouring of jazz music over rock music continues in music colleges in Sweden.

Is it possible and desirable to learn to play rock in a traditional school setting? One argument against teaching rock music is, for example, that rock music cannot be institutionalized. On the other hand, it is easy to argue in favour of rock music within various school settings because of the elements of motivation and interest present amongst the students, and because of youth music's great prevalence and importance. If it is decided also to include rock music in formal music teaching in the future, one critical question will be how the teaching should be conducted – it is almost impossible to unite it with the music teaching which has grown up within the classical tradition. The training of music teachers is, of course, of central importance to the view that schools in the future will take as regards rock music. It is reasonable to expect that the demand for music teachers to be open and have understanding and insight will be emphasized in the multicultural society which is developing. Musicians and teachers of the future must thus learn to understand and cope with many different learning situations, and the question is whether music colleges *can* or *should* have responsibility for providing this competence during young people's years at school.

References

Björnberg, A. (1984) *There's Something Going On – om eolisk harmonik i nutida rockmusik* [*About Aeolian Harmony in Today's Rock Music*], Multiplay, 31 papers on music. Jan Ling dedication paper, Göteborg: Göteborgs Musikvetenskapliga institution, Göteborgs universitet.

Bouij, C. (1998) 'Swedish music teachers in training and professional life', *International Journal of Music Education*, 32: 23–30.

Brändström, S. (1999a) 'Music education as investment in cultural capital', *Research Studies in Music Education*, 12: 49–58.

Brändström, S. (1999b) 'Music teachers' everyday conceptions of musicality', *Bulletin for the Council of Research in Music Education*, 141: 21–6.

Brändström, S. and Wiklund, C. (1996) 'The social use of music and music education', *Canadian Music Educator,* 37(3): 33–8.

Campbell, P.S. (1995) 'Of garage bands and song-getting: The musical development of young rock musicians', *Research Studies in Music Education*, 4: 12–21.

Ericsson, C. (1996) *Elevkultur – Skolkultur i musikundervisningen* [*Pupil Culture – School Culture in Music Teaching*], Lund: Musikhögskolan i Malmö, Lunds Universitet.

Fornäs, J., Lindberg, U. and Sernhede, O. (1988) *Under rocken – Musikens roll i tre unga band* [*Beneath the Rock – The Role of Music in Three Young Bands*], Stockholm: Symposion.

Georgii-Hemming, E. (1999) *Om viljan att spela och lusten att skapa egen musik* [*Of the Will to Play and the Passion to Create: The Music Making of Music Teacher Students*], masters thesis, series D-uppsats 1999:01, Örebro: Örebro Universitet, musikhögskolan i Örebro.

Gullberg, A-K. (1999) *Formspråk och spelregler: En studie i rockmusicerande inom och utanför musikhögskolan* [*Playing by the Rules: A Study of Rock Music Making within and outside the School of Music.*], licentiate thesis 1999:12, Piteå: Luleå tekniska universitet, musikhögskolan i Piteå.

Hargreaves, D. (1986) *The Developmental Psychology of Music*, Cambridge: Cambridge University Press.

Johansson, K.G. (1995) *Rockens historia* [*The History of Rock*], Teaching Compendium, Musikhögskolan i Piteå.

Lilliestam, L. (1995) *Gehörsmusik* [*Music Played by Ear*], Göteborg: Akademiförlaget AB.

Lilliestam, L. (1997) 'On playing by ear', *Popular Music*, 15 (2): 195–216.

Lilliestam, L. (1998) *Svensk rock – musik, lyrik, historic* [*Swedish Rock – Music, Lyrics, History*], Göteborg: Bo Ejeby Förlag.

Olsson, B. (1993) *SÄMUS en musikutbildning i kuturpolitikens tjänst? En studie om en musikutbildning på 1970-talet* [*SÄMUS – Music Education in the Service of a Cultural Policy? A Study of a Teacher Training Programme during the 1970s*], dissertation, Göteborg: Göteborgs universitet.

Olsson, B. (1997) 'The social psychology of music education', in D. Hargreaves and A. North (eds) *The Social Psychology of Music*, pp. 290–307, Oxford: Oxford University Press.

Ruud, E. (1997) *Musikk og identitet* [*Music and Identity*], Oslo: Universitetsforlaget AS.

Säljö, R. (2000) *Lärande i praktiken: Ett sociokulturellt perspektiv* [*Teaching and Learning in Practice: A Sociocultural Perspective*], Stockholm: Bokförlaget Prisma.

Sloboda, J. (1985) *The Musical Mind: The Cognitive Psychology of Music*, Oxford: Clarendon Press.

Steward, S. and Garratt, S. (1984) *Signed, Sealed and Delivered*, London: Pluto Press.

Chapter 14

Priorities in Voice Training: Carrying Power or Tone Quality[1]

Allan Vurma and Jaan Ross

The voices of 42 students studying classical opera singing at the Estonian Academy of Music were investigated to find any objectively definable qualities possibly correlating with the length of training. Each student's singing of a four-bar seven-word initial phrase from a well-known Estonian classical solo was recorded. The recordings were digitalized and subjected to acoustic analysis yielding the long-term average spectrum (LTAS) for each voice studied. It turned out that the longer a singing student had been trained professionally, the higher was the level of the so-called 'singer's formant' in her/his LTAS. Subsequently, the voice quality in each recording was evaluated by four experts using a five-point scale, where five points marked the best quality and one point the poorest. It turned out that the average ratings did not show any positive correlation with the length of training; rather, a slightly negative trend (not statistically significant) could be observed. The results seem to support the critical remarks made by some Estonian specialists about domestic teaching of vocal music perhaps being inadequate in some respects (Pappel, 1990). The teaching process seems to be focused on the development of those qualities which enable the singer to be audible in large concert halls and with a symphony orchestra, while the importance of timbral qualities recedes into the background.

Introduction

As a rule, young people admitted to study opera singing have a good natural voice. Before entering the academy they have usually been spotted for their pleasant voice, either in music lessons at school or at an amateur singing studio. In Estonia, singers' training at the Academy of Music lasts for six to eight years, but it is relatively short in comparison with the violinists and pianists, who have been practising their respective instruments for 12 years *before* starting their studies at the academy.

The level of teaching of professional singers varies considerably across different schools. Students of classical western opera frequently make a beeline either for Carlo Bergonzi's private studio in Milan or for the Hochschule für Musik in Vienna, as these are the schools where teaching is based on the experience of generations. A high level of competition among teachers as well as students, and permanent contact with top-level musical life and scientific research, guarantee most of the graduates future success on the world's stages.

There are also less advanced schools where the teachers have not been part of international musical life at a high level. In addition, they may not exactly be masters of their profession. Combined with the limited choice of students, it may leave many young singers with unresolved problems of voice treatment. Consequently, these singers are left with greatly reduced opportunities to be employed by better opera houses. This was, unfortunately, the situation in Estonian vocal pedagogy in the 1980s and early 1990s, as reflected in several critical articles published in the Estonian musical press (for example, Pappel, 1990). Young singers were criticized for deficiencies in technical skills, unrestrained vibrato and awkward coloratures. In addition, it was pointed out that the compulsory singing of 'big', vocally demanding arias was beyond the under-graduates' capabilities, skills and knowledge. As a result, many students who had trained for longer were observed to have improved on the power and operatic timbre of their voices, yet at the expense of tonal smoothness, free phonation and the expression of musical subtleties.

The present study has been inspired by the necessity to find out whether the subjective impression described above could, by any means, have an objective reason. We hypothesize that vocal training in Estonia has perhaps been focused on the development of such qualities that could be associated with the carrying power of the voice, while less attention has been paid to its timbral qualities.

Carrying Power

Carrying power is what makes a voice audible in large opera houses or concert halls, in the presence of a symphony orchestra (Vennard, 1967). As an opera singer traditionally performs in a large hall with an orchestra and without amplification systems, the carrying power of the voice is of primary importance. It has been found that, although the region of sound pressure variation is broadly the same for both trained and untrained singers, in a performance situation the trained singers can make themselves heard better than the untrained ones (Sundberg, 1997). Singers make their voice carry by employing a special vocal technique, usually acquired during training, that enables them to sing in a sufficiently loud voice with a minimum of physical effort. While trying to make the voice carry better, it is useful to remember that the human auditory system is most sensitive to frequencies in the range between 2 and 4 kHz (Fletcher and Munson, 1933), hereafter referred to as the MS (that is, the most sensitive) area.

A high level of partials in the MS area makes the voice more audible even with the accompaniment of a symphony orchestra. A symphony orchestra reaches the maximum level in its sound spectrum at about 450 Hz, only to decrease rapidly as the frequency rises. Therefore, a singer's voice with strong partials in the MS area can be heard clearly through the orchestral accompaniment (Sundberg 1987, 1991).

What are the articulatory means by which a singer can reach a high level of partials in the MS area of his/her voice spectrum? The voice spectrum depends on the activity of the vocal folds, as well as on the shape of the vocal tract. As we know, the human voice is produced by a periodical opening and closing of the space between the vocal folds (glottis), caused by the pressure of the airflow from the lungs. The result is the so-called 'voice source' (Sundberg, 1977), the ideal spectrum of which consists of harmonic components uniformly decreasing by 12 dB per octave (Baken, 1997). Of course, the real spectrum displays certain deviations from the ideal. The amplitude of the voice source fundamental is sensitive to the strength of the flow pulse, that is, the stronger the flow pulse, the larger the amplitude of the voice source fundamental. The level of the higher partials in the voice source spectrum depends on how rapidly the air stream changes during the flow pulse; rapid alterations in a wave translate to stronger high-frequency components in the wave's spectrum (Baken, 1997, p. 158). The rapidity of change in the airflow, in its turn, is in positive correlation with the amplitude of the flow pulse, the skewing of the pulse waveform and the length of the glottis closed phase. (Due to the inertia of the air column, the closing time of the glottis is shorter than the opening time and the displayed glottal waveform is steeper at onset.)

Mainly by the force keeping the vocal folds apart, different types of phonation can be distinguished, such as pressed, normal, flow and breathy phonation (Sundberg, 1995). Pressed phonation is characterized by a great force keeping the vocal folds apart, a long glottis closed phase in each cycle, a high sub-glottal pressure of the air stream, and yet a narrow amplitude of the glottal pulse. The spectrum of such a voice displays a low amplitude of the F0 and, due to the weak pulse, a relatively low level of sound pressure is generated. Pressed phonation, besides demanding a strong effort from the singer, is the most deleterious to the vocal organs (Benninger et al., 1994). In breathy phonation, however, the force affecting the vocal folds is too weak to allow complete closure of the glottis, so that during the cycle the airflow never actually reaches zero. The sub-glottal air pressure is low, the amplitude of the flow pulse and the air consumption are high, while the level of sound generated is low. The maximum energy can be transferred to the voice in the case of flow phonation, for which a relatively low sub-glottal pressure is combined with a strong flow pulse and a high overall energy level. Flow phonation is characterized by a shorter closed quotient (CQ being a measure of the amount of time the vocal folds are together as a proportion of the entire open/closing cycle (Titze, 1994b)) than pressed phonation, but it is longer than the CQ typical of breathy phonation (Titze 1994a). During transition from a flow phonation to a pressed one, the displayed pulse waveform becomes more skewed to the right as a result of an increase in the proportion of higher partials in the voice source spectrum (Hillman et al., 1990).

Consequently, both flow and breathy phonation enable a higher fudamental frequency (F0) amplitude in the voice source spectrum than pressed phonation. The level of higher partials in the spectrum can be increased by means of a stronger airflow, that is, by singing louder, as well as by using a more pressed type of phonation. For a singer, the most desirable regime would involve singing with a flow phonation which enables them to generate the maximum sound without increased risk of damaging the voice. In addition, flow phonation is characterized by a rather high level of higher partials in the voice source spectrum.

Apart from the activity of the vocal folds, the voice spectrum of a singer depends on the shape of the vocal tract, which functions as a filter. A special feature found in the voice spectra of male singers, as well as female singers with low voices (Bloothooft and Plomp 1984, 1985), is the so-called 'singer's formant'. The singer's formant is produced by the frequencies of the third, fourth and fifth formants of the singing voice moving so close to each other that the resulting cluster appears as a salient consolidated region in the spectrum. The average frequency of the singer's formant depends on the voice category, being approximately 2.4 kHz for basses, 2.6 kHz for baritones, 2.8 kHz for tenors, and 3.0 kHz for altos, even though individual differences may be considerable (Dmitriev and Kiselev, 1979; Sundberg, 1997). Amateur choir singers, as a rule, do not use a singer's formant (Ternström and Sundberg, 1989). The same applies to the performers of old Estonian folksongs (Ross, 1992).

The strength of the singer's formant also depends on the voice category, being somewhat weaker in basses than in tenors. The articulatory way to achieve the singer's formant lies through dilation of the pharyngeal opening so that it becomes a great deal wider than the tracheal one. This happens if a dilated pharynx is combined with a low laryngeal position. It has been suggested that, in addition, there could possibly exist other, still undiscovered ways of producing a singer's formant, which do not require a low larynx (Detweiler, 1994; Sundberg, 1997).

Sopranos differ from other voice categories due to their relatively high F0 range. Their higher spectrum partials can reach up to 700–1000 Hz (F5 up to C6) or even higher. Theoretically, it may thus happen that in a sung vowel the target value of F1 may be lower than F0 (for spoken /u/ and /i/, for example, the approximate F1 values are 350 and 300 Hz, respectively). A problem occurs, however, at high fundamental frequencies. The problem is caused by the harmonics – which, as we know, are integral multiples of F0 in a musical sound – being so widely spaced that some of the formants may not be energized at all (Acker, 1987; Raphael and Scherer, 1987). If, for example, the F0 is 1 kHz, such resonance frequencies of the vocal tract as 500 Hz or 1.5 kHz cannot have much effect on the sound spectrum. In this case sopranos may resort to the so-called 'formant tuning' technique, which involves trying to make the formants and harmonics coincide, resulting in a considerable boost to vocal intensity. Articulatorily, the frequency of the first formant can be raised either by opening the mouth wider or by retracting its corners (like smiling) and using a raised larynx, but this is considered an incorrect vocal technique by several singing teachers. It should be remembered that articulatory changes alter the quality of the sung vowels (Sundberg, 1997). It is possible that the strength of the singer's formant is increased if the fundamental and the first formant are placed in a harmonic relationship (Simonson, 1992). Indeed, good sopranos have been found to use a higher energy level in the 2–4 kHz spectral region than lesser sopranos (Leino and Toivokoski 1994–95). Yet the universal value of the formant tuning technique is questionable as, in attempting to achieve maximum intensity on every note, the voice may lose its smoothness, and a male voice could become too similar to a female one (Carlsson and Sundberg 1992; Titze 1994b).

Voice Quality

It is not easy to find objective terms to define voice quality. In general, it is understood to mean the presence of qualities in the voice which enable the singer to perform music of a certain genre in a near-to-ideal way. The kind of singing voice considered acceptable largely depends on cultural background. Apart from the western classical style, there are various popular styles, such as spiritual, blues, jazz, gospel, rap and rock, requiring vocal techniques (particularly so-called 'belting') dramatically different from the classical one (Benninger et al., 1994, p. 241). In sharp contrast, there are also the singing traditions of various non-European cultures, practised, for example, in Turkey, Iran, Tibet, China, and various African countries. It is empirically possible to find vocal techniques that enable the singer to produce different style-specific sounds without doing much harm to the vocal mechanism, even in the case of a professional singer (Benninger et al., 1994).

As for the western classical style, it is represented by different schools of thought, the principles of which may be conflicting. For example, physiological alterations within the vocal tract, which the German school sees as concomitant to vowel modification, are avoided by the Italian school, as is the low-positioned larynx (Miller, 1977, pp. 91 and 139). At the same time it is admitted that even classical operatic singing may be damaging to the vocal tract if performed incorrectly (Sataloff, 1997, pp. 735–53). One of the techniques potentially detrimental to the quality of the voice is so-called 'forced' singing, whereby the singer exceeds the physical optimum of voice production. Forced singing may result in undesirable changes in the voice quality, making the voice 'dry', 'tense', 'unaesthetic', 'uneven' or 'tremulous' (Ljush, 1988, p. 105). This kind of voice problem may also be caused by attempts at singing vocally demanding music without sufficient technical preparation (Brown, 1996, p. 220).

The vocal characteristics possibly connected with the timbral quality are often described metaphorically by means of various figurative expressions. Each of these characteristics is generally defined by the activity of a definite part of the vocal mechanism (Benninger et al., 1994). Laryngeal activity, for example, is behind such tonal qualities as 'breathy', 'pressed', 'strident', 'edgy', 'harsh', 'firm', 'clear', 'mellow' and 'warm'. The heavy/loud to light/soft scale is also connected with the laryngeal regime. On the other hand, vocal qualities conditioned by the shape of the vocal tract can be associated with such adjectives as 'dark', 'soblike', 'woofy', 'squeezy', 'narrow', 'shrill', 'balanced' or 'bright'.

How the listener evaluates the voice quality may also relate to the continuity in tonal parameters perceived during the performance. As we know, the sound flow is regularly perceived as being divided into segments, for example, words and phrases for speech, or motifs for music. Every such segment has a beginning and an end. In a musical performance it is vital not to violate continuity within a segment (motif), while discontinuation should be used to mark segment boundaries. Discontinuation can be brought about by changes in timbre, loudness or pitch. A singer should control all essential parameters perceptible in the voice, avoiding accidental changes marking unintended segment boundaries (Sundberg, 1994, pp. 106–22).

Another factor possibly affecting the voice quality is the age of the singer. The human vocal mechanism usually matures by the 20th or 21st year of life. Puberty normally changes the female voice between the ages of 12 to 16.5 years, and the male voice between the ages of 13.5 to 18 years (Sataloff, 1997). Men usually experience age-conditioned vocal degeneration from the age of 60, while for women it is, as a rule, connected with the menopause. Ageing may account for loss of the chest register, a narrowing of the vocal compass, certain timbral changes, some loss in voice control, intonational problems, and quavering (Benninger et al., 1994).

A complex evaluation of voice quality by describing all its potential parameters, as well as giving due consideration to cultural background, may turn out to be a voluminous task. Yet the solution can be facilitated a great deal by using competent expert ratings. If all of the experts share the same cultural background and deal with voice problems professionally every day, listening to and, in some cases, working to shape the singing voice (such as those of professional singers, singing teachers and critics), there is good reason to believe that their perception of tonal quality is essentially similar.

Procedure

The aim of this project was to carry out an objective study of the singing voices of the students studying opera singing at the Estonian Academy of Music in 1994, in order to find out whether certain more or less clearly discernible features – either measurable acoustically, like the strength of the singer's formant, or attainable by expert ratings, like tonal quality – could in any way depend on the length of vocal training. The target group consisted of 42 students, including 18 sopranos, 8 mezzo-sopranos, 6 tenors, 6 baritones and 4 basses. The length of training varied from one to ten years. The students were tutored by 12 teachers in all. The age of the students varied from 19 to 35 years. Forty students of the total number were native Estonian speakers, while two were native Russian speakers fluent in Estonian.

The musical material used represented the first four bars (seven words) of the well-known song 'Ei saa mitte vaiki olla' by the Estonian composer Miina Härma (Example 14.1). The phrase was recorded by each student twice, once in E minor and once in A minor. The F0 range, based on a standard, equally tempered tuning, was 165–247 Hz for males and 330–494 Hz for females in the E minor version, and 220–330 Hz for males and 440–660 Hz for females in the A minor version. Three students (two basses and one baritone) of the 42 refused to sing the A minor version, considering it too high for their voices. This refusal was rather unexpected from the baritone; his instructor, however, pointed out the somewhat low, 'basso'-like character of this student's voice. The song from which the extract is taken is ballad-like, with a simple melody and a narrow pitch range (a pure fifth for the phrase in question). It belongs to the repertoire of every classically trained Estonian singer.

Ex. 14.1   A phrase from the well-known song 'Ei saa mitte vaiki olla', by the Estonian composer Miina Härma

Ei saa mit - te   vai - ki ol - la   lau - lu - vii - si   lõ - pe - ta

The recordings were made in a room with a very short reverberation time. The room was chosen in order to avoid possible artefacts in the recordings, which might have been caused by longer reverberation. On the other hand, the room could not be considered a hostile acoustic environment for the singers since, in general, they were familiar with its acoustic properties and, as expected, had learned to cope with them. The recordings were accomplished with an ML19 directional microphone (with the irregularity of the frequency characteristic not exceeding 1.5–2 dB below 5 kHz) and a Sony TCD-D3 tape recorder. The distance between mouth and microphone was 60 cm.

The measurements were obtained in the Laboratory of Phonetics and Speech Technology, at the Institute of Cybernetics, Tallinn, Estonia. The recordings were analysed acoustically using the KAY Elemetrics Company CSL workstation.

The sampling frequency was 16 kHz. Before sampling the recordings were lowpass filtered with a cutoff frequency of 8 kHz. LTAS were calculated for each recording using the Hamming window. 1024-point FFT was used, which corresponds to the filter bandwidth of 23 Hz.

The students' use of the singer's formant technique was estimated from the LTAS by means of the following procedure. First, two peaks were located in the spectrum, the first of which was observed in the MS area, that is, somewhere between 2 and 4 kHz, while the other was below 1 kHz, the area which usually corresponds either to the F0 or to the first formant. Next, the ratio of the first peak to the second was calculated. The higher the resulting value, the stronger the singer's formant in the voice studied and, consequently, the better the voice carries. It was decided to measure the level of the singer's formant relative to the largest maximum in the spectrum because there may occur quite large differences in overall level between different voice productions and, therefore, their comparison with each other does not seem justified.

After this we tried to attain the rate of formant clustering (the singer's formant) used by each student, by calculating the distance between their third and fourth formants in their recordings. The formant frequencies were found using the LPC (linear predictive coding) formant history. The shorter the distance between F3 and F4, the more reason there is to believe that the student has been using the singer's formant. Figure 14.1 illustrates two examples of formant frequency analysis by means of the LPC formant history technique. In the first example (the left panel), the distance between F3 and F4 is small, which refers to the singer's use of the singer's formant. In the other example (the right panel), the formant distance is larger, which is characteristic of a speaking voice.

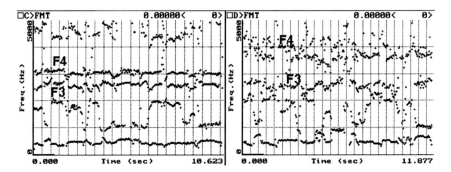

On the left panel, the singer uses the singer's formant technique (the distance between F3 and F4 is small); on the right panel, the singer is not using the singer's formant technique (the distance between F3 and F4 is considerable).

Figure 14.1   Two examples of formant frequency analysis, performed by LPC formant history technique

In order to estimate the voice quality, four experts were consulted. All four teach at the Estonian Academy of Music, and two of them have past experience of heading the Department of Singing. Although the exact criteria of evaluation were not specified, the profession and shared working experience of the experts provide reason to believe that their standards of voice quality evaluation are based on western classical operatic singing and do not differ too much. The experts were instructed to evaluate the tonal quality for each recording, using a five-point scale, so that the best quality would get a 'five' and the poorest rating would be 'one'.

Results

The results of the acoustic analysis of the recordings are presented in Table 14.1, grouped by gender (female and male), voice categories (sopranos, mezzo-sopranos, tenors, baritones, basses), and by tessitura (the keys of E minor and A minor). For each group, the average frequency of the singer's formant (fm2, Hz), its level in relation to the LTAS peak (sform, dB), and the normalized distance of F3 and F4 [(F4–F3)/F3], with standard deviation, have been calculated.

According to the LTAS shapes, the results of the acoustic analysis fall into the following categories (Figure 14.2). First, spectra with a distinct triangle shape, with a high sound level (between –4 and +10 dB) in the MS area, that is, between 2 and 4 kHz (Figure 14.2, top left). Such a spectrum is characteristic of five of the male voices, auditorily perceived as bright and sonorous. There is good reason to believe that these singers use the singer's formant technique. The second type (Figure 14.2, top right) is characterized either by two separate peaks located relatively far from one another, or by a medium energy level (between –6.3 and –9.5 dB) in the MS area. This group includes 11 male singers who are supposedly not so consistent in their use of the singer's formant. The shapes of the LTAS for the female singers (Figure 14.2, bottom left) typically resemble each other much more than those of the male singers. Their maximum energy level in the MS area was –12 to –25 dB, without any distinct peaks. And finally, presented in the right-hand bottom part of Figure 14.2 is the spectrum of the ordinary speaking voice, with no singer's formant to be distinguished.

In order to measure the obvious correlation between the relative distance between F3 and F4 and the strength of the singer's formant, the Pearson Product Moment Correlation Coefficient was used. Table 14.2 presents the coefficient as calculated separately for male and female voices, both performing in E minor and A minor. The results were statistically significant ($p < 0.05$) for all cases. The positive correlation was stronger for the male voices ($p < 0.01$).

Our next point of interest was the possible correlation between the strength of the singer's formant and the average length of professional training, which could vary from one to ten years. Regression analysis indicates (Figure 14.3) that the

Table 14.1   Average data on the singer's formant frequency (fm2, Hz), its level (sform, dB) and the normalized distance between F3 and F4 [(F4–F3)/F3]

	Minor key	Number of voices	fm2 (Hz)	Standard deviation	sform (dB)	Standard deviation	(F4–F3)/F3 (%)	Standard deviation
female	E	26	3337	569	–18.4	3.5	38	6.2
female	A	26	3065	560	–18.4	3.7	43	6.3
male	E	16	2717	338	–8.4	4.9	26	5.5
male	A	13	2732	304	–6.1	8.9	25	5.5
soprano	E	18	3456	572	–17.7	3.4	39	6.7
soprano	A	18	3165	592	–17.9	3.7	44	6.2
mezzo-soprano	E	8	3127	555	–20.0	3.4	36	4.8
mezzo-soprano	A	8	2840	429	–19.5	3.7	39	4.5
tenor	E	6	2612	339	–10.1	7.5	27	6.3
tenor	A	6	2914	359	–6.2	12.4	26	6.6
baritone	E	6	2734	359	–7.2	2.4	24	6.3
baritone	A	5	2585	154	–5.0	5.6	24	5.4
basso	E	4	2848	344	–7.8	2.4	23	2.2
basso	A	2	2552	33	–7.5	6.3	23	0.3

The results presented in Table 14.1 enable the following conclusions to be drawn:

1. In female voices, the singer's formant is higher than in the male voices, the respective frequencies being 3337 Hz (female) and 2717 Hz (male) in E minor, and 3065 Hz (female) and 2732 Hz (male) in A minor.

2. The sound level corresponding to the singer's formant is higher for the male than for the female singers (the average values being –8.4 dB (male) and –18.4 dB (female) in E minor, and –6.1 dB (male) and –18.4 dB (female) in A minor, respectively).

3. In the female singers, the relative distance between F3 and F4 is greater than in the male singers (the average values for E minor being 38 per cent (female) and 26 per cent (male), while for A minor they are 43 per cent (female) and 25 per cent (male), respectively).

4. In the mezzo-sopranos, the singer's formant occurs at lower frequencies than in the sopranos (the average values being 3127 Hz (mezzo-soprano) and 3456 Hz (soprano) in E minor, while in A minor they are 2840 Hz (mezzo-soprano) and 3165 Hz (soprano), respectively).

5. In the male voices, no positive correlation could be ascertained between the voice category and the frequency of the singer's formant, as when moving from lower to higher voices in E minor the frequency of the singer's formant was – contrary to expectations – seen to drop (the average values being 2848 Hz for basses, 2734 Hz for baritones, and 2612 Hz for tenors).

longer the period of study, the stronger the singer's formant. The correlation is proved statistically significant ($p < 0.05$) for both male and female voices in both voice ranges studied (E minor and A minor). For the females who had

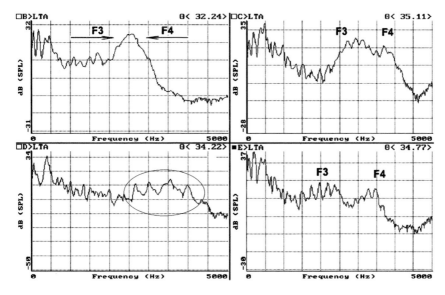

A male singer using the singer's formant technique (top left); a male singer using the singer's formant technique inconsistently (top right); a typical female singer (bottom left); a singer who does not use the singer's formant technique (bottom right).

Figure 14.2   The shape of the LTAS of different recorded voices

Table 14.2   Correlation between the level of the highest peak between 2 and 4 kHz in the LTAS and the distance between F3 and F4, normalized with respect to F3, in the spectra of male and female voices, performing in two different voice ranges (the keys of E and A minor, respectively)

	Key	**Correlation coefficient** (Pearson Product Moment Correlation)	*p* value
Male	E min	−0.637	0.008
	A min	−0.717	0.006
Female	E min	−0.533	0.005
	A min	−0.407	0.039

studied western operatic singing from one to two years, the average maximum level in the MS area was −20.5 dB, while for the females who had studied for seven years or more, the average maximum level increased to −15.6 dB. For male singers the corresponding levels were −11.6 dB and −2.5 dB.

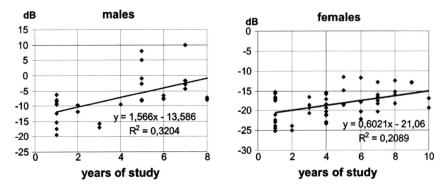

Horizontal axis: number of years studied; vertical axis: level of the highest peak between 2 and 4 kHz in the LTAS in relation to level of the highest peak below 1 kHz in the spectrum; dots correspond to individual singers.

Figure 14.3   Level of the singer's formant in the voice spectrum as a function of the length of training, approximated by linear regression

Expert ratings of the voice quality were collected for every recording. Of the five-point scale, 'one' as the poorest grade was never used. The sums of the ratings given to each recording by the four experts ranged from 9 to 20 points. In order to estimate inter-judge reliability, correlation was calculated for each pair of rating lists (out of the total six) produced by the four experts. The correlation coefficients calculated ranged from 0.37 to 0.47; we decided that the criteria were similar enough for our purposes, indicating fairly robust inter-judge reliability.

Figure 14.4 demonstrates that there is practically no correlation between the average expert ratings and the length of voice training, as the curve of linear regression generally stays level as the period of study lengthens, or even shows a slight fall. Consequently, according to average expert ratings, the quality of voices that had been trained for longer was not any better than that of the beginners. We also assume that the test group was not affected significantly by the age factor. Individuals from 19 to 35 years of age are, on the one hand, physiologically mature; on the other hand, the effects of ageing on their voices are not very significant (except in the ossification of some cartilages, which normally begins during the twenties (Sataloff, 1997)).

Discussion

A good opera singer should have a voice that carries well enough to be heard in large halls, or with the accompaniment of a big orchestra, without amplification

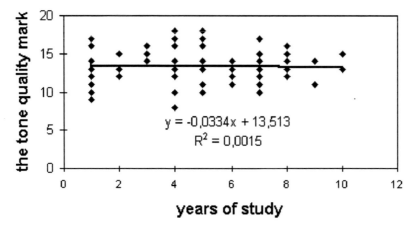

Horizontal axis: number of years studied; vertical axis: the sum of the marks (on a five-point scale) by experts; dots correspond to individual singers.

Figure 14.4   Average voice quality, estimated by four experts, as a function of the length of training, approximated by linear regression

systems. At the same time, the singer should be able to sing for hours without doing harm to her/his vocal mechanism, while the voice should still be flexible enough to correspond to the character of the music being performed. Some singers can cope with the above challenges better than others.

Our analysis of the voices of the students studying classical opera at the Estonian Academy of Music permits the conclusion that the longer a student has been trained in singing, the higher is the level of overtones between 2 and 4 kHz in their voice spectrum. This characteristic of the spectrum can be associated with the better carrying power of the voice and its increased audibility with an orchestral background, as well as with a certain timbral brightness. In order to achieve this, singers used the singer's formant technique, clustering the frequencies of F3, F4 and F5. Expert ratings did not reveal any correlation between the quality of a singing voice and the length of its professional training, which seems to indicate that during vocal training more attention is being paid to the development of the carrying power of a student's voice than to the improvement of its timbral qualities.

Two issues of methodological character may need brief comments below, as they are directly related to the relevance of the results obtained in the present study. The first issue is concerned with the choice of test stimulus. Our main aim here was to use an excerpt which would be familiar to all students, including the beginners, in order to ensure that the students would not experience any difficulties in reading the music. The piece of music used was a simple melody with a narrow pitch range (Example 14.1), which may raise issues as to whether it could have been associated with folksong repertoire rather than with operatic singing, and therefore whether voice production more appropriate to folksongs could have been applied by the students. However, the particular musical excerpt possesses several features which are not characteristic to the local folksong idiom, but clearly belong to the western classical tradition. For example, the second phrase of the melody (not included in Example 14.1) contains a modulation to the parallel major, a feature not typical to Estonian folksongs.

The second comment is related to the evaluation of the students' voices by the expert panel. In a limited community (like a small country, and the Academy of Music in that country in particular), it is hardly possible to avoid the situation where justified guesses will be made by judges with respect to the origin of evaluated material, even when all possible measures have been taken in order to ensure the objectivity of the evaluation process. However, the small dispersion of the correlation coefficient values in paired comparisons of lists produced by different judges, as well as the consistent level of positive scores, demonstrate a reasonable consensus in the evaluation process between the panel members. This, as it seems to us, allows the results of the evaluation to be considered reliable.

Finally, it does not seem entirely surprising that the duration of vocal training should lead to increases in carrying power, and yet to no discernible change in tonal quality. As a rule, the students are chosen for entrance to the Academy of Music on the basis of their promising ability; that is, their tonal quality. Vocal training should serve to ensure that tonal quality is preserved throughout the singing range, as well as under vocally taxing conditions, such as filling a large concert hall or being heard over an orchestra. It should be noted that the success or failure of the Estonian Academy of Music to prepare well-trained singers also depends on the size of the pool from which the students can be selected, and that until very recent years this has mostly been restricted by the limits of the country, the population of which equals less than 1.5 million inhabitants.

Note

1. Parts of this paper have been presented at the Finnic Phonetics Symposium in Pärnu, Estonia, 11–14 August 1998, and published in the Proceedings of the Symposium: Linguistica Uralica, Vol. 34, No. 3, pp. 283–7, 1998. The present chapter is an abridged version of the article published in *Musicae Scientiae*, 4(1): 75–93 (2000). Reprinted with permission of the editor.

References

Acker, B.F. (1987) 'Vocal tract adjustments for the projected voice', *Journal of Voice*, 1: 77–82.

Baken, R.J. (1997) 'An overview of laryngeal function for voice production', in R.T. Sataloff (ed.), *Professional Voice: The Science and Art of Clinical Care*, pp. 147–165, New York: Raven Press.

Benninger, M.S., Jacobson, B.H. and Johnson, A.F. (eds) (1994) *Vocal Arts Medicine: The Care and Prevention of Professional Voice Disorders*, New York: Theime Medical Publishers.

Bloothooft, G. and Plomp, R. (1984) 'Spectral analysis of sung vowels I', *Journal of the Acoustical Society of America*, 75: 1259–64.

Bloothooft, G. and Plomp, R. (1985) 'Spectral analysis of sung vowels II', *Journal of the Acoustical Society of America*, 77: 1580–88.

Brown, O.L. (1996) *Discover Your Voice: How to Develop Healthy Voice Habits*, San Diego, London: Singular Publishing Group.

Carlsson, G. and Sundberg, J. (1992) 'Formant frequency tuning in singing', *Journal of Voice*, 6: 256–60.

Detweiler, R.F. (1994) 'An investigation of the laryngeal system as the resonance source of the singer's formant', *Journal of Voice*, 8: 303–13.

Dmitriev, L. and Kiselev, A. (1979) 'Relationship between the formant structure of different types of singing voices and the dimension of supraglottal cavities', *Folia Phoniatrica*, 31: 238–41.

Fletcher, H. and Munson, W.A. (1933) 'Loudness: Its definition, measurement, and calculation', *Journal of the Acoustical Society of America*, 5: 82–108.

Hillman, R.E., Holmberg, E.B., Perkell, J.S., Walsh, M. and Vaughan, C. (1990) 'Phonatory function associated with hyperfunctionally related vocal fold lesions', *Journal of Voice*, 4: 52–63.

Leino, T. and Toivokoski, R. (1994–95) 'Miten laulajaan äänenlaatua voidaan mitata' ['How can we measure the voice quality?'], *Laulupedagoogi*, 1994/95: 29–45.

Ljush, D. (1988) *Rashvitije i sohranenije pevcheskogo golosa* [*Development and care of the singing voice*], Kiev: Muzichna Ukraina.

Miller, R. (1977) *English, French, German and Italian Techniques of Singing: A Study in National Preferences and How They Relate to Functional Efficiency*, Meluchen, NJ: The Scarecrow Press.

Pappel, K. (1990) 'Vokaalprobleemidest kaheteistkümnendal tunnil I–IV' ['About vocal problems in the last minute I–IV'], *Reede*, 4: 11; 7: 11; 13: 11; 15: 11.

Raphael, B.N. and Scherer, R.C. (1987) 'Voice modifications of stage actors: Acoustic analyses', *Journal of Voice*, 1: 83–7.

Ross, J. (1992) 'Formant frequencies in Estonian folk singing', *Journal of the Acoustical Society of America*, 91: 3532–9.

Sataloff, R.T. (1997) 'Clinical anatomy and physiology of the voice', in R.T. Sataloff (ed.), *Professional Voice: The Science and Art of Clinical Care*, pp. 111–30, New York: Raven Press.

Simonson, D. (1992) 'Harmonic relationship between sung pitch, the first vowel formant and the singing formant. A study in enhancing acoustical efficiency in singing', *Voice*, 1: 103–24.

Sundberg, J. (1977) 'The acoustics of the singing voice', *Scientific American*, 3: 82–91.

Sundberg, J. (1987) *The Science of the Singing Voice*, Illinois: DeKalb.

Sundberg, J. (1991) *The Science of Musical Sounds*, London: Academic Press.

Sundberg, J. (1994) 'Perceptual aspects of singing', *Journal of Voice*, 8: 106–22.

Sundberg, J. (1995) 'Vocal fold vibration patterns and modes of phonation', *Folia Phoniatrica et Logopaedica*, 47: 218–28.

Sundberg, J. (1997) 'Vocal tract resonance', in R.T. Sataloff (ed.), *Professional Voice: The Science and Art of Clinical Care*, pp.167–84, New York: Raven Press.

Ternström, S. and Sundberg, J. (1989) 'Formant frequencies of choir singers', *Journal of the Acoustical Society of America*, 86: 517–22.

Titze, I.R. (1994a) *Principles of Voice Production*. Englewood Cliffs, NJ: Prentice-Hall.

Titze, I.R. (1994b) 'Acoustics of the tenor high voice', *Journal of the Acoustical Society of America*, 95: 1133–42.

Vennard, W. (1967) *Singing, the Mechanism and Technique*, New York: Karl Fisher.

PART 4

Researching Musician Identity and Perception

Chapter 15

Rethinking Voice Evaluation in Singing

António G. Salgado

Introduction

It is generally accepted in the history of western art singing that vocal specialization and labelling appeared in the nineteenth century as a consequence of the loss of the *Bel canto* tradition and ideals. *Bel canto* consisted of the ability to communicate human emotions by singing precisely notated musical phrases with a wide range of qualities based on the exclamatory vowels – 'ah' for pleasure, 'ee' for disgust and hatred, 'oo' for fear and horror – as a means of interpretation, extending across a wide range of several octaves (Manén, 1974). The *Bel canto* singer was supposed to be able to sing a vast array of qualities covering all different kinds of vocal compartments. According to Hahn (1920), the voice was 'meant to be moulded in an infinite degree, passing through all the colors of the sound prism'. Later, singers gradually began to have to cope with operatic roles which required more specialized qualities of sound, and this led to a process of training the voice which was more influenced by the technical demands of the music and less connected to the fundamental role of the voice as the expression of emotion (Newham, 1998).

Whilst *Bel canto* singers were intent on mastering the art of extending the different possible emotional qualities and the imaginative characteristics of each note, later singers sought to specialize in the perfection of a single operatic quality of voice and they resisted trying to extend their range beyond what was required of the particular operatic role. What has become known as traditional voice evaluation (TVE) was born out of this context, where a distinct vocal quality was allotted to a role and was increasingly constrained to a specific pitch range. Indeed eventually, rather than a role requiring a certain type of voice, composers wrote for the specific voice type. So, the label became the requirement, rather than a particular type of singer being chosen for a specific role. This sense of compartmentalization became increasingly fixed, with clear labels emerging – *heroic tenor, coloratura soprano*, and so on. These labels did vary according to the tastes of particular periods, but nowadays they have become much more stable, with most singers and teachers having a model for what constitutes a heroic or coloratura voice.

The current chapter explores the impact of TVE on vocal formation and vocal education. It considers how conservatoires and academies of music deal with vocal evaluation and how people within the profession of singing are affected by their training and subsequent categorization. The research was carried out drawing on the research methodology of Interpretative Phenomenological Analysis from social psychology. In other words, a methodological approach from another discipline was adopted to explore the current issue.

As a consequence of the historical situation explained above, at very different levels of vocal education and career, students and singers want to understand their vocal identity. They search for evaluation, classification, *a label*. The wish to be identified with a timbre of voice can lead to individuals desiring to sound like someone they have heard before: a teacher or a great singer. Common concerns include: 'How do I sound?', 'What type of voice do I have?', 'Am I a soprano or a mezzo?', 'Which repertoire is the most appropriate for my voice?' Despite the pertinence of these questions, it is often very difficult to give the singer a *straight* and *fair* answer, for there are indeed many issues to be considered and a single label cannot possibly capture all of them. This is in part the aim of the current chapter: to identify the components that make up the singer and the singing voice and also to explore how individuals feel about the TVE labels.

Given the questions provoked by TVE, it seemed essential to investigate what impact giving the voice a particular specification has on the singer, in particular:

- How does a person's creation of a vocal identity come about through the multiplicity of choices that the art of singing poses?
- How does the singer experience a sense of self within the process of singing (of course, just as in everyday life, where there is great variability in individual presentation and perception, the sense of the singer's self is not as rigid as the imposed labels of 'lyric soprano' or 'high baritone' would suggest)?
- How, in fact, do singers cope with the labelling process of singing and what alternatives may be available?

The analysis presented here is based on the data from a series of 40 interviews, with 20 students at conservatoire level and 20 professional singers, working and studying in Portugal, England and Austria, where answers to the questions outlined above were sought.

Analysis

Through qualitative semi-structured interviews, and then Interpretive Phenomenological analysis (see Smith et al., 1999) several key findings on TVE came to light, summarized as follows:

1. The majority of professional singers (62 per cent) and students (76 per cent) reported having had problems with TVE.
2. The singers commented that because of the voice type they had been categorized into, they had often encountered problems in their learning process.

The students' problems were identified as follows:

- Fifty-two per cent said their voices have often been wrongly evaluated and they had been put into a vocal category that they felt not to suit them. Because of this situation, they had often changed voice classification during their study period. This appeared to have occurred at a rate of 20 per cent during their vocal studies with the same teacher, and at a rate of 40 per cent when they actually changed vocal teacher.
- The changes in categorization led to a very confused self-identification. This was seen as a result of the different quality of sound required for the new categorization, and the different types of roles and repertoire that fall within the new voice classification. After the change of category, 36 per cent of the students interviewed had to deal with such different vocal and emotional qualities that some of them finally considered the possibility of giving up singing altogether.
- Thirty-four per cent of the students ended up suffering from severe vocal stress when they tried to manage the vocal difficulties imposed by the 'different' repertoire. Among the main reasons for this situation were severe voice disorders, self-discouragement and depression.

Outside of the training environment, of course, vocal identity is no less of an issue. As a result of this research, it was brought to light that in professional work, singers have to manage their voices in order to 'negotiate' the set of roles that their vocal categorization dictates. A number of professional singers felt that their voices did not fit all of these roles, but because of their specific operatic contract – 'to sing all lyric roles', for instance – they tried to fit with the external view of who and what they should be as a singer. The reality was that sometimes they ended up performing repertoire that did not suit them at all. Or, otherwise, they were not allowed to perform repertoire that, though it would suit them individually, did not fit with the vocal category they were pushed into.

The problems identified by the professionals can be divided into five main themes:

1. At the very beginning of their professional lives, when auditioning for agents and theatres, 45 per cent of the singers interviewed said that they had problems knowing which categorization to apply for.

2. Even when they were accepted according to a particular label (lyric tenor, for instance) it was impossible for them to cope (vocally or emotionally) with all the different challenges that the vocal categorization dictated. This situation often led to a more complex one, a professional one, where the singer had to cancel or change his/her contract with the opera house. Here, the potential consequences were dire: an end to a job, a breach of contract, self-discouragement and often consequent personal depression. In some of these cases, the situation was responsible for major, and even irreparable, vocal disorders.

3. Thirty-nine per cent were not allowed to perform repertoire that, though it would have suited them individually, did not fit with the vocal category they had been pushed into and, consequently, according to the contract they were engaged with, they could not perform it. This situation also often led to a more complex one, where a role would suit the singer individually and could have helped in the progress of his/her career, but, because it belonged to a different TVE, meant that colleagues and the management of the opera theatres would not allow them to audition for the role.

4. Forty-seven per cent of the singers stated that they regarded their voice specialization as an imprisonment.

5. Thirty-five per cent of the interviewed singers confessed that they somehow felt they did not fit within any of the categorizations offered by TVE. As a result, 30 per cent of the singers interviewed had considered the possibility of stopping their careers for a period of time while they tried to cope with the three major difficulties that appeared through all these different situations: voice disorders as a result of a wrong use of the voice, self-discouragement as a result of a loss of self-identification, and depression as a result of a working conflict or an irreparable voice disorder.

Discussing Voice Classification and Evaluation

According to the findings above, TVE seems, if not an unnecessary, then at least an insufficient and, perhaps, undesirable way to shape the voice, the personality, and the process of self-identification in singing. So, it seems important to eliminate the weaknesses of the traditional model by redressing the present TVE processes, and at the same time beginning to identify what parameters might be adequate to build on the strengths of the existing labels for the voice to assist singers with their sense of vocal identity.

From the results, it seems that TVE should not be, as a model of voice classification and as a process of self-identification, regarded as being more valid then any other approach, and perhaps it should appear as a final stage in the training process and of particular interest to the student and to the teacher in the process of shaping the voice as well as, critically, the personality. To label a voice as *bass-buffo*, for instance (as stated by a singer at one of the interviews), made it impossible, for a long period of time, for one man to establish a vision of himself and of his voice that could serve the multiple and different characters and interpretations he felt he was able to express. The single compartment of being only one type of voice was an imprisonment for him.

Of course, it is important to know how the voice sounds and what its real boundaries are so that damage is not done and so that realistic targets are set. Therefore, it is important to research voice evaluation with the intention of being able to assess, in a more tolerant and objective way, the diversity of human voices and, at the same time, find a grounded vocal identity that will accommodate the multiple manifestations and different expressions that the voice will assume in the process of singing. Turning to some of the most recent approaches in voice therapy, alongside some recent biological and technical advancements, it seems that there is potentially a new and far more objective way forward. For instance, the following questions seem like pertinent points of departure:

- What is general and common to all voices and can therefore be a starting point of vocal work for everybody?
- What can be objectified and measurable about the voice and might therefore constitute valid and contributory evidence for vocal self-identification?
- What other domains of expression could possibly contribute towards a more clear and objective way to help singers in their process of self-identification and self-expression?
- What method(s) or voice conception(s) may contribute more effectively to establish a polycentric vision of the psyche and of the voice by which a person, in the creative process of singing, is able to experience – not as a fixed being, but rather as a different persona at different times?

Voice therapy workers (for example, Ida Kerelova, who worked in the UK some years ago but has now established the International School for the Human Voice in the Czech Republic; Paul Newham, who directs the Royal Society of Arts Examinations Board Diploma in Voice Movement Therapy in London, UK and Boston, USA) have been using an approach in which the singer starts the process of voice-work in a general way, based on general principles of voice use and self-identification which aim to free the body and voice for openness and fullness of expression. Within this approach, the singer starts the singing process by exploring the different registers (modal or chest register, falsetto or head register, whistle and vocal fry registers); by practising the tones with all the significant changes of the vocal tract, vocal resonance, and vocal support (breath support is included here, but also the ability to hear support, structure support, and so on); and working on all combinations of the other components and parameters by which one's voice can be affected such as pitch, pitch fluctuation (vibrato), intensity, attack, support, register, resonance and timbre. They believe that this process culminates in allowing the singers to vocalize all aspects; that is, to work with all emotional resources and all the timbres they are capable of producing. It means that rather than just working the 'beautiful' part of the voice ('correct', even, legato line), the singers will understand that ugliness, fearfulness, fearlessness, sadness, strangeness, and other qualities can and should be perceived as a part of the learning process and contributory to the creative processes of singing and vocal timbre.

In some other approaches, the singing student works deliberately at cultivating self-awareness: awareness of the body, of its structure, of its gesture and movement, and of the qualities of the voice. By exploring these areas, the aim is that the student becomes more self-aware, coordinated and 'in control'. Examples of such approaches include the Alexander Technique (Alexander, 1987) adapted as a vocally-orientated framework (for example, in the work of London-based singing teacher Ron Murdoch (for more information, see Newham, 1998)). By moving from the general to the specific and by addressing the issue of self-awareness from the start of the training process, it seems that the student may become more aware of the many nuances occurring in vocal quality, and also explore the corresponding kinesthetic perception, or physical sensation, of the sound produced, as well as the emotional and psychological issues expressed. Through all of these means the singer seems to be potentially more able to use the singing voice to express himself/herself in an open and multiple way, and to identify his/her personal process with the process of singing itself, by combining the physical and emotional aspects. However, it is imperative that these alternatives to TVE are systematically studied to see whether they are objectively better for the singer. This would be a critical step for the researcher interested in these issues.

Other approaches do try to bring further knowledge to the process of voice-objectification and evaluation in singing, through more experimental and scientific methods based on laboratory research instruments. Of course, in a short chapter such as this, there is no space to give an exhaustive account of all existing labels of voice, or the many different approaches to voice-work currently used. Nevertheless, it is important to examine some of the information that could possibly shed new light on the present discussion. Below, the conclusions established by Husson (1962), based on the results of the *Chronaxie Recurrentielle* (CR), serve as an example of a more objective exploration of the voice. (The CR is an electrical tool which measures the excitability of the vocal folds through the recurrent nerve, which is exactly the same as the excitability of the branch of the spinal nerve which innervates the sterno-cleido-mastoideus muscle, and which is very easy to access, being directly under the skin of the neck.) As Husson (1962) wrote: 'It is a very important prognostic for the beginner's voice and a very important diagnostic for the singer's voice since it gives the exact determination of the singer's physiological vocal range, based on the excitability of the recurrent nerve.' It is surprising, given its usefulness, that CR has not been more widely adopted, especially since it is not an invasive technique.

According to the CR results:

1. The classification of a voice range has nothing to do with timbre or intensity, qualities that basically determine the different categories of voice specialization in TVE (range, timbre and intensity).
2. The classification offered through CR is continuous, whereas TVE classification focuses on the existence of separate types (biotypes) of voice.
3. Voices of 'intermediate' ranges appear (they are intermediate in relation to the categories fixed by TVE classification).

Again, more study is required, but CR shows that the employment of scientific techniques might be very helpful to the singer. As the approaches of researchers such as Newham and Husson show, it seems that by examining the singer's vocal production from a physiological and psychological perspective might be a productive way to maximize the potentiality of vocal classification. Of course, in the short term, the issues of repertoire and the historical conventions of the opera house will persist, but perhaps these more integrated and proactive attempts by practitioners to understand the voice and the singer in greater detail will help to overcome the problems of TVE.

References

Alexander, F.M. (1987) *The Use of the Self*, London: Victor Gollancz.

Hahn, R. (1920) *Du Chant*, Paris: Editions Pierre Lafitte.

Husson, R (1962) *Le Chant*, Paris: Presses Universitaires de France.

Manén, L. (1974) *The Art of Singing*, London: Faber Music.

Newham, P. (1998) *Therapeutic Voice Work*, London: Jessica Kingsley Publishers.

Smith, J.A., Jarman, M. and Osborn, M. (1999) 'Doing interpretative phenomenological analysis', in Murray, M. and Chamberlain, K. (eds) *Qualitative Health Psychology: Theories and Methods*, pp. 219–40, London: Sage.

Chapter 16

Assessing Vocal Performance[1]
Daniela Coimbra and Jane W. Davidson

Introduction

If a performer is 'an exhibitionist' engaged in 'carrying out notable feats' (Oxford English Dictionary), it seems that there may be particular circumstances that help him or her to develop performance skills. This is an issue which should be of central interest to the music practitioner, especially the teacher. The current chapter goes some way towards exploring the skills involved in classical vocal performance by investigating the relationship between the performer and the audience in the context of student musical examinations. An aim of the research was to explore the criteria used by expert audiences when making judgements of young singers, in order that some insight might be gained into what experts expect of student performers. But, more relevantly here, the entire project enabled us to look at the communication process between performer and audience to explore whether or not the singers were aware of the audience's thoughts about their performance and whether or not the audience members had an awareness of how they were communicating themselves to the performers. The chapter draws on work published by the authors, mainly in Davidson and Coimbra (2001), which gives detailed analysis of the assessors' questionnaires. But we refer the reader also to further publications drawing on the same data set for further information: a detailed analysis of the students' questionnaires and reports is presented in Kokotsaki et al. (2001).

Contextualizing the Research Project

To date there has been little research interest in the topic of how audiences assess classical music performance. Of the existing studies within the western art music tradition in the US and Europe, research evidence shows strong (subconscious) racial preferences, with judges preferring performances by people of like races (Elliott, 1995; Green, 1997). Gender stereotypes have also been found to have strong influences, such as male trumpeters being rated more highly than un-stereotypical players like female trumpeters (O'Neill and Boulton, 1996). At a psychological level, these biases obviously need to be understood if we are to understand how audiences operate, and, also if a fair and suitably objective means of assessing performance is to evolve, such effects need to be investigated.

Performers and audiences in completely authentic performance situations have rarely been studied. In terms of judges evaluating students, the only study we have been able to identify that occurs in a real musical assessment situation at higher education/professional standard is an out-moded and empirically flawed study by Manturzewska (1970). She did, however, explore judging consistency in a detailed examination of the International Chopin Piano Contest in Warsaw. She revealed that when evaluators heard tapes of the contestants in a random order, with surreptitious repetitions, there was very little correlation between their ratings. The order of the performances seemed to have a significant effect on appraisal of performance quality. For instance, if a performance followed a particularly mistake-ridden interpretation, it would tend to receive high marks.

Manturzewska's study also raised a number of questions related to 'in group' versus 'out group' biases in judgement. That is, she found that assessors who knew the candidates awarded them more generous marks. This is clearly an issue that needs further and systematic study.

Wapnick et. al. (1997) carried out a brief study of university entrance auditions for singers and discovered that singers who were more animated, smiled more often and established more eye contact with the audience were rated as more attractive and generally as better performers.

Thus it seems important to consider the role of non-verbal communication in the performer–audience interaction. Some research highlights the importance of this form of communication. For example, Davidson (1991, 1993, 1994), in a series of studies about the content of body movements in musical performance, discovered that musical intentions were more clearly revealed in physical gestures than in musical sounds, suggesting the critical perceptual role of the body in understanding and communicating a musical work to the audience. Sundberg (1982), in a study of speech, song and the emotions, argued that there is a connection between the psychological emotion to be transmitted, the performer's external body movements and the acoustic consequences of the gesture of the speech organ – the internal body movements of the vocal tract which result in varying the timbre of the singing tone.

In spite of the fact that some performers and teachers are aware of the importance of body movement in conveying musical expression, the extent to which body movements are considered important criteria is not clear. Thus the study described here aimed to explore the extent to which evaluative audiences consciously use this non-verbal information in their communication.

The problem of how to gather information about assessors' criteria in music evaluation was an outstanding question for the research project. Tuncks (1987) addressed the issue by proposing a model of evaluation to be done by using a 'goodness of fit' method of comparison between the performance to be assessed, and the ideal performance that the assessors are asked to have in mind. Contrastingly, Thompson et al. (1998) developed a technique to explore the constructs used by assessors in the adjudication of music performance. Saunders and Holahan (1997) developed formal multiple choice rating scales in the evaluation of high-school instrumental performances. Since it is evident that there might be a number of different approaches to finding out what criteria assessors apply during the assessment process, our research developed drawing on a number of different techniques in an attempt to maximize the depth of data collection. Grids and questionnaires often require careful piloting before the experimenter can be sure that he or she is asking the right sort of questions. Qualitative semi-structured interviews, however, provide a good forum for asking exploratory questions out of which issues can emerge, and several interviews can be cross-referenced for similar thematic content. Thus, we focused on such qualitative techniques combined with rating scale assessments of individual aspects and then overall scores for the performances.

As for additional points which came to our attention when planning our study, it is noteworthy that in Saunders and Holahan's work it was discovered that both teachers and assessors discriminate readily between levels of technical and artistic attainment, and use these two distinct categories to determine an area of 'performance error'. In the recommendations emerging out of their research the authors suggest that in order to obtain a more objective level of evaluation, the repertoire presented by the student should be standardized: that is, all being assessed should perform the same repertoire so that direct comparisons can be made. We wondered whether this would be an issue for our assessors.

Again, surveying previous literature, we discovered that no explanation of how the elements that are said to constitute musical performance quality are judged had been attempted in the existing body of research. There is an acknowledgement that performances comprise both technical merit and aesthetic appeal like Saunders and Holahan's work describe, yet there are no indications about what stocks of knowledge are being drawn upon when assessments are made. So the work we report in this chapter was an attempt to explore what these criteria may be. Thus, in application, the results of the current study could inform practitioners about how best to assess musical performance and, moreover, how to design measures of musical performance suitable for a specific population.

The Research Design and Procedure

Working with Robin Bowman, Head of Vocal Studies at the Guildhall School of Music and Drama in London, 21 second-year vocal studies students' mid-term performance assessment procedures were investigated. Here, quantitative data were collected, providing overall scores so that ordering effects and variability in scoring between assessors could be examined. Also qualitative data were collected so that individual assessor style and criteria could be extrapolated.

The mid-term assessment context has been chosen primarily for ethical reasons, in that we did not wish to put the students under unnecessary duress, perhaps jeopardizing their degree results. Mid-term examinations are 'real' in that they are used as indicators to staff and students about likely finals outcomes, but they do not contribute to the final grading. A panel of four highly experienced singer/ assessors sat in judgement of the students.

Of the four assessors, three were 'insiders', that is, they work in the Department of Vocal Studies: two were female, and taught a number of the students in one-to-one settings; one was male and Head of Vocal Studies, and knew all of the students well, but did not teach any of them singing. The last assessor that took part in the experiment was regarded in a different light for he knew none of the students, nor did he teach any of them singing. In this way, he was an 'outsider' and we referred to him in the study as the 'external assessor'. This meant that we could study the effects of 'insider' versus 'outsider' knowledge in the assessment process.

The assessors were provided with two sheets of paper for each candidate. On the first, they were asked to make free comments about the student's performance of each of three pieces sung by the student, a number of songs agreed by the Head of the Vocal Studies Department in accordance with the course requirements at that stage in the degree course. Thus, the task was believed to be completely appropriate to the student's level of training.

At the bottom of these 'open-ended' assessment sheets we asked the assessors to award a grade. The Guildhall usually grades students on an A to E letter ranking. We allowed the assessors to use this, but also we displayed comparative banding for percentage grades and degree classifications so that various comparative statistical tests could be undertaken. There were no specific written criteria for the degree bands, but none of the assessors asked for clarification, so we were intrigued to explore what features they believed constituted each category.

After the singer's performance was completed and he/she left the concert room, one further sheet of specific questions was completed by each assessor. These questions asked:

- if the assessor knew the student, and if so, in what capacity;
- how well they knew the pieces being presented;
- whether the assessors felt that the repertoire was appropriate to the candidate;
- what were the major strengths and weaknesses of the performance; and
- what impressions were they left with, and were these impressions different to their initial thoughts.

We sketched these questions to explore the influence of the previous knowledge on assessment, what the assessors considered to make a good/bad performance and what struck them most about the singer. In other words, we were trying to establish their rating criteria.

Then, the assessors were asked to participate in a round table discussion, during which time each assessor was asked to state her/his opinion. After this procedure, the original marks were read out and were modified at this point, if necessary, by the individual assessor.

This whole procedure was devised in consultation with Robin Bowman as a means of preventing one assessor from dominating the joint report which was to be given to each singer – again, a regular practice at the Guildhall School. We realized that our particular means of data collection would have an effect on the assessment procedure, but since we were most interested in the assessment criteria rather than the dynamics of the assessment protocol, we did not feel that the imposition of a systematic round table discussion negatively affected the assessment procedure. On the contrary, the assessors stated that they enjoyed and learned from this means of data collection.

In order to establish a final grade for the singer, the average score (the *mean*) of the four individual marks was calculated. These quantifiable data were then subjected to statistical analyses and constitute part of the results we shall discuss here. In the round table discussion, the assessors not only summarized their own written reports, but they offered comments in order to construct a collaborative final report which was transcribed by the first author who sat in the concert room with the assessors throughout the performances. This collective report was eventually given to the students along with their grades. All performances were recorded on video and all discussions were tape-recorded.

Detailed qualitative analyses were made of the assessors' report sheets and the discussion material. These analyses were based on Interpretative Phenomenological Analysis as outlined by Smith (1995). This technique involves the researcher in a detailed and re-iterative process in which a written transcript of the tape-recorded discussions and free-response written questionnaires were subjected to a process of theme extrapolation. Although time-consuming, this technique enabled a lot of detailed to be collected.

Results

Here, a general overview of the results is presented, since the aim of this chapter is a detailed description of an empirical investigation, rather than offering details of how to undertake an analysis. However, this general perspective draws the reader's attention to the fact that much data were generated in this work, and thus hopefully illustrates the importance for both psychologists and practitioners of this kind of investigative approach.

In summary, the results demonstrate individual differences between the assessors. Indeed, as can be seen in Table 16.1, the 'external' assessor's grades were not only the highest, but also showed the smallest amount of variation (smallest deviation from his average score) of the four adjudicators. The fact

Table 16.1   **Mean scores and standard deviations for each assessor**

	Mean (%)	Standard Deviation
Assessor A	56.35[a]	5.96[ab]
Assessor B	56.10[a]	6.47[b]
Assessor C	59.90[b]	5.48[ab]
Assessor D 'external'	61.30[b]	3.60[a]

Note: Mean scores are the average percentages and standard deviations are the variability of the individual scores which contribute to the average. The different superscripts indicate those scores that are significantly different from one another according to the results of a statistical analysis.

that he did not know the students may have led him to approach the task in a more general manner, assessing the overall work of all the students, and thus rating all the students more similarly and at a slightly higher level than the other assessors. On the other hand, it may be that he was just a more generous evaluator than the other assessors. This need to seek out reasons for obtaining differences in results is of course one of the skills necessary in research. In order to make sense of the 'external' adjudicator's findings more fully, the qualitative analysis yielded extra information. It showed that this assessor focused his assessments more on general artistry than on individual technical aspects of each student, and it could be that he was using slightly different criteria for assessment than the other assessors.

The two females (Assessors B and C), by contrast, awarded the lowest average scores, and the qualitative data revealed that they focused more on specific technical details of singing for each student. A possible justification for their scoring differences, other than them being less generous markers, could be that the two are singing teachers in the Guildhall School and so in their everyday practice focus more on specific and technical aspects of the performance, possibly losing a more general perspective of the performance which would also consider general artistry. Additionally, as teachers they may show a tendency never to be satisfied and expect more from students either in the present exam or in future performance. Again, all interpretative possibilities need to be considered when interpreting the results.

The highest scores within the group of internal assessors came from the Head of Vocal Studies (Assessor A). In his written reports he seemed to be more protective of the students, often referring to both their personal and vocal improvement, and looking to a more positive future, saying things like 'a good performance for a second year student'. This qualitative interpretation of his scoring focuses our attention on another aspect of the assessment. It can be seen that the Head of Vocal Studies has a closer personal relationship with the students than the other assessors, for example he stated that he knew all individuals fairly or very well. So this could have affected his marking.

In the statistical analyses of the scores obtained, no gender differences were noticed in the ratings of the students, that is neither male or female assessors favoured male or female students in their assessments of their singing. Although this finding is at odds with the previous literature on gender biases in judgement, we regarded this finding as being positive.

The final agreement of marks was decided in the round table discussion, and our transcripts of the discussions suggest that a code of assessment criteria was shared between all four assessors. There were no extreme differences of view or arguments emerging during these discussions – though the differences that exist in the quantitative and qualitative data hint that different individuals do focus on different elements when making assessments. In the section which follows, the qualitative analysis, we explore the themes which emerged from the round table discussions and the open-ended questionnaires we gave the assessors. From these we, as the researchers, were able to formalize a set assessment criteria.

Qualitative Analysis

We believed that the best way to establish the criteria being used in the assessment process was to consider how the assessors wrote and spoke about the assessing process, so this section is based on analysing transcripts of discussions and looking in detail at the written comments made on the open-ended assessment forms. Because of the personal nature of some of the comments made, we have decided not to identify which assessor is passing judgement.

Repertoire

Repertoire was regarded as a factor that could improve or impair performance considerably. All assessors wrote that the more appropriate to the technical capabilities of the voice the repertoire is, the better the singer can convey the contents of the music to the audience. For example:

> Perhaps the repertoire is too demanding for what she is able to achieve technically.

Technical Control

The assessors were very concerned about how the voice and body were controlled. That is, how the technical aspects of singing were embodied. For instance:

> At the moment, what we hear is a good voice. Everything else is slightly lacking: not enough connection, support, and engagement with body and brain. [...] At the moment, the small voice and big physique don't match.

> [...] Physically she is doing too much: it's too tense.

Additionally, the assessors aimed for the integration of the different vocal registers, in order to obtain a homogeneous voice, as we can see in the following examples:

> She needs to be careful to integrate the voice more and not let soft singing lose its intensity.

Perhaps the most significant sub-theme to emerge from the technical issues was the concept of vocal support.

> There is quite shocking neck tension and an overall lack of support. The tension begins to make the voice wobble [...] Whilst the potential is very impressive we feel as though it will be compromised unless the physical tensions are removed.

The single most striking and surprising issue to emerge from considering the assessors' reports, however, was the emphasis they all placed on the physical appearance of the singers.

The Body and Appeal

Comments of this type were very often of a personal nature. Here are two indicative examples:

> A big guy. With a high lyrical voice.

> A rather puppet-like physical appearance.

'Bodily Communication'

The assessors also focused heavily upon bodily communication, and more specifically aspects related to the use of facial expression and eye contact, as shown in comments such as:

> A self-possessed beam.

> A visual 'performing' element missing. A problem of self-image: Does he need/ want to develop as a performer?

> 'Very appealing visual/facial expression', or on the contrary, 'Eyes dead. Blank face.'

In summary, one could say that the body was regarded not only as the physical support of the singing process, but also as a means of expression and so a primary means of communication with the audience. From these comments it is evident that the physicality of singing and how this interfaces with the performer's inner mental processes – what we believe the assessors' label of 'artistic communication' to mean – are key criteria in the assessment process.

Indeed, the next most strongly emergent theme employed by all of the assessors was 'artistry'. Here, we try to deconstruct what they mean by this term by the issues they raised to discuss allied to its use.

Artistry

Communicating meaning to the audience The meaning of the song or aria's message was a central concern. The assessors consistently commented on how well the students knew the meaning of the words. This was to help them internalize the content and therefore the right emotion to convey to the audience.

> If he had the words inside him, it would have been easier. German, not yet – careless.

After understanding the emotional content of the piece, it seems necessary to identify with this meaning. The assessors suggest that ideally the interpretation should be 'heartfelt', and 'from the centre of the person'. The consequence of these terms seems to be that an expressive performance is created emerging out of the individual's personality and presentation of it on stage.

The interaction with the audience The next criterion which emerged from all the assessors' reports allied to artistry was the absolute significance of the singer showing that he/she was committed to interacting with the audience.

From the assessors' comments it seems that the singer's introduction shows that the audience is important to the process of performance – an immediate channel for communication is established, as we can observe in the following examples:

Positive statements:

> General confident presentation – professional feel to her performance.

> Engaging opening gambit.

Negative statements:

> A relaxed, almost diffident approach.

> Introductions – Boring.

Connected to the concept of singer–audience interaction, there was much discussion of the singer's 'presence' – the assessors referred to it as the singer's projection of the 'self' on the stage.

Presence

The more focused the singer is on transmitting the musical intention, the more the assessors seem to be captivated and willing to interact, and, therefore, consider the singer as being 'appealing'.

If the singer is not sufficiently 'present', the assessors feel either that there is a lack of energy or interest, or that the singer is hidden behind the song's message. Lack of energy or interest in acting is then considered as a lack in part of the performance itself:

> A lovely sound, but rather disappointing as she doesn't get involved as an artist.

On the other hand, if the singer overacts and distracts the audience from the contents of the song, the assessors feel that the singer is focused more on his/her 'self' than on the contents of the song itself, hence lacking the desirable involvement:

> ... ultimately tiring to listen to because of the over giving.

> He is very comfortable with himself, but may be too comfortable?

Performing Personality

Stage presence was the means through which the singers showed their personalities, but from the descriptions given, it seems that the stage presentation revealed only part of the personality, the side connected with an outward focus. All assessors talked about the most successful performers sharing a particular kind of personality trait, one that was 'large' and 'projected'. Their descriptions were combined with concepts of acting.

> The Barber was transfixing. Lots of intelligence, self-possession and humility here.

> I am just flooded with pictures of Sarah Black, his girlfriend – Why not? This is the reality of this song.

> This is an engaging performing personality showing great intensity. It is all engaged and heartfelt with the self.

These data suggest that, on the one hand, the singers have to be authentic to themselves and the audience members, yet, on the other hand, they have to be public in their presentations. So, a slightly ironic and complex presentation is required – personal, yet sufficiently external to be public:

> [referring to the major strength of the performance] She found the inner self and the voice in the last piece.

> Beautiful multi-layered poised sincerity.

> Deeply felt performance – partly real and partly excellent role-playing.

Overall, the concept of artistry appears to be the most important factor for the enhancement of the performance. When looking to the profiles of those students who achieve the highest marks, expressions such as 'engagement', 'appealing', 'charming', 'commitment' and 'depth of feeling' were always present. Not only that, even with the students who were not rated so well, comments were always made about their artistry, and it was evidently seen as a significant factor in the assessment of the quality of the performance:

> Half of this mark is for the high quality of artistry. There is much greater concern about the vocal ability.

The data reveal that the assessors do share a clear code of assessment criteria, though it is implicitly held rather than explicitly articulated in their discourse. The presence of someone who did not know the students at all – the 'external' assessor – proved to be useful, since it showed some striking similarities between all the judgements, highlighting a shared cultural expectation. Of course, biases should be considered in the assessment process, and in our discussion we see that the female assessors were more technically biased, seemingly due to their backgrounds as singing teachers.

General Conclusion

According to the results of the two sets of data analysed, the four assessors appeared to have common criteria of assessment. It is important to mention, however, that the assessors belong to the same cultural milieu, and that perhaps in other cultural situations their comments would be of a different nature. It is certain that to some degree the students must share in this code for many of them score well, and so in accordance with the criteria. However, if the code is not equally understood or shared, it could create a gap between assessment and performance. Perhaps it is important for both teachers and students that the technical and artistic criteria are systematized in such a way that would reflect the concerns of all the teachers involved and be perceptible to the students. The consequences of this systematization would be profitable for both parties. The students would have a more practical knowledge of how to develop as musicians and performers and therefore improve their competitive advantage; the teachers have the opportunity to reflect on their evaluation process and, if needed, update their criteria, adjusting their evaluation to the present evolution of the performance process. However, we do have empathy for Guildhall's aim to not become rule-bound. They resist publicizing specific rating criteria to their students for fear that the students and teachers will simply try to abide by the model, and so not develop individuality.

Implications of the Research

We believe that our study has given important insights into the assessment process. Also, despite the fact that our tools shaped the process of assessment usually carried out in the Guildhall School of Music and Drama, since assessors do not fill in such lengthy report sheets for each student, we believe they have proved to shape the process positively. On the one hand, they have enabled us to find which assessment criteria emerged, and, on the other hand, they enabled the assessors to systematize and reflect on their assessment process and its implications.

Performance can be considered as a skill and therefore finding the most appropriate way of planning, developing and practising it, taking into account its internal mental aspects (musical, emotional), external (communication) and physical (gestures, face, bodily expression and posture) elements are clearly necessary to develop the communication of these ideas. We hope that practitioners reading this chapter might be inspired to develop their own projects drawing on some of our methodologies or indeed our findings. Useful directions we now wish to pursue in future work include:

1. the singers' personality and emotional management in performance;
2. singing performance as a communicative act;
3. a bodily approach to training the singing voice.

Note

1. This chapter is based on the authors' already published research (see references), drawing particularly on the article: Davidson, J.W. and Coimbra, D.C. (2001), 'Investigating Performance Evaluation by Assessors of Singers in a Music College Setting', *Musicae Scientiae*, V: 33–54, and appears with the full permission of the Editor.

References

Davidson, J.W. (1991) *The Expressive Movements in Musical Performance*, doctoral dissertation, City University, London.

Davidson, J.W. (1993) 'Visual perception of performance manner in the movements of solo musicians', *Psychology of Music*, 21: 103–13.

Davidson, J.W. (1994) 'Which areas of a pianist's body convey information about expressive intention to an audience?' *Journal of Human Movement Studies*, 26: 279–301.

Davidson, J.W. and Coimbra, D.C. (2001) 'Investigating Performance Evaluation by Assessors of Singers in a Music College Setting', *Musicae Scientiae*, V: 33–54.

Elliott, C.A. (1995) 'Race and gender factors in the assessment of musical performance', *Bulletin of the Council for Research in Music Education*, 127: 50–57.

Green, L. (1997) *Music, Gender, Education*, Cambridge: Cambridge University Press.

Kokotsaki, D., Davidson, J.W., and Coimbra, D.C. (2001) 'Investigating the assessment of singers in a music college setting: The students' perspective', *Research Studies of Music Education*, 16: 15–32.

Manturzewska, M. (1970) *Reliability of Musical Performance Evaluations of Musical Experts* (translations of several documents submitted and published through various Polish academic journals), personal communication.

O'Neill, S. and Boulton, M. (1996) 'Boys' and girls' preferences for musical instruments: A function of gender?' *Psychology of Music*, 24: 171–83.

Saunders, T.C. and Holahan, J.M. (1997) 'Criteria-specific rating scales in the evaluation of high school instrumental performance', *Journal of Research in Music Education*, 45: 259–70.

Smith, J.A. (1995) 'Semi-structured interviewing and qualitative analysis', in J.A. Smith, R. Harre and L.V. Langenhore (eds), *Rethinking Methods in Psychology*, pp. 9–26, London: Thousand Oaks; New Delhi: Sage.

Sundberg, J. (1982) 'Speech, song and emotions', in M. Clynes (ed.), *Music, Mind and Brain: The Neuropsychology of Music*, pp. 44–57, New York: Plenum.

Thompson, W., Diamond, C. and Balkwill, L. (1998) 'The adjudication of six performances of a Chopin étude: A study of expert knowledge', *Psychology of Music*, 26: 154–74.

Tuncks, T.W. (1987), 'Evaluation in music education: The value of measurement/the measurement of value', *Bulletin of the Council for Research in Music Education*, 90: 53–9.

Wapnick, J., Darrow, A.A., Kovacs, J. and Dalrymple, L. (1997) 'Effects of physical attractiveness on evaluation of vocal performance', *Journal of Research in Music Education*, 45(3): 470–79.

Chapter 17

Starting a Music Degree at University
Stephanie E. Pitts

Introduction

Students moving from school to university are faced with numerous changes in their everyday circumstances, which might include living away from home, making new friends, interacting with larger groups of students, and studying one subject as opposed to the broader school curriculum. For music students, in particular, the shift from being one of only a few 'expert' musicians at school to finding themselves amongst a much larger group of similarly skilled people presents a challenge to their sense of self-identity, and can cause them to question knowledge and ability that they have previously taken for granted.

Research in psychology and in education has paid remarkably little attention to this transition, despite the benefits that greater awareness of this change in students' lives and understanding could bring for schools and universities. It has been said that 'no mission is more vital to the success of higher education than ensuring the rapid transition of these new students to a university culture' (Cook and Leckey, 1999, p. 159), and an awareness of the differences and overlap between school and university culture must surely form part of that mission. Beyond such practical concerns, investigating the effects of these personal, social and musical changes offers insight for music psychologists on the perceptions that young musicians hold of themselves and others, so contributing to the wider question of what it means to be a musician.

This chapter presents data from an interview study in which 'A' level music students (final year of secondary school – Year 13) and first-year undergraduates were asked to reflect on their perceptions of themselves as musicians, and the way in which these affected their experience of school and their expectations of university education. The study is first set in context, drawing on research into general student experience and specific musical transitions, before data are reported and discussed, and some recommendations for practitioners and researchers offered.

The Research Context

The first year of a degree course has been recognized as 'make or break year' (Oldham, 1988), and whilst the majority of students will thrive in their new environment, some will need support to meet the social and academic demands they encounter (Rickenson and Rutherford, 1995, p. 163). A recent study of withdrawal rates amongst first-year students noted that course difficulties and living away from home were the most commonly cited reasons for leaving university, with social concerns dominating for first term leavers, and academic worries assuming greater importance later in the first year (Rickenson and Rutherford, 1996, p. 215). Students are more likely to seek help from their personal tutor within their department, rather than using the university counselling service (ibid., p. 216), yet this system is compromised on the students' part by an unwillingness to take up lecturers' time with personal problems (Grayson et al., 1998, p. 244), and on the lecturers' part by a feeling that they are ill-equipped to deal with potentially complex and distressing cases (Easton and Van Laar, 1995, p. 176). Whilst excellent advice to lecturers can be found (Lago and Shipton, 1994; Grant, 1999), the tutorial system is under pressure from increases in student numbers, meaning that 'students may go through their entire degree course without regular and continuing personal contact with an academic supervisor' (Williams, 2000, p. 11).

Booth, in his study of 201 students beginning history degrees at the University of Nottingham, cites students' generally low awareness of course content and demands as accounting in part for 'the dislocation frequently expressed by newcomers' (Booth, 1997, p. 209). Booth's questionnaire survey revealed that whilst most students had a strong rationale for choosing to study history, with 98 per cent professing a long-standing interest in the subject, choice of institution was a secondary consideration. Despite this, the students placed considerable emphasis on the perceived quality of teaching in rating their experience of the course, offering the familiar judgements that a good lecturer is enthusiastic and approachable, whilst bad lecturers dictate notes and appear uninterested in their subject (cf. Marsh, 1987, p. 257; Ramsden, 1992, p. 73):

> History students newly-arrived at university regard their teachers as a principal element in their progress as historians, and look to them to share their expertise and love of the subject and provide the advice and support necessary to sustain the interest and the high level of personal motivation which they see as essential to effective learning. (Booth, 1997, p. 215)

As yet, no comparable body of research exists to document music students' expectations of university, although parallels can be drawn with work on other transitions, from primary to secondary school (Mills, 1996) and from music student to music teacher (Beynon, 1998; Austin and Reinhardt, 1999; Dolloff, 1999). In both these phases, a questioning of musical knowledge and skill takes place, generated by comparison with new peers in different circumstances. These musical attributes are a significant part of the identity of students choosing to study music at university, and analysis of data from the current project revealed a resultant sense of insecurity amongst the students interviewed (Pitts, 2000).

Many were generously inclusive in their definitions of musicality, and yet highly critical of their own abilities and entitlement to be called 'a musician'. Their sense of musical identity had been brought into question by the transition from school to university, but in some cases that process of change had ultimately reinforced their commitment to music and their determination to pursue a music-related career.

The academic and personal challenges of beginning a university course are difficult to separate, and indeed the students interviewed for this research all cited making new friends as one of their primary concerns. This preoccupation with the friendliness of new environments is supported in the literature, with Berndt (1999) stating that the supportive function of self-disclosure and shared perceptions between friends is essential to the emotional security and well-being of adolescents:

> Friends' support enhances adolescents' self-esteem and improves their ability to cope with stressful events. Intimate conversations in which a friend shares personal information also give adolescents a better understanding of other people and a broadened perspective on the world. (Berndt, 1999, p. 57)

If friends are 'allies in navigating through ... the world' (ibid., p. 51) it is not unreasonable that students should feel anxious about having to make new friends at a time when they are negotiating an unfamiliar environment. The importance of friends in late adolescence means that friendships forged are likely to be strong and significant, whilst lack of friends 'gives rise to more intense feelings of loneliness than can be found at any time in earlier years' (Schaffer, 1996, p. 327). This aspect of adaptation to university might be seen as beyond the remit of academic departments, who are principally concerned with the development of their students as individuals, rather than as part of a group. However, the psychological importance of friends, and the frequency with which concern was expressed by participants in this study, highlights the necessity of fostering a friendly atmosphere with introductory events, approachable staff, and well-publicized and accessible support networks.

Method

Participants in this study consisted of 11 'A' level (16+ years-old, advanced level schools examination) music students (seven female; four male) from a Derbyshire secondary school, and nine first-year undergraduates (eight female; one male) studying music at the University of Sheffield. Each subject completed a questionnaire which asked for biographical details, views on experiences or expectations of university, perceptions of music and its importance, and answers to the question of what makes a musician. An interview followed, in which ideas from the questionnaire were discussed in greater detail. Questionnaires were returned in all but two cases, and all interviews were tape-recorded and transcribed for analysis. The interviews took place in March 2000 for the 'A' level students and April 2000 for the undergraduates, at which stage of the academic year the school students were making university choices, and the undergraduates were into the second semester of their course.

The sample of students interviewed were largely, but not exclusively, from a classical tradition, with musical interests including folk guitar, jazz and African drumming, as well as classical, popular and contemporary music. All played at least one instrument, usually more, to a high standard, averaging Grade VI–VIII of the Associated Board Practical Music Examinations for the A level students and Grade VIII or above for the undergraduates. (These are typical standards for specialist music students at these levels.) Almost all were members of orchestras, bands and choirs whilst at school and had experience of performing solo and chamber music, and a smaller proportion had a strong interest in composition. The students were drawn from A level and undergraduate seminar groups that I was teaching at the time, which ensured a similar bias across the participants; all were familiar with my teaching style, and were used to talking to me, albeit in rather different circumstances. Any concern that the students might have been unwilling to speak honestly about their experiences appears to have been unfounded, and indeed the students' articulate and insightful responses were a clear reminder of the importance of listening to students and allowing them to offer fresh perspectives on their music education.

Data have been analysed according to emergent themes, with comparisons made between the A level (Y13) and undergraduate (UG) students, and between those declaring a long-term interest in music and those who expect to stop playing within the near future. The concepts of musicianship and musical identity revealed in the data have been explored fully elsewhere (Pitts, 2002), and the focus for this chapter will be on the implications for music practitioners in secondary and higher education.

Results and Discussion

Music at School

Without exception, participants in the study were enthusiastic about the performance opportunities they had experienced at school, and agreed that music was a busy and rewarding part of their lives. Most had chosen to study A level music because they had enjoyed it at GCSE (General Certificate of Secondary Education, taken typically at 16 years of age and thus usually two years prior to A level), although some expressed reservations about the extent to which the syllabus accommodated their musical interests, particularly where these were in popular music or music technology. These students were among the last to follow the 'traditional' music A level course, and it will be interesting to see if this perspective changes for current and future cohorts, who will experience the potentially more integrated and practical approach of the new revised syllabuses that have recently been introduced. For the A level students in this study, musical involvement took place not just in school, but also through county and national youth ensembles, meaning that for many of them, evenings and weekends were taken up with musical activities:

> I play double bass in the school orchestra, Peak District String Orchestra, County Youth Orchestra and County Windband. I have played in a few big bands, including one in Derby, and guitar-wise I've not done much, but bass guitar I've played in a few rock groups. … I just like playing, doing concerts and things, and the social side as well. (Y13)

> We always had Chorale on a Monday, for an hour and a half, everybody did that without a choice, whether they liked it or not, and most people didn't to start with, and everybody sort of got to like it in the end. We'd have Chamber Choir on the Tuesday lunchtime, 'cello quartet rehearsal on Tuesday sometimes; Wednesdays I would have an African drumming lesson sometimes, then we'd have a 'cello quartet rehearsal again, possibly, string quartet sometimes on a Wednesday if necessary, and then Sinfonietta. Thursday – Thursdays were hell, guitar lesson and all sorts of other stuff. Fridays I didn't actually do anything; oh no, I had a piano lesson on Fridays. … Then Saturdays I'd have Midland Youth Orchestra, possibly with Chamber Orchestra beforehand, and Sunday, about once a month, I'd have County Youth Orchestra, possibly again with Chamber Orchestra afterwards. Then it would go back to Monday. (UG)

These descriptions are representative of the range and extent of the participants' musical lives while at school, illustrating that for many, the move to university meant leaving behind many valued activities. Indeed, those students not intending to study music at university tended to see their future involvement in terms of returning to existing ensembles, rather than forging new links once they were away from home.

Around half the undergraduate students stated that music was the main thing they had been involved in at school, explaining this with reference either to ability – 'it was the only thing I was good at' – or to interest – 'I just liked music, so I did it all the time'. Participants in the undergraduate group were more likely than the school students to state that they were single-minded about music, so it is possible that this impression had occurred with hindsight, since it was not shared by those students currently involved in other A level studies.

Anticipating Music at University

Of the 11 A level students in the study, seven were intending to take degrees that included music, whether through acoustic engineering, music technology, performing arts, or music alone. Another two were undecided, and later settled for their other subjects, history and pharmacology, whilst the remaining two never intended to take music, choosing nursing and business courses respectively. Not surprisingly, those planning to take music-related degrees had slightly clearer ideas about the kind of people, activities and opportunities they would find within a university or college music department, although these ranged from hazy impressions to idealistic projections:

> Going on my experiences of music college, it's a very relaxed atmosphere, very non-judgmental. Because of the way musicians are, there are great characters, so people just accept who you are, not expect you to conform. (Y13)

> I think the attitudes towards it [will be different], because it will be the only thing you're doing, so it will be like dedicated musicians who'll be there, instead of people worrying about what other subjects they've got to do as well. I think there'll be more diversity in the course, like doing conducting, and there'll be kind of jazz and composing, which we don't do, so I think that will be good. (Y13)

The expectation that university departments are populated by 'dedicated musicians' seemed to be encouraging to those students who planned to join those communities, whilst being somewhat off-putting to those who were not. The image of the eccentric music student was commonly held, with the undergraduate participants expressing varying levels of disappointment or relief that their peers had turned out to be 'not quite so bizarre in a lot of ways'.

Choosing the university itself had been influenced by a variety of factors, including the location and its associated social scene, advice from teachers, family and friends, and first impressions formed on interview or open days. Courses were generally expected to be wide-ranging and include coverage of new and familiar things, and some students commented that, on paper, there was little to choose between the programmes offered by different music departments: 'you can't tell a lot from the course titles, because it's often more to do with the lecturer and the way it's taught'. Potential music students also shared the more general concerns of new undergraduates; managing finances, living away from home and adjusting to the demands of the course. Making friends was also a consideration mentioned by all the participants, although the existing undergraduates reported that this had been less of a problem than they had anticipated, and attributed this to the shared ideals and interests found within a music department.

In summary, students intending to study music at university were usually open-minded and optimistic about the prospect, whilst expressing some reservations about losing the performing opportunities and sense of expertise they were accustomed to from school. Consistent with the literature on university choice (Keen and Higgins, 1990; Moogan et al., 1999), the decision-making process was lengthy, but often dependent on potentially unreliable factors, such as the friendliness of the students on open days.

Experiencing Music at University

Recalling their initial impressions was obviously reliant on the undergraduates' memories (a problem addressed in part by an ongoing diary study), and opinions about how the first term of the course met their expectations varied:

> It's completely different from what I did expect, but I don't actually know what I was expecting. ... I think I was expecting a lot of history and sort of set works and things like that, which is what we get more this [semester]. I was hoping for more composition, but that hasn't happened, but then again that will do next year, so that's okay. (UG)

> Actually I thought we'd have a lot more time when you actually have to be here doing different stuff. I expected to be here a lot more often; not as much as you are at school, but more than we are. (UG)

On this subject, data from the two groups were reasonably consistent, in that the A level students had only broad ideas about what they expected from a university course, whilst the undergraduates were generally unable to suggest improvements or changes to the first year they had experienced. This is perhaps not surprising, given that both groups of students were more acclimatized to the school culture, in which decisions about what and how to learn are largely the province of teachers. Some of the undergraduate participants reported a sense of confusion over the differences between school and university learning, particularly where they had submitted work which would have fulfilled A level requirements, but did not adopt the more independent approaches of university work:

> I was concerned about the work; I think everybody is to start with. Nobody knows what to expect, what the standards are, and because you're having to do a lot of the work yourself, rather than the lecturer do it and you just reproduce it on another bit of paper, you don't know quite what's expected of you, and that was quite worrying to start with. (UG)

Although this student's language suggests that she now understands the need to go beyond 'reproducing' lecture notes, she was not alone in her uncertainty about requirements and assessment procedures. Whilst some expressed a readiness for the self-discipline and flexible organization that university learning offers, others were surprised by the relatively small proportion of time devoted to lectures, and tended to exclude rehearsals and concerts from their calculations of how much work they did each week. Comparison with the hectic schedules of the school students goes a long way to explaining these feelings, as students are used to being occupied in directed activities for much of their week, and take time to adapt to the new pattern of existence at university.

The undergraduate students, reflecting on the social and personal changes intrinsic to starting at university, all reported some anxiety about the transition, ranging from financial and practical concerns to more subject-based worries, particularly whether their performing ability would be 'good enough' for university. Some were aware that their skills might be different from their peers, particularly those who had strengths in composing rather than performing, whilst others reflected in more confused ways on the experience of being one of a larger group of musicians:

> With the oboe playing, because there are five oboists in our year and I'm not used to having five oboes around, so it's made me want to practise more because I want to get into orchestras, so yes, I think competition in performance helps me, it spurs me on. But in the history and things like this, I don't know if this is just me, but I'm trying to work at my own level rather than compete with other people, because I know there are people who are going to come out with Firsts, and I'm not. (UG)

This recognition that varied backgrounds and interests lead undergraduates to have different strengths and priorities is another area which will need further thought as students from the new AS/A2 system, where modular assessments led to an award at the end of each year of Advanced level study, enter university. With more opportunity to develop specific strengths, students no longer have an obvious means of comparison with their peers as was the case when an exchanging of A level grades seemed to take place during the first weeks of term. Lecturers, too, will need to be aware of the greater range of musical expertise and specialisms which the broader access opportunities of AS/A2 syllabuses may foster, and the implications this could have upon music degree courses cannot yet be fully evaluated.

Conclusions and Implications

Increasing understanding of students' views of music in school and university can only be beneficial to music educators at all levels. Whilst the confusion and ambiguities expressed by many of the students indicate that structuring courses according to students' needs and ideas is an impossible task to fulfil completely, there is certainly more room for acknowledging students' views than is standard practice at present. Student evaluation of existing provision has become commonplace in universities in recent decades (Marsh, 1987), but the pressure of timetabling and assessment deadlines in schools means that there are few opportunities for students to reflect on music provision at an earlier stage. Where investigations of student opinion do take place, as in Spencer's (1993) study of the first cohort of GCSE music students to reach university, students sometimes appear remarkably conservative in their views:

> There needs to be more of an effort to bridge the gap between those who plan learning and those who undergo learning in music at an advanced stage. The

opportunities the GCSE offers to students to be imaginative and adventurous are, it seems, not being taken by pupils; nor, it has to be said, are they being encouraged by teachers. ... In the choices of challenge for composing and of repertoire to perform, we tend to find an emphasis on the safe, the unenterprising and the easily assessible. (Spencer, 1993, p. 83)

Whilst things may have changed in the years since Spencer's investigation, the principle remains the same: students need to be encouraged to take risks in their learning, and to look beyond assessment to find a true purpose and direction for their music education. This adds yet another task to the already complex roles of teachers in secondary and higher education, but the dangers of overlooking this broader vision of music in education are far-reaching. Undergraduates who evaluate their music degrees in terms of quality of teaching, workload and difficulty of assessment, are products of the political interventions in education that characterized the late twentieth century, reducing all learning to measurable outcomes (Pitts, 2000). By encouraging students to reflect on their own learning from an early stage, teachers can foster the spirit of true enquiry and education within schools, and so remain resistant to the narrow views of schooling that threaten to proliferate.

The research reported here illustrates the need for closer links between schools and universities, to assist students in bridging that gap by fostering understanding and common purpose between institutions. There is much potential for replication and extension of this study, using more participants, and including other categories of students, such as those who continue to participate in music at university whilst studying another subject. Without a doubt, however, this investigation has revealed the need for practical support at an individual level, as students go through the intense and sometimes overwhelming process of adapting to their new personal, social and musical circumstances. The magnitude of change that faces new university students demands careful handling if the enthusiasm for music that informs students' choice of degree is to be sustained within and beyond university.

References

Austin, J.R. and Reinhardt, D. (1999) 'Philosophy and advocacy: An examination of preservice music teachers' beliefs', *Journal of Research in Music Education*, 47(1): 18–30.

Berndt, T.J. (1999) 'Friendships in adolescence', in M. Woodhead, D. Faulkner and K. Littleton (eds), *Making Sense of Social Development*, pp. 51–71, London: Routledge/Open University.

Beynon, C. (1998) 'From music student to music teacher: Negotiating an identity', *Studies in Music*, 17: 83–105.

Booth, A. (1997) 'Listening to students: Experiences and expectations in the transition to a history degree', *Studies in Higher Education*, 22(2): 205–20.

Cook, A. and Leckey, J. (1999) 'Do expectations meet reality? A survey of changes in first-year student opinion', *Journal of Further and Higher Education*, 23(2): 157–71.

Dolloff, L.A. (1999) 'Imagining ourselves as teachers: The development of teacher identity in music teacher education', *Music Education Research*, 1(2): 191–207.

Easton, S. and Van Laar, D. (1995) 'Experiences of lecturers helping distressed students in higher education', *British Journal of Guidance and Counselling*, 23(2): 173–8.

Grant, A. (1999) *Helping Students in Difficulty: A Guide for Personal Tutors and Other Staff*, Leicester: University of Leicester.

Grayson, A., Miller, H. and Clarke, D. (1998) 'Identifying barriers to help-seeking: A qualitative analysis of students' preparedness to seek help from tutors', *British Journal of Guidance and Counselling*, 26(2): 237–53.

Keen, C. and Higgins, T. (1990) *Young People's Knowledge of Higher Education*, London: HEIST/PCAS.

Lago, C. and Shipton, G. (1994) *Personal Tutoring in Action: A Handbook for Staff Involved in Working With and Supporting Students*, Sheffield: Sheffield University Counselling Service.

Marsh, H.W. (1987) 'Students' evaluations of university teaching: Research findings, methodological issues and directions for future research', *International Journal of Educational Research*, 11: 257–388.

Mills, J. (1996) 'Starting at secondary school', *British Journal of Music Education*, 13(1): 5–14.

Moogan, V.J., Baron, S. and Harris, K. (1999) 'Decision-making behaviour of potential higher education students', *Higher Education Quarterly*, 53(3): 211–28.

Oldham, B. (1988) 'The first year – make or break year', *Journal of Further and Higher Education*, 12(2): 5–11.

Pitts, S.E. (2000) *A Century of Change in Music Education*, Aldershot: Ashgate.

Pitts, S.E. (2002) 'Changing tunes: Perceptions of music and musicians amongst school and university music students', *Musicae Scientiae* 6(1): 73–92.

Ramsden, P. (1992) *Learning to Teach in Higher Education*, London: Routledge.

Rickenson, B. and Rutherford, D. (1995) 'Increasing undergraduate student retention rates', *British Journal of Guidance and Counselling*, 23(2): 161–72.

Rickenson, B. and Rutherford, D. (1996) 'Systematic monitoring of the adjustment to university of undergraduates: a strategy for reducing withdrawal rates', *British Journal of Guidance and Counselling*, 24(2): 213–25.

Schaffer, H.R. (1996) *Social Development*, Oxford: Blackwell.

Spencer, P. (1993) 'GCSE music: A survey of undergraduate opinion', *British Journal of Music Education*, 10(2): 73–84.

Williams, E. (2000) 'Tears and Fears', *Guardian Education*, 14 March: 10–11.

Chapter 18

Tracing a Musical Life Transition[1]

Karen Burland and Jane W. Davidson

Introduction

The aim of the current chapter is to report a study which investigated events that have influenced the careers and lives of a group of talented musicians. This research followed up a study carried out by Davidson, Sloboda, Howe and Moore (1991–93), in order to discover what has happened to some of the participants eight years after being involved in the original study, examining in particular the transitional phase from training to professional life. Semi-structured telephone interviews were conducted with 18 of the 'specialist' musicians, and these were analysed using Interpretative Phenomenological Analysis (IPA). The analysis revealed several themes that seem to be of key importance in determining the successful transition from training to professional life, and a tripartite model of success has been proposed. The central importance of music to self-concept seems to be the primary factor responsible for the successful transition to the pursuit of a professional career. Positive experiences (with others and within the music education institutions), and the development of coping strategies seem to influence, and work with, self-concept, and so contribute to the success of the transition. The findings contradict the belief that only practice makes perfect, or that the influence of others is the most significant factor in development. This chapter has important implications for the education of talented musicians, and is of interest methodologically, showing how individuals can be traced over a long period of time.

The underlying argument of any discussion concerning development is that of the nature–nurture debate: is development caused by innate, genetic factors, or is it influenced by the environment? The study of giftedness and talent is no different in this, and psychologists seem to agree that whilst innate factors may have some role to play – such as an inherited potential for a particular quality – there is little evidence to confirm the suspicion. There is, however, a wealth of evidence suggesting that the experience of the child shapes who she/he becomes, thus highlighting the importance of environmental influences. It is for this reason that the current chapter begins with a review of literature that will consider the impact of external influences rather than speculate about the possibility of inherited talents.

Research into musical development has focused primarily on the early years, considering environmental factors that contribute to the child's motivation to continue their instrumental studies. Parents are considered a vital influence in early musical development (Manturzewska, 1990; Csikszentmihalyi et al., 1993) for many reasons, including the provision of high levels of support (Sosniak, 1990; Sloboda and Howe, 1991; Kemp, 1996), and obtaining regular feedback from teachers (Sloboda and Howe, 1991). Furthermore, parents of talented children are initially responsible for the initiation of systematic practice skills through their active support and the rewards they provide on the acquisition of such skills (Ericsson et al., 1996). The role of teachers in the development of gifted children is also highly important. The teacher's personality is vital (Csikszentmihalyi et al., 1993; Davidson et al., 1998), and the feedback teachers provide is important. Without adequate feedback, improvement will be minimal, and efficient learning impossible (Csikszentmihalyi et al., 1993; Ericsson et al., 1996). The influence of peers on the developing child is crucial, especially as the child approaches adolescence. Evidence suggests that the gifted child is best located in an educational setting where they are surrounded by like-minded peers for three reasons: first, the child needs companionship with someone of his/her own ability (Freeman, 1985); second, they require the stimulation and motivation of being with others of the same ability (Feldhusen, 1986); and third, they work at a faster pace than 'normal' children in the classroom, thus being with similar ability peers will enable them to progress faster (Freeman, 1991). One final factor in relation to this is the importance of 'idols within touching distance' (Hall, 1960). It is suggested that role models close in age and expertise to the student have more influence on the talented child than a master in the field (Sosniak, 1990). Sosniak believes that slightly older students in the field are used for setting goals and skills to be mastered, and the younger child can identify with the older, simply because they are aware that they are not alone in the amount of work they have to dedicate in the pursuit of excellence. One final factor influencing musical development is motivation. Intrinsic motivation ('interest in and liking of the activity under question of its own sake', Sloboda, 1990, p. 169) is considered to be one of three contributory factors in the development of talent (Howe, 1990), the others being experience and practice. Similarly, 'task commitment' related to intrinsic motivation is considered an important factor in Renzulli's Three-ring Conception of Giftedness, the other factors being creativity and above-average ability (Renzulli, 1986). Self-concept is also thought to contribute to an individual's motivation to persevere with certain activities. Researchers suggest that those students who equate ability with achievement are more likely to want to succeed in order to protect their self-esteem, rather than wanting to master the task for its own sake (Covington and Omelich, 1979).

Life-span Development

Theories of the development of talent suggest that the individual has changing and adaptable needs as they grow older, and some psychologists suggest that development may end in late adolescence, believing that early development provides the individual with the necessary traits to deal with changes in later life (Piaget and Inhelder, 1969). Other research challenges this view, however, suggesting that the individual changes and grows throughout the life-span (Erikson, 1959). The transition from adolescence to adulthood is considered the most significant of the life-span changes, and is thought to be stressful for both the individual, and those around him/her (Gecas and Mortimer, 1987). Gecas and Mortimer believe this is due to the changing roles that occur during this stage of development, such as the transition from school to work, or the shift from relationships with peers and parents, to an intimate relationship, for example. This is thought to be reflected in a child's musical development (Bamberger, 1982). Bamberger describes what she terms the 'midlife crisis' – a period of transition from early expertise to excellence in adulthood. For some, this transition will be successful, after a difficult period of reassessment, but for others it signifies the end of their careers because they were not able to pass through the transitional period successfully. Another explanation for this phenomenon is the difference between adolescents and young adults in terms of assimilation and accommodation (Haan, 1981). It is suggested that adolescents are, on the whole, assimilatory, but, due to the demands of young adulthood, such as buying a house, or advancing a career, the individual becomes more accommodatory – if the accomplishments are to be successful, they must agree with the self's desires and capabilities.

In specific relation to music, Manturzewska (1990) has proposed a sequence of six stages in the life-span development of the professional musician. Relevant to the current study are stages 2 and 3. In the second stage (intentional, guided music development: 6–14 years of age), the child gains basic technical and performance skills, alongside musical knowledge, due to an increase in intrinsic motivation – a need to learn. Throughout this stage, the child undergoes enormous development, and by the end of the phase should be able to tackle an ambitious musical repertoire and will have given their first musical performances.

The third stage of development (formation and development of the artistic personality: 12/13–23/24 years of age) involves the child seeking models and ideals, and they gradually join the professional community. Teachers continue to play a vital role, in the 'master–student' relationship, and the teacher concentrates on the technical aspects of performance in addition to the development of the entire personality. However, for those who do not find a 'master', their personalities and beliefs develop within the environment and peer groups. It is suggested that the lack of a 'master–student' relationship can reflect negatively in the student's artistic and professional development. The stage is completed with graduation from a higher music academy, and the period that follows is characterized by the student trying to establish himself/herself within the professional field. For those who have a good teacher, their transition is likely to be successful due to the amount of support and assistance provided. However, for those who do not, the transition is likely to be erratic and may not have the anticipated outcome of an artistic career.

By studying these models of development, it is clear to see how life transition and change is dependent upon experience, the influence of other people, and the individual's personality.

The Original Study

From 1991 to 1993, Davidson, Sloboda, Howe and Moore conducted research investigating motivating factors in children's musical development (Howe et al., 1995; Davidson et al., 1996, 1997, 1998; Sloboda et al., 1996). Data were collected from interviews with five different groups of children, each defined by a different level of musical ability, and their parents. These data indicated that environmental influences were critical determinants of musical success. For instance, the results revealed that children who had successfully acquired musical skills were those whose parents had offered high levels of support. The children of those parents who had received regular feedback from the teacher, or were present in the lessons, were the most successful learners. A further observation indicated that by the early teenage years the 'specialists', rather than any of the other groups, began to require less social support and became more autonomous in their commitment and motivation.

Teachers were also found to play a vital role in the development of the child's musical skill. The data revealed that for the high achievers, the first teacher was perceived positively in terms of personal characteristics – as friendly and chatty, and as a good player. Conversely, for those who had given up, the first teacher was viewed as unfriendly, and as a bad player. It is suggested that in the initial stages of instrumental learning it is important for the teacher to establish a friendly rapport with the children, who are likely to perceive them as being supportive, thus increasing the child's motivation to learn. However, this role changes in later stages of instrumental learning when the child is concerned with finding a role model in order to improve himself/herself, and so a personal rapport with the teacher is less important.

A final finding of the Davidson et al. research concerns the relationship between type of practice (formal – scales, exercises – or informal – messing around, playing favourite tunes) and achievement; the high achievers practised the most, whilst the low achievers hardly practised at all. Furthermore, the relationship between achievement and informal practice was less strong than that for formal practice.

The study reported here was undertaken for three reasons:

1. The findings of the original research highlight the influence of other people in the acquisition of high-level musical skills, and emphasize the role of practice and its importance to the development of musical expertise. However, the data have been quantitatively analysed and do not account for the individual's unique experience, or consider the impact of those important factors identified in the study on the individual's personal and musical development. Thus:
2. Due to the nature of the original analysis, the data cannot consider the psychological and emotional effects of studying music, especially in the case of the 'specialists', for whom music study is quite intensive, and the influence of that experience on their motivation.
3. Generally, much research has concentrated on studying early musical development, but little considers the musical development that occurs in young adulthood – in the transition from training to professional life.

Thus we investigate what has happened to the highly successful musicians from the original empirical study of 1993, investigating the events that have influenced their careers. The study is concerned with the psychological and musical development of the participants, and aims to discover those factors important in the transition from training to professional life. In doing so, it aims to understand more fully how talented young musicians, or 'specialists', are able to maximize their musical potential and become professional performing musicians. In order to achieve these aims, a qualitative study was undertaken to maximize our understanding of individual experiences.

The Empirical Approach

In order to explore what had happened to the children displaying high potential in music, 20 people aged 17–26 from the 'specialist' group in the original study (Howe et al, 1995; Davidson et al., 1996, 1997, 1998; Sloboda et al., 1996), and who had attended Chethams Music School in Manchester, were contacted. This took place eight years after the original interviews so that most were in the adult 'transitional' phase (24 years of age). Participants were selected through a process of snowballing; a small number of contact numbers provided by Chethams was used to contact some musicians, and these provided numbers of other individuals. Of the participants, 13 were male, and 7 were female. Fourteen of these are currently pursuing professional performing careers, whilst the remaining 6 are not. It was felt appropriate to work with these participants despite the unequal divide between those still pursuing a music career and those working in a domain other than music performance because according to school records (personal communication with J.M. Leach, and records of Alumni) 60 per cent of students stay in professional music: the sample was representative of the school's predicted impact on the music profession. Fewer females than males participated on the same basis, representing the information in the school Alumni records. Each individual was interviewed over the telephone, and these interviews were recorded and later transcribed. The interview schedules were compiled using questions from the original interviews, and questions specifically designed for the current study (see Appendices 1 and 2 to this chapter). Two interview schedules were designed – one for those in pursuit of a professional performing career, and one for those who have moved away from music. The main aim of the interview was to gain insight into the musical and psychological development of the individual since the time of the original study, examining their motivation to pursue music or not, and to explore the psychological impact of pursuing music to a professional level at a specialist music school and at conservatoires. The interview further considers the extent to which other people have influenced the individual, and the changing role of significant influences such as parents and teachers. Furthermore, the changing role and importance of music are considered.

The interviews were designed as semi-structured interviews to allow the interviewer to derive specific information whilst having the freedom to further discuss and elaborate any interesting issues that may arise. Semi-structured interviews also enable the interviewer to modify the order of questions based on what seems appropriate to the conversation and to leave out questions that seem inappropriate (Robson, 1998).

The interviews were conducted over the telephone, which was logistically easier as the participants are now at many different locations in the UK. Like face-to-face interviews, telephone interviews have a high response rate and allow for clarification at times of misunderstanding. They also have the advantage of fewer interviewer effects and a lower tendency for socially desirable responses (Robson, 1998).

The interviews were analysed using IPA (Smith et al., 1997). This particular technique was used because it is a method that enables participants to tell their own story, in their own words, through self-reflection. This process involved organizing the interview data into clusters of themes allowing important comparisons to be drawn between the participants. In order to confirm the analysis, an individual external to the research confirmed the final themes arising from the raw data.

Results of the Empirical Work

Analysis of the interviews reveals that there are differences between the experiences of musicians still in pursuit of a performing career, and those who are not. Therefore, in order to examine which factors are the most important to the successful development of musical talent, comparisons were drawn between the two groups. Fourteen of the total sample of 20 are still actively involved with music. This group of individuals are still in pursuit of a professional performing career, and are either studying within the education system, intending to pursue a music career, or are now earning their living from being a professional performing musician, in the ranks of a professional orchestra, for example. From this point forward, this group will be referred to as PPC (those in pursuit of a professional performing career).

The individuals who are no longer in pursuit of a professional performing career either have a career linked to music in some way, such as teaching, or are working in a domain unrelated to music. The majority of members in this group rarely play their instruments. From this point forward this group will be referred to as PNC (those in pursuit of a non-performing, or non-music-related career).

Analysis of the interviews revealed key themes important to the development of these individuals, which were highly consistent with the areas highlighted by the original study, and with other research findings:

1. influence of other people (teachers, parents, peers);
2. impact of institutions (music school, college, university);
3. the importance of motivation (interfacing key others as external motivation, with intrinsic motivation).

Note that indicative citations will be used here. There is no attempt to give all instances of a particular theme or issue. In quoting examples of transcripts, an alias for the participant is given and the participant's group (PPC or PNC).

Influence of Other People

It emerged from the analysis that the roles played by other people, and the impact they have on the individual, are quite different for the two groupings. Perhaps one of the biggest differences between them is the nature of the support provided by parents, teachers and peers, as summarized in Table 18.1.

It appears that the influence of peers, parents and teachers can be both positive and negative. PPC seem to perceive their interactions with other people as positive, using them as opportunities for learning, and for inspiration and motivation. PNC, however, perceive parental, teacher and peer support negatively, and this influences the way they assess their abilities and experiences. One particularly interesting example of how others can influence the developing musician is the case of Bobby; several years of his musical training were influenced by an idol, and this impacted on Bobby's musical and personal development.

Table 18.1   The influence of others

1. Influence of others	Evidence
Parents	
1.1 PPC: parents highly supportive on a general level	'By just saying 'we believe in you' and that's enough for me.' (Georgina: PPC)
1.2 PPC: for some, parents provide security for the developing musician	'They are my sort of base on the planet as it were, they're my feet on the ground.' (Simon: PPC)
1.3 PNC: sense of obligation to parents	'I really felt the pressure of I've got to show my parents that they have not whilst still in pursuit of a career in music wasted all their money and time, especially my father.' (Jade: PNC)
Teachers	
1.4 PPC: current teachers play really important role in development, but emphasis is on extra-musical activities	'She really influenced me in loads of things I did later on – she's influenced me not to completely focus on singing, not to focus on music … and she felt strongly that if you had a brain then you should go to University.' (Andrew: PPC)
1.5	'Both my teachers have been into promoting us, their students, as much as themselves, they're always wanting to see the CV and the repertoire list, and making sure that we're promoting ourselves properly.' (Graham: PPC)
1.6 PNC: teachers did not meet the requirements of the student	'He wanted it done in one way, and it felt totally unnatural and unmusical … there were things I could do that he couldn't … and he was a bit resentful of that.' (John: PNC)
Peers	
1.7 PPC: peers an important source of motivation, inspiration and support	'You're just drawing on each other's imaginations all the time, and in that sense it often gets the very best out of me.' (Peter: PPC)
1.8	'At least they know what makes me tick … I find it difficult to relate to people who just don't understand what drives me to do the things I do.' (Simon: PPC)
1.9 PNC: peers are used as a means of negative social comparison	'Not good [musician] from most people's points of view, because I'm not emotional, and most people say that you have to be able to put expression into the piece and stuff, and I'm sure they've got more logic than me, and they're probably right, so I'd say no, probably not [a good musician].' (Ian: PNC)

I liked to hang out with him and stuff because he was doing it, and he was a professional musician ... and I looked up to him ... there was a certain period when my influence from him was actually bad I think ... because ... I thought that I just wanted to play like him and even slightly be like him as a person as well.' (Bobby: PPC)

It appears that this person was one of Bobby's first peer contacts with the music world, and he seems to have been captured by its appeal – perhaps by observing a friend in the business, Bobby thought that he needed to adopt his idol's musical and personality characteristics in order to succeed. There is clearly a danger here because it is important as a musician to exert individuality, and imitating someone's personality at such a young age can be risky. The influence of his idol even stretched as far as Bobby's motivation to succeed:

I didn't really care about achieving anything he hadn't achieved, or going any further – I didn't really have my own goals ... and once I realized that I could achieve ... different things that I wanted to achieve, I think that was a turning point. (Bobby: PPC)

The danger seems to be that in idolizing someone, personal goals are limited to their achievements. It appears that Bobby had a struggle to remove the influence of his idol, and consequently he now has a greater awareness of what he wants to achieve.

Impact of Institutions

It emerged that the institutions to which the participants belonged had a particular impact on the individuals and their musical development. The influence of institutional setting on PNC seems to have been a key contributory factor in their decision not to pursue a professional performing career (see Table 18.2).

This evidence suggests that PNC's experiences of competition, pressure and intellectual boredom within the educational settings have contributed to their decision not to pursue a professional performing career. Whilst PPC have also had negative experiences within the institutions, they seem to have developed methods for coping with them, as detailed later. Of all the participants in the current study, one – Ian – is the only person no longer involved with music in any form. Ian seems to have had negative experiences within the music institution, and felt incredibly pressured to succeed.

If you do it every day of your life for eight years, you can get sick of it, so to speak, not sick of music, I'm just sick of learning it, and having to study it intensively ... You get pressured to practice, and you get pressured to do it more as it goes along. (Ian: PNC)

Table 18.2   The impact of institutions

2. Impact of institutions	Evidence
2.1 PNC: increasing disillusionment with institutions or the music industry	'It had all become a rat race of who you know, and who you last spoke to, and … it didn't necessarily depend on how good you were.' (Maggie: PNC)
2.2 PNC: the tendency of institution to favour a select few had a debilitating effect	'There was little general support for people unless you were an international soloist when you arrived.' (Maggie: PNC)
2.3	'I suppose that's why I didn't take it seriously, because they had people pegged out from the very beginning.' (Jade: PNC)
2.4 PNC: institutions don't always cater for the needs of unique individuals	'I didn't need particularly to practice that much – I'd do about an hour a day, and everybody else was doing 5 or 6 … and I was getting bored.' (John: PNC)

Ian is the only participant who explicitly states diminished enthusiasm for studying music. It seems that he felt increasing pressure from the school, and the culmination of this was that he no longer wished to pursue music. Ian used the environment of the school as a means of social comparison, through which he judged himself negatively, particularly in relation to emotion and music.

> They all seemed to be, a lot of them enjoyed the school anyway, and they all enjoyed music, and I was the one not particularly into … I was the least into music than the lot of them. (Ian: PNC)

Ian clearly perceives himself as different to his peers, and it seems that he felt inadequate, and like an impostor simply because he didn't have the same passion for music. Consequently, he seems to consider himself a less able musician. This is further emphasized by his lack of confidence in his musical ideas and playing, and the fact that he seems very submissive to the viewpoints of others, as detailed in Table 18.1, 1.9 above. Perhaps for these reasons, music is not a major part of Ian's self-concept (see below), and it is likely that these factors in combination have contributed to his move away from studying music.

The Importance of Motivation

Whilst all factors discussed in the current chapter contribute to the participants' motivation to pursue a professional performing career or not, the interviews revealed different forms of motivation in each group. The members of both groups are still motivated to be involved with music, but the precise nature of their motivation and engagement is quite different (see Table 18.3).

Table 18.3 The importance of motivation

3. Importance of motivation	Evidence
3.1 PNC: Enjoyment on a general level is the primary concern; they no longer want the burden of technical concerns	'I ... just want to enjoy it rather than getting totally weighed down with what angle my fingers are at.' (Maggie: PNC)
3.2 PPC: experience direct fulfilment from music	'[Music has brought] unbelievable amounts of pleasure.' (Mark: PPC)
3.3	'At the end of the day, I really enjoy doing it [music], definitely. There's no doubt about that, I just would have jacked it in ... So, it's definitely because I really enjoy doing it.' (James: PPC)
3.4 PPC: very strong intrinsic motivation	'It drives me so totally, I think, the whole nature of the beast. It drives me in the way that I want to do things, I want to do something new.' (Simon: PPC)
3.5	'There is a physical response, a necessary response to do it.' (Carl: PPC)

It is clear that PPC and PNC are distinguished by their types of motivation: for PNC, enjoyment seems to be the primary motivating force, but PPC seem driven to pursue a performing career by powerful intrinsic motivation. Simon is one of the more successful participants, and in his interview he described how much he relies upon his parents for security and as a contact with reality (see Table 18.1, 1.2), and it seems that his motivation to pursue music as a career is related to the centrality of music to his sense of self, as a form of expression.

> It's [music] sort of a rather fundamental part of life because it's there, and it's important, and I can do things with it that I can't do when I talk to people ... I can

just play better and I can move people, which I can't do when I talk to them.
(Simon: PPC).

As 4.1 and 4.5 in Table 18.4 further demonstrate, Simon has also developed his
own means of coping with the difficulties associated with being a musician,
recognizing the need for a balanced lifestyle and the importance of developing
other skills. By doing so, it seems that Simon feels he has more to offer music,
approaching it from a different, more mature perspective, both emotionally and
psychologically.

'Methods for coping', such as those developed by Simon, is one of three
themes that emerged to complement the themes discussed so far, which were
largely anticipated owing to the evidence previous research studies (Howe et al.,
1995; Davidson et al., 1996, 1997, 1998; Sloboda et al., 1996). The three themes
are:

1.   Methods of coping
2.   Music and communication
3.   Music as a determinant of self-concept

Methods of Coping

For the purposes of the current study, 'methods of coping' refers to either
physical measures taken by the musician, such as changing instrument, or a
more internal response, whereby the individual uses the surrounding environment
in a positive way. For example, rather than concentrate on the negative impact of
pressure or competition, experiences such as these are perceived by PPC as
valuable learning experiences. These methods of coping manifested themselves
in several forms (see Table 18.4).

What seems important about these different methods of coping is that all PPC
display a number of the above strategies (see the discussion about Simon above,
for example). There was no evidence, however, that PNC had developed any
methods for coping within the music institutions. It can be assumed, therefore,
that the presence of methods for coping, such as those described above, are a
contributory factor to the successful transition from training to professional life.

Music and Communication

One of the strongest distinctions between the two groups is that PPC use music
as a vehicle for communication. There appear to be two main forms of
communication that music adopts for this group: one is a means for communicating with other people, and the other is as a channel for emotional experience.

Table 18.4   The development of coping strategies

4. Methods of coping	Evidence
4.1 PPC: changing first study instrument to regain individuality and increase future opportunity	'I was on my own as a harpsichordist, so I got to do everything. I got to play things, I got to organize groups ... So, I made some huge mistakes, but I had some great successes.' (Simon: PPC)
4.2 PPC: developing positive ways for reflecting on experiences within institutions	'Because you're against all these people who are so much better than you, so much older than you, and who were actually beginning a professional career ... you begin to listen and hear things in a totally different way.' (Graham: PPC)
4.3	'I think what Chethams and College did was probably just open my eyes and give me much more worldwide experience.' (James: PPC)
4.4 PPC: learning to deal with the disappointments associated with being a musician	'I can accept that if I get kicked out in the first round of one [competition], it's not going to set me back too much, psychologically anyway. You have to – there are more disappointments in life than there are the good things.' (Graham: PPC)
4.5 PPC: recognizing the need for a balanced lifestyle, to enable them to approach music from different perspectives	'At least if you go away and do something else like a music degree ... or even bum off round the world for three years, you gain valuable experience ... you become once removed from the instrument, and then when you come back to it, your depth of understanding ... your feeling of ... internal satisfaction is greatly increased.' (Simon: PPC)
4.6 PNC: concerned with personal development, concentrating on different skills	'I was beginning to discover other talents that I had, and I guess I wanted to make use of those and develop those.' (Maggie: PNC)

Significantly, the majority of PNC do not use music in this way, or to the same extent as PPC. Of the six people in PNC, only one – John – makes any direct connection between music and emotional release. The ways in which music is

Table 18.5 Music and communication

5. Music and communication	Evidence
5.1 PPC: music is fundamental; it offers opportunities to express themselves and stir others, a skill not offered in language	'It's [music] sort of a rather fundamental part of life because it's there, and it's important, and I can do things with it that I can't do when I talk to people ... I can just play better and I can move people, which I can't do when I talk to them.' (Simon: PPC)
5.2 PPC: music is a channel for releasing negative emotions	'I've had quite a few bad things that have happened to me, and it's [music] been a form of release, therapeutic and relaxing.' (Georgina: PPC)
5.3	'I'm sometimes not very good at expressing things in words, expressing feeling ... whereas my playing I can just do it all the time, and I'm quite happy to put myself on the line when I'm playing and let people see me in a way that I won't do when I'm talking.' (Melissa: PPC)
5.4 PPC: music transcends ordinary levels of emotion	'I mean the freedom you get when performing is akin to other sorts of spiritual thing like prayer, which people consider to be important, and I consider I get more out of doing music than I would out of things like prayer.' (Andrew: PPC)
5.5 PPC: music is a way of communicating with others	'[Music] is a really special thing really, because you can do it with people that you don't really know very well, which you can't really do in any other way.' (Bobby: PPC)
5.6 PPC: music is a sharing experience	'I think it's [music] so liberating – there's no kind of prejudice in it – it's just pure expression from one person to another ... there's no prejudice or racial thing about it, it's an all encompassing thing.' (Patrick: PPC)

thought to be a powerful vehicle for communication are summarized in Table 18.5.

As detailed in Table 18.5, PNC do not describe music as having such powerful associations for them. One interpretation of this, therefore, is that the emotional, psychological and spiritual significance that music has for PPC contributes to their motivation to pursue a professional performing career. To contradict this generalization, however, one PNC, John, still relies on music as a means of releasing negative emotions.

> Good music has the ability to take me to a better space, I'd say. A better space within myself ... it's like all of the bad emotion in me just tightens up and explodes, and just totally goes, and then I'm just feeling totally light, and totally ready to dance, and so it sort of shatters any stress I've got. (John: PNC)

John's response to music is completely different to that of PPC in that his response when listening to music is very physical, probably due to the type of music in which he is interested (dance). John was a particularly interesting participant, in that having developed very quickly as a musician (four years) and displayed great potential at Chethams for a successful performing career, he has rejected classical music as a profession, and now works in the education division of a specialist music technology company. In his spare time, John composes dance music, from which he eventually wishes to earn his living. John did not complete his studies at music college, and his experiences with teachers and within the musical institutions were mainly negative, resulting in intellectual boredom, and a subsequent move away from classical music.

> There were things that I could do that he couldn't, and he was well-known for being one of the most technical recorder players in the world ... and I could play faster than him ... he was a bit resentful of that. (John: PNC)

> I'd do about half an hour a day, everybody else was doing five or six hours a day, and I had hours to kill, and I was getting so bored. (John: PNC)

John has an exceptional talent, and contrary to what might be expected, it appears that the school did not cater for his skill. John feels that he did not need to practise, which suggests that his programme of instrumental training was not demanding enough to challenge him. Furthermore, he clearly did not respect his teacher as a musician, which has also influenced his move away from music

Music as a Determinant of Self-concept

During the discourse that took place in the interviews, the participants were constructing stories of the self, rather than explicitly stating facts about themselves. In this way, it is possible to consider the self-concepts of these individuals, and it seems that the strongest distinction between the two groups is the impact that music has on their self-concepts. Self-concept refers to the perceptions, interpretations, and evaluations that an individual has about the self, and his or her talents and abilities (Feldhusen, 1986). For both groups of musicians, music is clearly a determinant of self-concept, although the extent to which it plays a role varies between the two groups (see Table 18.6).

Table 18.6   Music and self-concept

6. Music and self-concept	Evidence
6.1 PPC: perceive themselves and their feelings in terms of music	'I know when I haven't played for a while I start to doubt myself as a person.' (Mark: PPC)
6.2 PPC: music contributes to a sense of well-being	'[Music is] a great comforter. Sometimes when I have had a bad class at RADA, I'll go and play and always be reminding myself, "Hey I can do some things right."' (Carl: PPC)
6.3 PPC: music offers security	'I think it is always something that's there, you can't get away from it, and it will always be there, and that's nice in a way.' (Bobby: PPC)
6.4 PPC: many feel they have a personal affinity with their instruments	'I feel I always wanted to play the oboe since I was young and it's the most natural thing to me. Playing the oboe is literally the most natural thing I can do.' (Andrew: PPC)
6.5 PNC: music will always be important to self-concept due to years of involvement, but they have diminished passion for music	'It's [music] definitely part of my make-up, and I don't think I'll ever lose that, there's no reason to, but it's not something that really controls me ... I still absolutely love it ... I think I just lost the desire to make my living out of playing the fiddle.' (Maggie: PNC)

It could be considered that the contrasted ways in which PPC and PNC perceive themselves in relation to music have contributed to their decision to pursue a professional music career or not. It seems, therefore, that music as a major determinant of self-concept is vital if the transition from training to professional life is to be successful.

The themes discussed above demonstrate how the experiences of PPC and PNC are clearly different, and it can be assumed that they play a key contributory role to the musicians' motivation to pursue a professional performing career. In order to gain depth of understanding of the precise nature of the participants' experiences, several isolated cases have been considered, and it is clear to see that the difference between PPC and PNC lies mainly in three elements: the influence of others, the centrality of music to self-concept, and the development of methods for coping. If we consider the difference between John and Ian (both PNC), for example, the main difference seems to be the importance of music to self-concept, which may explain why John has not completely moved away from music – he has simply focused his attentions away from classical music, and onto commercial dance music.

Tripartite Model of Success

It appears that the influential factors determining whether the transition from training to professional life is successful are highly connected. By examining the individual experiences, comparing PNC and PPC, it appears that certain elements must be present in the transitional phase. Therefore, we propose a model of success illustrated in Figure 18.1.

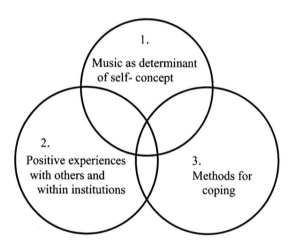

Figure 18.1   Tripartite model of success

This model proposes that the three elements are all dependent upon one another and that without one element, the musician's transition from training to professional life will not be successful. All elements of the model are equally important, and the presence of all elements is likely to enhance the likelihood of success. If, however, one element of the model is absent, success is unlikely. The centrality of music to self-concept is the most crucial element, as it contributes to the intrinsic motivation of the musician; experience allows the musician to develop the necessary tools to persevere with difficult periods, and, equally, the development of methods for coping help the individual to adapt to new experiences and challenges. Hence, each of the above elements is dependent on the others.

In order to illustrate the model further, the experiences of two individuals (PPC and PNC) are considered.

Figures 18.2 and 18.3 demonstrate how the model of success works for two individuals (PPC and PNC). The detail inside the rings show the experiences and behaviours which meet the criteria of the model, and that outside the model, in the case of John, demonstrates those areas of his experience and development that do not meet the necessary criteria. Figures 18.2 and 18.3 highlight that Simon (PPC) fulfils all the necessary criteria of the model, whilst John (PNC) does not. Interestingly, Ian does not fulfil any of the criteria of the model, perhaps reflecting his complete move away from music. The fact that music is still a strong determinant of John's self-concept may explain why he now focuses on creating commercial dance music, rather than rejecting music completely. The model of success can be used as a brief guideline to explain why the transition from training to professional life is successful for some, and not for others, and may be used to predict which individuals are most likely to succeed. The findings of the current study contradict theories that propose that only practice makes perfect, or that the influence of key others is the most significant

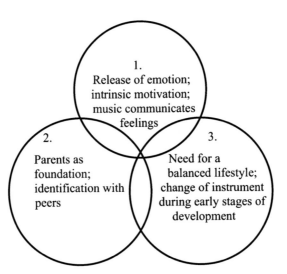

Figure 18.2   Tripartite model of success for Simon (PPC)

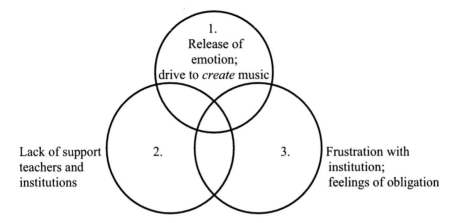

Figure 18.3   Tripartite model of success for John (PNC)

factor in the development of musical expertise. We would argue that the most crucial factor as the musician enters the transitional phase from training to professional life is music as the central determinant of self-concept, because it seems to provide the necessary motivation to persevere. Key others and the development of coping strategies are important in this model because they influence the self-concept of the individual, and if one element is absent, the musician's transition will be unsuccessful.

Discussion and Conclusion

The Importance of Music to Self-concept

The most important factor influencing whether the musicians in the current study went on to pursue a professional performing career is the role of music as the central determinant of self-concept, as it has an adaptive function for them, and it seems that the importance of music to self-concept develops during the later stages of training. Within this, crucial factors influencing the centrality of music to self-concept are the enjoyment and passion for music that PPC seem to experience, and, to further enhance their enjoyment, it seems paramount that PPC have freedom, independence and a balanced lifestyle, including non-musical as well as musical activities. Finally, intrinsic motivation is also highly important, since self-concept and the ability to survive in the industry depend on it. It is possible that the changes occurring in this developmental stage are related to changes in personality traits at this time (Kemp, 1996). Kemp, for example, suggests that particular personality traits 'are continuously adjusted and committed to music because of what it offers them in terms of meeting emotional and symbolic needs that are deeply embedded within their personalities' (Kemp, 1996, p. 28). Clearly, in order to establish the extent to which personality change influences the transition from training to professional life, further investigation is required.

Influence of Others

Experiences with other people (teachers, parents and peers) and the music education establishments clearly shape the musician and his or her self-concept in an ongoing manner, and this seems to influence whether they proceed through the transitional phase successfully. Parents remain important throughout the development of the musician, but their role changes – from one of support and encouragement, to that of providing a contact with reality and a sense of security. Their influence continues into adulthood, although too much pressure from parents throughout the child's development can be detrimental to the developing musician. Furthermore, teachers become an increasingly important influence, shaping the individual both musically and psychologically. The implications of this for parents and teachers are threefold: first, parents and teachers need to recognize the influence and impact of their actions on the developing musician. Talented children are considered more sensitive than other children (Albert and Runco, 1986; Freeman, 1990), and therefore too much negative action, or too little attention, can have disastrous effects on the developing child. Second, teachers and parents need to ensure that the child is given the freedom and space to explore their musical ideas, and indeed other experiences, in order to be well balanced, because this can enhance their musical experience. It is perhaps more important, however, that the musicians themselves recognize the need for a balanced lifestyle, because it seems that music can so easily become part of the whole person, perhaps to the detriment of other abilities, such as interpersonal skills. Finally, teachers should further be aware that the students' requirements of them change as they approach the transitory period (Sosniak, 1990); they may be required to offer practical help and encouragement, which can help maximize the musician's potential for success as a professional.

A further point to be considered relating to the education of talented musicians refers to the institutions in which they are studying. Due to the feelings of anxiety often experienced by students within their settings (Freeman, 1985; Sloboda, 1990), the specialist music schools and colleges need to recognize the requirements of all students, not simply a select few. It seems desirable to encourage, or even push, exceptionally gifted students enough that they have to work hard each day to achieve their targets, but not so much that they feel too pressured.

One final conclusion is that peers also play an important role, and their influence particularly towards the end of the training period, and during the transitory phase, is vital. Peers provide support, encouragement and understanding to one another (Freeman, 1985; Sosniak, 1990), and this is perhaps more important when they initially finish their training and begin the pursuit of a professional career – a period of difficulty, and much uncertainty. Furthermore, peers can inspire one another when they work together on small joint projects (Feldhusen, 1986), which is perhaps something that should be considered throughout specialist music education.

Conclusions

The study has provided some useful insights into the young specialist musician, and it has demonstrated the changes that have occurred in the lives of these participants since the original study: teachers, parents and peers continue to play an important role, although the nature of their influence has adapted alongside the needs and developments of the musician. The development of methods for coping seem crucial in overcoming the many hurdles experienced during education and the transitional phase, and perhaps more importantly, music's role within the individual's self-concept is vital. The implications of the study seem mainly targeted at parents, teachers and institutional policy, but they also have relevance to the students themselves, since it is perhaps necessary for them to have an awareness of the factors contributing to their success as a musician in order that they seek the appropriate support and encouragement. Furthermore, the findings provide a foundation on which additional, and more extensive, research can build.

Appendix 1: Interview Schedule 1 – Background Information

1. Name:
2. Age:
3. Year of study:
4. Current place of study/course:
5. Main instrument: Length of time played: Age started:
6. Other instruments: Length of time played: Age started:
7. Why did you want to learn/start playing your main instrument?
8. Why did you want to learn/start playing the other instruments? (if applicable)
9. Why did you decide to focus and improve on your main instrument?
10. Has there been some kind of turning point that has influenced your decision to study music to a high level, and perhaps further?
11. What kinds of activities have you been engaged in with your main/other instruments throughout your musical career?
12. What activities are you currently engaged in with your main/other instruments? What kind of commitment do they require?

13. What courses have you completed? (University, college, etc.)
14. What, or who, do you think your key influences have been? In what aspect of your life have they played a role? To what extent?
15. What role have your parents played in decisions you have made? (studying, jobs, other)
16. Do any other people play an important role in your life?
17. What are your current goals and ambitions?
18. What are your long-term musical goals?
19. Do you think music will always play an important role in your life?
20. What do you think makes a good musician? (qualities/strengths/weaknesses)
21. Do you think you have these qualities?
22. What do you think studying music to a high level has offered you? What skills has it provided?
23. Are there any negative aspects to studying music to a high level? Have you had any experiences that have made you think this? How have you coped with these difficulties?

Appendix 2: Interview Schedule 2 – Transitional Questionnaire

1. How has your playing been going recently/since we last met for an interview?
2. What playing have you been doing? (concerts/rehearsals/gigs/practice)
3. How much have you been playing? How is your playing time divided into rehearsals and formal practice – time scales?
4. How is your practice going?
5. What progress do you think you have made?
6. How do you think that has been achieved?
7. What form has your practice taken?
8. How have you been feeling when you've been playing?
9. How have your lessons been?
10. What has your teacher said about your playing?
11. Have you had a lesson that has been particularly good or bad?
12. How has this affected your playing?
13. How would you describe your relationship with your teacher? What are your perceptions of your teacher? How does this influence your playing?
14. How do you feel about the quality of your playing in general at the moment? Why do you think that is?
15. Do you think you could improve that feeling? How?
16. Is there anything you feel needs improvement? What?
17. How do you think you will go about overcoming the problem?
18. Do you have a target that you are working towards at the moment?
19. How do you feel about it?

20. How do you think the event will go?
21. How central would you say music is to you at the moment, spiritually, psychologically, and socially?
22. How does this compare with other things you do? (sport/hobbies)
23. How are the academic elements of the course going?
24. How much work have you been doing for them?
25. How does this compare to the amount of time you have spent practising?
26. Why do you think you divide your time in this way? (priority/enjoyment)
27. Have you had any feedback on the work you have done? Has that been positive or negative?
28. In what way has this affected you?
29. How much are you enjoying the module?
30. What else have you been doing aside from work on your degree? What time have you spent pursuing other interests? How do you feel when engaging in other activities?
31. Do you find that other aspects of your life carry over into your music? Have there been any instances of this since we last met? In what way has it affected your playing?
32. What do you think you want to do after you complete your degree?
33. How realistic do you think it is that you will do that? Do you think you have to achieve anything in particular before you are able to do so? How do you think you will go about preparing for that?
34. Do you think music will always play an important role in your life?
35. What do you think music has brought you, for good or ill, since I last met with you?
36. What do you think your biggest achievement has been since we last spoke/ in the last few weeks?
37. What do you want to have achieved by the next time I speak to you? Do you think that's possible? How will you try to achieve that goal?
38. Would you now summarize your thoughts and feelings about your playing, and music in general, in the last few weeks.

Note

1. This chapter is based on an article by Burland and Davidson that appears in *Music Education Research*: Burland, K. and Davidson, J.W. (2002) 'Training the talented', *Music Education Research*, 4: 121–140. It is reproduced with full permission of Carfax Publishing.

References

Albert, R.S., and Runco, M.A. (1986) 'The achievement of eminence: A model based on a longitudinal study of exceptionally gifted boys and their families', in R.J. Sternberg and J.F. Davidson (eds), *Conceptions of Giftedness*, pp. 332–56, Cambridge: Cambridge University Press.

Bamberger, J. (1982) 'Growing-up prodigies: The midife crisis', in D.H. Feldman (ed.) *Developmental Approaches to Giftedness*, pp. 388–413, San Fransisco: Jossey-Bass.

Covington, M.V. and Omelich, C.L. (1979) 'Effort: The double-edged sword in school achievements', *Journal of Educational Psychology*, 71: 169–82.

Csikszentmihalyi, M., Rathunde, K. and Whalen, S. (1993) *Talented Teenagers: The Roots of Success and Failure*, Cambridge: Cambridge University Press.

Davidson, J.W., Howe, M.J. and Sloboda, J.A. (1997) 'Environmental factors in the development of musical performance skill over the life span', in D.J. Hargreaves and A.C. North (eds), *The Social Psychology of Music*, pp. 188–206, Oxford: Oxford University Press.

Davidson, J.W., Howe, M.J.A., Moore, D.G. and Sloboda, J.A. (1996) 'The role of parental influences in the development of musical performance', *British Journal of Developmental Psychology*, 14: 399–412.

Davidson, J.W., Moore, D.G., Sloboda, J.A. and Howe, M.J.A. (1998) 'Characteristics of music teachers and the progress of young instrumentalists', *Journal of Research in Music Education*, 46(1): 141–60.

Ericsson, A., Tesch-Römer, E. and Krampe, R. (1996) 'The role of practice and motivation in the acquisition of expert-level performance in real life', in M.J.A. Howe (ed.), *Encouraging the Development of Exceptional Skills and Talents*, pp. 149–64, Leicester: The British Psychological Society.

Erikson, E. (1959) *Identity and the Life Cycle*, New York: International University Press.

Feldhusen, J.F. (1986) 'A conception of giftedness', in R.J. Sternberg and J.E. Davidson (eds), *Conceptions of Giftedness*, pp. 112–27, Cambridge: Cambridge University Press.

Freeman, J. (1985) 'Emotional aspects of giftedness', in J. Freeman (ed.), *The Psychology of Gifted Children: Perspectives in Development and Education*, pp. 247–64, Chichester: John Wiley.

Freeman, J. (1990) 'The intellectual gifted adolescent', in M.J.A. Howe (ed.), *Encouraging the Development of Exceptional Skills and Talents*, pp. 89–108, Leicester: The British Psychological Society.

Freeman, J. (1991) *Gifted Children Growing Up*, London, Portsmouth: Heinemann Educational Books.

Gecas, V. and Mortimer, J.T. (1987) 'Stability and change in the self-concept from adolescence to adulthood', in T. Honess and K. Yardley, *Self and Identity: Perspectives across the Lifespan*, pp. 265–85, London: Routledge and Kegan Paul.

Haan, N. (1981) 'Adolescents and young adults as producers of their development', in R.M. Lerner and N.A. Busch-Rossnagel (eds) *Individuals as Producers of Their Development: A Life-Span Perspective*, pp. 155–82, New York; London: Academic Press.

Hall, R. (1960) Sleeve note to *Masters of Irish Music: Martyn Byrnes*, Leader Sound.

Howe, M.J.A. (1990) *The Origins of Exceptional Abilities*, Oxford: Basil Blackwell.

Howe, M.J.A., Davidson, J.W., Moore, D.G. and Sloboda, J.A. (1995) 'Are there early childhood signs of musical ability?' *Psychology of Music*, 23: 162–76.

Kemp, A.E. (1996) *The Musical Temperament: Psychology and Personality of Musicians*, Oxford: Oxford University Press.

Manturzewska, M. (1990) 'A biographical study of the life-span development of professional musicians', *Psychology of Music*, 18: 112–39.

Piaget, J. and Inhelder, B. (1969) *The Psychology of the Child*, London: Routledge and Kegan Paul.

Renzulli, J.S. (1986) 'The three-ring conception of giftedness: A developmental model for creative productivity', in R.J. Sternberg and J.E. Davidson (eds), *Conceptions of Giftedness*, pp. 53–127, Cambridge: Cambridge University Press.

Robson, C. (1998[1993]) *Real World Research*, Oxford: Blackwell Publishers.

Sloboda, J. (1990) 'Musical excellence – how does it develop?' in M.J.A. Howe (ed.), *Encouraging the Development of Exceptional Skills and Talents*, pp. 165–78, Leicester: The British Psychological Society.

Sloboda, J.A. and Howe, M.J.A. (1991) 'Biographical precursors of musical excellence: An interview study', *Psychology of Music*, 19: 3–21.

Sloboda, J.A., Davidson, J.W., Howe, M.J.A. and Moore, D.G. (1996) 'The role of practice in the development of performing musicians', *British Journal of Psychology*, 87: 287–309.

Smith, J.A., Flowers, P. and Osborn, M. (1997) 'Interpretative phenomenological analysis and the psychology of health bad illness', in L. Yardley (ed.), *Material Discourses of Health and Illness*, pp. 68–9, London: Routledge.

Sosniak, L.A. (1990) 'The tortoise, the hare, and the development of talent', in M.J.A. Howe (ed.), *Encouraging the Development of Exceptional Skills and Talents*, pp. 165–78, Leicester: The British Psychological Society.

Chapter 19

Flawed Expertise:
Exploring the Need to Overcome the
Discrepancy between Instrumental
Training and Orchestral Work –
the Case of String Players

Daina Langner

Background

Alongside general rising standards of competence in musicians emerging from music colleges, the number of applicants for professional orchestral positions is increasing from year to year (Rinderspacher, 2000). Focusing on string players, this chapter examines how these individuals train and then cope with the auditioning process. A situation has arisen in which players train largely for a solo career, but then the reality is that, if they are lucky, they may gain employment in the rank and file of the second violins in an orchestra. As violin professor H. Schneeberger (Noltensmeier, 1997) comments: 'Twenty to twenty-five years ago, we could quite happily advise violin players to apply for positions as concertmasters, but today we should really sometimes be telling them that they should be glad to find a place in one of the last seats of a good orchestra'. Thus, the situation nowadays is that musicians who excel in solo performance tend to be those who are increasingly selected for the orchestra, with solo audition playing being the most common part of these musicians' training (Griffing, 1994). The majority of successful auditionees fill tutti positions within the orchestra and are hence no longer required to perform solos.

It is not surprising, therefore, that orchestral auditioning panels criticize the fact that auditionees neglect to prepare the excerpts (extracts from orchestral works, employed in the audition process) thoroughly. In the final round of auditioning, an alarming discrepancy emerges: musicians with highly-trained abilities in solo playing, but a startling lack of preparation for the practical demands of orchestral playing (this notion is based on personal communication and participation in orchestral auditioning panels). Orchestral work may at the glance appear less demanding than solo performance; in reality, however, the body of orchestral literature contains works of as great a difficulty, and demanding of just as much skill (albeit of a somewhat different kind), as solo pieces (Noltensmeier, 1997).

Musicians, it appears, experience the transition from a solo to a group role in very different ways. Some are relieved to have a position. Others, however, have difficulties integrating into their section and miss the challenge of solos. The award of a place in an orchestra is typically followed by a one-year trial period, during which anecdotal reports indicate that failure is more often due to problems of integration rather than to insufficient ability. Such cases of social failure indicate the importance of adapting to the orchestral group situation for successful and permanent integration into the orchestra, and suggest that training institutions should perhaps consider some of these issues in more detail. It was on these grounds that the investigation described in this chapter was undertaken.

The TICOM Study

Popular belief among orchestral musicians is that problems of integration and adaptation, and indeed greater individualism, occur more evidently and frequently among violinists than among other string players. Such differences, if they do in fact exist, would surely be most evident between violinists and double bassists. The reason for this supposition lies in the different roles these two instruments tend to take in orchestral music. The parts double bassists are required to play in art music are by no means solos, but rather supporting parts. The instrument has a primarily accompanying function. Double bassists will not generally have ambitions to be soloists. They are required to take a supporting role within the group from the very beginning. Are violinists, then, more individualistic than double bassists? Or are particularly good musicians, regardless of which instrument they play, more individualistic than their colleagues? Or are differences not to be found between either instrument groups or different levels of musical competence, but rather are equally distributed across all instruments and competence levels? These were the main questions of the TICOM study (Test of Individualism and Collectivism of Orchestral Musicians) reported here. This study examines personality traits, focusing on those closely connected to individualism and collectivism. Individualism can be defined as a person's perception of self-development and variety of life choices as basic requirements for personal happiness and satisfaction. By contrast, collectivism can be defined as the sense of belonging to a group, with membership of this community being the basis for personal happiness and satisfaction (Triandis, 1995; Triandis and Gelfand, 1998). Individualism, then, would imply a greater reluctance to work simply as a member of the group (here, the orchestra), and a pursuit of one's own personal development.

General Method

The TICOM study investigated 121 music students from 12 German music academies during 1998–99. The students were divided into groups according to whether their main instrument was violin or double bass, and according to their level of competence – the 'best' and the 'good' groups. The criterion for the 'best' group was that a student had in the last three years, with their main instrument, taken part in a minimum of one national or international competition, in which she/he had successfully reached at least the second round. The 'good' group were students who were successfully completing their performance courses, but who had not achieved competitive success. There were four groups in all: best violinists, good violinists, best double bassists and good double bassists. The questionnaire consisted of particular scales based on a commercially available and standardized German version of the Personality Research Form (PRF; Stumpf et al., 1985), one of the most commonly used personality questionnaires; scales from the Achievement Motivation Inventory (LMI, Schuler and Prochaska, 2000), a newly developed personality questionnaire; and scales based on Test of Individualism and Collectivism (TIC; Triandis, 1995). These scales have been developed with large numbers of test participants, and are believed to be robust tools to measure particular personality traits (for example, displayed levels of dominance). Potential traits are characterized in statements which the participant is required to rate on a seven-point scale of agreement, running from one (strongly disagree) to seven (strongly agree).

In a statistical analysis of all seven-point rating scales, collected for every participant, the factors 'instrument' (violin/double bass) and 'competence' (best/good playing standard) were examined. Potential differences in mean (average) scores across 'instrument' × 'competence' were calculated. This type of test allowed the following questions to be posed:

1. Are there significant differences in the mean scores for the personality traits between violinists and double bassists?
2. Are there significant differences in the mean scores for the personality traits between the good and the best students?
3. Finally, is there an interaction between the two factors 'instrument' and 'competence'?

Results

Applying statistical tests to the data, an effect of 'competence' appeared in every trait for which significant differences were found (these results are shown in Table 19.1). The 'best' students demonstrated higher mean scores in every trait except affiliation, in which they had lower mean scores. Affiliation bears an inverse relation to the other traits studied; and so it implies a seeking out of the

Table 19.1   Traits that showed significant effects ($p < .05$)

Affiliation (PRF)	High scores in this trait indicate a tendency to seek the company of other people.
Dominance (PRF)	High scores indicate the tendency to aim to reach the top of a given hierarchy or occupy a leading position in the group.
Exhibition (PRF)	High scores indicate that the person enjoys being in the limelight, receiving favourable attention, etc.
Status orientation (LMI)	A sense or consciousness of, consequently self-orientation according to, status.
Competitiveness (LMI)	A need to compare oneself with, and the desire to achieve more than, others.
Vertical individualism (TIC)	Emphasis on free choices and liberty of development, differing from horizontal individualism in that vertical individualism implies an acceptance of hierarchical relations between individuals.

company of other people and an ability to cooperate well with them, while the other traits imply higher individualism and the assumption or acceptance of a competitive or hierarchical relation.

A significant main effect of 'instrument' did occur, but for only two traits: dominance and exhibition. Here, violinists had higher scores than double bassists. Significant interactions between competence and instrument also appeared for two traits: dominance and status orientation. Analyses of variance yielded significant main effects for instrument, competence, and their interaction. Inspection of the mean values of the four groups of participants (see Figure 19.1) suggests that the main difference is between best violinists and the other three groups. This was confirmed by an additional *post-hoc* test, the Newman-Keuls test ($p < 0.01$).

Emerging from this result, it must be asked; why are best violinists more dominant than others? This difference cannot be attributed to competence alone, since 'best' double bassists did not report more dominance than 'good' double bassists. Male and female violinists showed similar patterns in this scale, so gender cannot be an explanation for the finding. Undertaking further analyses, the age at which these musicians began to play their instrument appears to have had an effect. The violinists began at an average age of six years. The earliest starting age in my sample was three years, and the latest nine years. The double bassists began at an average age of ten years with a variance of 4.2; thus, a much larger variance than that for the violinists. The earliest starting age for the

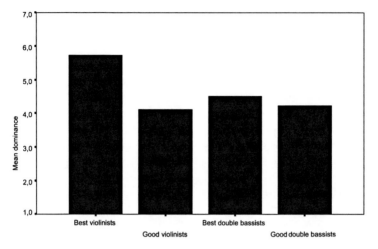

Figure 19.1   The mean scores for dominance for the four groups of musicians

double bassists was three years, and the latest 20 years. It is important to note that these figures, unlike those for the violinists, do not refer to the present instrument, but to the first instrument they played at all. The double bassists played instruments ranging from the drum to the trombone, flute, violin and saxophone. Many of the girls played the harp. The average age at which they started to play the double bass itself was 16 years. The variance of 2.5 for the figure 'starting the double bass' is small in comparison to that for 'starting to play an instrument', but still much larger than that for the violinists. The minimum and maximum ages exhibited quite a large gap: the youngest was 11 years old, the oldest 30.

In the case of the violinists, the considerably lower average age of starting to play the instrument is a factor which separates all violinists from all double bassists. Further factors are responsible for differences within the instrument groups.

Ericsson et al. (1993) have established that the 'best' violinists differ from the 'good' violinists in that they do a much larger amount of practice during early adolescence. The role of teachers, parents and peers in encouraging them in these activities is a very significant one (Sloboda and Howe, 1991; Davidson et al., 1996; Sloboda, 1997). If progression in expertise is praised by such people, this in turn increases self-confidence and possibly also the level of dedication, leading to a form of 'virtuous circle'. During this long period, such development might well go hand-in-hand with increased levels of dominance, tendency to exhibitionism, consciousness of status, competitiveness, and so on. Increased amounts of practice have the effect of encouraging this virtuous circle, which can go to explain the difference between the 'best' and the 'good' violinists.

This 'virtuous circle' effect, however, also – at least in principle – takes place among the double bassists, which gives rise to the question as to why it is only the 'best' violinists who demonstrate such markedly increased levels of the personality traits I have investigated. Here we find ourselves returning to the question of the age difference at the time of starting the instrument. The effect of the 'virtuous circle' of practice and praise on a musician's personality may well be more marked if it takes place in childhood and adolescence, as is the case for the vast majority of violinists. From around 18 years of age, however, the personality is considered to be largely formed (see Kemp, 1996 for an overview). As the average age for the double bassists starting to play their instrument is 16, there may have been little opportunity for the 'virtuous circle' to have effected changes in their personalities.

The 'best' violinists' high levels of dominance, exhibition and so on may be the result of the simultaneous occurrence of three factors: early starting age (factor specific to instrument group); increased levels of practice (factor separating 'good' violinists – less practice – from 'best' violinists – more practice); and the 'virtuous circle' effect (more pronounced for the musician who practices more, and having a greater effect on personality development for the younger musician, both of which are the case for the 'best' violinists).

Conclusion

The TICOM study established that the 'best' violin students (those who had the best chances of gaining a place in an orchestra later on) exhibited differences from 'good' violin students in personality traits which are closely connected to greater degrees of individualism. These differences, however, are at odds with the requirements for orchestral musicians. This expertise effect on personality, along with the heavy emphasis on solo work at the music academy, could well be responsible for many an orchestral violinist coming down to earth with a bump once successfully past the audition stage, and hence past the point at which success is measured almost exclusively by solo ability. Carl Flesch (1929), the doyen of modern violin pedagogy, commented as follows on the rude awakening of the orchestral violinist: 'Nearly every orchestra violinist, once upon a time, has dreamed of becoming a celebrated soloist. ... An orchestra violinist of this type, therefore, will and must always be discontented with his [sic] lot.'

The dilemma for the training of professional musicians, then, is: how to devote adequate attention, within violin lessons, both to perfecting musical/ technical skills on the instrument and to the demands of the students' later working life? Musical training offers the opportunity to study orchestral playing, chamber music and training of orchestral excerpts as subsidiary subjects. If the professor responsible for the main instrument, who represents the greatest musical influence on the students in the training stage, harnesses the early enthusiasm of the young musician for the youth orchestra, he/she will be able to transform this childhood enthusiasm into a musically productive and lasting interest in these subsidiary subjects. There is also the potential – and the need – for new orchestra-related subjects in the curriculum. We see, then, that there exists a need to arouse interest among music students – at every stage of training – for orchestral as well as solo repertoire, as it is orchestral literature with which most of them will primarily occupy themselves in the course of their professional work later on. It is particularly important that music professors inspire this interest; however, this is a difficult task in the face of current structures in music academies, which inevitably put orchestral training at a disadvantage. The mission statements of music academies often commit them to encouraging in students a 'distinctive interpretive personality, which is convincing in live concert performance – in both solo and ensemble contexts' (see, for example, 'Learning Outcomes', Royal Academy of Music, London, 2000). Nevertheless, these are perhaps overreaching aims in the current work environment, and in light of the fact that there is such huge competition for relatively few positions.

This current research project has indicated two important points which are of great urgency to the music practitioner:

1. different types of musicians show different personality traits;
2. the traits displayed by the best and most soloistic of players means that they are most likely to become employed through audition in an orchestra, yet be least suited to, and equipped for, the demands of the job.

This leads to the question that it is surely time to think about creating structures in music teaching in which a concentration on orchestral training for all orchestral instruments would in fact be advantageous to them. Solo violin concertos are not the only way to provide the musical and technical training professional musicians require.

The orchestras could also change their auditioning practices so that they are recruiting the 'right sort of attitude' as well as playing technique for the job.

The TICOM study has demonstrated that the practice of searching for the conventionally 'best' violinists, relying on audition methods which concentrate on solo playing to the exclusion of all other skills, naturally increases the likelihood that those players eventually selected for the orchestra will, similar to the 'best violinists' group in our study, be those who tend to have difficulties in adapting to a group situation and be, to refer again to Flesch, 'discontented with their lot'. However, the TICOM study analysed only *average* values for the groups of participants. This means that within the 'best violinists' group there will be violinists who have more and less difficulty in adapting to a group, that is, more 'individualist' and more 'collectivist' types, respectively. Thus, there do exist violinists who combine very high levels of musical and technical competence with skills of social competence in group conditions. Hence, it would make a lot of sense to introduce a systematic element into the audition process that is capable of selecting those with both the highest level of technical competence and the greatest ability to adapt to groups. One suggestion of the current research, therefore, would be to include in the audition process a test of ability to integrate speedily into a group. One possible way of testing such ability, which would not be at all problematic or difficult to organize, would be to arrange a quartet from the orchestra, remove the second violinist, and replace him/her with the applicant; then, to present the applicant with a piece of music with which he/she is unfamiliar. This procedure would test both sight-reading ability and competence in adaptation to the group, which are precisely the abilities required in the everyday working life of an orchestra member.

Old habits die hard: conservative modes of thought which suggest that solo work is the only adequate means of training a future orchestra member, or testing the orchestra applicant on his/her technical competence at audition, are clearly still very powerful within the musical world in Europe. On the other hand, the Metropolitan Opera in New York has already effected radical changes in the audition process. Aware that is it not necessarily 'soloist'-types who are most fitted for orchestral work, the Met now completely omits solo works from the audition procedure, instead preferring to test applicants on orchestral excerpts at each stage of the audition.

If many more orchestras were to take up a similar practice, musical training would be freed from the necessity of preparing students for an audition concentrating only on solo works, and would consequently be able to provide the students with a training more closely resembling the reality of their future orchestral career. Likewise, the procedure I am suggesting would bring the requirements of the audition closer to the demands of the real work situation, which would in turn have a positive effect on musical training. Such changes will necessitate more adaptation, on the part of students and structures, in the case of violin, viola and cello than in the case of the double bass; this is often apparent from the differing requirements the music academies set their auditionees in these two cases. For example, the double bassists, in contrast to the other three string instruments, must prepare for the entrance exam for the Royal Academy of Music in London 'two excerpts from orchestral repertoire' and are required to perform a sight-reading test, neither of which appear in the auditions for the other strings ('Audition Requirements', Royal Academy of Music, London, 2000).

Music academies certainly have the potential and the duty to arouse and channel students' interest in orchestral works. The aims of the academies, conceived at the top of the tree, to train students to the highest level 'in both solo and ensemble contexts' ('Learning Outcomes', Royal Academy of Music, London, 2000) should be able to arrive undiluted at, and be capable of realization in, the actual work of training. However, the main impetus for change must come from the orchestras. Bizarrely, their current practices are more suited to the support of music academies' structures, and to the prolongation of the academics' predicament, than to the fulfilment of their own requirements. And without change on the part of the orchestras, music academies are given neither the carrot nor the stick to persuade them to revise their own practices.

References

Davidson, J.W., Howe, M.J.A., Moore, D.G. and Sloboda, J.A. (1996) 'The role of parental influences in the development of musical ability', *British Journal of Developmental Psychology*, 14: 399–412.

Ericsson, K.A., Krampe, R. and Tesch-Römer, C. (1993) 'The role of deliberate practice in the acquisition of expert performance', *Psychological Review*, 100: 363–406.

Flesch, C. (1929) *Die Kunst des Violinspiels*, Berlin: Ries & Erler.

Griffing, J. (1994) *Audition Procedures and Advice from Concertmasters of American Orchestras*, unpublished dissertation, Ohio State University, UMI ON: 9427653.

Kemp, A.E. (1996) *The Musical Temperament*, Oxford: Oxford University Press.

Noltensmeier, R. (1997) *Grosse Geigenpädagogen im Interview* [*Interviews with Great Violin Teachers*], Kiel: Götzelmann.

Rinderspacher, A. (2000) 'Zum Thema Nachwuchs' ['About young professionals in music'], *Orchester*, 4: 10–15.

Royal Academy of Music London (2000) 'Audition Requirements', available at: <http://www.ram.ac.uk/pages/2.htm>; 'Learning Outcomes', available at: <http://www.ram.ac.uk/pages/6.htm>.

Schuler, H. and Prochaska, M. (2000) 'Entwicklung und Konstruktvalidierung eines berufsbezogenen Leistungsmotivationstests' ['Development and Constant Validation of an Achievement Motivation Inventory'], *Diagnostica*, 46(2): 61–72.

Sloboda, J.A. (1997) 'Begabung und Hochbegabung' ['Talent and giftedness'], in H. Bruhn, R. Oerter and H. Rosing (eds), *Musikpsychologie: Ein Handbuch*, pp. 565–78, Reinbek: Rowohlt.

Sloboda, J.A. and Howe, M.J.A. (1991) 'Biographical precursors of musical excellence: An interview study', *Psychology of Music*, 19: 3–21.

Stumpf, H., Angleitner, A., Wieck, Th., Jackson, D.N. and Beloch-Till, H. (1985) *Deutsche Personality Research Form*, Hogrefe: Göttingen.

Triandis, H.C. (1995) *Individualism and Collectivism*, Boulder, CO: Westview Press.

Triandis, H.C. and Gelfand, M.J. (1998) 'Converging Measurement of Horizontal and Vertical Individualism and Collectivism', *Journal of Personality and Social Psychology*, 74: 118–28.

PART 5

Adopting Innovative Research Approaches

Chapter 20

A New Method for Analysing and Representing Singing[1]

Stefanie Stadler Elmer and Franz-Josef Elmer

Introduction

This chapter offers new perspectives on the analysis of song-singing for research in psychological and cross-cultural contexts (for example, ethnomusicology). So far, the traditional methods turn out to be culturally or even ethnocentrically biased. The aim of this research and of the newly devised method was to gain reliable and valid analysis and descriptions of various kinds of singing as the basis of acoustic tools.

In the last decades, there has been a growing interest in cultural issues and in socio-cultural processes that promote individuals' acquisition and internalization of cultural products and rules. One such product that exists in every human culture is the social tradition of song-singing that is mediated and transformed from one generation to the next. From early on in life, children familiarize with the musical conventions, especially with the child-directed practice of children's songs (for example, lullabies). At amazingly early ages children produce vocal musical sounds such as recognizable songs and song fragments. For instance, children's productions of the traditional German song '*Hopp, hopp, hopp, Pferdchen lauf Galopp*' are reported by Stern (1965 [1914]) about Günter at age 1.10 years, by M. and H. Papoušek (1981) about Tanja at age 1.1 years, and by Stadler Elmer (1997) about Ursina at age 1.8 years. These children performed vocal sounds that were structured in such a way that the intended song was easy to identify. Of course, these early products were not yet properly organized with respect to all of the complex and hierarchical rules that make up a song. The learning of a culture's song-singing rules is a lengthy process of enculturation that basically includes linguistic (lyrics) and musical (melody) rules, both combined by meter (pulses that are periodically stressed and unstressed), and social rules that regulate participation by jointly matching and synchronizing vocal pitches.

In children, the vocal structures are in progress towards integrating these rules. When stimulated to participate in recurrent and joyful singing rituals, young children readily adapt their vocal structures to these joint activities. Usually, the adult guide is able to recognize the newly acquired song fragments in the child's vocalization as a response to their communication and shared musical experiences. Moreover, the adult's interpretation and understanding of the child's singing is based on cultural concepts or knowledge. With this situated cultural knowledge, a minimum of cues is sufficient in identifying the child's intended (musical and linguistic) meaning in her or his vocalization.

Usually, there is no need to reflect on this functional tendency for misinterpreting pre-cultural behaviour. On the contrary, interpretation by cultural categories or concepts helps to reduce the wealth of perceptually available information, allows distinctions among objects and events, and adds meaning to them. In this sense, musical training aims at gaining and refining categorical perception and musical concepts within a given cultural system. It is a collectively shared semiotic system, and akin to language; it provides the very basis for communication and the social practice of sound-making.

Siegel and Siegel (1977b) showed that highly trained musicians had a strong tendency to rate out-of-tune stimuli as in-tune. Their attempts to make fine, within-category judgements were highly inaccurate and unreliable, whereas they differentiated well between musical categories. The musicians were not aware of their biases in categorizing stimuli in terms of musical concepts. Since these authors proved that non-musicians have great difficulty in discriminating even between musical categories (1977a), they conclude the phenomena of categorical perception to be a result of musical training; it is functionally similar to phonemic categories for speech.

Many developmental and learning theories, especially the ones in the tradition of Piaget (see, for example, Beilin and Pufall, 1992; Smith, 1996), favour structural approaches in the sense that actions are analysed as organized units in order to study underlying mental processes and structural changes. According to such theoretical approaches, we consider singing as a complex organized action whose structures are guided mentally (for example, Imberty, 1996; Stadler Elmer, 1998). Whenever we want to describe and explain unconventional singing, either by children or by people from other cultures, we are faced with a rather paradoxical situation. Psychological investigations into musical issues require musical knowledge. But it is this knowledge that turns out to be an obstacle in understanding children's, novices', and general non-western musical behaviour and cognition. Musical training implies strong biases towards culturally established meanings and symbols which may not be present in the phenomena. Seashore (1938) impressively demonstrated the discrepancies between a singer's interpretation of a score and the listener's judgements of intonation. He concludes that: 'It is shockingly evident that the musical ear which hears the tones indicated by the conventional notes is extremely generous and operates in the interpretative mood. ... the matter of hearing pitch is largely a matter of conceptual hearing in terms of conventional intervals, ...' (p. 269). Deviations from expected pitches are tolerated and are a means for aesthetic expression, particularly in artistic singing with vibrato (cf., for example, Seashore, 1938; Sundberg, 1982).

To conclude, it appears that researchers need musical knowledge for understanding musical phenomena, but this knowledge may misrepresent the phenomena due to the highly culturally influenced mind that tends to overestimate cultural meaning which might not be intended by the producer of music. The problem we discuss in this chapter is, therefore, to cope with our musical mind in a way that allows us to minimize its high propensity of cultural interpretation.

First, we discuss the traditional methods for analysing and representing 'musical' products, especially singing, and its shortcomings. Second, we show that computers can be used as excellent research tools to eliminate the researcher's musical mind at an important stage in the research process. Third, we propose to reduce the detailed acoustic data by a notation system that is more differentiated than the conventional one. Then, we illustrate this method with an example of a young western child's song-singing. The utility of the method is discussed by comparing it with a professional musician's transcription of the same song-singing.

Beyond general delight of children's singing, scientific interest in this behaviour can be traced back to the beginning of this century. Yet, the fleeting and transient nature of singing and the related problems of assessing its intricate nature seem often to have kept researchers from conducting systematic investigations. Our method promises to open new ways of gaining insights into psychological processes in this cultural domain.

Traditional Methods for Analysing Singing

In his review of the ways singing can be assessed, Welch (1994) distinguishes between 'machine-based' and 'human-based' analyses. Welch's term 'machine-based' analyses refers mainly to those methods which assess the underlying physiological bases of singing such as electrolaryngography. By 'human-based' analyses he refers to auditory ratings done by professional musicians about 'goodness of fit' with regard to the rules of the musical culture.

Besides these two methods, researchers want to study *what* children sing and how the structures of their singing change as a matter of progressive adaptation to their socio-cultural surrounding through learning and development (see, for example, overviews by Atterbury, 1984; Anderson, 1991; Stadler Elmer, 2000b, 2002). However, the nature of such enculturation processes is a key interest in the fields of development, education, and cultural learning in psychology. In a cross-cultural and ethnomusicological context, it would be important to have research tools that permit some kind of culture-free and reliable access to the actual musical productions.

Heinz Werner (1917), in his pioneer work on children's singing, already had to deal with the following two problems: analysing a form of singing that does not yet adhere to adult conventions, and representing the sounds' transcription on paper. He analysed recorded singing by repeated listening, and he used quarter pitch notes for representing inaccurate singing. It appears that most researchers since have pursued the same procedure. That is, if possible, they record and then auditorally analyse the singing, using conventional musical notation with some additional symbols such as quarter pitch notes and a cross sign for speechlike reproductions (for example, Moog, 1967, 1968; McKernon, 1979; Davidson et al., 1981; Davies, 1986, 1992; Kelley and Sutton-Smith, 1987; Davidson, 1994). This method, thus, approaches song-singing on the basis of purely auditory analysis. Sometimes, assistance from professional musicians is mentioned (for example, Davidson, 1985), and musical instruments are used as a means of comparing and improving conceptualization. Nevertheless, this procedure does not prevent categorical perception. Somewhat surprisingly, automatic tuners are only rarely used (Flowers and Dunne-Sousa, 1990; Stadler Elmer, 1990). Such apparata are made for tuning musical instruments; they receive sounds, analyse them, and show the results immediately in the form of a light flashing on a temperate half-tone keyboard bar. Although it is a useful supplement to a purely auditory analysis, it is tedious because it only reacts to immediate input and is able to handle only broad pitch categories.

Papoušek and Papoušek (1981) tackled the problem of analysing early pre-musical and prosodic vocalization with detailed and extensive procedures. They applied several acoustic methods that are widespread in speech analysis, and combined them with auditory analysis represented by musical transcriptions. By that, the resulting representations show a wealth of information about a sung performance's structure. Papoušek and Papoušek use this combined method of auditory and acoustic analyses not only for explicit singing contexts with children but also for highlighting musical elements in preverbal communication (for example, M. Papoušek, 1996). In fact, their solution for analysing and representing singing is closest to what we propose in this chapter.

There are other ways computer-assisted tools are used in the context of singing analysis. For example, in order to specify 'good' from less competent singers, Sergeant (1994) proposed some acoustic features that he gained with the aid of a computer program (devised by David Howard at the University of York) that extracts the fundamental frequency of the sung response. This program seems to work in a manner similar to the one presented below. However, the author was interested in analysing acoustic features of children's single pitch matching and in comparing trained with untrained voices at the basis of single sounds produced. He was neither interested in analysing larger vocal units such as song-singing nor in working out a notation system for such larger units. The same is true for research that focuses on only selected acoustic features but not singing as an entire musical event with regard to vocal pitch and timing. For instance, Trehub et al. (1997) were interested in quantifying the average pitch level at which parents produced infant-directed songs. They asked a musicologist to identify the tonic or principal pitch (of the song's key) which was then measured by computer tools, yielding the fundamental frequency. They focused on a single parameter and were neither interested in the organization of pitches and time, nor in the stability of the tonic's fundamental frequency, that is, changes of the musical key, throughout a performance.

Limitations of the Traditional Methods

Analytic methods that are based on purely auditory analysis have two major limitations. The first and most restrictive one lies in the aforementioned analyser's propensity to preconceptualize and categorize unconventional singing into musical concepts. Since we know that children, novices and people with a non-western education do not have full perceptual and conceptual command of western musical concepts and of rules in the same way as trained individuals habitually do, a description of their vocal expressions should take this fact into account. Auditory analyses and transcriptions solely based on musical concepts presumably are biased towards overestimating the cultural concepts and rules. They do not adequately capture the relevant developmental or learning phenomena.

The second limitation is related to the first one. Since conventional music notation allows only the kind of singing which already somehow fits into this preset frame of symbols and categories to be represented, all singing that is outside this traditionally narrow interpretation of this concept or that has not yet been sufficiently adapted to the cultural forms of expression, such as poor, out-of-tune, or non-western-style singing, cannot be assessed by these methods. So far, this problem has been tackled by verbal descriptions of children's poor or not so well-developed song-singing, or by employing descriptions using roughly ascending and descending lines or some additional symbols within the frame of the traditional musical notation system.

There is a long tradition of using computer-assisted methods for speech analysis (for example, Hess, 1983; Tohkura et al., 1992), especially with regard to acoustic features of intonation (speech melody or prosody) (for example, Helfrich, 1985; Hart et al., 1990). These methods were applied, for instance, to substantiate acoustically prosodic features of adult's infant-directed speech ('motherese') (Fernald and Simon, 1977; Garnica, 1977) and became influential in this domain (for example, Fernald and Simon, 1984; Fernald and Kuhl, 1987; Fernald et al., 1989). Further applications concern prosodic analysis of infant–parent dialogues (for example, Papoušek and Papoušek, 1989; M. Papoušek, 1994, 1995) and developmental aspects of children's speech (for example, Smith and Kenny, 1998). Whereas computer-assisted methods for analysing acoustic features of speech melody are widespread, they are only rarely applied systematically to analyse and represent sung performances. When applied to singing, they tend to evaluate only single and isolated parameters (for example, Trehub et al., 1997). Moreover, although singing and speaking share some common features, they differ markedly in the conventions on how to organize temporally the pitches together with the syllables of the lyrics. Methods for speech analysis have to be adapted to the specific nature of singing. For example, the analysis of singing has to account for the fact that each syllable can have a different average pitch level (which is less important in prosody), and that the syllables are more or less metrically timed. The variations of pitch within a syllable is an important feature of prosody, but it is ignored in traditional methods of singing analysis. In order to account for different patterns of pitch variation, we use different symbols for assessing the sung pitch quality (see Table 20.1, and Figure 20.2 later in this chapter).

As an exception, Papoušek and Papoušek (for example, 1981) and M. Papoušek (for example, 1981, 1996) examined vocalizations (infant directed speech and singing, young children's singing) with regard to several structural aspects. They combined acoustic with auditory analyses for the same vocalized unit. However, they used acoustic measures, but represented the musically relevant features (pitch and time) with conventional music notation. As discussed above, for certain research purposes we consider musical notation not appropriate for describing actually performed song-singing.

In doing research that focuses on children's and novices' singing and its process of enculturation, we are, thus, faced with the following epistemological and methodological problem: *How can we analyse and represent adequately the organization of pitch and time in preconventional singing since it does not yet fit into the frame of our musical notation system and conceptual conventions connected with it?* Similarly, this question applies to research carried out in cross-cultural contexts involving musical sound patterns that do not follow the habitually used musical concepts and rules.

Our aim was, thus, to devise a method that would allow not only more objective and reliable measures with computer-assisted analyses of sung performances, but also to develop a system for representing the organization of the musically relevant features by more differentiated symbols than the culturally given musical notation system. This method should provide reliable descriptions of a sung performance's constituent components, first and foremost the configuration of pitches, and their timing, together with the sung syllables or lyrics.

The Advantage of Computers: The Elimination of the Musical Mind

During the twentieth century, important progress was achieved in developing and improving the technical recordings of sounds, and for the last few decades computers have served as excellent research tools in achieving a high quality in the acoustical analysis of sounds. These technical possibilities permit and support a deconceptualization of our culturally coined perception and conception of complex sound phenomena such as human speech and singing. To be clear, the problem as we see it is not a matter of subjectivity in conceptualizing singing.

Two trained musicians may easily come up with close agreements about the way a sung melody is transcribed. Such expert agreements may be taken as inter-subjective valid results. But in our view, it is the shared cultural background, that is, the musical mind, that coins conceptual hearing and comprehension. Thus, we see the primary advantage of computer tools as being their function as an *external control* on the basis of acoustical criteria to conceptualize singing. Apart from this, this tool permits researchers to achieve reliable and valid data without interference from the musical mind, since analysis no longer relies on hearing only. For instance, by analysing a sung tune on the basis of each single syllable and its acoustical data, the culturally defined relations among the sounds that usually affect our listening can be eliminated. Although analysed as single events, as a consecutive series they yield a complex structure showing syllables with their pitches and their timing.

A Computer-aided Method for Analysing and Representing Singing

Here we describe the new method we devised for analysing and representing pre- or unconventional singing. Although we exemplify this method within the context of an investigation into a young child's song-singing, it is also applicable to various other research problems that require musical analyses with respect to the organization of pitch and time in a more differentiated, reliable and valid way.

Any computer-aided method assumes (i) that the singing is recorded on an audio or video tape and (ii) that the computer is able to record and digitize audio data from a tape. In order to aid the process of analysis, the appropriate software is necessary. It should be able to provide information on the timing and on pitch for certain singing events selected by the researcher. The first task can be done by virtually any sound recorder and editor, whereas the second task needs special software. Our solution is a combination of a commercially available sound recorder with a self-written program for pitch analysis. For more details see Appendix 1 to this chapter.

Figure 20.1 is a typical output of a pitch analysis program. The upper part shows the envelope of the sound. It gives some information on loudness. The lower part gives the raw pitch data. Only sounds that reach a certain loudness-threshold can be analysed.

This raw data has to be further processed for two reasons. First, the pitch analysis program offers too much data by showing all the wavy details of the pitch curves. For most research questions, the amount of information provided is too rich. Hence, the researcher has to choose a useful reduction of the information to a limited set of categories of pitch curves that is relevant to the research question. Second, the print-out of our program shows that certain important information is missing that would be necessary for a valid description of the

```
A4 = 435 Hz, filter = 200..600 Hz, duration = 2
```

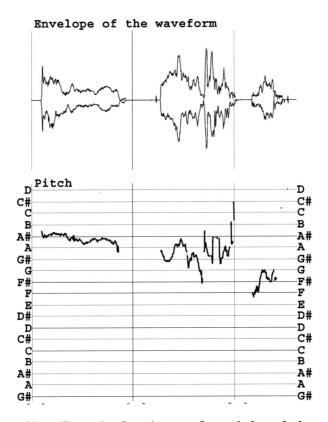

Figure 20.1   Example of a print-out of our pitch-analysing program

data. Such information concerns, for example, joint singing, breathing (to determine the phrases), the syllables of the lyrics, and the identification of the singer's voice.

In the context of our research on young children's song-learning processes, we have produced a list of categories represented by the symbols shown in Table 20.1. The first five symbols define our categories with respect to the relevant parts of the pitch curves. The symbol W stands for syllables that are spoken and not sung. The symbol X means that it is not possible to gain reliable data on pitch from the computer tools because of a strong disturbance. The symbol H stands for 'help' and indicates that the syllable is sung by the researcher or presenter of the song and not by the child. Joint singing events are symbolized by an additional circle around the centre of the symbol. The encircled symbol

Table 20.1   Table of symbols

Note: In the case of joint singing, a circle is drawn around the centre of the symbol that is the geometrical centre, except for symbol 2 and 3 where it is the dot. In the graphical representation of a song actually sung, the x and y coordinates of the position of the symbol's centre denote the onset time and the pitch, respective of the corresponding syllable.

Code	Symbol	Description
1	●	Stable pitch
2	╱ ╲	Stable pitch, ending with upward or downward glissando
3	╱ ╲	Stable pitch, starting with upward or downward glissando
4	╱ ╲	Unstable pitch, but clear upward or downward glissando
5	│	Unstable pitch with glissandi in any direction and/or unidentifiable, fuzzy pitches within context of singing (prolonged vowel)
6	W	Pitch of a spoken syllable
7	X	Estimation on the basis of disturbed signals
8	H	Syllable sung by the researcher
+10	○	Joint singing

represents the louder of the two singer's production. Note that in other research contexts, for example an ethnomusicological one, other symbols and categories may be more appropriate.

An Example

As an example of this new method's outcome, Figure 20.2 shows our graphic representation of a girl's song-singing at age 4.5 years. It is an excerpt that came out of an acquisition process that occurred in a natural context of song learning. (For more detailed results obtained by this method, see, for example, Stadler Elmer, 1998, 2000a, 2000b, 2000c, 2002, Stadler Elmer and Hammer, 2001). As the figure's title indicates, it is the girl's second solo performance of this song, and, including all its previous events, this song counts as the eighth event. The learning situation is reflected by the fact that this event is initially guided by a trained female singer who instructed this song. We selected this example for illustrating such natural occurrences as it is a transition from guided singing to joint singing, and finally to solo singing. Note that all this happened within a short period of time, namely 8.9 seconds.

Each syllable of the song's lyrics produced is categorized by one of the above-mentioned symbols. The horizontal and vertical position of a symbol's centre define the time onset and the pitch, respectively. The vertical extension of symbols 2–5 represents the pitch range of glissandi. Syllables belonging to the same phrase are connected by a dotted line. The end of a phrase is determined by breathing.

It should be emphasized that the symbols are placed in a time and pitch *continuum*. Therefore, they are not restricted to western categories even though the vertical axis has tics for the well-tempered scale (A4 calibrated at ~435 Hz), and the horizontal axis counts the regular beats of the tics (here 120 beats per minute). These scales of the axes provide information on the western conventions. Where possible, the tonic triad (do, mi, so) is marked by dotted horizontal lines for a further orientation. Also, for orientation, the actual song model is drawn in thin lines connecting small dots. It stands for an idealized depiction of the pitch organization that was repeatedly presented to the child. In order to reduce confusion, the timing of the song model's syllables is set identical with the timing of the syllables actually produced. Since the pitch organization of the song model is given according to the well-tempered scale and serves as a normative account, one can easily see the pitch deviations of the syllables actually produced. For example, Figure 20.2 shows that the strong deviation from the song model at the beginning of the third phrase corresponds to many (and sometimes large!) glissandi. Such large glissandi that lack a stable state with respect to pitch, are also observed by Sergeant (1994) in children's pitch matching with untrained singing voices.

Below the time axis, the onset of each syllable and ending of each phrase are shown in thick vertical and horizontal lines, respectively. Additionally, a transcription of the lyrics produced is shown. Here, one can easily see rubati or metric irregularities. In the present example, all syllables of the song model are quarter notes, except for 'still', 'Blu-', and 'men' that count half notes.

(i) Mathy, (ii) song 5, (iii) perf. 2, (iv) event 8, (v) 8.9 secs.

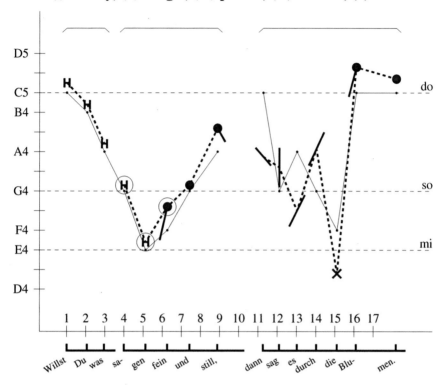

The title gives information about (i) the singer, (ii) the song, (iii) the numbers of at least partially solo singings of this song by this singer, (iv) the number of times this song occurred while the child was present, and (v) the total duration in seconds. The legend of symbols is listed in Table 20.1. For more details, see the main text. Note that syllables 8–11 are the transcriptions of what is given (or not) in the raw data shown in Figure 20.1.

Figure 20.2 **An example of the graphical representation of a song actually produced by a girl at age 4.5 years**

Because the manual drawing of such graphical representations would be tedious work, we have condensed the whole of the information from Figure 20.2 into a small data file from which a special computer program produced a graphical representation. As an example, Appendix 2 to this chapter shows the data file from which Figure 20.2 is made.

The detailed description shows that this girl is already familiar with the song model: she took over the entire song's lyrics correctly, and additional similarities are given in the first part of the song, where she had been given support by the more competent singer. After the transition from joint to solo singing, she shows some adjustment to the model's melodic contour. In the second part, the similarity is obvious in the contour of the last three notes where she adapts to the model by exaggerating the interval of a fifth with a large leap upwards and by ending with the two closely pitched notes. Interestingly, the gross deviations from the model's melody occur at the beginning of the second phrase, and there we see four symbols that indicate unstably produced pitch qualities. For a solid interpretation of the more psychological aspects of her song-learning process, we would, as a minimum, need information about her previous and her subsequent singing of this song.

Utility of the New Method

In order to illustrate what the traditional method might yield with the same material represented above, we asked a professional musician to listen to the song-singing and to transcribe it. The result is shown in Figure 20.3. We deliberately did not give special instructions because our aim was to see the well-known effects of categorical perception with our material. It would be worth studying how special instructions and special training can improve the analytical hearing of musicians. Now let us compare the outcome of the traditional method with our method. The first five notes, where the presenter sung or dominated joint singing (see symbol H and joint singing), are fairly identical. In what follows, taking into account the glissandi in Figure 20.2, the sixth and eighth note can be interpreted as roughly being within the same pitch category. Thus, we may say that pitch representation of the first part of the song does not considerably differ between the two methods. Note that the musician's perceived melody suit the song model well, showing his understanding of the musical meaning. But in the second part, where the child's sung pitches are less stable, we see considerable discrepancies between the computer-aided method and the musician's transcription. The first three notes illustrate the aforementioned musician's categorical perception, namely by adjusting the half-tone deviations to a key assumed to be F major. The fourth note even deviates approximately two semitones from the symbol gained by the aid of the

The transcription was made by a professional musician who has been conducting children's choirs for many years.

Figure 20.3   Musical transcription of the same vocal production on which Figure 20.2 is based

computer analysis. Therefore, the musician's transcription proves to be wrong, even on the assumption that the key would be F major. The estimation of the disturbed signal (see symbol X) seems almost agreed, whereas the last two notes again differ clearly between the two methods. With respect to the song's produced *temporal pattern*, the musician's representation shows that he perceived temporal categories of two values, namely, either one or two beats. In contrast, the representation gained by computer-aided analysis shows some temporal variations that would not be well represented by a two-value timing category system.

This brief comparison shows that the musician's transcription of pitch agrees with the outcomes of the new method as long as the sung melody suits the conventions, as is the case with the trained singing voice in the initial part of the song. Since the child is producing this song only for the second time (cf. performance 2), we cannot expect her performance to be the same quality as a competent singer. Note that just one part of her singing is unstable, with the largest deviations in pitch from the song model. Yet, the musician's representation of her singing suggests a rather nice melody overall, except for one note where he was not sure. This reflects the well-known 'categorical perception' (see 'Introduction' to this chapter). When comparing with the newly proposed method, it is obvious that the traditional method does not account for the singer's unstably produced pitches. Rather, the musician's use of the conventional music notation a priori limits the scope of perceiving and describing the phenomena.

Not only does the new method use more differentiated tools by using symbols to represent pitch qualities in a continuous time and pitch coordinate system, but also the results are gained by combining analytic hearing with acoustic data given by the computer program. Thus, the basis for analysing and describing the phenomena is more reliable than pure auditory perception. Moreover, it allows the representation of the organization of three pertinent components (pitch, lyrics, time) of a sung performance as a structural entity, rather than as isolated parameters.

Concluding Remarks

Musical practice is communication, and written symbols play an important role as a medium for the conservation and transmission of musical meaning. The music notation system helps the composers to communicate musical meaning, and the notation is intended as a guideline for interpretation by musicians. In a different way from the artistic contexts and musical practice, scientific communication about melodies actually produced has to be as precise and unequivocal as possible. Like the discrepancy between written and spoken language, the sung melody requires a description that accounts for possible deviations from the idealized conventions represented by musical notation. These divergent criteria for coding and decoding musical meaning explains why we cannot expect the musical notation to describe adequately actual performances.

What is lacking is some kind of symbolic system similar to those where speech is represented by letters for reading, and by phonetic letters for spoken sounds.

As discussed in this chapter, the main research problem with preconventional singing is eliminating the culturally coined musical mind that tends to overestimate cultural concepts in perceived phenomena. Moreover, for certain research questions we need to go beyond evaluating the single acoustic parameters provided by computers and analyse and describe the organization of larger behavioural units. In order to solve these problems, we devised the proposed method that uses acoustic measures for representing detailed structural aspects of song-singing, which are more differentiated and reliable than music notation.

By proposing to combine auditory with acoustic analyses for the analysis of singing, we follow the approach already introduced by H. and M. Papoušek (for example, 1981). Their microanalyses of musical elements in infants' and parents' vocalizations have not yet been seriously transferred to research in singing. A combined method uses a computer program that provides various acoustic measures on the sounds' pitches and timing. Together with listening, we obtain a computer-aided analysis that has clear advantages over the pure auditory analysis. For describing actually produced melodies, it allows control and even elimination of the listener's musical mind while analysing a sung melody.

In addition to what the Papoušeks' proposed, we emphasize using a more differentiated symbolic system for reducing the detailed acoustic information rather than the traditional music notation system. The computer-aided detailed information makes it possible to go beyond the given western musical categories of pitch and time by exploiting the entire continua of these parameters. This way, the culturally given category boundaries are dissolved. Nevertheless, a reduction of the detailed information obtained by the computer is still necessary if we want to describe and understand more than a single and isolated parameter. However, any methods for reducing the acoustic data should be subordinate to the research questions. In our research context of children's singing development, we distinguish between several kinds of stable and unstable pitches and depict these categories with symbols that are placed in the coordinate system.

We illustrated our method by an example of a young girl's song-singing, and we demonstrated its utility by comparing its outcome with the one achieved by the musician's traditional method. This demonstration shows the expected bias towards categorical perception and, moreover, the traditional method cannot account for unstably sung pitches nor for pitches in-between the given categories.

The example confirmed that the proposed method not only provides external control of perceived stimuli, but also allows communication of the analysed data by a symbol system that is more adequate for describing singing than the conventional musical system and selected acoustic parameters.

In this way, it is now possible to study a series of interesting issues related to vocal musical expression and underlying cognition. First, short- or long-term changes in the structure of vocal musical expression as they adapt towards our western musical conventions can be investigated. Second, in research contexts that focus singing in the light of learning and development, underlying organizational rules of vocal musical expression can be studied with respect to pitch and time. (For more details see Stadler Elmer, 1998, 2000a, 2000b, 2000c, 2002.) Furthermore, our method might be useful in ethnomusicological research.

Despite these advantages, we are far from claiming that the new method would provide an ultimately true or objective description of what we observe or perceive. Although the paradoxical relation between knowledge and understanding on the one hand and perception or observation on the other is reduced at one stage in the research process, it reappears elsewhere. The reason for that lies in the fact that we have to give meaning to the data computers provide. Hence, we need socio-cultural knowledge on the phoneomena. Interpretation already starts with distinguishing between the relevant and irrelevant data, for example, noise from sung sounds. More critical are the problems in determining intended events from observed events in the interpretation of the data. How can we decide to what extent structures of a child's sung performances represent his/her mental representation or are destorted by a lack of vocal control? Such questions need to be addressed in subsequent research. Eventually, as with any microgenetic method (Catán, 1986; Siegler and Crowley, 1991), the proposed method is time-consuming. The researcher has to decide whether the research questions justify gaining data at microanalytic levels or not.

Nevertheless, overall this method provides more reliable and differentiated access to vocal productions that would appear 'wrong' or 'out-of-tune' to a naïve listener. It facilitates consideration of certain questions that could not be otherwise addressed, for example, regarding structural changes across time in the song production of individuals, or investigations of relationships among a number of aspects of song production, learning and development. *What* is sung has its own regularities to be discovered in future research.

Appendix 1: Description of our Computer Tools

Here we describe our computer tools and how we get timing and pitch information from our audio data. The software, including a tutorial, is available from the authors on request. Note that our tools, especially the self-written pitch analysis program, are optimized for analysing the singing of young children.

For our study we used two different PCs (an old one with a 386 processor plus an arithmetic processor and MS Windows 3.1 as the operating system as well as a newer one with a Pentium processor and MS Windows '95). Both PCs are equipped with sound cards. Because the sound recorder delivered with the operating system is rather limited in its functionality, we used a commercial (shareware) sound recorder and editor (CoolEdit V1.31 from Syntrillium Software) which is widespread. Our self-written pitch analysis program communicated with the sound recorder by constantly listening for data sent by the sound recorder to the clipboard (that is, a part of the memory accessible by all running applications).

Description of the Sound Recorder

In order to extract information on time and pitch, the following features of CoolEdit are important:

- On the screen the sound signal is drawn as a function of time. From this one immediately gets the timing of the onset of the syllables that are sung staccato because the syllables are clearly separated by silence.
- Parts of the recorded data can be played back between selected time points. This is important for obtaining information on the timing of syllables which are not clearly separated by silence.
- A selected part can be copied onto the clipboard. This is how we deliver data to our own pitch analysis program.
- A large variety of manipulative functions (amplification, designable filters, and so on) is available to improve the signal-to-noise ratio.
- A spectral analysis of the data can be obtained either as a curve of spectral intensity versus frequency for selected time points or as a colour-coded sonogram of the whole data. We use the spectral analysis as a complementary method in cases where our pitch analysis program does not yield reliable data.

Note that these features may be also available in other commercially available sound editors and recorders.

Description of our Pitch Analysis Program

Extracting the pitch from an audio signal means finding the fundamental frequency (F_0) of a periodic signal. In the literature, a huge variety of methods have been reported for this problem. For an overview of the most important ones, see the monograph by Hess (1983). Basically, the methods can be divided into two subgroups: spectral methods and temporal methods.

A *spectral method* is based on the calculation of the *power spectrum*. Any audio signal can be thought of as the sum of the sinusoidal oscillations of different frequencies. The power spectrum gives the strength of oscillation for each frequency. The spectrum of a strictly periodic signal (which is not necessarily sinusoidal) contains only the oscillation with the fundamental frequency and/or oscillations with integer multiples of the fundamental frequency (that is, the harmonics). Graphically such a spectrum is characterized by very sharp peaks appearing equidistantly. Note that the fundamental frequency is often not present (for example, in the voice of an opera singer with its typical formant around 3000 Hz). But the distance between two consecutive higher harmonics also defines the fundamental frequency and, therefore, pitch. Non-periodic and noisy signals are characterized by a relatively flat and broad spectrum. A power spectrum is usually calculated for a finite interval at an arbitrary point on the time axis. A sonogram is a graphical presentation of the spectra of all time points. The x-axis is the time axis whereas the y-axis is the frequency axis. The intensity of an oscillation of a certain frequency at a certain time is coded by a grey scale or a colour code. Periodic signals manifest themselves typically by the appearance of stripes parallel to the time axis. The averaged distance between the stripes is a measure of the pitch. A vibrato, for example, leads to wavy stripes.

The sound recorder we use is able to perform spectral analysis and shows sonograms. But it is a very tedious task to obtain quantitatively the pitch from this spectral analysis as a function of time. Therefore, we use its capacity to perform spectral analysis only for a comparison with uncertain results or in cases where our pitch analysis program fails to yield reliable results.

Temporal methods do not perform any spectral analysis. The main reason for avoiding a spectral analysis is to save computation time. Temporal methods can be very fast because they usually need only integer arithmetics. For this reason we have chosen a purely temporal method that should run fast even on an older PC without a numeric processor. An algorithm, working within the time domain, has to look for some characteristic features which reappear periodically. We have chosen the absolute minimum of the waveform or alternatively the absolute maximum.

The fundamental frequency is given by the inverse of the time difference between two consecutive events of the characteristic feature. The main problem with a temporal method is overcoming the confusion between characteristic features that seem to be similar. This is especially important for periodic signals where the fundamental frequency does not appear. Such a signal is characterized by a waveform that resembles a landscape with many hills and valleys having different heights and depths. But, eventually, the valleys and hills of the same depths and heights reappear defining the fundamental frequency. One of the strategies we used in our algorithm to tackle this problem is a restriction of the expected pitch to a certain interval given by the user of the program. Since we are analysing the singing of young children, this problem is not a very serious one because in these signals the fundamental frequency is usually present. Nevertheless, with this kind of data the program sometimes computes the wrong octave. It should be noted that all pitch analysis methods have serious problems analysing polyphonic signals. Thus, getting the pitch of two singers singing with roughly the same loudness is almost impossible.

After the analysis, the waveform of the data as well as its pitch pattern are shown graphically on the screen as a function of time. The program calculates and shows pitch only when the amplitude of the signal is larger than a certain threshold. If the program does not succeed in calculating the pitch, it draws the last successfully calculated pitch in red. This may lead to red horizontal lines which can be taken only as a very crude approximation of the actual pitch (if it exists). The pitch curve is shown together with horizontal lines that mark tempered pitches based on a freely definable calibration of the middle A4 that can be set in the range between 430 to 450 Hz. By moving the mouse cursor, one gets the pitch in Hz as well as the nearest note on the tempered scale and its deviation in cents for any point on the time scale. The result can be either printed or stored as a list of readable data on the hard disk.

Figure 20.1 gives an example of a print-out from our pitch analysis program. The heading text line shows (i) the frequency on which the tempered scale in the lower part is based, (ii) the expected pitch range (given in Hz), and (iii) the duration of the sample. The upper plot shows the envelope of the waveform. The horizontal line in the middle means no wave, that is, silence. The pitch is shown below the envelope. Note that pitch is only calculated when the distance between the upper and lower envelope is large enough, that is, when the sound is loud enough. When the loudness occasionally drops below the threshold, especially just before the end of a syllable (here, for example, just before the 2-second line and near ~2.5 seconds), the results may be spurious. The thin and short horizontal line near ~1.82 seconds means that the program could not calculate a reliable value for the pitch. Therefore, as explained above, it draws the last successful calculation. With unclear or equivocal sounds, it is useful to apply spectral analysis as a complementary method.

Appendix 2: Example of the Data Representation of the Singing Structure

The ASCII-text file from which Figure 20.2 is drawn reads as follows:

Mathy, song 5, perf. 2, event 8, 8.9 seconds
3
3
8 24.5 24.5 0.04 Willst
8 23.4 23.4 0.53 Du
8 21.4 21.4 0.98 was
5 1.32
18 19.3 19.3 1.50 sa-
18 16.4 16.4 2.06 gen
13 16.5 18.2 2.63 fein
1 19.3 19.3 3.21 und
2 22.2 21.5 3.94 still,
7 4.69
4 21.2 20.3 5.13 dann

5 21.2 19.2 5.55 sag
4 17.2 18.8 6.01 es
4 20.3 22.0 6.51 durch
7 14.8 14.8 7.05 die
3 23.8 25.3 7.55 Blu-
1 24.7 24.7 8.59 men.
8.89

The first line is the title. The number in the second line counts the number of phrases (here three phrases). Each phrase is headed with a line containing the number of syllables and the ending time (in seconds) of the previous phrase. The line of each syllable contains (in this sequence) the symbol code (see Table 20.1), two numbers carrying information on pitch, the onset time (in seconds), and the syllable of the lyrics. The very last line contains only the ending time of the last phrase. *Information of pitch* is coded in the following way. The number before the decimal point is the pitch on the well-tempered scale where zero denotes C3. The digit behind the decimal point counts the (upper) deviation in cents divided by ten. Thus 17.2 means F4 plus 20 cents, whereas 15.7 means E4 minus 30 cents. Symbols 2–5 and 12–15 require two different numbers of pitch information because they denote the starting and ending pitch, whereas this distinction is not necessary for all the other symbols. Therefore, starting and ending pitch coincide and are represented by two times the same value (as an example, see the first five syllables).

Note

1. This chapter is a version of work published in *Psychology of Music* and appears with the full permission of the Editor.

References

Anderson, J.D. (1991) 'Children's song acquisition: An examination of current research and theories', *The Quarterly Journal of Music Teaching and Learning*, II(4), 42–9.

Atterbury, B.W. (1984) 'Children's singing voices: A review of selected research', *Council for Research in Music Education*, 80: 51–63.

Beilin, H. and Pufall, P. (eds) (1992) *Piaget's Theory: Prospects and Possibilities*, Hillsdale, NY: Lawrence Erlbaum.

Catán, L. (1986) 'The dynamic display of process: Historical development and contemporary uses of the microgenetic method', *Human Development*, 29: 252–63.

Davidson, L. (1985) 'Tonal structures of children's early songs', *Music Perception*, 2(3): 361–74.

Davidson, L. (1994) 'Songsinging by young and old: A developmental approach to music', in R. Aiello (ed.) *Musical Perceptions*, pp. 99–130, New York: Oxford University Press.

Davidson, L., McKernon, P.E. and Gardner, H. (1981) 'The acquisition of song: A developmental approach', documentary report of the Ann Arbor Symposium: *Applications of Psychology to the Teaching and Learning of Music*, pp. 301–17, Reston, VS: Music Educators National Conference.

Davies, C.V. (1986) 'Say it till a song comes', *British Journal of Music Education*, 3(3): 279–93.

Davies, C.V. (1992) 'Listen to my song: A study of songs invented by children 3–13', *British Journal of Music Education*, 3(3): 279–93.

Fernald, A. and Kuhl, P.K. (1987) 'Acoustic determinants of infant preference for motherese speech', *Infant Behavior and Development*, 10: 279–93.

Fernald, A. and Simon, T. (1977) 'Analyse von Grundfrequenz und Sprachsegmentlänge bei der Kommunikation von Müttern mit Neugeborenen' ['Analyses of fundamental frequencies and duration of sements in the communication of mothers and newborns'], research report, Munich: Institut f. Phonetik u. sprachliche Kommunikation der Universität München.

Fernald, A. and Simon, T. (1984) 'Expanded intonation contours in mothers' speech to newborns', *Developmental Psychology*, 20(1): 104–13.

Fernald, A., Taechner, T., Dunn, J., Papoušek, M., de Boysson-Bardies, B. and Fukui, I. (1989) 'A cross-language study of prosodic modifications in mothers' and fathers' speech to preverbal infants', *Journal of Child Language*, 16: 477–501.

Flowers, P.J. and Dunne-Sousa, D. (1990) 'Pitch-pattern accuracy, tonality, and vocal range in preschool children's singing', *Journal of Research in Music Education*, 38(2): 102–14.

Garnica, O.K. (1977) 'Some prosodic and paralinguistic features of speech to young children', in C.E. Snow and C.A. Ferguson (eds), *Talking to Children: Language Input and Acquisition*, pp. 63–88, Cambridge: Cambridge University Press.

Hart, J.'t., Collier, R. and Cohen, A. (1990) *A Perceptual Study of Intonation: An Experimental-phonetic Approach to Speech Melody,* Cambridge: Cambridge University Press.

Helfrich, H. (1985) *Satzmelodie und Sprachwahrnehmung: Psycholinguistische Untersuchungen zur Grundfrequenz* [*Speech Melody and Speech Perception: Psycholinguistic Research on the Fundamental Frequency*], Berlin: W. de Gruyter.

Hess, W. (1983) *Pitch Determination of Speech Signals: Algorithms and Devices*, New York: Springer.

Imberty, M. (1996) 'Linguistic and musical development in preschool and school-age children', in I. Deliège and J. Sloboda (eds), *Musical Beginnings: Origins and Development of Musical Competence*, pp. 191–213, Oxford: Oxford University Press.

Kelley, L. and Sutton-Smith, B. (1987) 'A study of infant musical productivity', in J.C. Peery, I. Weiss Peery and T.W. Draper (eds), *Music and Child Development*, pp. 35–53, New York: Springer.

McKernon, P.E. (1979) 'The development of first songs in young children', in D. Wolf (ed.), *New Directions for Child Development*, Vol. 3, pp. 43–58, San Francisco: Jossey-Bass.

Moog, H. (1967[1963]), *Beginn und erste Entwicklung des Musikerlebens im Kindesalter*

[*Beginning and Early Development of Musical Experience in Childhood*], Ratingen: Henn.

Moog, H. (1968) *Das Musikerleben des vorschulpflichtigen Kindes* [*Experiencing Music by the Preschool Child*], Mainz: Schott.

Papoušek, M. (1981) 'Die Bedeutung musikalischer Elemente in der frühen Kommunikation zwischen Eltern und Kind' ['The significance of musical elements in the early communication between parent and child'], *Sozialpädiatrie in Praxis und Klinik*, 3(9): 412–15, 3(19): 468–73.

Papoušek, M. (1994) *Vom ersten Schrei zum ersten Wort: Vorsprachliche Kommunikation zwischen Mutter und Kind als Schrittmacher der Sprachentwicklung* [*From the First Cry to the First Word: Preverbal Communication between Mother and Child as Pacemaker of Language Development*], Bern: Huber.

Papoušek, M. (1995) 'Origins of reciprocity and mutuality in prelinguistic parent-infant 'dialogues'', in I. Markova, C. Graumann and K. Foppa (eds) *Mutualities in Dialogue*, pp. 58–81, Cambridge: Cambridge University Press.

Papoušek, M. (1996) 'Intuitive parenting: A hidden source of musical stimulation in infancy', in I. Deliège and J. Sloboda (eds), *Musical Beginnings. Origins and Development of Musical Competence*, pp. 88–112, Oxford: Oxford University Press.

Papoušek, M. and Papoušek, H. (1981) 'Musical elements in the infant's vocalization: Their significance for communication, cognition, and creativity', *Advances in Infancy Research*, 1: 163–224.

Papoušek, M. and Papoušek, H. (1989) 'Forms and functions of vocal matching in precononical mother-infant interactions', *First Language*, 9: 137–58.

Seashore, C.E. (1938) *Psychology of Music*, New York: McGraw-Hill.

Sergeant, D. (1994) 'Towards a specification for poor pitch singing', in G. Welch and T. Murao (eds), *Onchi and Singing Development*, pp. 63–73, London: David Fulton.

Siegel, J.A. and Siegel, W. (1977a) 'Absolute identification of notes and intervals by musicians', *Perception & Psychophysics*, 21(2): 143–52.

Siegel, J.A. and Siegel, W. (1977b) 'Categorical perception of tonal intervals: Musicians can't tell sharp from flat', *Perception & Psychophysics*, 21(5): 399–407.

Siegler, R.S. and Crowley, K. (1991) 'The microgenetic method. A direct means for studying cognitive development', *American Psychologist*, 46(6): 606–20.

Smith, B.L. and Kenny, M.K. (1998) 'An assessment of several acoustic parameters in children's speech production development: Longitudinal data', *Journal of Phonetics*, 26: 95–108.

Smith, L. (ed.) (1996) *Critical Readings on Piaget*, London: Routledge.

Stadler Elmer, S. (1990) 'Vocal pitch matching ability in children between four and nine years of age', *European Journal for High Ability*, Vol. 1: 33–41.

Stadler Elmer, S. (1996) 'Die Entwicklung des Singens: Eine kritische Diskussion der Beschreibungs-und Erklärungsansätze' ['The development of singing: A critical discussion of the theoretical and empirical approaches'], *Zeitschrift für Entwicklungspsychologie und Pädagogische Psychologie*, 28(3): 189–209.

Stadler Elmer, S. (1997) 'Die Anfänge des musikalischen Erlebens und Erkennens' ['The beginnings of musical experiences and cognition'], in J. Scheidegger and H. Eiholzer (eds), *Persönlichkeitsentfaltung durch Musikerziehung*, pp. 35–49, Aarau: Musikedition Nepomuk.

Stadler Elmer, S. (1998) 'A Piagetian perspective on singing development', *Jahrbuch der Deutschen Gesellschaft für Musikpsychologie*, Bd. 13, pp. 108–25, Göttingen: Hogrefe.

Stadler Elmer, S. (2000a) 'Liedersingen mit Kindern: Strukturgenese im sprach-musikalischen Ausdruck' ['Song singing with children: A structural genetic approach to the vocal musical expression'], in S. Hoppe-Graff and A. Rümmele (eds) *Entwicklung als Strukturgenese [Development as Geneses of Structures]*, pp. 157–95, Hamburg: Verlag Dr Kovac.

Stadler Elmer, S. (2000b) *Spiel und Nachahmun – Über die Entwicklung der elementaren musikalischen Aktivitäten*, ['*Play and Imitation – The Development of Elementary Musical Activities*'], Aarau: HBS Nepomuk.

Stadler Elmer, S. (2000c) 'Tradierung von Kultur am Beispiel des Singens' ['Transmitting Culture – the Case of Singing'], in N. Knolle (ed.), '*Musikpädagogische Forschung*' ['*Research in Music Education*'], pp. 152–82, Essen: Blaue Eule.

Stadler Elmer, S. (2002) *Kinder singen Lieder – über den Prozess der Kultivierung des vokalen Ausdrucks [Children Sing Songs – Cultivating one's Vocal Expression]*, Berlin: Waxmann.

Stadler Elmer, S. and Hammer, S. (2001), 'Sprach-melodische Erfindungen einer 9-jährigen' ['Inventions of lyrics and melodies by a nine-year-old girl'], *Zeitschrift für Entwicklungspsychologie und Pädagogische Psychologie*, 33 (3), 138–56.

Stern, W. (1965[1914]) *Psychologie der frühen Kindhei*, Heidelberg: Quelle & Meyer.

Sundberg, J. (1982) 'Perception of singing', in D. Deutsch (ed.) *The Psychology of Music*, pp. 59–98, New York: Academic Press.

Tohkura, Y., Vatikiotis-Bateson, E. and Sagisaka, Y. (eds) (1992) *Speech Perception, Production and Linguistic Structure*, Washington: IOS Press.

Trehub, S.E., Unyk, A.M., Kamenetsky, S.B., Hill, D.S., Trainor, L.J., Henderson, J.L. and Saraza, M. (1997) 'Mothers' and fathers' singing to infants', *Developmental Psychology*, 33(3): 500–507.

Welch, G.F. (1994) 'The assessment of singing', *Psychology of Music*, 22: 3–19.

Werner, H. (1917) 'Die melodische Erfindung im frühen Kindesalter' ['Melodic invention in the early years of childhood'], report no. 182 of the Kaiserlichen Akademie, Wien: 1–100.

Chapter 21

The Fears and Joys of New Forms of Investigation into Teaching: Student Evaluation of Instrumental Teaching

Ingrid Maria Hanken

Introduction

The quality of teaching is of vital concern to institutions of higher music education, and in particular the teaching of the student's principal instrument. Many years of good instrumental teaching are needed to qualify for a career as a professional musician, and the years students spend in higher music education institutions are crucial in this respect (Manturzewska, 1990; Sosniak, 1990; Ericsson, 1997). Recognizing this, many institutions have implemented strategies for monitoring and improving the quality of teaching. Student evaluation of teaching is one such strategy which is used commonly in higher education in many countries.

But *is* student evaluation a useful means for improving this particular kind of teaching? Or is there a danger that it might have a negative effect on the teacher–student relationship and confuse the roles? Can student evaluation of individual instrumental teaching actually be counterproductive? In this chapter I will discuss these questions, drawing from a research study that I conducted at an academy of music a few years after student evaluation of teaching was introduced as a mandatory procedure.

Student Evaluation in a Dyadic Relationship

Research on higher music education confirms that a close and personal relationship normally develops between instrumental teachers and their students (Kingsbury, 1988; Nettl, 1995; Nielsen, 1998). In such dyadic teacher–student settings, developing and preserving a good working relationship between the two parties is vital. Tiberius and Flak (1999) claim that in every relationship between teacher and student there will be some disappointment and negative emotions. Dyadic teaching and learning represent a special challenge, however, because '… the overt civility of dyadic relationships can mask unexpressed tensions and … these tensions, if not addressed, can increase to the explosive point, at which the relationship itself is destroyed' (p. 3). Therefore, they conclude, it is important to '... structure a relationship that can handle conflicts and tensions routinely and thereby prevent escalation' (p. 5). Student evaluation can be understood as one such routine that may be built into the teacher–student relationship for the purpose of unmasking tensions in a controlled manner, thereby enabling the parties to address problems constructively.

On the other hand, being subject to evaluation is not always pleasant; student evaluation reflects on the teacher's self-respect as a professional and can sometimes be experienced as wounding, threatening and demoralizing (Ryan et al., 1980; Moses, 1986; Seldin, 1989 and 1993; Strike, 1991; Braskamp and Ory, 1994, p. 128). For this reason the evaluation literature commonly recommends that student evaluation should be conducted anonymously. In individual instrumental teaching, however, it is often difficult, and perhaps not even very productive, to maintain anonymity. Given this, it is relevant to ask whether student evaluation of individual instrumental teaching might in fact, in some cases, *worsen* the teacher–student relationship.

Another relevant question is whether student evaluation is compatible with the roles of instrumental teacher and student respectively. Instrumental teaching is often described as learning by apprenticeship. Although learning by apprentice-ship can be defined and understood in different ways (Nielsen and Kvale, 1997), there is undoubtedly a strong professional authority ingrained in the role of the master. In his study of instrumental teaching and learning at an academy of music, Nielsen (1998) found that the student's professional trust in his or her teacher is an important basis for learning to take place. Is it possible to combine the student's need for a strong professional trust with the appraising and dispassionate attitude that student evaluation implies?

A Case Study

In 1994–95, student evaluation was implemented as a mandatory procedure at my own institution, the Norwegian Academy of Music. In the years since, many comments that I have received from both students and teachers indicate that student evaluation is regarded as somewhat problematic, especially when it concerns the student's principal instrumental teacher. However, little seems to be known about the use of student evaluation in this particular educational context. The extensive research undertaken on student evaluation of teaching has so far only addressed to a very limited degree the special form of teaching that individual instrumental tuition implies. The research undertaken at my own institution and reported below aims to assess whether student evaluation is indeed a useful means of improving individual instrumental teaching within institutions of higher musical education.

Given the lack of existing research, I chose to do an exploratory study. To understand how student evaluation works in a certain context, it is vital to understand the thoughts and feelings of the persons involved. I therefore conducted semi-structured qualitative research interviews (Kvale, 1996) with nine principal instrumental teachers with many years of teaching experience. The interviews with the teachers indicated that there were three different approaches to the use of student evaluation represented. I therefore chose one representative for each of these approaches (teachers A, C and H) and interviewed nine of their students (students a1–3, c1–3, and h1–3). The students had each completed a minimum of two years of study at the academy, and all had music performance as a central part of their programme.

Results

Both teachers and students in the study were of the opinion that, in reality, the students' evaluations were not anonymous. The teachers have such a limited number of students and normally know each of them so well that they can identify each one. While there may be ways of reducing the possibility of identifying the students, both students and teachers claimed that student evaluation might not serve its purpose if these were implemented. If the evaluation does not communicate the needs and opinions of *individual* students to the teacher, it will not be of much help to them in tailoring their teaching for particular students, they claimed. When discussing student evaluation in the context of principal instrumental teaching it is, therefore, important to understand that in most cases student evaluation in reality is *not* anonymous.

This raises a fundamental question: do students dare to be honest in their evaluations? If not, student evaluation may not serve any purpose.

The study revealed that many students find it difficult to be honest in their evaluations and identified three main potential difficulties: fear of hurting a teacher's feelings; fear of reprisals; and conflicting role expectations. Interview results relating to each of these are set out below.

Fear of Hurting the Teachers' Feelings

Fear of hurting their teachers' feelings was a serious concern for a number of students and teachers interviewed: 'It is something to do with the "chemistry" also, you are kind to each other. They are much more afraid of hurting the teacher in a way' (Teacher F). Teacher H indicated that students might be considerate in what they say: 'In a way you have to attach more importance to any hint of objection that crops up, and then decide whether this is only a considerate way of saying that this is hopeless, because they don't dare to express themselves more strongly.'

When asked whether they were afraid of hurting their teachers, several students admitted that this was a problem. Two of the female students implied that girls in particular might be afraid of hurting their teachers: 'Afraid of hurting the teacher, yes, we probably are. I think that's true. I don't know about the boys, but I have talked with a lot of girls, and I think many girls are afraid of hurting their teacher' (Student a1), and '… it is probably typical of girls that we care more about people. You feel it hurts to criticize someone' (Student c1).

But for some students this did not seem to be a problem. One of the male students said: '… you have to realize that getting a good education is *your own* responsibility. You can't be afraid of hurting a teacher. You have to tackle the problem yourself and try to criticize' (Student c2).

When the teachers were asked about their reactions to critical evaluations, some of them answered that normally they did not feel upset; they felt that they could handle whatever comments they received professionally. Others admitted that they could feel hurt when criticized. Teacher C described her reactions in this way: 'You are, quite naturally, a bit hurt by negative comments, especially when you believe you are as good as I believe I am. "What! I, who am 'world famous'?!" and so on. And it definitely hurts a bit.'

One teacher reported on his experience a few years earlier when several of his students had filed a complaint against him. This is how he described his reaction to being criticized:

> When you are as fond of the students as I actually was – I loved the job because of the students – then it comes as such a disappointment that you cannot describe it with words. … As a teacher, you have to find the balance between humility, self-confidence and *joie de vivre*. My self-confidence is still there, strangely enough, even if the *joie de vivre* received a blow that lasted several years. I still haven't got over it entirely. I felt as if something died inside me at that time. (Teacher J)

This experience has made him oppose the use of student evaluation, he said, because the thought of being evaluated makes him apprehensive, and he fears this will interfere with his teaching and make him a bad teacher.

The interviews with both students and teachers confirmed the closeness of the teacher–student relationship described in the literature on instrumental teaching. They also provided evidence that many of the principal instrumental teachers invest considerably more time and personal commitment in their students than would be expected. This personal relationship between teachers and their students can be understood as a fundamental trait of individual instrumental teaching. There seem to be at least two possible reasons for this. First, this type of teaching implies a one-to-one teacher–student relationship that often lasts several years, years that are of vital importance in a young musician's life. One student, for example, compared the relationship between teacher and student to a parent–child relationship when she described the bonds between them. Second, it seems that characteristics of the subject matter, the *music*, force both student and teacher to expose themselves emotionally, and therefore to come closer to each other on a personal level, as this extract from an interview reveals:

Teacher F: With regard to having a close relationship – a lot of people say that the teacher–student relationship should not become too personal, but I find that difficult to regulate. We talk a lot about real *feelings* during the lessons, not just 4th finger on F sharp … . We talk about what this music expresses. It might sound sentimental, but you have to open up your whole register of feelings, and then you cannot just sit there and keep a distance to the student. … you cannot be close in your teaching without being close as a human being.

Interviewer: And I suppose the students might feel the same way, and then they are perhaps afraid of hurting you?

Teacher F: Yes. That is the point exactly.

The interview results indicate that there might be a price to pay for the closeness between principal instrumental teachers and their students: students might not dare to voice any criticism because they are very anxious not to hurt someone they feel strongly attached to, and thereby risk destroying the openness and intimacy that is so vital in this type of teaching and learning relationship.

Fear of Reprisals

Another reaction to receiving a negative evaluation can be anger and hostility. Such feelings can in themselves be a strain on the relationship between teacher and student. In addition, they might lead to reprisals against the student. Several of those interviewed commented on the fact that instrumental teachers are in a position to retaliate in different ways, and that fear of reprisals might stop students from expressing any criticism of their teachers or their teaching.

> … the teacher can decide whether you are going to get a job engagement or not, then it is hopeless when you know that you will be studying with that teacher for the next three years. There is no question of making any criticism, as they know it will not improve things. The only thing that might happen is that the relationship might become worse. You will definitely be out of favour with the teacher. (Teacher C)

> … they will feel that they might insult me, or that I somehow might reject them if they have something negative to say. … in individual teaching, and in the *milieu* here as a whole, they are more careful not to come into conflict with anyone. … if they come into conflict with someone they may have the impression that it could harm their career. (Teacher E)

When students were asked whether this is something they worry about, some said that they had never thought about it, but others reported that fear of reprisals had actually kept them from being frank and open either with their present teacher or with former teachers.

The fact that students often, as one student put it, 'surf[s] on the contacts that his teacher has in the job market' implies that teachers have an instrument of power that they may potentially use against the student.

> ... you know very well that it is preferable not to get onto bad terms with your teacher, because then you will not get jobs. ... I am very much aware of the fact that if I got into a major conflict with her, I would have a problem getting those jobs, and those are jobs that I really want. Then it becomes just hopeless. (Student c1)

> ... because often if you get onto bad terms with your teacher, it implies that you will have difficulties in the freelance market and the like. It is a problem, really a problem. (Student c2)

Principal instrumental teachers can choose to use their contacts in the job market for the benefit of their students, or they can choose *not* to use them. It is not surprising, then, that students in some cases think it wiser to remain friendly with their teachers by refraining from criticizing them in an evaluation.

Conflicting Role Expectations

As we saw earlier, instrumental teaching is often described as learning by apprenticeship. I was therefore interested in finding out whether the roles of master/teacher and apprentice/student are perceived in a manner consistent with student evaluation.

One teacher's answer indicates that student evaluation is not a natural part of this teaching tradition:

> It is not the customary way of thinking, to let the students evaluate. I don't think it is common among my colleagues or myself. In this master–apprentice tradition you are what you *are*, namely in this case, a musician ... . It is not natural for the master to ask for an evaluation, because the master is, per definition, a master ... student evaluation is not perceived as natural within the master-apprentice tradition, it just isn't; you only destroy yourself. (Teacher C)

At the same time, both this teacher and most of the others interviewed were anxious not to be identified with a master role in the sense of someone who has all the answers. Several of them rather expressed a strong wish to *reduce* their authority in relation to their students.

Some of the students interviewed also stated very clearly that they did not feel the authority of the teacher as a hindrance in the sense that the teacher would object to being evaluated. On the contrary, several commented on the fact that they perceived their present teachers as being anti-authoritarian and open to feedback and criticism. Nevertheless, it might not always feel natural for students to evaluate and be critical of their teachers. One student expressed himself this way: ' ... it is sometimes a bit ridiculous that you as a 20-year-old should criticize a teacher who has 30 years of experience. ... I have that much respect for [C's] experience not to criticize her teaching in this way. You have to accept it as it is' (Student c2).

Teacher J seems to agree. He claimed that student democracy has gone too far and that student evaluation is neither appropriate nor necessary: 'If we are supposed to have the best teachers in Norway here, I feel that, in a way, this student evaluation should be quite unnecessary' (Teacher J).

And even if teachers might wish to play down their authority, the students might not perceive it in the same way. One of the students interviewed pointed out that teachers might not realize how strong their authority in reality is, and that they perhaps underestimate their power over the students:

> At least I feel that in this master–apprentice relationship in which we actually find ourselves, the teacher has a lot of power. ... this power is not obvious to the person possessing it, only to the one who might be exposed to it. I have been teaching enough myself to know that you don't feel very powerful when you stand there in front of a class or student, but nevertheless you are, because it is your agenda, it is your word that counts. It is easy to forget, all too easy to forget that when I teach. And I suppose it is as easy to forget for an instrumental teacher, also because he has such a friendly relationship with his student. (Student a1)

Furthermore, evaluating the teacher might for some students be incompatible with having great professional confidence and trust in their teachers, a trust that seems to be fundamental in learning by apprenticeship.

> In my opinion, to put up too much resistance against the teacher or the type of system he has just doesn't work, especially in the type of teaching tradition that we have. I think you have to decide to go along with him entirely, or otherwise you have to find yourself another teacher. (Student a1)

One teacher expressed somewhat the same attitude when looking back to his own student days:

Teacher E: It is a question of faith, to subject oneself to teaching. It is a question of *believing* in it.

Interviewer: Believing in what the teacher has to offer you?

Teacher E: Yes, for me it was. I had to make a choice: either I was suspicious and distrustful, or I just had to 'swallow' what he came with. And then, in a way, you have put behind you that dispassionate and critical attitude. You have to have faith in the person and trust that this will work out.

The results of the exploratory interviews indicate that there might be some role expectations built into this kind of teaching that can make it difficult for students to have a dispassionate and appraising attitude towards their own teachers. The teacher's professional authority per se sometimes seems to be an obstacle, even if the teachers themselves do not necessarily stress their authority or expect any reverence. The reasons for this may lie with the need of students to have complete faith in their teachers as professional authorities. But the results also indicate that some teachers might feel that student evaluation is alien to the kinds of roles they and their students have within this teaching tradition.

Discussion

We have seen that the teacher–student relationship plays a decisive role in students' development towards becoming professional musicians. Students' professional trust in their teachers is a fundamental condition in this relationship. In his book, *Personal Knowledge*, Michael Polanyi (1958, p. 53) underlines the importance of this almost blind trust when he writes: 'You follow your master because you trust his manner of doing things even when you cannot analyse and account in detail for its effectiveness.' It seems, however, that it is not always easy to combine this trust with a more democratic relationship and a dispassionate and appraising attitude; both teachers and students might feel that student evaluation confuses the roles.

Individual instrumental teaching normally creates closeness between teacher and student, but it also *presupposes* closeness to succeed. The results of this study indicate that students might be very anxious not to destroy this intimacy and confidence. In this situation student evaluation can be a double-edged sword. On the one hand, it can help students to express any negative feelings they might have in a regulated and accepted context and thereby help to reduce any tension in the dyadic relationship. Gaining insight into the needs and feelings of individual students can also enable teachers to adapt their teaching to those needs and feelings and thereby prevent future disappointment and frustration. On the other hand, it seems that student evaluation in some cases actually results in a deterioration of the relationship, because the teacher cannot handle negative evaluations and feels hurt or even becomes hostile. In other words, student evaluation can actually be counterproductive.

Students seem to be painfully aware of this possible outcome and their strategy, at least in some cases, seems to be to keep quiet. They prefer to live with the problems rather than tackle them by criticizing, or they change teachers if it becomes too much of a strain. In many cases this fear of the teacher's reaction might be groundless. Most teachers probably handle criticism professionally and do not let the student notice any negative reactions. But at the same time, some students' tales of experiences they have had trying to voice criticism to teachers over their years of study give grounds for concern. The interviews underline how important it is for teachers to have a highly developed professionalism and ethical awareness in their roles as teachers. If this is absent or inadequate, student evaluation may result in a worse situation for the students.

Instrumental teachers are, of course, only human beings and in my experience they generally invest enormous amounts of time, commitment and professional reputation in their work as teachers. Disappointment and anger are therefore understandable reactions when students are dissatisfied or do not want to accept what the teacher is able to offer. In such a close relationship both parties are dependent upon each other for support and acknowledgement. As the Danish philosopher Knud Eilert Løgstrup (1997) says, in every relationship we hold something of another human being's life in our hands: We are each other's destiny and therefore have power over each other. The teacher is the student's destiny, but the student is also to a large extent the teacher's destiny. The truth of this is clearly evident in the experience and feelings of Teacher J in response to his experience of student criticism.

Intimate relationships involve the revelation of oneself to another, and for that trust is a precondition. 'Acknowledgement, respect and consideration can only develop between persons who dare to expose themselves to each other in the conviction that they will not be rejected by the other part' (Bergem, 1998, p. 80). Criticism and negative evaluations can easily be regarded as a rejection of what one stands for both as a teacher and as a musician, and a natural reaction to this might be a feeling of hurt or anger. For this reason, it is crucial that teachers be aware of the ethical demands that are ingrained in their roles as teachers. The teacher is always the stronger party in a relationship that is asymmetric per definition, no matter how close it might be. This imposes on teachers an ethical responsibility towards their students; they have to control their own reactions, and put their own needs aside in favour of their students' needs.

In this chapter I have highlighted the problems associated with student evaluation in this particular educational context. This must not be interpreted as a total rejection of the whole idea of using student evaluation to improve instrumental teaching. The results of this study certainly do not justify such a conclusion. It is, however, vital for all parties involved to understand that such problems can occur in order to counteract them. The results make clear that there are ethical as well as psychological issues that need very careful consideration when implementing student evaluation of instrumental teaching.

References

Bergem. T. (1998) *Læreren i etikkens motlys* [*The Teacher in the Light of Ethics*], Oslo: adNotam Gyldendal.

Braskamp, L.A. and Ory, J.C. (1994) *Assessing Faculty Work: Enhancing Individual and Institutional Performance*, San Francisco: Jossey Bass.

Ericsson, A.K. (1997) 'Deliberate practice and the acquisition of expert performance: An overview', in H. Jorgensen and A.C. Lehmann (eds), *Does Practice Make Perfect? Current Theory and Research on Instrumental Music Practice*, pp. 9–51, Oslo: Norges musikkhøgskole.

Kingsbury, H. (1988) *Music, Talent and Performance: A Conservatory Cultural System*, Philadelphia: Temple University Press.

Kvale, S. (1996) *InterViews: An Introduction to Qualitative Research Interviewing*, Thousand Oaks: Sage.

Løgstrup, K.E. (1997) *The Ethical Demand*, Notre Dame: University of Notre Dame Press.

Manturzewska, M. (1990) 'A biographical study of the life-span development of professional musicians', *Psychology of Music*, 18: 112–39.

Moses, I. (1986) 'Student evaluation of teaching in an Australian university: Staff perceptions and reactions', *Assessment and Evaluation in Higher Education*, 2: 117–29.

Nettl, B. (1995) *Heartland Excursions: Ethnomusicological Reflections on Schools of Music*, Urbana: University of Illinois Press.

Nielsen, K. (1998) 'Musical apprenticeship: Learning at the academy of music as socially situated', unpublished PhD thesis, Aarhus University.

Nielsen, K. and Kvale, S. (1997) 'Current issues of apprenticeship', *Journal of Nordic Educational Research*, 173: 130–39.

Polanyi, M. (1958) *Personal Knowledge*, London: Routledge and Kegan.

Ryan, J.J., Anderson, J.A. and Birchler, A.B. (1980) 'Student evaluation: The faculty responds', *Research in Higher Education*, 4: 317–33.

Seldin, P. (1989) 'Using student feedback to improve teaching', *New Directions for Teaching and Learning*, 37: 89–97.

Seldin, P. (1993) 'The use and abuse of student ratings of professors', *Chronicle of Higher Education*, 46: 40.

Sosniak, L.A. (1990) 'The tortoise, the hare, and the development of talent', in M.J.A. Howe (ed.), *Encouraging the Development of Exceptional Skills and Talents*, pp. 149–64, Leicester: BPS Books.

Strike, K.A. (1991) 'The Ethics of Evaluation', in J. Millman and L. Darling-Hammond (eds), *The New Handbook of Teacher Evaluation*, pp. 356–73, Newbury Park, CA: Corwin Press.

Tiberius, R.G. and Flak, E. (1999) 'Incivility in dyadic teaching and learning', *New Directions for Teaching and Learning*, 77: 3–12.

Chapter 22

A Role for Action Research Projects in Developing New Pedagogical Approaches to Aural and Musicianship Education

Nicholas Bannan

Introduction

This chapter weaves together two distinct threads which deserve attention in music education research. First, it outlines some of the new influences from the field of evolutionary psychology which mesh with neurological research to suggest fruitful avenues for the development of innovative pedagogical practice; and second, it exemplifies the potential of the technique of action research as a means of refining and evaluating influences on the musical thinking and behaviour of teachers and learners. Action research involves a number of interconnected cycles of research planning, acting, observing and reflecting. It is viewed as being particularly appropriate to educational research since it deals with practical concerns and regards the participants and researcher as joint collaborators. Robson (1993, p. 441) presents a simplified model of action research which is useful here to explain the research process:

1. *Data collection* and the generation of hypotheses
2. *Validation* of hypotheses through use of analytical techniques
3. *Interpretation* by reference to theory, practice and practitioner judgement
4. *Action* for improvement that is also monitored by the same research techniques

Action research strategies are particularly appropriate where the social interaction of musicians has an important role in the pedagogical method.

The practices developed, modified and recorded in the research on which this chapter focuses have acquired the generic title 'Harmony Signing'. The Harmony Signing project illustrates the means by which an innovative programme for developing aural and musicianship skills was tested and refined through a series of action research projects. The motivation for the projects was to devise a consistent and powerful new pedagogical tool able to endow enriching musical experience across a wide variety of aptitudes and ages, transcending prejudices that kinaesthetic and social approaches of this kind are 'only for children' or 'only for the gifted' by ensuring that:

- the learning spiral offered by the approach connected in a consistent manner the simplest possible starting-point to an advanced level able to support the work of budding professionals;
- the techniques involved and the observation and discussion of their effectiveness were informed by research into the psychology of music, and especially kinaesthesia and musical aspects of social intelligence.

The pedagogical system became known for practical purposes as Harmony Signing, though not all activities involved either the experience of harmony or communication through gesture. Nevertheless, the central place in this approach of kinaesthetic learning and group improvisation directed by cheironomy (Gerson-Kiwi, 1980) led to this designation being adopted. 'Harmony Signing' is nearing readiness to be independently tested in a variety of music-educational environments including schools, choral groups, academies and conservatoires.

Why Action Research?

'All research starts with identifying a problem' (Kemp, 1992). Research in music and music education, as much as anywhere else, involves pursuing answers to questions. But certain approaches to research are specifically concerned with the process by which the questions to be asked are best defined. Action research in particular is associated with this solipsistic pattern of renewed inquiry and redefinition. Action research proceeds differently to experimental or observational projects in that the participants can control the agenda by which the researcher defines, by mutual consent, the problems and the means by which they are to be addressed and the resulting data interpreted. 'To positivists this seems like a dereliction of responsibility' (Adelman and Kemp, 1992). This study accepted the further necessary remove from standard social science models by assuming that the discourse within which change would be attempted and tested would be the media of music and gesture themselves. The development of Harmony Signing and associated pedagogy has thus represented a sequence of encounters which have largely eschewed the spoken and written word. It is central to the research position which gave rise to Harmony Signing as a principle to hypothesize that verbal interaction inhibits the acquisition of musical thinking and feeling. A research method was therefore devised appropriate to this theory. The richest experiences in the development of Harmony Signing which have most left their mark on the present state of its pedagogical methods have been those in which the capacities of the system developed organically within the rules inferred by participants from previous work and without reliance on spoken instruction.

Why 'Harmony Signing'? – Theoretical Influences on the Focus of the Research

The pedagogical concerns which motivated the conditions in which 'Harmony Signing' arose and developed have drawn heavily on existing projects (Bannan, 1988, 1994, 1996, 1997, 1998a, 1998b, 2000b, 2000a) involving children's vocal creativity and evolutionary models of voice acquisition. The influence of practitioners of hand-sign technique from Guido d'Arezzo via Curwen to Dalcroze and Kodály is acknowledged, as is Gerson-Kiwi's (1980) account of their antecedents in the Ancient World. Hypotheses under investigation elsewhere underpinned assumptions basic to Harmony Signing: that music and social communication are specific intelligences (Gardner, 1983); that the mind of *homo sapiens* developed under evolutionary pressures which determined links between oral/aural communication and manual dexterity (Mithen, 1996), and that musical behaviour played its part in the psychological adaptations which made this possible (Scherer, 1992; Vaneechoutte and Skoyles 1998; Cross, 1999); that musical behaviour is instinctive and universal (Wallin, 1991) and forms the substrate of speech (Tomatis, 1991); that music is 'contagious' in comparison with the serial nature of speech (Deacon, 1997; Merker, 2000), and is thus processed differently in the brain. While instinctive gestural and musical responses are widely accepted as of significance in infant and early childhood development (Woodward, 1992; Locke, 1993; Papoušek, 1996; Minami and Nito, 1998), there would appear to be an inferred 'sell-by date' operating in music education whereby movement-based and interpersonal learning are phased out and musical experience tends towards either the individual, the analytic, or the passive (this trend was observable, for instance, in the learning sequences prescribed by the National Curriculum for England at the time (2000) that the version of Harmony Signing described in this chapter emerged). Harmony Signing could be seen as a 'right-brain' compensation for such 'left-brain' tendencies. Finally, the 'game-playing' experiences of childhood (Bjørkvold, 1992; Bailey and Farrow, 1998) can be maintained through appropriate pedagogy as prime motivators of musical participation.

A resulting concern was to foster musical learning and interaction in which music itself predominated as the communicative medium. The project was not in its own terms able to yield results sufficient to confirm that verbalization (spoken or written) 'switches off' the perceptual and productive mechanisms which could be seen to represent 'musical thinking and feeling'. But what did occur in much of the interaction of the various participant groups is consistent with this hypothesis and has allowed the development of a tool for primarily non-verbal teaching and learning which is ripe for more formal investigation.

A Brief Developmental History of Harmony Signing and the Project

Harmony Signing began almost accidentally. At one of the regular rehearsals of the Reading University Children's Choir in the summer of 1996, a group of six singers aged 7–10 were engaged in devising an a cappella arrangement of the song *Shenandoah*. They had experimented with generating chords to accompany the melody, and worked out who should sing what, but lacked a means of controlling how and when the chords should change. A simple three-sign system was proposed by which one member of the group would show which chord was required as the melody unfolded. This remains the fundamental feature of Harmony Signing, though a considerable edifice of pedagogical and practical procedure has grown from it.

Since it was clear that volunteer child singers could make use of such a technique, both responding to it as participants and operating it as leaders, it seemed logical to share this with teacher education students at the university. As each new group was introduced, further levels of possibility were revealed, and the need to document and organize the consequences became clear. This provided the opportunity to arrange sessions designed to illustrate what occurred when different participants were introduced to the technique. Over the period September 1996 to August 1999, the following groups contributed to the Harmony Signing project:

- A children's choir
- Music education undergraduates
- Education undergraduates without specialized musical knowledge
- Postgraduate music education students at two different institutions
- Advanced young musicians (11–18) with Dalcroze experience
- Intermediate young musicians (10–15) on instrumental courses
- Members of a youth choir (14–18)
- Members of an adult chamber choir
- Pupils aged 9–10 in a state-maintained primary school
- A group of teachers with musical responsibility in Rudolf Steiner schools
- Members of a barbershop chorus
- Participants in workshops at a barbershop convention

Each new group was selected on the basis of providing different conditions in which Harmony Signing might adapt (or be adapted) to meet the differing needs and expectations of participants:

- with greater or lesser musical experience;
- of widely differing ages;
- within groups with differing gender profiles;
- with varied experience of musical leadership roles;

- with varied stylistic experience;
- with varying involvement in vocal performance and pedagogy.

Some Illustrations of Harmony Signing Practice

The issue originally addressed was how to develop a consistent and flexible pedagogical tool which exploits social and spacial intelligences (Gardner, 1983) and kinaesthesia in developing participants' feel for harmony and their confidence to explore music through vocal improvisation. Teaching was generally sequenced as follows, depending on length and frequency of session, ability of students, and so on:

1. Creating triads: working with scale notes 1/3/5 (doh/me/soh) in three groups to voice the tonic triad. The signer holds the left arm horizontally across the chest, palm down and fingers extended.
2. Moving to the subdominant: (see Figure 22.1): (The harmonic vocabulary now available allows the signed accompaniment of a simple melody such as the opening bars of the theme music to the film 'Chariots of Fire'.)

---

1 (doh) 'anchors' (elbow)
3–4 (me–fah) rises only a semitone (wrist)
5–6 (soh–la) rises a whole tone (fingertips)

The signer raises the arm through a 90-degree arc to a vertical position, fingers pointing upwards.

Figure 22.1   Moving to the subdominant

---

5 (soh) 'anchors' (elbow)
3–2 (me–ray) falls a whole tone (fingertips)
1(8)–7 (doh–ti) falls only a semitone (wrist)

The signer lowers the arm through a clockwise arc until the fingers are pointing vertically downwards towards the ground.

Figure 22.2   Moving to the dominant

3. Moving to the dominant (see Figure 22.2).
4. Working with the primary triads: tonic-subdominant-dominant. (The harmonic vocabulary of three primary triads related by simple voice-leading allows the performance of a basic boogie-woogie blues; or the accompaniment to a melody such as the eighties pop song *Wimoweh*.)
5. Composing with three chords and verbal texts. (Beginning with a single word such as 'Amen' or 'Alleluia', the signer communicates changes of syllable, cut-off to silence and re-entry with the right hand while signing chord choice with the left arm. Melisma becomes available where right-hand action signals no change of syllable while left arm movement signals change of chord.)
6. Developing the use of inversions (see Figure 22.3).

The sign for inverting is: right hand, palm upward placed across the chest *below* the left-hand position (as if gently holding an object between the palms). Raising the right-hand signals inversion of the chord to the next position: lowering signals the opposite.

		doh			
3	soh	soh	soh		soh
2	me	me	me	me	me
1	doh		doh	doh	doh
				soh	

The same exchanging of pitches can be employed on the subdominant and dominant chord positions to create a rich harmonic potential with simple means which establishes through internalization and practical experience the important difference of role between:

- chords with different roots;
- different inversions of the same chord

Figure 22.3   Developing the use of inversions

7. Moving a melody part against chords: working with suspensions (see Figure 22.4).
8. Modulation: the cut-and-paste technique; exercises in modulating away from and back to the tonic (see Figure 22.5).

Involves employing standard Kodály handsigns (assuming a movable doh) to signal with the right hand *anticipations, suspensions* and *free melodic movement*. Beginners can experiment with neighbour-note decoration (*appoggiaturas, auxiliaries, turns, etc.*), for example:

```
        Soh_____ : La_____ : Soh_____
[RH] me–fa–me–ray–me : Fa_____ : Me____
        Doh_____: Ti___: Doh_____
[LH Chords]
        I_____IV____V___I (susp.)___
```

Figure 22.4   Moving a melody part against chords

Modulation is achieved by pointing clearly with the right-hand index finger at the position representing the chord which is to be moved, as a means of activating 'cutting-and-pasting'. Thus a subdominant chord can be 'dragged' to the central, tonic position: notes 1/4/6 (doh-fa-la) then become 5/1/3, and are treated as the tonic; which allows the subdominant position (finger pointing up) to be occupied by a new subdominant.

Figure 22.5   Modulation

The basis of this is to establish the understanding that every tonic is defined by its relationship to its dominant and subdominant, just as the present mediates between the past and the future, or a given generation has both parents and offspring. A series of 'cut-and-paste' manoeuvres of this kind can help develop security with cycle-of-fifths modulation.

9.   Free modulation 'journeys' through cutting-and-pasting (see Figure 22.6).

Modulation is combined with other aspects of Harmony Signing to allow expressive experimentation and develop a sense of tonality.

Figure 22.6   Free modulaton 'journeys' through cutting-and-pasting

10. Some sample polyphonic material accessible through Harmony Signing
     (see Figure 22.7).

Experienced signers can perform melodies and harmony together (in four
parts).

Examples might be:

- Grüber   Silent Night
- Chopin   Etude in E major, Op. 10 No. 3

**Figure 22.7   Some sample polyphonic material accessible through
           Harmony Signing**

(Signers who have reached this level of competence will be able to transfer
skills which allow them to convey 'known' music (such as the examples
given in Figure 22.7) to improvising freely with participants. This can aid
the development of confidence in composing, as well as permitting
experimentation with stylistic features such as chromatic combinations
and dissonances, and so on.)

11. Signers able to achieve step 10, working with similarly experienced singers
     or instrumentalists, can use the technique as a basis for free composition
     of their own devising.

The steps illustrated above comprise the initial stages of Harmony Signing
which evolved within the time-frame of the action research reported. Further
signs and procedures have since developed, including representation of the
secondary triads, and turning the primary triads into minor versions of themselves.
    What the *signer* does is only part of this method. Simple voice-leading
principles which are learned simultaneously with the signs that represent them
allow participants to create rich and functional harmonic textures. This is initially
achieved vocally, though instrumental work can also develop from it. Most
important of all are the procedures through which participants learn to 'locate':
to know which note of the scale or triad they are performing, thus building a
sense of melodic and harmonic function. This skill is built through games in
which, initially, the teacher's aural skills in guiding participation are essential –
in turn, the same skills will be acquired by participants through the experience
these activities endow. But vital to the success of these principles is that pupils

lead the session: 'Harmony Signing' is collective and democratic, and founders when teachers are afraid to pass on 'their' responsibility. Indeed, it is through having the opportunity to lead that participants begin fully to understand the relationship between musical part and whole. This 'knowledge' develops through experience rather than analytic explanation.

'Harmony Signing' owes much to experience gained in projects employing Music Technology (Bannan, 1998a), while itself eschewing hardware of any kind, and, indeed, offering a pedagogy which compensates in its interpersonal, bodily holistic practices for the somewhat private and analytic features of pupil engagement with Information Technology (IT) workstations. Its adoption of 'cut-and-paste' techniques and other aspects of IT architecture (for instance in communicating modulation, or nesting motifs within harmonic relationships) is acknowledged: Harmony Signing is of our time, 'post-electronic' – unplugged music IT.

The Aims and Methodology of the Action Research Project

The aim of the project was to create an innovative teaching tool with flexibility and potential, the properties of which addressed concerns raised in the literature reviewed. The two principal strategies were:

- developing a scaffold of concepts and procedures through the written recording of practice, in which I variously participated and observed (supported by occasional video recording), and through subsequent discussion with participants (both 'performers' and 'signers');
- setting targets for potential new developments arising from the practice and reports of practitioners, especially where variations in practice emerged according to differences in client groups.

A secondary issue developed alongside these principal aims, in which the action research procedures designed to investigate Harmony Signing gave rise to new data and analysis, which led in turn to the recognition that participation in Harmony Signing can itself provide useful diagnostic information for the teacher regarding how students are developing in their musical perceptions and responses. This gave an additional dimension to the predicted outcomes of the project, which sought to illuminate the processes by which a scaffold of musical thinking and feeling could be established. An antidote was also sought to the commonly encountered phenomenon represented by young musicians with highly developed physical skills and advanced instrumental technique whose musicianship, judged as the capacity to discriminate intervals and chords, to improvise and sight-sing, are by contrast poorly developed or non-existent; a position which first motivated Dalcroze more than a century ago.

A significant stimulus to the development of Harmony Signing was thus to explore means of restoring expressive and spontaneous vocal work in the classroom and teaching studio. It is no accident that the foundations of the system owe much to the improvised vocal harmony of Southern Africa and Polynesia, in which part-singing develops from an instinctive capacity to complement the performance of others (Blacking, 1987; Dargie, 1991), as opposed to prevailing practice within the western tradition characterized by conformity and fidelity to the notation of composers. Harmony Signing encourages the generation of new music in a manner which empowers individuals to share their musical thoughts with others in real time (see step 11, above). In so offering the opportunity for the pupil to create and lead, it sidesteps the rote learning and focus on notation which can represent a narrow, teacher-dominated function.

The Assessment of Musical Behaviour in Teachers and Pupils

The reflective methodology of this project, involving 'live' observation, video analysis and discussion with participants, began to reveal distinct differences in musical thinking and feeling in signers and participants. For instance, in relation to participants' existing levels of harmonic experience (for example, music graduates and teachers, as opposed to children and adult amateurs), the self-consciousness of the 'expert' as opposed to the 'novice' affected the capacity to operate and even to value work of this kind:

> It would seem that the more expertise had been developed in thinking about harmonic relations and properties on paper, the less able such participants were to allow intuition to take over. What noticeably defeated such musicians was the modulation exercise in which a chord changes role as one tonic is replaced by another: those for whom this process had always been inwardly represented through work on the keyboard or musical stave found themselves having to visualise or 'finger' the operation in order to discover what notes to sing! Such strategies were never evident in younger participants, even where they possessed advanced musical performance skills. It would seem that paper study of the kind carried out in University degrees and Conservatoire diplomas is responsible for demanding only one form of musical thinking. In view of the fact that this constitutes the training route through which so many of our future teachers qualify in their subject, the need for a bridge which allows re-entry into the instinctive musical world of the child and amateur could not be clearer. (Bannan, 2000a)

Positivists should note that a 'control' for this comparison was made available through teaching the movements to participants without telling them why or what they would obtain. Such 'innocent' users proved more effective than some musically skilled leaders.

As important was the *quality* of movement observed in signers. Some communicated fluently, clearly hearing, feeling and 'showing' in an integrated perceptual and productive continuum. Others were jerky, as if each experience was separated on a 'lattice' (Wishart, 1996), and did not arise from coherent self-representation of musical ideas. Such signers presented information unhelpfully, as if trying to trick participants rather than cooperate with them, as in a game of 'scissors-paper-stone'. Different approaches of this kind shed light on related inhibitions of musical performance and aural discrimination in the same individuals.

In addition, Harmony Signing began to address differing needs, since the shaping of the pedagogy itself in its most advanced forms has responded to what exponents have said and done:

- an 18-year-old university applicant in music who stated that she understood fully the characteristics of *suspension* for the first time as a consequence of experiencing them as a participant and signer;
- 15-year-old students preparing for composing assignments who found the capacities of chromatic inflection around diatonic harmony opened up new expressive opportunities;
- members of a children's choir aged 9–10 with limited understanding of notation who were able to work out vocal arrangements of melodies using Harmony Signing;
- members of an adult chamber choir who had never been taught harmonic function who were able to develop their personal contributions to blend and tuning;
- teenage participants whose capacities to think physically in the system more than matched those of the author, and who were keen to propose refinements and test it to its limits.

Implications for Teacher Education

Harmony Signing poses questions and challenges to those who educate music educators:

- Do we provide an effective model for teaching *through musical thinking and feeling*?
- Are we sensitive to the differing modes of thought which our pupils bring to bear on engagement with the same experiences?
- Do we allow pupils the generative and leadership opportunities in music which formed the foundations of their acquisition of language as children?
- Are we in danger of attempting to teach music through high-level concepts which we only mastered ourselves as adults?

Where employed in teacher education programmes, the capacities which Harmony Signing provide focus on adapting the experience and skill of music graduates to modes of thought and feeling able to engage the whole personality of pupils in a supportive social context. The pedagogy guides personal creativity in group situations under controlled conditions, fulfilling Bickerton's (1990) conditions for language evolution of both *communicating* to others and *representing* to the user; and Sacks' (1989) similar observation that deaf signing conveys both meaning and emotional motivation. Such interpersonal skills and sensitivities, developed within a dedicated music pedagogy, can be of immense benefit to entrants to the profession.

The Role of Action Research in Pedagogical and Curricular Development

The value of action research methods to a study of this kind is the means it offers to allow participants to break new ground. Even the research and development model of the inventor (or, indeed, the artist or composer) represents a process in which all ideas emanate from one mind. This is much less so with the *atelier* approach. Without the teamwork implicit in the various phases of the project, some of the most valuable aspects of Harmony Signing would not have evolved; nor would the opportunity to evaluate its potential for eliciting evidence of instinctive behaviour. Indeed, one of the most interesting aspects of this work has been its capacity to feed ideas back into the evolutionary psychology models which first influenced its development; it may well be that close observation of 'Harmony Signing' activities allied to the use of MRI or PET scanning could yield valuable information about the nature of musical responses and different modes of musical thinking and feeling.

Action research can, then, represent a valuable tool for the definition of questions in preparation for laboratory and quantitative research. It can contribute to the identification of needs, in individuals or processes. It can allow the replication of activities in circumstances which allow one to discover variables one might not have predicted, so as to be able to determine better-informed experimentation. And it allows participants (as opposed to subjects) the preservation of authenticity of experience such that behaviour is not inhibited by unnatural roles or circumstances: the organism is studied in its usual environment. All these factors helped make the Harmony Signing project a valuable means both of developing the pedagogy involved, and of giving insight into aspects of musical behaviour which require further study. Such methods merit application to other curricular and pedagogical investigations in places where music education is practised.

Conclusions

Harmony Signing is now being written up as a method, and the outcomes of the project have begun to be published (Bannan, 1999, 2000a). Experience and evaluation suggest that it can have a valuable role in the development of musicianship and aural skills in participants from age 7 (when groups of children are likely to be able to pitch their voices with sufficient accuracy and confidence) through to advanced students at university and conservatoire level. A case could be argued for including pedagogy of this kind in teacher education programmes. Harmony Signing allows participants to develop composition and improvisation skills, aural discrimination and part-singing experience to high levels without recourse to notation, and has proved a useful tool in the education of both classroom teachers and ensemble directors.

In addition to its potential as a pedagogical tool, there is growing evidence of its having diagnostic properties with respect to how participants engage in music and how holistic musical thinking can be developed as a solution to certain frustrations and inhibitions. These concerns, in addition to the approach itself, now require the more rigorous testing of experimental research.

References

Adelman, C. and Kemp, A. (1992) 'Case study and action research', in A.E. Kemp (ed.), *Some Approaches to Research in Music Education*, pp. 111–37, Reading: International Society for Music Education.

Bailey, R. and Farrow, S. (1998) 'Play and problem-solving in a new light', *International Journal of Early Years Education*, 6(3): 265–75.

Bannan, N. (1988) 'Singing, synthesis and creativity', *Music Teacher*, January: 8–9; February: 19–21; April: 18–20; May: 29–32.

Bannan, N. (1994) *The Voice in Education*, London: Rhinegold Publishing.

Bannan, N. (1996) 'The children's choir as research laboratory', unpublished paper in support of the ISME Research Commission Poster Session, 22nd ISME World Conference, Amsterdam.

Bannan, N. (1997) 'The consequences for singing teaching of an adaptationist approach to vocal development', in *Proceedings of the First International Conference on Music in Human Adaptation*, pp. 39–46, VirginiaTech/MMB Music Inc.

Bannan, N. (1998a) 'Aural feedback, vocal technique, and creativity', in B.A. Roberts (ed.), *The Phenomenon of Singing*, pp. 11–19, Newfoundland, Canada: Memorial University Press.

Bannan, N. (1998b) 'Out of Africa: The evolution of the human capacity for music', in C.V. Niekerk (ed.), *Proceedings of the 23rd International Society for Music Education*, World Conference, pp. 26–33, Pretoria: University of South Africa Press.

Bannan, N. (1999) 'Harmony Signing', in *Yamaha Education Supplement*, No. 30, p. 27, Christchurch: CODA Music Trust.

Bannan, N. (2000a) 'A gestural language for the representation and communication of vocal harmony', in B.A. Roberts (ed.), *The Phenomenon of Singing II*, pp. 11–19, Newfoundland: Memorial University Press.

Bannan, N. (2000b) 'Instinctive singing: lifelong development of 'the child within', *British Journal of Music Education*, 17(3): 295–301.

Bickerton, D. (1990) *Language and Species*, Chicago: University of Chicago Press.

Bjørkvold, J-R. (1992) *The Muse Within: Creativity and Communication, Song and Play from Childhood through Maturity*, trans. W.H. Halverson, New York: HarperCollins.

Blacking, J. (1987) '*A Commonsense View of all Music*', Cambridge: Cambridge University Press.

Cross, I. (1999) 'Is music the most important thing we ever did? Music, development and evolution', in Suk Won Yi (ed.) *Music, Mind and Science*, pp. 10–39, Seoul: Seoul National University Press.

Deacon, T. (1997) *The Symbolic Species*, London: Allen Lane.

Dargie, D. (1991) *Xhosa Music*, Cape Town: David Philip.

Gardner, H. (1983) *Frames of Mind*, New York: Basic Books.

Gerson-Kiwi, E. (1980) 'Cheironomy', in S. Sadie (ed.), *The Grove Dictionary of Music and Musicians* (vol. 4), pp. 191–6, London: Macmillan.

Kemp, A. (1992) 'Approaching Research', in A.E. Kemp (ed.), *Some Approaches to Research in Music Education*, pp. 7–18, Reading: International Society for Music Education.

Locke, J. (1993) *The Child's Path to Spoken Language*, Cambridge: Harvard University Press.

Merker, B. (2000) 'Synchronous chorusing and human origins', in N. Wallin, B. Merker and S. Brown (eds), *The Origins of Music*, pp. 315–28, Cambridge, MA: MIT Press.

Minami, Y. and Nito, H. (1998) 'Vocal pitch-matching in infants', paper presented at *Respecting the Child in Early Childhood Music Education*, seminar of the ISME Early Childhood Commission, University of Stellenbosch, South Africa.

Mithen, S. (1996) *The Prehistory of the Mind*, London: Thames & Hudson.

Papoušek, H. (1996) 'Musicality in early infancy research: Biological and cultural origins of early musicality', in I. Deliège and J. Sloboda (eds), *Musical Beginnings*, pp. 37–55, Oxford: Oxford University Press.

Robson, C. (1993) *Real World Research*, London: Blackwell.

Sacks, O. (1989) *Seeing Voices: A Journey into the World of the Deaf*, London: Picador.

Scherer, K.R. (1992) 'Vocal affect expression as symptom, symbol and appeal', in H. Papoušek, U. Jürgens and M. Papoušek, *Nonverbal Vocal Communication: Comparative and Developmental Approaches*, Cambridge: Cambridge University Press, pp. 43–60.

Tomatis, A.A. (1991) *The Conscious Ear*, Barrytown, NY: Station Hill Press.

Vaneechoutte, M. and Skoyles, J.R. (1998) 'The memetic origin of language: Modern humans as musical primates', *Journal of Memetics – Evolutionary Models of Information Transmission*, 2: available at: <http://www.cpm.mmu.ac.uk/jomemit/1998/vol2/vaneechoutte_m&skoyles_jr.html>.

Wallin, N. (1991) *Biomusicology*, New York: Pendragon.

Wishart, T. (1996) *On Sonic Art*, Amsterdam: Harwood Academic Publishers.

Woodward, S. (1992) 'The transmission of music into the human uterus and the response to music of the human fetus and neonate', unpublished doctoral dissertation, University of Cape Town, South Africa.

Chapter 23

A New Approach to Pursuing the Professional Development of Recent Graduates from German Music Academies: The Alumni Project

Heiner Gembris

Introduction

The Alumni Project started from two different angles. The first was concerned with the developmental aspects of musical careers. Musical development is arguably a life-long process; therefore, the developmental psychology of musical abilities and careers needs a perspective which covers the whole life-span. There is a considerable amount of research concerning musical development in childhood and the teenage years (cf. Hargreaves, 1986; Deliège and Sloboda 1996; Gembris, 2002), but research about the career development of musicians in adulthood or about ageing musicians is very limited. Those few studies that have dealt with the development of professional musicians have focused on the course of musical biographies of instrumentalists (for example, Manturzewska, 1990), the acquisition and maintenance of expertise (Krampe, 1994), personality and temperament (Kemp, 1996), retired instrumentalists (Smith, 1988, 1989), job perceptions and well-being (Kivimäki and Jokinen, 1994), and the career of outstanding singers (Rexroad, 1985). There is virtually no developmental research about a very important and decisive phase of careers, namely the transition from the music academy to the professional life as instrumentalist or singer.

The other starting point of the Alumni Project was the observation that only a few graduates manage to make a smooth transition from being students at a music academy to establishing their professional lives. Many singers and instrumentalists who had aimed for a career as a vocal soloist or orchestral musician experience tremendous problems in getting engagements or secure positions. This situation often does not change even after a longer period of time. Naturally, this has to do in part with the generally unfavourable situation for musicians on the job market. Of course, the music business in every country has its specific national characteristics. The following observations characterized the situation in Germany, which may be somewhat different from that of other countries.

Job Market for Musicians

Despite the fact that Germany has a varied and rich cultural scene which includes 130 musical theatre stages, around 50 professional orchestras and 30 festivals, the situation regarding the start of a musical career after graduation is generally difficult. The main reason is the increase in the numbers of trained singers and instrumentalists along with the simultaneous decrease in job opportunities in choirs, orchestras and opera ensembles. This decrease is due to the problematical financial situation, which brings about the merging or dissolution of orchestras. Also, new vacancies may simply not be filled. For example, the number of artistic personnel working in musical theatres dropped by 1392 (8 per cent), from 17 423 to 16 031, between the 1993/94 and the 1996/97 seasons. Theatre orchestras, opera choirs and vocal soloists were among the most affected (Rinderspracher, 1999, p. 47). Between 1991 and 1998, a total of 1136 (9.3 per cent) of orchestral positions were lost due to the merging and dissolution of orchestras. Of course, these developments have a negative impact on the employment opportunities and job perspectives of the 4000 instrumental musicians who are currently being trained as orchestral musicians in German schools of music. While, according to official statistics, only 16 musicians on average applied for each orchestral position in 1980, in 1988 there were already 52 applicants for each position. Between 1992 and 1995, the average across 400 to 500 job opportunities per year was 57 applications (Rinderspracher, 1999, p. 54). But because not all orchestras provide data for statistical surveys, the real number of applicants could be much higher. According to the insights and experiences of music agents, there may be an average of 200 to 300 applicants per position. Recently, in an extreme case reported by a music agent to the author, there were more than 700 applicants for one violin position in a renowned orchestra.

Singers face similar problems. Currently, only very few female singers (especially sopranos) have the chance to receive a contract for the stage, because there are essentially more female singers coming from the music academies than there are available positions. In contrast, only very few male singers enter professional training, and theatres experience a certain shortage of male singers. Therefore, the career opportunities for male singers are generally somewhat better. These facts highlight some aspects of the situation of the job market for instrumentalists and singers in Germany. It may be that the situation in other countries is somewhat different.

In recent years, some European countries have initiated a number of interesting and important projects to investigate the changing job market for musicians, and to improve the training at the music academies. For instance, the Higher Education Funding Council for England (HEFCE) evaluated the patterns of employment of conservatoire graduates and the implications for desirable patterns of future training (HEFCE, 1998, p. 11). The Professional Integration Project (PIP, 2000;

Barnes and Holt, no date), a cooperative of British conservatoires and university music departments, fosters the professional integration of music graduates. The Leonardo Working-Group on Professional Integration of Musicians and the 'Promuse' project of the Association Européen des Conservatoires, Académies de Musique et Musikhochschulen (ACE) pursue similar ideas and examine the areas of professional integration and continuing education in order to offer music students and professional musicians better professional opportunities. Another project deals with the phenomenon of 'feminization' of professional music life in Scandinavia (that is, the increasing number of female musicians in orchestras) and its consequences for the traditionally male hegemony in music performance, and so on (Annfelt and Stendal, no date).

Extra-musical Personality Factors

In addition to the labour market, success in a musical career has to do not only with the degree of someone's musical qualification, but also with extraneous and personality-related aspects. That outstanding musical qualifications are a prerequisite for a successful career requires no mention. At the same time, experts in the area of stage performance and musical theatre emphasize time and again the importance of personality, charisma and stage presence. Personality traits like introversion, fearfulness and so forth have at times been operationalized and researched in psychology. However, we cannot claim from those empirical studies regarding personality of musicians (for example, Kemp, 1996) which personality characteristics will allow one musician to be more successful than another. One problem is that personality characteristics such as charisma and stage presence are perceived with high inter-individual agreement, and they may constitute central criteria for the evaluation of musicians. However, even experts in the area of stage performance are unable to clearly define these characteristics. Despite their real-life importance, these concepts are elusive. One reason is that psychology does not provide appropriate concepts for them. This renders them an interesting topic for investigation.

Also, we do not know how the professional lives of those singers and instrumentalists who have successfully undergone the necessary training, but afterwards do not find the employment as musicians or soloists they were aiming for, continue. This is exactly the situation in which the majority of graduates from music academies find themselves.

With regard to the career prospects of instrumentalists and singers, these circumstances pose difficult and unresolved problems. Certainly, people in other domains of work also suffer from unemployment. In contrast to other professionals, however, musicians have an additional issue: that they might have started to play their instrument when they were six, seven or eight years old. Thus, since childhood they have invested considerable amounts of time and money in instruments, lessons and practice. During their artistic training in schools of music or music academies, their sense of individuality and of being special because of their musical aptitude has been strengthened. It is likely that their identity, personality, and long-term goals as professional musicians are heavily tied up with their musical activities. When it becomes impossible to work as an instrumentalist or singer, the next question is not only one of finding a different livelihood, but also how an artist's personality can change his or her professional identity and adapt to the new situation.

The Alumni Project: Research Questions

In light of the context above, Alumni Project research questions are as follows:

- What happens to professional singers and instrumentalists who have finished their training at music academies?
- What factors contribute to a smooth transition from school to professional life?
- How does the phase between graduation and entrance into professional life proceed?
- How do musicians experience this transition and how do they cope with it?
- How well do the demands of professional life match the qualifications acquired at the music academies?
- What conclusions can we derive from our results to improve the training of musicians?

From these questions, it is possible to gain insights into the transitory phase between training and professional life; to explore those extra-musical factors that decide whether the transition from training to professional life is successful and how successful it is; to examine how musicians experience and cope with the transitory phase between training and professional life. From these discoveries, insights regarding correspondences between the training curriculum at the academies and demands of the employment market should be possible, and so the development of a set of suggestions for more realistic training and career counselling for future musicians.

Methods

The Alumni Project consists of three different parts, or modules, all of which are currently being investigated (see Figure 23.1):

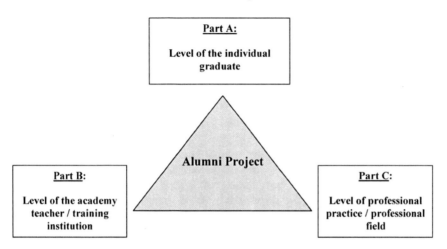

Figure 23.1   The design of the Alumni Project

- Part A: Level of the individual graduate
- Part B: Level of the academy teacher / training institution
- Part C: Level of professional practice / professional field

Part A: Data Collection among the Graduates

At four music academies, a random sample of 20 graduates will be taken, with five students from each of the departments of voice, wind, string, and piano. Restricting the research to these groups of instruments seems justified because they represent the majority of the students. The data collection among the graduates will be carried out in two distinct phases. During the first phase, initial interviews will be conducted; the second phase consists of a longitudinal study.

Phase I: Initial interview   Individual interviews will be conducted with the graduates after their final exams. The interview will comprise three parts:

1. Data regarding the participants' musical biography and training background up to the present will be elicited using a semi-structured survey.
2. The quality of training, practical applicability, duration of academy training, and so on, will be examined.
3. Characteristics will be measured using standardized personality inventory (NEO-FFI; Borkenau and Ostendorf, 1993) and a self-concept scale (Ferring and Filipp, 1996). We assume that the characteristics measured with these inventories are relevant for success in a musical career.

Phase II: Longitudinal survey   Following the initial interview, and for a duration of two years, every six months the graduates will receive by mail a standardized survey (four surveys in total). Each survey will address the professional, personal, social and financial situation of the graduate: contacts with agents, applications, auditions, professional experience, professional and personal plans, estimates of future perspectives, occupations and jobs in non-music fields, and so on.

Part B: Data Collection among the Academy Teachers

In order to investigate how questions touching upon professional life are incorporated into the training of future instrumentalists and singers, interviews will be conducted with academy teachers. We want to find out:

- to what degree academy teachers are concerned with the career prospects of their students;
- whether this problem already affects the selection of students;
- to what degree it plays a role in curriculum development;
- and the possibilities academy teachers believe they have for increasing the chances their students have on the job market.

Part C: Data Collection in the Professional Field

Two groups will be surveyed, among them representatives of the music profession and experts in the musical employment market, namely agents of public and private agencies who place musicians and singers, as well as conductors and choir directors, and others who contract musicians. Informants will be interviewed using a guided interview technique. This information will be supplemented with statistics and other data (for example, German stage performance association; Federal Labor Bureau) to see how the employment situation has evolved over the last 10 years. This data collection is focused on the following questions:

- What are the practical musical and non-musical demands that agents and other decision-makers (conductors, choir directors, theatre directors) in the musical employment market impose on the graduates?
- According to which criteria are potential applicants hired and contracted?
- What kind of experiences do representatives have with applicants, and what prognosis can they make regarding the employment opportunities of graduates?

Based on preliminary thoughts and communications with experts, interview schedules for the three areas of the project have been developed.

Preliminary Results from Interviews with Agents for Musical Theatres

A few preliminary results from the work with Part C cast some light on the huge potential of this study. The results are based on five interviews with agents with the Central Stage, Film, and Television Placement Agency (ZBF), one of the most important employment agencies for artists in Germany. The interviewees are experts with specialisms in the placement of vocal soloists and choir singers for opera houses. Hence, these individuals possess a comprehensive knowledge of the job situation for opera singers. The interviews were subjected to a qualitative thematic content analysis (see references to such techniques in Chapters 11 and 16 in this volume). The following results concern the question of which abilities and characteristics both male and female singers must have, according to the agents, in order to be successfully placed as a soloist with an opera house.

Obviously, outstanding vocal qualities are a necessary prerequisite. This includes a good vocal disposition, an expressive voice, appealing timbre, good technique and breath control. However, in addition there are a number of other extra-musical factors involved, which are summarized as follows:

- **Physical characteristics**
  - Attractiveness
  - Youthfulness
  - Good health
  - Resilience to physical strain
  - Good posture
  - Vivid eyes

- **Psychological characteristics**
  - Charisma
  - Vivacity
  - Strong motivation to present oneself
  - Resilience to psychological stress
  - Self-confidence
  - Ability to communicate with others

- **Professional characteristics**
  - Obsession for the theatre
  - Ability to act
  - Expressiveness
  - Clear diction
  - Willingness to work in a very insecure profession
  - High mobility and flexibility
  - Willingness to put work ahead of the family
  - Willingness to sacrifice and lead a lifestyle compatible with the job

Discussion

It stands to reason that these results are only tentative, because the pool of data they are based on is still small. Nevertheless, they already raise a number of questions that are relevant with regard to the developmental psychology and personality psychology of musicians, and also with regard to the ways in which music academies train their students.

One important question is: to what degree can the extra-musical abilities and characteristics that musicians' agencies deem important for a successful musical career actually be acquired and learned? A second question is: are these skills (or are they not) developed at the music academies to an extent where they can be taught at all? Physical properties like health and good looks can obviously not – or only to a minimal degree – be influenced through training. But disciplines such as performing arts medicine can inform students of career-related health and prevention issues. It is conceivable that one could create classes in which one learns to dress and behave properly in auditions (and on stage). Classes that teach stress management might also be helpful. What I think is most important is to inform students carefully at the onset of their training about the occupational practices, the employment situation and the extra-musical demands they are likely to face. This heightens students' awareness of the risks and problems associated with the professional career in music to which they aspire, and may prevent them from being led by fantasies and illusions.[1]

Note

1. I would like to thank Dominique Lafourcade, Charles Bodman Rae, John Sloboda, and Tor Anders Stendal for pointing me to other recent or ongoing European projects concerned with similar issues. I also grateful to Andreas Lehman for his comments and help with the translation. This project is now complete and further details can be obtained at: www.uni-paderborn.de/ibfm

References

Annfelt, T. and Stendal, T.A. (no date) '"The job goes to the best musician", Researching in negotiations about sex and music in Norwegian music education', unpublished paper, Norwegian University of Science and Technology/Faculty of Arts, Trondheim Conservatory of Music, Department of Interdisciplinary Studies of Culture.

Barnes, J. and Holt, G. (no date) *Making Music Work: Professional Integration Project: Fostering Professional Skills among those Studying Music in Higher Education*, London: Royal College of Music.

Borkenau, P. and Astendorf, F. (1993) NEO-Fünf-Faktoren Inventar (NEO-FFI), Göttingen: Hogrefe.

Deliège, I. and Sloboda, J. (1996) *Musical Beginnings: Origins and Development of Musical Competence*, Oxford: Oxford University Press.

Ferring, D. and Filipp, S.-H. (1996) 'Messung des Selbstwertgefühls: Befunde zu Reliabilität, Validität und Stabilität der Rosenberg-Skala' ['Measuring self-esteem: Findings concerning the reliability, validity and stability of the Rosenberg scale'], *Diagnostica*, 42: 284–92.

Gembris, H. (2002) *Grundlagen musikalischer Begabung und Entwicklung* [Foundations of Musical Abilities and Development], Augsburg: Wissner.

Hargreaves, D.J. (1986) *The Developmental Psychology of Music*, Cambridge: Cambridge University Press.

Higher Education Funding Council for England (HEFCE) (1998), *Review of Music Conservatoires*, HEFCE Report 98/11, available at: <http://www.hefce.acc.uk/pubs/1998>.

Kemp, A. (1996) *The Musical Temperament: Psychology and Personality of Musicians*, Oxford: Oxford University Press.

Kivimäki, M. and Jokinen, M. (1994) 'Job perceptions and well-being among symphony orchestra musicians: A comparison with other occupational groups', *Medical Problems of Performings Artists*, 9(4): 73–6.

Krampe, R.Th. (1994) 'Maintaining Excellence: Cognitive-motor Performance in Pianists Differing in Age and Skill Level', dissertation, Studien und Berichte des Max-Planck-Instituts für Bildungsforschung, 58, Berlin.

Manturzewska, M. (1990) 'A biographical study of the life-span development of professional musicians', *Psychology of Music*, 18: 112–38.

Professional Integration Project (PIP) (2000) Royal College of Music, Prince Consort Road, London SW7 2BS, available at: <http://pipdbs.rcm.ac.uk>.

Rexroad, E.F. (1985) 'Influential factors on the musical development of outstanding professional singers', dissertation, University of Illinois at Urbana-Champaign (University microfilms order no. 8511664).

Rinderspacher, A. (1999) 'Daten und Fakten zur Situation der Orchester und Musiktheater', in A. Eckhardt, R. Jakoby and C. Rohlfs (eds), *Musik-Almanach 1999/2000: Daten und Fakten zum Musikleben in Deutschland*, pp. 47–55, Kassel: Bärenreiter/Bosse.

Smith, D.W.E. (1988) 'The great symphony orchestra – A relatively good place to grow old', *International Journal of Aging and Human Development*, 27(4): 233–47.

Smith, D.W.E. (1989) 'Aging and the careers of symphony orchestra musicians', *Medical Problems of Performing Artists*, 4(2): 81–5.

Chapter 24

What Music Psychology is Telling Us about Emotion and Why It Can't Yet Tell Us More: A Need for Empirical and Theoretical Innovation

Matthew M. Lavy

Musical practice has changed dramatically over the last few thousand years; music's function in societies has changed, and even the societies themselves have changed. Despite all the changes, however, one apparently immovable constant has been music's extraordinary power to evoke emotion. In the days of the ancient Greeks, this power was evidenced by tales such as the Orpheus legend; and it has been recounted by philosophers, writers and musicians throughout the ages. In recent years, this canon has been supplemented by a catalogue of recent psychological work on response to music. We now have an abundance of evidence to indicate not only that people regularly use music deliberately as a mood induction tool (for example, Sloboda, 2000), but also that listening to music in everyday circumstances can lead to moderated mood and altered cognition (for example, Bruner, 1990). For evidence of the centrality of music to the emotional lives of many Americans, at least, we need look no further than Frey (1985), whose massive survey reported that 8 per cent of all crying episodes in the USA were evoked either directly or indirectly by music. Large-scale surveys have confirmed that music is capable of catalysing intense feelings of sadness and joy, which can occasionally lead even to strong physical reactions or overt physical behaviour, such as shouting, screaming or crying (Gabrielsson and Lindström, 2000); less extreme physical reactions, such as piloerection and lumps in the throat, are just a few of the commonly cited musically induced phenomena (for example, Sloboda, 1991). Emotional responses to music are correlated with physiological functioning, as evidenced by measurable effects on the sympathetic and parasympathetic systems (for example, Iwanaga and Tsukamoto, 1997; Krumhansl, 1997) and by detectable changes in neural activity (for example, Panksepp, 1997; Gerra et al., 1998). As a complement to these findings, clinical observation and the success of music therapy in helping patients with psychophysiological complaints ranging from autism to dementia (see, for example, Bunt, 1994) also stand testament to music's power to affect psychological and physiological state.

In the light of these observations, it is hardly surprising that the search for an explanation of music's evocative power has been a quest for many involved with music, not least for the music psychologist, whose promise is to bring scientific objectivity to this somewhat inscrutable subject. This chapter presents a brief review of some of the discoveries made by music psychology over the last few decades and considers two theories that have been invented to explain them. It then attempts to identify a problem with many present conceptualizations of emotional response to music, and suggests that a fundamental philosophical realignment is required if music psychological research is to reveal anything about emotional response to music that the music practitioner does not already know.

Characterizing Emotion in Music

A common trend amongst music psychologists interested in studying emotional response to music empirically has been the attempt to identify and isolate musical parameters that might be responsible for music's various effects on listeners. Over the years, this approach has proved reasonably fruitful: an armoury of robust and complementary experiments has indicated beyond a shadow of doubt that the broad emotional characterizations of music as perceived by listeners familiar with western musical idioms is for the most part mediated by a rather small number of parameters, such as mode, intensity, timbre and tempo.

Findings concerning mode should come as no surprise to any music practitioner: listeners tend to associate major keys with positive emotions, and negative ones with negative emotions (for example, Hevner, 1936; Scherer and Oshinsky, 1997). The ability to discriminate the valence of emotional expression on the basis of mode has been noted in children as young as three years old (Kastner and Crowder, 1990), so if it is a learned ability, it is learned very early in musical life. As for tempo, listeners tend to associate fast music with joy and vividity, and slow music with sadness or solemnity.

By mediating level of activity in quite a literal sense, tempo interacts with other parameters, such as mode, melodic contour and intensity, in the generation of perceived emotional expression (for example, Rigg, 1940). Intensity (that is, sheer volume) alone has not been shown to be unambiguously associated with any specific emotional expression, but it is frequently cited as an important parameter nonetheless.

Perhaps the most reliable finding involving intensity concerns an interaction with tempo: a high intensity makes fast music seem more energetic than its lower-intensity counterpart, whereas slow music appears more serious or solemn; a low intensity, on the other hand, makes slow music appear sadder, more contemplative and gloomy than its louder counterparts (for example, Wedin, 1972).

The effect of timbre is somewhat more complex and cannot easily be summarized, but one relatively unambiguous finding has been that timbral quality of a musical sound consistently affects perception of emotional tension (for example, Nielzen and Olsson, 1993).

Studies that have investigated the influence of musical parameters on perceived emotional expression and drawn conclusions such as those summarized above have gathered and analysed data using a variety of techniques. Some of these have involved measuring physiological correlates of emotion, such as blood pressure, pulse rate, or skin conductance, in the hope of finding evidence for a direct relationship between the state of a particular musical parameter and the evocation of emotion in a listener. Most, however, have relied on introspection for their data, asking listeners to rate musical extracts on a variety of semantic scales, to match extracts with predefined lists of adjectives, or sometimes even to give free reports of feelings or thoughts whilst listening. Some studies have used real music in their experiments, others have used specially designed stimuli, and yet others have used hybrid techniques involving systematic manipulation of real musical examples. Each of these approaches is plagued by methodological problems of varying degrees of severity, as has been discussed several times elsewhere (see, for example, Rigg, 1964; Dowling and Harwood, 1986; Sloboda, 1996). Perhaps the most pervasive problem is the difficulty of demonstrating that a listener's ability to perceive emotional expression in music necessarily equates to evocation of emotion. After all, just because a listener perceives a musical passage to be, say, sad or joyful, it does not necessarily follow that the emotion is actually induced in the listener. This issue is partly addressed, of course, by attempts to measure physiological correlates of emotion; it is also one to which we will return shortly. Despite these partially unresolved difficulties, research on broad emotional characterizations of musical parameters is yielding an impressive corpus of extremely useful data.[1]

All of the research mentioned so far has been concerned with general emotional characterizations of music, looking at those parameters that tend to remain constant throughout a piece (for example, music is slow, or is in the minor key or has a bright timbre). Perhaps the single most important characteristic of music, however, is its dynamic quality – the fact that it constantly changes over time. Certainly, this is crucial to the entire edifice of western tonal musical structure, which is built on a dynamic flux of tensions and resolutions both in the melodic and harmonic domains (see, for example, Schmuckler, 1989; Narmour, 1990, 1992).

Concomitantly, although music undoubtedly has the power to moderate mood, and although characterizations of static attributes of a musical work may be at least partly responsible for this – the difficulty of equating perception of expression and emotion evocation notwithstanding – emotional response to music can be intense and momentary. In recent years, therefore, much music psychological research in the field has concentrated on the dynamic aspects of musical structure that may be responsible for the evocation of emotions. Here, too, consistent patterns of results have emerged: a growing body of evidence indicates that certain small-scale musical structures, such as appoggiaturas and suspensions, reliably evoke emotional responses in accultured listeners (for example, Sloboda, 1991; Waterman, 1996, 1997) and that these listeners reliably detect and respond emotionally to changing levels of tension that emerge as a piece of music unfolds (for example, Krumhansl, 1996). Perception of structure is not the only source of musical dynamics to have been the subject of extensive research: another concerns timing deviations in performances, where perceived emotionality of a performance has consistently been found to be correlated with deviations from strictly accurate timing patterns (Repp, 1997; Sloboda, 1997). As serious research in this area is a relatively new phenomenon, there are few established research methods; a particularly troublesome issue for investigators in this field has been the need to develop means of capturing listeners' momentary responses without disturbing the listening experience. Developments in computer technology have made a huge difference here, and have effectively provided a de facto research paradigm in which listeners 'track' perceived tension – or some other dimension – in real time. Within this paradigm results take the form of fluctuating continuous data in one- or two-dimensional space, derived from the position of a joystick or a computer mouse, or the pressure applied to a pressure-sensitive device (for example, Madsen and Fredrickson, 1993; Schubert, 1998). Stimuli tend to be real musical extracts, often manipulated in some way.

The extensive data fast amassing concerning both perceived emotional characterizations in music and emotion evocation as a result of the dynamics of musical structure constitute a formidable canon, and go some way to fulfilling the goal of building a corpus of knowledge about musically evoked emotion that transcends subjectivity. Despite these encouraging signs, however, all work that attempts to isolate musical parameters – static or dynamic – that may be responsible for the evocation of emotional responses is confounded by an apparently inescapable paradox: however strong the evidence for agreement between listeners, there exists an equally powerful body of evidence to suggest that two accultured listeners can respond to the same piece of music in vastly different ways; furthermore, the same listener can respond in a different way to the same piece of music at a different time. As Sloboda (1992, p. 38) put it, one can 'listen to the same recording on two difference occasions and be moved to tears on one of them, while remaining completely detached on the other'. The implication for research on broad emotional characterization of music is grave: perception of emotional expression encoded within musical parameters certainly does not inexorably lead to the evocation of those emotions in a listener. As for musical dynamics, it would appear that listeners may be moved by musical moments, but not under all circumstances! In short, it would appear that musical antecedents of emotion are not universally definable. Therefore, all this research may tell us a lot about the general consensus of accultured listeners, which perhaps in turn tells us much about musical convention, but it does not necessarily tell us anything about musical evocation of emotions.

Extra-musical Factors

While music psychologists have devoted their efforts to revealing what musical parameters might be responsible for the evocation of emotional reactions, many researchers in fields more closely allied to social psychology have devoted their energies to considering the extra-musical factors that may impinge on emotional response to music, and thereby accounting for the lack of intersubjectivity. Results, mostly based on analysis of listener introspections, have demonstrated that the extent to which people are moved, even by the most paradigmatically emotionally expressive music, can depend on their mood (Sloboda, 1992), the situation in which the music is heard (Konečni, 1982), or even the motivation for listening (North and Hargreaves, 2000). In addition, listeners are frequently moved by a piece of music if it reminds them of previous periods in their lives, whether by bringing to mind specific episodes (for example, Baumgartner, 1992) or general eras (for example, Schulkind et al., 1999), regardless of the musical content. In short, when emotional responses are attributed to music, it is often not the music at all that causes the response but something completely different which happens to be associated with the music in the listener's mind. These observations, of course, tell us nothing about the interaction between emotional characterizations, musical dynamics and extra-musical stimuli – an issue that surprisingly little work has addressed – but they do serve as a useful complement to the plethora of music-based research, and at least serve to put many of the findings into perspective.

Two Theoretical Accounts

The difficulty of reconciling what has been discovered about the evocative properties of music with what is known about the idiosyncrasies of listening is symptomatic of a more general problem that besets much research in the field, namely that despite the wealth of empirical data, there exist few theoretical accounts of emotional response to music within which the empirical data may be understood. Although several psychologists, philosophers and musicologists have presented theories that impinge on the subject, very few have written from a music-psychological perspective. As a result, experimental work remains somewhat phenomenological: whilst we know a great deal about a number of isolated phenomena, we have very little understanding about how these phenomena interact within a wider frame.

Although some empirical researchers have grounded their work in terms of more general theories of emotion, hardly any attempt has been made to weave the various facets of emotionality in music into a single coherent picture that could constitute the needed 'wider frame' upon which future work could be based. Music psychologists seem to have been particularly reluctant to embrace findings concerning the influence of extra-musical phenomena when considering emotional response to music. In practice, the music psychologist and his experiments can tell us little more about the parameters and processes involved in emotional response to music than can any music practitioner or, for that matter, a reasonably thoughtful listener. Of the few theoretical accounts of emotional response to music that do exist, by far the most thorough – and most often cited – is that of Meyer (1956), which presents a detailed analysis of the structures that underlie much of western tonal music and considers how these features interact to evoke emotional reactions in listeners.

Meyer made a great contribution to music psychology by lucidly describing the dynamic of western tonal music as a series of unfolding tensions and resolutions; he demonstrated that listening to such music involves the constant generation of expectancies on many levels, which are confirmed or violated as the music unfolds. Although Meyer's thesis is largely musicologically inspired, he grounds emotional response to music in a broader psychological context by invoking a theory of arousal suggested by MacCurdy (1925). Crudely, the idea is that arousal is a physiological phenomenon triggered by the repression of instinctive behaviour. A habitual smoker, for example, feels nothing when he puts a hand in a pocket and withdraws a cigarette, but can become quite agitated if he feels in his pocket and finds the cigarette packet to be empty. In musical terms, Meyer argues that expectancy violations in music are particularly prone to the evocation of emotional reactions because 'emotion or affect is aroused when a tendency to respond is arrested or inhibited' (p. 14) and unlike in the real world, where unresolved tendencies are 'dissipated in the press of irrelevant events ... in art inhibition of tendency becomes meaningful because the relationship between the tendency and its resolution is made explicit and apparent'(p. 23). This conception of music and the listening process fits well with cognitive models of emotion (for example, Ortony et al., 1988), and a variety of empirical studies have shown it to be rather robust. It can certainly account for much of the empirical data concerning musical tension. The vast number of empirical studies based on or inspired by Meyer's work even today stand testament to the great debt owed to him by music psychologists studying emotion.

Whilst being an extremely important work for music psychologists, Meyer's theory has one serious (self-declared) limitation: it only concerns itself with emotional responses to structural characteristics of western tonal music. As it is not generalizable enough to embrace other musical genres, or to explain responses that are not directly related to the dynamics of musical structure, it remains an insightful discourse on what is likely to be a significant source of emotional response to music for a listener steeped in the western musical tradition, but is too narrow in scope to form the basis of a general framework within which empirical work can be understood and upon which it can build.[2] It cannot help reconcile broad emotional characterizations of musical parameters with the idiosyncrasies of listeners' personal histories and cultures.

For a more general theory, we turn to Dowling and Harwood (1986). Their theory is not nearly as detailed as that of Meyer – it is not intended to be – but it does offer a wide overall perspective on what it is to which listeners might be responding when they respond emotionally to music, taking into account both the emotionally evocative characteristics of western music as reported by music psychology and the influence of idiosyncratic histories of listeners as studied by social psychologists. Drawing both on the work of the philosopher Charles Peirce (1931–35) and on a review of the core experiment literature, Dowling and Harwood model emotion in music as existing on three levels; index, icon and symbol. Music acting as index is said to evoke responses by provoking associations in a listener's mind between that music and something extra-musical. Indexical association can be sparked as a deliberate compositional ploy, such as in the use of the French and Russian national anthems in Tchaikovsky's *1812 Overture*, or the taped fire sirens in *Poème electronique* by Varèse; alternatively, they may belong exclusively in the domain of a particular listener, for whom a particular piece of music might spark related memories.[3] Either way, music acting as index works in a Pavlovian (1927) way, and can evoke emotion to the extent that the associand constitutes an emotional stimulus for the listener.

The iconic level represents the sounds and patterns of a musical surface, or the ebb and flow of a musical line; drawing heavily on Langer (1951, 1953), Dowling and Harwood suggest that 'music mimics the form ... of emotional life' (p. 206). In support of this notion, they present a thorough review of the empirical research on emotion characterizations in music, covering similar ground to that reviewed earlier in this chapter. If the concept of iconic ebb and flow seems somewhat amorphous, that is allegedly because 'the representation of emotion in musical icons is necessarily vague' (p. 207). In contrast to icons, symbols are emotional by virtue of their place and function within a musical structure: Mandler's 1984 theory of autonomic arousal is cited as the basis for a conceptualization of western music much akin to that of Meyer (1956). The symbolic level of representation, therefore, is only available to an accultured listener, who has an understanding of the musical idioms in question. Between them, index, icon and symbol are intended to cover the whole gamut of musical features to which listeners might respond emotionally. Theoretically, any empirical findings involving emotion and music may be categorized as belonging to one of its three domains.

Dowling and Harwood are by no means alone in their tripartite categorization; the distinctions they draw between index, icon and symbol reflect broadly the implicit distinctions made by many empirical researchers in the field. Even the brief taxonomy of empirical work in the field given in this chapter reveals the three distinct branches: one contains studies of the way in which listeners associate musical works with extra-musical concepts (indexical associations); another, of the various parameters that affect 'emotionality' of a musical surface (icons); yet another, of musical structure and its ability to evoke emotional responses in the accultured listener (symbols). The distinction between the second and third branches may not always be entirely clear – empirical work inspired by Meyer sits somewhere in the middle as it concerns both the (iconic) flow of a musical line and the dynamics of musical (symbolic) structure – but the first branch is almost entirely segregated from the rest of the tree, not least because it is the branch of least interest to music psychologists.

A False Dichotomy

However closely the distinction between index, icon and symbol maps on to empirical research, it does not fare so well when considered in the light of the phenomenon of emotional response itself. Not only does the difficulty of placing Meyer's work (and the empirical evidence that supports it) show the distinction between icon and symbol to be artificial at best, but also music theory and plain common sense conspire to indicate that symbol and index can often be interchangeable. For example, a perfect cadence, which is both a highly recognizable and conventional musical unit, is certainly part of a symbol structure – in itself encapsulating a complete expectancy generation and resolution cycle – but also has the potential to act indexically, because as a recognizable token, a closed unit, it could well spark associations both cultural and idiosyncratic for a listener.[4] It seems plausible, in fact, that, in many circumstances, emotional response to musical structures such as perfect cadences could be understood much better as a phenomenon allied to indexical association than to one allied to the tensions and resolutions of a musical dynamic. In short, whilst the distinctions may broadly reflect the landscape of phenomenologically inspired empirical research, they do not well represent any essential reality.

The theoretical distinction between index, icon and symbol as sources of emotion is really the product of a more fundamental distinction made by many current conceptualizations of emotional response to music, one hinted at already in this chapter; namely, the distinction between sources of emotion that are ascribed to music itself, so-called intrinsic sources, and those sources that are only tangentially related to music, so-called extrinsic sources. It is within this dichotomy and the widespread assumption of its validity that the real problem lies. Of course, it is inevitable that aspects of a research area as wide in scope as emotional response to music will attract researchers working within different, possibly even incompatible paradigms, and it is certainly not cause for alarm that researchers whose agenda is primarily social will be interested in music's place in the emotional lives of listeners, whereas those whose interest lies squarely within the realm of music will concentrate more on the emotion-evoking properties of musical parameters. For the music psychologist, however, the distinction between intrinsic and extrinsic sources of emotion is often not an epistemological but an ontological one. It is not assumed merely to be different paradigmatic agendas that cause some researchers to concentrate on extrinsic factors while others study intrinsic factors; rather, underlying the dichotomy seen in the empirical and theoretical work has been the assumption, often explicitly asserted, that intrinsic and extrinsic sources of emotion are ontologically distinct entities. At first glance, the assumption does not seem entirely unwarranted; after all, a suspended fourth in western tonal harmony is obviously a very different thing to, say, a memory of childhood. As sources of emotion, however, the two are not so very different. The empirical data provide no reason to believe that responses evoked by extrinsic sources and those evoked by intrinsic sources are different phenomena. It is particularly interesting to note that from the perspective of emotion psychology, they are in fact very, very similar indeed.

None of this theoretical pedantry would be of significance to the empirical world were it not for the fact that the theoretical assumptions permeate empirical research in the field. Music psychologists investigating intrinsic sources of emotional response make heavy use of music theoretic concepts. Such concepts, which have evolved over several hundred years, provide countless pre-built units and dissection routines that can be used to categorize and control individual musical parameters, in the hope of isolating those that encode emotional signals. As has already been noted, the approach has for the most part been rather successful. Unfortunately, this success, coupled with a belief that there exists an absolute distinction between intrinsic and extrinsic sources of emotion, has led to a strange insularity amongst many researchers: musicologically inspired research need not be exasperated in its failure to account for idiosyncratic response differences that depend on listeners and situations, because these can be considered to be caused by extrinsic factors, relegated to the realm of the indexical, and are therefore irrelevant to the pursuit of discovering how intrinsic factors evoke emotions. This position, albeit in a somewhat different context, is exemplified eloquently by the philosopher Peter Kivy:

> Of course, the Grosse Fuge might arouse anger in some listener or other by reminding him of an angry encounter with his boss; so too, however, might the tranquil strains of the Spring Sonata ... This is a familiar enough phenomenon; but it has nothing whatsoever to do with the expressiveness of the music except by accident. (1989, p. 157)

A listener's reaction to extrinsic sources of emotion may not be exclusively musical, but they are intrinsic to the listening process; surely it is extrinsic factors, such as cultural context and previous experience, that help give so-called intrinsic factors their evocative power. It seems that, through all the categorization, one aspect of emotional response to music that has been largely forgotten is the listener. For the majority of researchers, the fundamental question has inevitably been: 'What are the features of music that evoke emotional responses?' By contrast, very few have asked the question: 'what are the features of listeners that make them interpret music as an emotional stimulus?' It is hardly surprising that, with a few exceptions, work in this field takes little account of the more general emotion theories: what is the need for an emotion theory when the object under scrutiny is music and not the listener?

If musicologically inspired research is ever simultaneously to form a satisfactory understanding of why certain musical parameters and the dynamics of musical structure appear to be sources of emotion, to resolve the difficulty of relation perception of musical expression to evocation of emotion, to address listener idiosyncrasy and to leave phenomenology behind, it will have to be situated within a model of emotional response to music at the heart of which is placed the listener. Such a model must avoid arbitrary categorizations based on a priori concepts and musicological or philosophical assumptions. It must not see response to music as a phenomenon that is somehow special and isolated from other facets of human emotion; instead, it must seek to situate what we know about emotional response to music squarely within the frame of everyday human experience, and embrace findings of emotion psychologists working in non-musical domains. Only then might music psychology be able to tell music practioners and listeners alike more than they already instinctively know about music. Thankfully, a growing interest in the study of emotion within the field of music psychology, coupled with increasing awareness of the perennial problems, offers more than a glimmer of hope that progress is on the horizon.

Notes

1. A rather more extensive review of such work may be found in several places elsewhere, such as Dowling and Harwood (1986). A recently published book on music and emotion, edited by Sloboda and Juslin (2001), provides a thorough review of the field from a number of different perspectives.
2. To be fair to Meyer, he emphatically did not present his theory as a framework for empirical research. In fact, he virtually rejected the possibility that the subject could usefully be studied using empirical psychological methods.
3. Dowling and Harwood provide by way of illustration an excerpt from Proust (1934) in which recognition of a violin sonata sparked memories of a love affair from years before.
4. This latter point has been made lucidly by Cooke (1959) in his well-known thesis on musical meaning.

References

Baumgartner, H. (1992) 'Remembrance of things past: Music, autobiographical memory, and emotion', *Advances in Consumer Research*, 19: 613–20.

Bruner, G.C. (1990) 'Music, mood, and marketing', *Journal of Marketing*, 54(4): 94–104.

Bunt, L. (1994) *Music Therapy: An Art Beyond Words*, London: Routledge.

Cooke, D. (1959) *The Language of Music*, Oxford: Oxford University Press.

Dowling, W.J. and Harwood, D.L. (1986) *Music Cognition*, San Diego: Academic Press.

Frey, W.H. (1985) *Crying: The Mystery of Tears*, Minneapolis: Winston Press.

Gabrielsson, A. and Lindström, S. (2000) 'Strong experiences of and with music', in D. Greer (ed.), *Musicology and Sister Disciplines: Past, Present and Future*, pp. 100–108, Oxford: Oxford University Press.

Gerra, G., Zaimovic, A., Franchini, D., Palladino, M., Guicastro, G., Reali, N., Maestri, D., Caccavari, R., Delsignore, R., and Brambilla, F. (1998) 'Euroendocrine responses of healthy volunteers to "techno-music": Relationships with personality traits and emotional state', *International Journal of Psychophysiology*, 28(1): 99–111.

Hevner, K. (1936) 'Experimental studies of the elements of expression in music', *American Journal of Psychology*, 48: 248–68.

Iwanaga, M. and Tsukamoto, M. (1997) 'Effects of excitative and sedative music on subjective and physiological relaxation', *Perception and Motor Skills*, 85(1): 287–96.

Kastner, M.P. and Crowder, R.G. (1990) 'Perception of the major/minor distinction: Emotional connotations in young children', *Music Perception*, 8(2): 189–201.

Kivy, P. (1989) *Sound Sentiment: An Essay on the Musical Emotions*, Philadelphia: Temple University Press.

Konečni, V.J. (1982) 'Social interaction and musical preference', in D. Deutsch (ed.), *Psychology of Music* (1st edn.), pp. 497–516, New York: Academic Press.

Krumhansl, C.L. (1996) 'A perceptual analysis of Mozart's Piano Sonata K282: Segmentation, tension, and musical ideas', *Music Perception*, 13(3): 401–32.

Krumhansl, C.L. (1997) 'Can dance reflect the structural and expressive qualities of music? A perceptual experiment on balanchine's choreography of Mozart's divertimento no. 15', *Musicae Scientiae*, 1(1): 63–85.

Langer, S.K. (1951) *Philosophy in a New Key: A Study in the Symbolism of Reason, Rite and Art*, London: Oxford University Press.

Langer, S.K. (1953) *Feeling and Form*, London: Routledge and Kegan Paul.

MacCurdy, J. (1925) *The Psychology of Emotion*, New York: Harcourt Brace.

Madsen, C.K. and Fredrickson, W. (1993) 'The experience of musical tension: A replication of Nielsen's research using the continuous response digital interface', *Journal of Music Therapy*, 30: 46–63.

Mandler, G. (1984) *Mind and Body*, New York: Norton.

Meyer, L.B. (1956) *Emotion and Meaning in Music*, Chicago: University of Chicago Press.

Narmour, E. (1990) *The Analysis and Cognition of Basic Melodic Structures: The Implication-realization Model*, Chicago: Chicago University Press.

Narmour, E. (1992) *The Analysis and Cognition of Melodic Complexity*, Chicago: Chicago University Press.

Nielzen, S. and Olsson, O. (1993) 'The influence of duration on verbal-attribute ratings of complex protomusical sounds', *Music Perception*, 11(1): 73–86.

North, A.C. and Hargreaves, D.J. (2000) 'Music preference in everyday life: Arousal- or typicality-based goals?', paper presented at *The Effects of Music*, a conference of the Society for Research in Psychology of Music and Music Education, 8–9 April.

Ortony, A., Clore, G. and Collins, A. (1988) *The Cognitive Structure of Emotions*, New York: Cambridge University Press.

Panksepp, J. (1997) 'The affective cerebral consequence of music: Happy vs sad effects on the EEG and clinical implications', *International Journal of Arts Medicine*, 5(1): 18–27.

Pavlov, I. (1927) *Conditioned Reflexes*, London: Oxford University Press.

Peirce, C.S. (1931–35) *Collected Papers*, Harvard, MA: Harvard University Press.

Proust, M. (1934) *Remembrance of Things Past, Volume 1*, trans. C.K. Scott Moncrieff, New York: Random House.

Repp, B.H. (1997) 'The aesthetic quality of a quantitatively average music performance: Two preliminary experiments', *Music Perception*, 14(4): 419–44.

Rigg, M.G. (1940) 'Speed as a determiner of musical mood', *Journal of Experimental Psychology*, 27: 566–71.

Rigg, M.G. (1964) 'The mood effects of music: A comparison of data from four investigators', *Journal of Psychology* 58: 427–38.

Scherer, K.R. and Oshinsky, J. (1997) 'Cue utilisation in emotion attribution from auditory stimuli', *Motivation and Emotion*, 1: 331–46.

Schmuckler, M. (1989) 'Expectation in music: an investigation of melodic and harmonic processes', *Music Perception*, 7(2): 119–93.

Schubert, E. (1998) 'Time series analysis of emotion in music', in *Proceedings of the 5th International Conference of Music Perception and Cognition*, pp. 257–63, Seoul.

Schulkind, M.D., Hennis, L.K and. Rubin, D.C. (1999) 'Music, emotion, and auto-biographical memory: They're playing your song', *Memory and Cognition*, 27(6): 948–55.

Sloboda, J.A. (1991) 'Music structure and emotional response: Some empirical findings', *Psychology of Music*, 19: 110–20.

Sloboda, J.A. (1992) 'Empirical studies of emotional response to music', in M. Jones and S. Holleran (eds), *Cognitive Bases of Musical Communication*, pp. 33–46, Washington, DC: American Psychological Association.

Sloboda, J.A. (1996) 'Emotional response to music: A review', presented at the Nordic Acoustical Meeting, 12–14 June, Helsinki.

Sloboda, J.A. (1997) 'What do we know about what makes us respond strongly to music? context, content and performance', paper presented at *Exploring Intense Musical Experience*, a conference of the Society for Research in Psychology of Music and Music Education, 15 March.

Sloboda, J.A. (2000) 'Everyday uses of music listening: A preliminary study', in S.W. Yi (ed.), *Music, Mind, and Science*, pp. 354–69, Seoul: Seoul National University Press.

Sloboda, J.A. and Juslin, P. (2001) *Music and Emotion: Theory and Research*, Oxford: Oxford University Press.

Waterman, M. (1996) 'Emotional response to music: Implicit effects in listeners and Performers', *Psychology of Music*, 24: 53–67.

Waterman, M. (1997) 'Intense but not emotional? The problems with describing experiences to music', paper presented at *Exploring Intense Musical Experience*, a conference of the Society for Research in Psychology of Music and Music Education, 15 March.

Wedin, L. (1972) 'A multidimensional study of perceptual-emotional qualities in music', *Scandinavian Journal of Psychology*, 13(1): 1–17.

PART 6

A Final Note

Chapter 25

Musical Chills and Other Delights of Music

Jerrold Levinson

Preliminaries

Though in a number of respects the value of music goes beyond the pleasure it provides when appropriately attended to, the capacity to provide such pleasure, it should be admitted, is a significant part of that value.[1] To be sure, there are values that attach to both individual pieces of music and music as a whole that may not be measured in terms of pleasures afforded listeners, but such values will not be the focus of these reflections. Here and now it is the hedonic that will rule.

Some preliminary remarks are in order concerning the sort of attention that should be understood to be involved when speaking of pleasures properly afforded a listener by music. Such attention is close and concerted; it is locally focused, though globally context-sensitive.[2] Such attention is aesthetic, or appropriate to music as art; that is, what is precisely heard in the music plays a role in the generation of any resulting pleasure, so that the music serves, at least in part, as object of such pleasure.[3] Finally, such attention is stylistically and historically informed, at least on a tacit level, allowing a given piece of music to be heard as such, each characteristic – formal, expressive, rhetorical, representational – being registered for what it is.[4]

Varieties of Musical Pleasure

Let me signal at the outset some obvious dimensions of difference among musical pleasures. Musical pleasures differ in how active they are, how intellectual they are, how essentially physiological or physiologically centred they are. Musical pleasures differ with respect to intensity, for example, they may be acute or mild; with respect to duration, for example, they may be passing or long-lasting; with respect to durability, for example, they may be one-shot affairs or eminently repeatable; with respect to communicability, for example, they may be highly esoteric or widely shared. Musical pleasures differ in the different values thereof, for example, elevated or trifling, in the different moral qualities thereof, for example, humanizing or dehumanizing, and in the different social imports thereof, for example, solidarizing or exclusionary.[5]

Musical pleasures differ further in when they are taken, so to speak, relative to when the music to which they refer is heard. That is to say, though most musical pleasure, I would claim, arises from the real-time following of music in its formal and expressive evolution,[6] some musical pleasure is anticipatory, preceding audition, and some musical pleasure is recollective, occurring after audition.

One dimension of difference among musical pleasures may correspond to two contrasting modes of listening, or perhaps two contrasting stances towards the listening that is going on. On the one hand one may, without losing contact with the music in its full particularity, let a piece of music enfold one, envelop one, wash over one, so that one gives oneself over to it in a personal way, as to a lover, or perhaps a trusted therapist. On the other hand one may undertake to keep music at a distance, so to speak, observing its lapidary details, its emotional manoeuverings, its dramatic gestures as something external to and apart from the self that listens. Each mode carries with it distinct sorts of pleasure, ones that, manifestly, are not easily combined on a given occasion.

A question that presents itself at this point is the following: is there a one-to-one correspondence between musical pleasures and pleasurable musical features? That is to say, is it the case that for every musical pleasure there is a musical feature such that the pleasure is a pleasure in that feature? This seems unlikely. Of course, many instances will conform, and manifestly so, to the hypothesis in question; for example, pleasure in the intricacies of Bach's counterpoint, or pleasure in the mellifluousness of phrase in Mozart's late piano concerti, or pleasure in the sheer amplitude of Schubert's C major Symphony.[7]

But what of the pleasure of being simply carried away or transported by music? Naturally one can always say that it was the music as a whole, in all its concreteness, that transported one, but that does not imply that there is any particular feature, say, formal perfection, sensual beauty, or expressive depth, that has claim to being the object of the pleasure in question. And one could equally well postulate a sort of transportive virtue – evidently possessed by the music, given that it has transported one – and maintain that the pleasure of being transported is a pleasure in that power of the music, but that, I imagine, would convince no one. I conclude that even if most musical pleasures readily reveal themselves to be pleasures taken in or turning on particular musical features, logically this need not be true of all musical pleasures.

Panksepp's Research on Musical Chills

I come now to the main preoccupation of this chapter, namely, a curious response to music that is, I will assume, familiar to most consummate music lovers, and one that has interested at least this music lover for the longest time. It is the singular phenomenon of music-induced 'chills', the affect accompanying such 'chills', and the attitude taken toward such 'chills'. My point of departure is a recent scientific study of the phenomenon, conducted over a number of years by psychologist Jaak Panksepp, and presented in a 1995 article, 'The Emotional Sources of "Chills" Induced by Music'.[8]

The pleasure associated with such 'chills', where there is such, is clearly of a sort we can label *physiologically centred*. That is to say, musical pleasure in such cases revolves around a particular physiological effect; in the present instance, the skin-suffusing chill in question, where such effect is an integral part of the pleasure experienced.

Now one reason the 'musical chills' phenomenon is philosophically interesting is this: how can a mere tingle or shiver, so to speak, a mere bodily disturbance, be of appreciative significance? Any number of philosophers of art, most famously Nelson Goodman, have accustomed us to view as ridiculous – through the ridicule they have heaped on it – the idea that sensations might, as such, have a legitimate role in aesthetic response.[9] What good is a mere sensation, even an agreeable one, in the context of art? What does it tell of or testify to? Does it inform us of some matter of artistic fact? Does it illuminate some artistic relation of ideas? If neither then consign it, if not to the flames, then at any rate to the dustbin of appreciative theory. Such is the prevailing post-Goodmanian wisdom on this score. But it is not a view I completely share, hence my interest in musical 'chills'.

Turning then to Panksepp's study, let us begin with some of his attempts to characterize the target phenomenon:

> … the tingly somatosensory feeling that can be evoked by certain kinds of music; … the provocative and often delightful bodily experiences that deeply moving passages of music arouse in many people … a bodily 'rush' commonly described as a spreading gooseflesh, hair-on-end feeling that is common on the back of the neck and head and often moves down the spine, at times spreading across much of the rest of the body … (1995, pp. 172–3).

Panksepp notes that despite its intriguing nature, '… the prickly skin response usually called "shivers", "thrills", or "chills" in English has not received the experimental attention it deserves … .' He observes further that '… people rarely discuss the experience, and there is no unambiguous referent for it …' (1995, p. 173).

To take up that last point, there is indeed a terminological problem for what we wish to discuss, in that none of 'chill', 'thrill', or 'shiver' seems entirely apt to denote the phenomenon under investigation, each carrying connotations, whether of coldness ('chill'), or risk ('thrill'), or tremor ('shiver'), that are in some degree undesired. Possibly the term 'frisson' – a partly nativized immigrant from French – is the best of the designations available for this phenomenon. In what follows I frequently refer to 'musical *frissons*', although when discussing Panksepp's paper I use the term 'musical *chills*', as this is how Panksepp refers to the experience in question.

Experiments were conducted by Panksepp on undergraduates at a small Midwestern university in the USA Panksepp employed as his test material popular music of the 1970s and 1980s, items having been proposed by his subjects themselves as chill-inducing. Thus with few exceptions, the test selections were songs, mainly of the soft and hard rock variety. Ideally, of course, one would have preferred for such experiments textless selections devoid of program – what Peter Kivy calls 'music alone' – but the design of the experiment, in which selections were elicited from the student population, obviously was not conducive to that. Panksepp seems surprisingly unconcerned about the possible collateral effects of song lyrics, with the articulate ideas and sentiments they contain, on the phenomenon under study, but naturally it is a possible source of reservations about some of his results.

Here is one specific experimental result, rather emblematic of the study as a whole:

> The highest rate of reported chills was .5 chills/min/person for the beginning 3-min segment ... from Pink Floyd's album *Final Cut*, which, on average, yielded essentially the same number of chills as one's own song [that is, the selection provided by the subject himself/herself] ... it was clear that the majority of the chills to this piece occurred in response to the dramatic crescendo at the beginning of the second minute. (Panksepp, 1995, pp. 178–9)

As regards the most important general result of the study, it would seem to be this: 'Overall, the data support the thesis that sadness or melancholy is an emotional dimension more significantly related to the production of chills than is happiness' (Panksepp, 1995, p. 187). In other words, it is negative, rather than positive, emotion in music that appears more efficacious in inducing the chill experience.

Yet clearly some positively toned music in the study was found capable of inducing chills. This prompts Panksepp to the following speculation, one that would, if sustained, preserve a role for negative emotion in the generation of chills in all cases: '... it will be worth considering whether the chills provoked during happy music are caused by segments where happiness and sadness are inextricably entwined in bittersweet feelings' (Panksepp, 1995, p. 187).[10] I return to this conjecture further on, since I think it is on the right track.

Some Criticisms

Panksepp's studies targeted a number of different features plausibly thought to bear on the incidence of musical chills. These included:

● the gender of the listener;
● the degree of familiarity with the music;

- the degree of liking for the music;
- the emotional quality of the music; and
- the dynamic and tonal contour of the music.

Panksepp observed a strong correlation between chills and degrees of both familiarity and liking, a strong correlation between chills and both rise in volume and rise in pitch, a fairly strong correlation (which we have already noted) between chills and music of sad-melancholy-nostalgic character, and a weak correlation between chills and being female.[11]

To my mind, there are probable determinants of the chill experience that Panksepp's experiments did not target, ones that would admittedly be hard to investigate quantitatively. Two worth mentioning are the music's *fineness* of expression and the music's expressive *shape* over time. Panksepp seems not to have considered the possibility that fineness of expressiveness, whether glossed as depth or intensity or exquisiteness of expression, may be crucial in triggering the chill experience, rather than expressing of negative emotion per se. Panksepp seems also not to have considered the likelihood that a piece's temporal expressive structuring, that is, the pattern of succession of its individually expressive segments, contributes importantly to its chill potential, with some sorts of succession being more likely to elicit chills than others.

Recall now Panksepp's suggestion that music with the greatest capacity for inducing chills may well be of an emotionally hybrid or compound nature – that it is music in which positive and negative affects are in some manner or other interwoven. This connects to what I am inclined to propose, on the basis of my own musical encounters, as perhaps the crucial determinant of chill-inducingness, namely *poignancy* of expression, or perhaps, the expression of *poignancy*.

The profound truth about life – or at least one such profound truth – is that almost all situations, experiences and conditions actually encountered are in fact of mixed character. One is aware of the bad, if only peripherally, even when solidly engaged with the good, and one glimpses the good even when caught up in the bad, intermingled as they are in virtually anything. Nor is this necessarily regrettable, for the mutual focusing of positive and negative elements that results arguably ends up enhancing the appreciation of whatever good is being enjoyed. The essential poignancy of human life, one may suggest, resides in its mixed nature, in the indissociable union of its joys and ills, the unavoidable commingling of its pluses and minuses.[12] Thus, were we to assume that the prime determinant of musical frissons was poignancy of expression/expression of poignancy, it would not be surprising to discover that the music most reliably able to induce such frissons was not that of unmitigated despair, nor that of untroubled gaiety, but that in which there was some admixture of the two.[13]

Pieces Conducive to Chills or Frissons

Here is a list of pieces containing passages conducive to the production of 'frissons' or 'chills', at least in my experience: Brahms, String Quintet in G, Op. 111, first movement; Brahms, Piano Trio in B, last movement; Brahms, Intermezzo, Op. 118 No. 1; Schubert, Piano Sonata in C minor, D958, last movement, middle section; Schubert, Impromptu in A flat, Op. 90 No. 4; Chopin, Prelude Op. 28 No. 6; Chopin, Mazurka Op. 17 No. 4; Chopin, Etude Op. 25 No. 1; Scriabin, Etude Op. 42 No. 5; Sibelius, Symphony No. 5, first movement, coda; Fauré, Violin Sonata in A minor, first movement; Franck, Violin Sonata in A major; Schumann, Piano Concerto, first and third movements; Saint-Saëns, Piano Concerto No. 2, first and last movements; Poulenc, Sonata for Flute and Piano, first movement; Mahler, Symphony No. 5, fourth movement; Mahler, Symphony No. 6, first and third movements; Shostakovitch, String Quartet No. 8, first and second movements; Ravel, *Gaspard de la Nuit*, 'Ondine'; Strauss, *Don Juan*, opening; Strauss, *Four Last Songs*, first song.[14]

From the list so far it might appear that only highly charged music of the Romantic or early Modern period is capable of inducing frissons in this listener, but that is not the case. Here are some other pieces, of earlier vintage, that have this power: Beethoven, Piano Sonata in E, Op. 109, Andante; Mozart, Piano Concerto No. 20 in D minor, first movement; Mozart, Piano Concerto No. 23 in A, second movement; Vivaldi, Concerto for Four Violins in A minor; Vivaldi, Concerto for Two Violins in A minor, Op. 3, first movement; Schütz, *Saul, Saul, was verfolgst du mich?*; Bach, 'Erbarme dich' from the *St. Matthew Passion*;[15] and, somewhat surprisingly, Haydn's sunny Piano Sonata No. 60 in C, first movement, where certain chromatic bridge passages occurring in the exposition, recapitulation and development often produce the effect in my hearing of them.

It is interesting that passages with the capacity to induce chills need not even be heard, strictly speaking, for that capacity to be realized: it suffices in many cases for them merely to be run through vividly in aural imagination, courtesy of the mental CD player, for frissons to be produced. I was able to confirm this recently in my own case with the Scriabin Etude noted above. Also, it seems likely that, as a general rule, when one actively seconds or parallels music one is listening to by a sort of inner singing, frissons are more likely to occur. If so, this stands as yet another of the many rewards of active, as opposed to passive, involvement with music, though the reward itself, as has been noted, might fairly be described as passive in nature, being a sort of sufferance or submission.

The opening movement of Brahms' String Quintet in G, Op. 111 probably affords me the most sustained 'chill' experience of any piece that I know, and I would hope that I am not alone in this.[16] So why, then, does one particularly relish this chill, as it steals up one's spine and pervades one's body, suffusing it with a sort of oxymoronic warmth? It is, perhaps, pleasant in itself, and relaxing, but arguably no more so than having one's hair stroked, settling into a well-stuffed armchair, or devouring a nice *mousse au chocolat*.

No, what makes this musical chill something particularly welcome must be more than the mild bodily comfort it conveys. It seems, rather, to be an attendant sense of surrendering control, of letting go, of delivering oneself to a powerful force, a sort of guide to the terror and mystery of existence. Chills of this sort seem to announce themselves, for those of us who are susceptible to them, as the mark of a confrontation with some fundamental truth of life, communicated by the music that so moves us. Thus they are received, not as mere physiological disturbances, but as ones fraught with significance.

The echoes of religious experience here are fully intended. As has often been observed, the greatest music seems to provide a passable substitute for the sacred, for those who find themselves doxastically challenged in regard to the traditional demands thereof. For many music lovers the listening room is a kind of chapel, at least when certain items are on the order of service.[17]

There is also a connection here to the whole tradition of the sublime as an aesthetic reaction distinct from that of the beautiful, as in the writings of Burke, Kant and Schopenhauer. It is a nice question whether it is the apprehension of a sublime quality in some piece of music, for example, one of infinity or power or danger or transcendence, that is a precipitator of frissons, or whether, on the contrary, it is the registering of frissons that makes us perceive in some piece of music a quality of the sublime. In any event, the 'sublime' experience and the 'frisson' experience cannot be simply identified, since not all sublime, or awe-inducing, experiences involve frissons, and not all frisson experiences partake of the cognitive character of the sublime.

Anyway, contrast that movement by Brahms with a roughly contemporary piece, the *Russian Easter Overture* of Rimsky-Korsakov. Though colourful, imbued with feeling, well put together, and possessed of a degree of kinetic energy comparable to that of the Brahms, it is not, I would guess, a piece capable of inducing the 'chill' experience. Though enjoyable, even absorbing, as music it is simply too superficial. Its energy does not speak to or tap into anything profound in human nature. Thus it does not summon from the depths of the human psyche, as it were, these frissons that seem so full of import.

Further Criticisms

Let us return to Panksepp's study and consider now Panksepp's evolutionary-developmental speculations on the underlying cause and biological significance of musical chills. My interest here is not so much in whether these speculations are well founded, but in whether, if they are, this should affect the way in which those who are susceptible to musical chills need regard them.

> ... people are most likely to have chills to music that has moved them in the past ... however, since unfamiliar sad music was more likely to provoke chills than unfamiliar happy music, the evidence suggests that there are more primitive instinctual neuropsychic components that underlie the phenomenon ... I will argue that the chill ultimately reflects a property of ingrained neural systems of our old mammalian brain that monitor emotions related to social proximity and separation. (Panksepp, 1995, p. 195)

And further:

> We presently know a great deal about the neural circuits for separation distress that lead young animals to cry out when they are lonely and lost ... Internal feeling of coldness and chills when parents hear separation calls may provide increased motivation for social reunion. Thus the separation call may have been designed, during the evolutionary construction of the brain's emotional systems, to acoustically activate a thermally based need for social contact ... Sad music may achieve its beauty and its chilling effect by presenting a symbolic rendition of the separation call (e.g. a high-pitched crescendo or a solo instrument emerging from the background) in the emotional context of potential reunion and redemption. (1995, pp. 198–9)

The issue I want to raise is this: once we have scientific insight into the causes – neurophysiological, biochemical, evolutionary, or what have you – of musical frissons, what impact should this have on one's pleasure in experiencing them or being subject to them? Need such knowledge have a deflationary effect, serving to undermine our satisfaction? Once we realize the responses in question are just, supposing Panksepp's speculations to be on the mark, a legacy of our evolutionary past, an artefact of a mammalian brain still sensitive to the separation calls of errant young, must we rationally cease to regard them as sources of satisfaction, or as bearers of significance beyond the biological?

I think not. Supposing the underlying cause of musical frissons to be an approximation to the separation call of lonely adolescent mammals, this need not invalidate the other dimensions of such frissons in which their value seems to reside. For first, the pleasure in being so affected by the music, whatever its remote causes, is real, and can be justified in terms of the beauty or depth or poignancy of the music to which such pleasure remains a response. And second, that a reaction has certain underlying causes of an evolutionary sort in no way precludes its taking on also a certain significance for us, in no way prevents it from reflecting as well, on occasion, a listener's recognition of something important about life as some music seems to embody it.

But in fact I would suggest that the evolutionary reduction of our susceptibility to frissons proposed by Panksepp is rather unlikely, at least as applied to the sort of musical frisson that I have had primarily in mind in this essay. For there are really *two* species of frisson that need to be distinguished.

On the one hand there are those, of relatively short duration, that are for the most part timbrally and/or dynamically induced; that is, produced by sound quality as such, and typified by the effect on many persons of a strong and beautiful soprano voice. On the other hand there are those, of relatively long duration, that are for the most part melodically/harmonically/rhythmically induced; that is, produced by sound structure. Structural features that seem to conduce to frissons of this latter, relatively extended, sort include certain kinds of melodic sequence, certain kinds of harmonic progression, chromatic intensifications, pedal points, suspensions, delayed cadences, sustained tremolos, and leaping melodic lines.[18]

This is a good point to acknowledge as well the important role that specific performance of a given piece plays in the generation of musical chills, given a structurally based potential for that in the music itself. Undeniably, certain performances bring out the inherent chill potential of a piece better than others. (In the case of the Scriabin Etude Op. 42 No. 5, say, the performance by Ruth Laredo, on Nonesuch Records, is by far the best I am acquainted with in that regard.)

In any event, that the former sort of frisson rests on the precipitating music's resemblance to piercing calls of separation is perhaps plausible, but that the latter sort of frisson has its roots there as well is rather less plausible. For the latter sort of frisson exhibits more in the way of temporal shape, of tension accumulated and discharged, of build-up and overflow. Such frissons thus seem harder to ascribe merely to a particular timbre and volume of sound.

Sloboda's Research on Musical Chills

One researcher apart from Panksepp who has interested himself in musical frissons is the psychologist of music John Sloboda. In a 1991 study Sloboda attempts to identify the structural features associated with various pronounced physical responses to music.[19] The results of his study point to the following six features as strongly associated with musical frissons, or, as he prefers to call them, 'shivers': melodic appoggiaturas; melodic or harmonic sequences; enharmonic modulation; unprepared harmonic change; sudden dynamic or textural change; and early arrival of expected events.

Appropriating a central idea of music theorist Leonard Meyer, Sloboda conjectures that what ties such devices together is that they all involve perturbation or frustration of musical *expectations*. Though undoubtedly containing some truth, this conjecture seems an over-generalization. Consider just melodic sequences, which appear on his list of conducive features, or sustained tremolos, which appear on mine, neither of which seem to contribute to shivers primarily by countering expectations.

In a more recent study, Sloboda suggests that it is not unexpected musical turns per se that are conducive to emotional peaks such as shivers, but rather both the *degree* of unexpectedness of such events and the *density* of unexpected events in a given stretch of music.[20] This improves the explanatory power of the conjecture, to be sure, but without making it wholly adequate. The reason, as I have already intimated in discussing Panksepp, is that the explanation accords no place to the *registering of the expressiveness of the music and of the character of that expressiveness*. In other words Sloboda's explanation, though of a cognitivist rather than an evolutionary sort, is *insufficiently* cognitive, or, perhaps, insufficiently cognitively *complex*. No formula in terms of structural and expectational variables alone, which fails to acknowledge the role of perceived expressiveness, can be entirely predictive of frissons, especially the type of frissons that listeners most care about.

To illustrate this point I venture an explanation of this more cognitively complex sort of my experience of the Scriabin Etude Op. 42 No. 5. The tempo of the piece is fast, d = 84, and the expressive marking is *affannato*, or 'breathless'. The overall shape of the piece is roughly ABABA, and though the piece is passionate and agitated throughout, there is a significant contrast in tenor between the A and B sections, with the A section being troubled and despairing in character and the B section projecting, when heard in context, a more lyrical and hopeful state of mind.

Now when in this marvellous Etude B first succeeds A, my spirits momentarily lift, and I sense a will to cast off the cloud of doom conveyed by A, a striving toward something more positive, though with an undercurrent of anxiety that does not depart. But when B again gives way to A – or more precisely, when B is on the verge of giving way to a version of A even more desperate than before (measures 27–30) – I am overwhelmed by a palpable sense of the hopelessness of the aspiration transiently perceived in B. B appears to me to be overcome by A, to be recaptured by it, and I realize that all is indeed lost, that there was never really any hope for this doomed passion, and that despair has now uncontested domain. This is the juncture at which the occurrence of chills is for me almost inevitable; and then again, though less powerfully, at the second, less psychologically crushing, shift in the second half of the piece, from a more febrile version of B back to A (measures 46–7).

What I want to suggest is that only a quasi-narrative account of this sort, positing unarticulated or semi-articulated thoughts in the form of an emotional scenario, can be an adequate explanation of the potential of music such as this Etude of Scriabin's to induce frissons in a certain range of listeners. And though it would be quixotic of me to expect all listeners strongly moved by this music to confess to exactly the scenario I have sketched, I cannot help but think that the sense of the music such listeners would extract from their own experiences would be at least conformable to such a scenario.

The Value of Musical Chills or Frissons: First Pass

I return now to Panksepp, and to the lesson to be drawn from my reaction to his evolutionary explanations of musical frissons. The lesson, I think, is this: the value of frissons produced by music is highly dependent on one's *construal* of that physiological response, on what one *takes* one's response to a passage of music to mean (for instance, that one has indeed plumbed its expressive depths), or on what in the music one *takes* oneself to be responding to (for instance, its manifestation of some singular state of mind or emotional drama). That said, there are then two possibilities in a given instance. Either the construal is reasonable and justified, that is, the music has expressive depths and you have indeed plumbed them, or it is unreasonable and unjustified, that is, the music has no expressive depths or at any rate you have not plumbed them.

In the first case the claim of value for musical frissons seems sustainable, for in that case such frissons constitute direct acknowledgement of a quality inherent in the music. But I think that a claim of value, though naturally a lesser one, can be advanced even in the second case. For it seems that it is a thing of value for individuals to find experiences of being strongly affected by artworks to be of significance, even where such claims of significance cannot, in the last analysis, be upheld. There is no harm, and arguably some gain, in listeners investing such experiences with such significances, even when such significances cannot in fact be objectively demonstrated. And the reason for that is that life, of which appreciative experiences are a part, is thus made, in a familiar sense of the word, more *meaningful* for those listeners.[21]

At any rate, it seems clear that it is one's construal of musical frissons, whether ultimately justifiable or not, that is critical in giving them what status or value they have. It is helpful to compare the ordinarily delectable musical chills with which we have been concerned[22] with the obviously far from delectable chill that runs through you when you suddenly think, rightly or wrongly, that you have deleted a computer file on which you have been working for no small amount of time, or that which occurs when you sense that a burglar has just broken in through a ground-floor window of your house. It indeed appears to be the cognitive construal of the frisson – or the thought accompanying the frisson – that makes most of the difference between the cases.

On the other hand, it is not entirely clear that the chills in question are precisely the same, phenomenologically speaking. Those that occur in the course of musical engagement seem to blossom more slowly, to suffuse the organism more gently, to have softer edges, whereas those prompted by sudden perceptions of danger or loss seem more sudden and piercing – more truly 'chilling', as it were. Thus, even among bodily-based frissons to which we are subject, there may be phenomenological differences that suit certain of them to a role in experiences of value, while others are excluded, on the same grounds, from so taking part.

The Value of Musical Chills or Frissons: Second Pass

What position do we seem to have arrived at, then, on the appreciative standing of musical chills? More or less this: that it is chill sensations *to which certain thoughts attach*, or *to which we accord a certain significance*, that are of appreciative value, and not chill sensations per se. Such chill experiences might thus reasonably be described as having a *derived* value, one derived from what they are, or are at any rate thought to be, sensings *of*, for instance, the music's depth of expression, or its poignancy, or its communication of some fundamental truth of life, and so on.

But if so one might very well object that it is really the *thoughts* that count, not the sensation, thus ultimately acceding in, rather than challenging, the Goodmanian position according to which the sensation as such is both without value and irrelevant to value. If musical frissons are only valuable when conceptually framed in a certain way by the person experiencing them, to wit, as registrations or reflections of the quality or power of the music, then does not all the value in fact reside in the conceptualization – the thought that one is recognizing the quality or power of the music – apart from whether frissons accompanying such recognition take place?

Not quite. For what is important, and what registering chills while listening underscores, is the 'whole person' response to music of which such sensations are a part. Responses to music of the 'whole person', that is, ones that are cognitive, emotional, sensational, and behavioral at once, are arguably of greater value than more partial and isolated responses to the substance of the music being heard. Thus, even if such chills are valuable only when viewed or regarded in a certain way by those who experience them, those chills remain essential to the full experience of value in question. The chills are essential to the value of the response as a whole, one might say, because they represent a bodily seconding, a bodily confirmation of what is being registered intellectually at the same time. The marking of abstract recognitions by felt frissons arguably imparts a kind of 'added value' to musical experience. Such frissons stand as corporeal endorsements of what is concomitantly grasped in cognitive terms. Their special value, I suggest, lies precisely in the affirmation of wholeness they afford: of body and mind resonating together in response to a given musical utterance.[23]

The Experience of Musical Uplift

I want briefly to contrast the experience of chills from music and a related, though distinguishable, experience I will label the 'uplift' experience.[24] What do I mean by being 'uplifted' by music? Something like this: being transfigured, swept up, carried away, by the power of its movement and progression, by the force of its gesture or the vitality of its impulse. This experience is distinct from the 'chill' experience on which we have dwelled for some time, though it may possibly coexist with it. Yet in what does the specific pleasure of such experiences of uplift consist, beyond that afforded by good music generally?

I would suggest that it is often a pleasure in being reminded of, and made to reflect upon, the goodness of life – its seriousness, substantiality, and incomparable value. And I mean 'incomparable' rather literally: what, especially when it is threatened, seems remotely tradable against the good of living, of being alive, with at least some capacity for enjoyment or satisfaction? Certain music seems capable of having this effect on us through its musical content, that is, through the complex of its form and expression.

Some examples of music capable of furnishing what I call an 'uplift' experience, though not necessarily one accompanied by chills, are these: Mozart, *Jupiter* Symphony, Finale; Beethoven, *Emperor* Concerto, first movement; Beethoven, Seventh Symphony, first and last movements; Mendelssohn, *Italian* Symphony, first and last movements; Mendelssohn, *Octet*, first and last movements; Haydn, the opening Allegros of most of his later symphonies; and, to switch genres, John Coltrane's masterpiece 'Giant Steps'.

On the other hand, there is yet other music, of an undeniably pleasurable and exciting sort, that reliably provides, I submit, neither chills nor the uplift experience I briefly characterized above. For example, almost any of Scarlatti's fast tempo harpsichord sonatas, almost any of Rossini's opera overtures, and, switching genres once again, almost any of the early songs of the Beatles. Whether such pleasurable-but-neither-chilling-nor-uplifting music might usefully be divided into further categories remains a question for further thought.

This is the right moment to remark that some music, perhaps all good music, is capable of giving pleasure on occasion merely by reinforcing the marvel that music exists at all, filling in the interstices of ordinary life, pouring from radios and cassette players at the touch of a button, any time of day or night, filling the public squares in the persons of street musicians, and thus combining with all sorts of quotidian things so as to transform them and surround them with an aesthetic glow.

I don't, of course, mean to suggest that music is always welcome, even if it is of some value, especially when it comes upon one unbidden; music in such contexts can seem an act of aggression, or indicative of a decline in public civility. I mean only to underline what is, I think, the more frequent sense we have of music as a gift, wherever and whenever it occurs. This is perhaps the truth in Nietzsche's hyperbolic, yet curiously compelling, observation: 'Without music, human life would have been a mistake.'

Two Final Pleasures of Music

In closing I want briefly to mention two other distinctive, if not physiologically distinctive, musical pleasures. One is the pleasure of savouring comparatively certain musical 'expressive pairs', that is, themes or passages that display strikingly similar, if not identical, expressive characters, even though far from structurally or perceptually the same. Here are some pairs that have always struck me in this light:

- Wagner, *Lohengrin*, Act 3 Prelude, opening/Strauss, *Don Juan*, opening
- Brahms, Violin Concerto, finale, main theme/Bruch, Violin Concerto, finale, main theme
- Brahms, Piano Trio in B, finale, main theme/Franck, Piano Quintet, first movement, second theme
- Vaughan Williams, *Fantasia on a Theme by Thomas Tallis*, main theme/ Saint-Saëns, 'Organ' Symphony, finale, second theme

The pleasure involved in remarking and mulling over such resemblances is perhaps not far to seek, and has indeed a traditional pedigree. To recall the formula for beauty associated with Hutcheson, it is a matter of appreciating uniformity-amidst-variety. What is distinctive in such cases, of course, is that it is an *interwork*, rather than an *intrawork*, uniformity-amidst-variety, that is in question.

Finally, to cross over into the perhaps irredeemably individual, consider the pleasure of realizing that one has followed and enjoyed, hence arguably understood, an extended piece of music without consciously focusing on its large-scale form or explicitly attending to any of its large-scale relationships. Admittedly, this is a peculiar sort of pleasure, both idiosyncratic and, in a rather strong sense, theory-dependent. (It depends, in particular, on accepting something like the theory of basic musical understanding advanced in my 1998 book, *Music in the Moment*.) But offering it at this late juncture answers to at least three purposes.

First, it serves to remind us of the great *variety* of musical pleasures of which we avail ourselves, which may thus keep us from foreclosing prematurely on that variety in our theoretical reflections. Second, it illustrates the point that some musical pleasures are *generalizable*, in the sense of legitimately presupposed of or imputed to all, to echo Kant, whereas other musical pleasures are not. In other words, some musical pleasures testify fairly straightforwardly to music's proper value as music, and some not. Third, it allows us to see, perhaps, that some pleasures, while not signalling the presence of or serving as measures of musical value, are not automatically appreciatively *illegitimate* ones. They may or may not be, this being a question not entirely reducible to that of whether they are generalizable in the Kantian sense or not. Pleasure in reflecting philosophically on the nature or ground of one's more basic pleasure in music, of which the peculiar pleasure confessed to above is an instance – as well as a paradigm example of a meta-pleasure – need not detract from one's aesthetic involvement in music; it might in fact even be considered a part, if a fairly remote part, of the appreciation of music as art.[25]

Notes

1. For both sides of the issue, see Levinson (1996a) 'Pleasure and the value of works of art', in *Pleasures of Aesthetics*; and Levinson (1996b) 'Evaluating music', *Revue Internationale de Philosophie*, 198.
2. For a defence, inspired by Edmund Gurney, of the primacy of local focus in the aural comprehension of music see Levinson (1998) *Music in the Moment*.
3. For more on this aspect of aesthetic attention, see Levinson, Jerrold (1996) 'What Is Aesthetic Pleasure?', in *Pleasures of Aesthetics*.
4. For further admonitions in this vein, see Levinson (1996a) 'Musical Literacy', in *Pleasures of Aesthetics* and Davies (1993) 'Musical understanding and musical kinds', *Journal of Aesthetics and Art Criticism*, 51.
5. On the social import of jokes, which serve at the same time to bind together members of a given group while putting at a distance those of other groups, see Ted Cohen, 'Jokes', in Schaper (ed.) (1983) *Pleasure, Preference, and Value*; the lesson applies, with modifications, to musical communities that form around a given work, genre, composer or performer. On possible moral aspects of music see Levinson (1996b) 'Evaluating music', in *Pleasures of Aesthetics* and also Higgins (1991) *The Music of Our Lives*; Radford (1991) 'How can music be moral?', *Midwest Studies in Philosophy*, 16; and Savile (1993) *Kantian Aesthetics Pursued*, chapter 6.
6. See Levinson (1998) for support of this.
7. Recall Schumann's apostrophe of 'heavenly lengths'.
8. Panksepp (1995) 'The emotional sources of "chills" induced by music', *Music Perception*, 13, pp. 171–207. All page citations to this article are given in parentheses.
9. See Goodman (1968) *Languages of Art*.
10. Panksepp expands on this thought later on in the following manner: ' ... happiness and sadness work together, and the most moving music allows the two processes to be blended in such a way as to magnify our sense of ourselves as deeply feeling creatures who are conscious inheritors of the tragic view ...' (p. 198). I think there is something right about this, as my own reflections below will suggest.
11. That is, female subjects were generally more susceptible to chills than were male subjects, or they were more likely to report having them.
12. See Davies (1994) *Musical Meaning and Expression*, chapter 7, for related reflections. Similar thoughts are to be found in Nietzsche, as Anthony Storr notes: 'Nietzsche realized – no one more vividly – that the only life we know is constituted by opposites. Pleasure is inconceivable without pain; light without darkness; love without hate; good without evil ... .This is why the greatest art always includes tragedy ...' (Storr (1992) *Music and the Mind*, p. 158).
13. One might note here a resemblance between this idea of the poignant as reflecting

the essentially mixed nature of what life has to offer and the traditional notion of the sublime as involving a fusion of pleasure and pain or attraction and repulsion.

14. I should stress that the music of the song alone possesses this power, in my experience, apart from its text.

15. The caveat registered above in connection with the Strauss song applies as well to these works of Schütz and Bach.

16. According to anecdote, in composing this resplendent music Brahms was thinking of time spent at the Prater, an amusement park on the outskirts of Vienna, and the simple joys of life available there – including, as he was supposed to have remarked, 'the pretty girls'. But that sounds perhaps too earthbound a note for the almost superhuman affirmation and exhilaration bodied forth in the music.

17. 'Nietzsche realized that, for many people, the concert hall and the art gallery have replaced the church as places where the "divine" can be encountered' (Storr, 1992, p. 155).

18. Of course most such features will not by themselves produce frissons, if only because the specific musical embedding of such features, and their interaction with other features constitutive of a given passage, is absolutely crucial.

19. Sloboda (1991) 'Music structure and emotional response: some empirical findings', *Psychology of Music*, 19: 110–20.

20. Sloboda (1999) 'Musical performance and emotion: Issues and developments', in S.W. Yi (ed.) *Music, Mind, and Science*.

21. Compare Sircello, Guy (1989) *Love and Beauty*, p. 35: '... an enjoyable experience of a quality need not be a veridical experience. For example, even though I may enjoy dancing in part because of the feeling it gives me of my own sexiness, I may not be sexy at all when I dance; I may actually just be klutzy – however it may ultimately be determined or determinable whether I am "in fact" sexy or klutzy.'

22. At least they are so for the vast majority of music lovers who are subject to them; that is, they are experienced as mildly hedonic in tone. But I have discovered that there are listeners who in fact do not find chills from music delectable, but on the contrary, decidedly unpleasant and unwelcome. (My speculation is that these are listeners of a certain personality type, one that resists letting go or surrendering control in even the smallest measure.) Whether there is any scope, for such listeners, for cognitive framings of received chills rendering them more valuable is a difficult question, one I shall not address.

23. At the end of his article Panksepp (1995) offers a terminological suggestion worth pondering. 'In several seminar presentations of this work I chose to label the chill phenomenon as a "skin orgasm" on the basis of the assumption that there are underlying neurochemical similarities between the two phenomena ... if we wish to generate a scientific term for the chill phenomenon, the *skin orgasm* designation may have some merit' (p. 203). Panksepp's suggestion seems a happy one, and not just on the assumption of an underlying similarity in the neurochemical under-pinnings of the two phenomena. There are also significant resemblances of an experiential sort. Salient in the case of both is this clutch of characteristics: passivity, involuntariness, a threshhold aspect, an afterglow aspect, a welling-up aspect. One might add that the value of both experiences is dependent on the cognitive positioning of the experience on the part of the subject, even if this is probably more marked in the case of musical 'skin orgasms' than in the case of orgasms proper.

24. 'Euphoria' experience might be another apt label for it.
25. I want to thank audiences in London, Amsterdam, Montreal, Lucerne and New Zealand during 1998–99 for spirited discussion of the content of this paper. I thank especially Rafael De Clercq, Henk Borgdorff, David Davies, Hubert Eiholzer, Cynthia Macdonald, Roger Pouivet and John Sloboda for helpful comments.

References

Cohen, Ted (1983) 'Jokes', in E. Schaper (ed.) *Pleasure, Preference, and Value*, pp. 120–36, Cambridge: Cambridge University Press.

Davies, Stephen (1993) 'Musical understanding and musical kinds', *Journal of Aesthetics and Art Criticism*, 51: 69–81.

Davies, Stephen (1994) *Musical Meaning and Expression*, Ithaca: Cornell University Press.

Goodman, Nelson (1968) *Languages of Art*, Indianapolis: Bobbs-Merrill.

Higgins, Kathleen (1991), *The Music of Our Lives*, Philadelphia: Temple University Press.

Levinson, Jerrold (1996a) *Pleasures of Aesthetics*, Ithaca: Cornell University Press.

Levinson, Jerrold (1996b) 'Evaluating music', *Revue Internationale de Philosophie*, 198: 593–614.

Levinson, Jerrold (1998) *Music in the Moment*, Ithaca: Cornell University Press.

Panksepp, Jaak (1995) 'The emotional sources of "chills" induced by music', *Music Perception*, 13: 171–207.

Radford, Colin (1991), 'How can music be moral?', *Midwest Studies in Philosophy*, 16: 421–38.

Savile, Anthony (1993), *Kantian Aesthetics Pursued*, Edinburgh: Edinburgh University Press.

Sircello, Guy (1989), *Love and Beauty*, Princeton: Princeton University Press.

Sloboda, John (1991) 'Music structure and emotional response: Some empirical findings', *Psychology of Music*, 19: 110–120.

Sloboda, John (2000) 'Musical performance and emotion: Issues and developments', in S.W. Yi, (ed.) *Music, Mind, and Science*, pp. 220–38, Seoul: Western Music Research Institute.

Storr, Anthony (1992), *Music and the Mind*, New York: Free Press.

Index